Sissies and Tomboys

D1566732

Artwork by Javier Cintrón

Sissies and Tomboys

*Gender Nonconformity and
Homosexual Childhood*

EDITED BY

Matthew Rottnek

Property of Jose E. Muñoz

New York University Press

NEW YORK AND LONDON

NEW YORK UNIVERSITY PRESS
New York and London

© 1999 by New York University
All rights reserved

Chapter 4 reprinted from *Feminists Rethink the Self*, ed. Diana
Meyers (Boulder, Colo.: Westview Press, 1996). ©1996 by Westview
Press. Reprinted by permission of Westview Press. Chapter 6
reprinted from *Fort Da: Journal of the Northern California Society for
Psychoanalytic Psychology* 3, no. 1 (spring 1998): 34–43. Reprinted by
permission. Chapter 11 reprinted from *Under the Rainbow: Growing
Up Gay* by Arnie Kantrowitz (New York: St. Martin's Griffin,
1996). ©1996 by St. Martin's Press. Reprinted by permission of St.
Martin's Press, Inc. Chapter 13 ©1999 by Michael Lassell.

Library of Congress Cataloging-in-Publication Data
Sissies and tomboys : gender nonconformity and homosexual
childhood /
edited by Matthew Rottnek.
p.   cm.
Includes bibliographical references.
ISBN 0-8147-7483-0 (hardcover : alk. paper). — ISBN 0-8147-7484-9
(pbk. : alk. paper)
1. Gender identity disorders in children.   2. Psychosexual
development.   3. Sex role in children.   4. Homosexuality.
I. Rottnek, Matthew, 1968–   .
RJ506.G35S57   1999
618.92'8583 — dc21   98-53735
                              CIP

New York University Press books are printed on acid-free paper,
and their binding materials are chosen for strength and durability.

Manufactured in the United States of America

10 9 8 7 6 5 4 3 2 1

for Marty Duberman,
teacher and friend,
and
for Ken Corbett,
with gratitude

Contents

Acknowledgments   *ix*

Introduction   1

PART I: Gender Identity Disorder (GID) and the Normal

1   Diagnosis and Treatment of Gender
    Identity Disorder in Children   9
    Shannon Minter

2   Ethical Issues in Diagnosing and
    Treating Gender-Dysphoric Children
    and Adolescents   34
    Richard R. Pleak

3   Is Gender Essential?   52
    Anne Fausto-Sterling

4   Queering the Center by Centering the
    Queer: Reflections on Transsexuals and
    Secular Jews   58
    Naomi Scheman

PART II: Theorizing Gender Nonconformity

5   Homosexual Boyhood: Notes on Girlyboys   107
    Ken Corbett

6   Tomboys and Cowgirls: The Girl's
    Disidentification from the Mother   140
    Dianne Elise

7   Oh Bondage Up Yours! Female
    Masculinity and the Tomboy   153
    Judith Halberstam

8   Sexing the Tomboy   180
    Lee Zevy

PART III: Sissies and Tomboys Speak

9   My Life as a Boy   199
    Kim Chernin

10 Butch in a Tutu   209
    Sara Cytron, with Harriet Malinowitz

11 Such a Polite Little Boy   226
    Arnie Kantrowitz

12 Las Nenas con las Nenas, Los Nenes
    con los Nenes   236
    Lawrence M. La Fountain-Stokes

13 Boys Don't Do That   245
    Michael Lassell

14 The Boy Who Grew Up to Be a Woman   263
    Jody Norton

15 The Golden Book of the Civil War   274
    Paul Russell

    Select Bibliography   289
    Contributors   295
    Index   299

Acknowledgments

I am grateful to the many people who advised, informed, and/or supported me in the production of both the conference, "Sissies and Tomboys," and this volume: Brett Callas, Ken Corbett, Lucile Duberman, Martin Duberman, Jeffrey Escoffier, Frances Goldin, Steven Goldstein, Janice Irvine, Richard Isay, Esther Katz, Suzanne Kessler, Sandra Kiersky, Harriet Malinowitz, Christian McEwen, Diana C. Miller, Richard Pleak, Kelley Ready, Jeff Roth, Carole Vance, Ron Winchel, the contributors, and conference participants. For their financial and in-kind support of the conference, I thank the Bills Foundation and the Graduate School and University Center of the City University of New York. For their work in the production of this volume, I thank Despina Papazoglou Gimbel, Daisy Hernandez, and Eric Zinner.

Introduction

In 1973, homosexuality was officially depathologized with a revision in the Diagnostic and Statistical Manual (*DSM*) of psychiatry. In 1980, a new diagnosis appeared: Gender Identity Disorder of Childhood. This diagnostic shift separated gender from sexuality—an important advance—but it also reinscribed a traditional male/female gender binary with corresponding appropriate masculine and feminine behavior. With the diagnosis of Gender Identity Disorder (GID), cross-gendered behavior or cross-gendered identification in children—for example, cross-dressing, playing with toys traditionally associated with the opposite sex, a desire to be of the opposite sex, or a belief that one is of or will become the opposite sex—if sufficiently rigid, and if accompanied by sufficient psychic distress, may be deemed illness.

Children diagnosed with GID are "extreme" cases—they are deeply unhappy and may say things such as, "I hate myself," "I don't want to be me," "I wish I were a girl (boy)[1]," "I wish I were dead."[2] These children's distress has been accounted for in various ways. Some theorists, such as George Rekers, see GID as a prehomosexual stage which, if treated in a timely manner, may prevent the development of a later homosexual orientation. Here, homosexuality-as-pathology is simply reconfigured as a childhood disorder. Other theorists, such as Susan Coates, see GID as part of a more pervasive underlying disorder having to do with mother-child relationships. A boy[3] in distress because of an unavailable or character-disordered mother may try to *be* Mommy—that is, dress and act like her—since he cannot be *with* her.[4] But why is gender scapegoated? If Coates is correct, why isn't the child's condition named for the causal factor(s) of the psychic distress—for example, anxiety around abandonment or separation or some other family dynamic, rather than for the gender experience of the child?

The stigma of illness, particularly for children, is harmful, and when focused on such a central component of identity—their experience of gender—the repercussions may be so strong as to significantly interfere with their development. The existence of GID as a psychiatric diagnosis is an opportunity to examine how gender conformity is being enforced on models of development and how social and institutional standards reflect, as Eve Sedgwick has said, "the overarching, relatively unchallenged aegis of a culture's desire that gay people *not be*."[5]

We need to open a conceptual space in which to look at the experience of homosexual childhood in a way that respects and values gender diversity and homosexual development and in a way that values homosexuals as human beings. This volume[6] begins to do so by looking at such questions as: How does persistent gender essentialism influence the manner in which children with gender identities and behaviors considered deviant are being handled in the context of family, school, medical institutions, and society? What does homosexual childhood look like? What is the relationship between the unique gender experience of homosexual, or prehomosexual, children and the problematized gender atypicality of children diagnosed with GID? Is the difference one of degree or of kind? Is it possible that creative, sensitive children are being diagnosed with a disorder when their cross-gendered characters may be a manifestation of their temperament, imagination, or constitution? To what extent is psychiatry's ignorance of the distinct experiences of homosexual, transgendered, and transsexual childhood behind this diagnosis? Is psychiatry, with the diagnosis of GID and diagnostic criterion of gender dysphoria, simply recreating a stigmatization that we experienced with homosexuality in the fifties and sixties?

To begin to address such questions, we first need to interrogate the conceptualization of "the normal" which pervades the literature on GID. Second, we should allow for—even expect—a certain degree of anxiety and conflict about growing up homosexual and gender-nonconforming in a traditional culture. And third, we need to embrace gender diversity both theoretically and practically.

The very concepts of gender "nonconformity" and gender dysphoria assume a normal or acceptable range of gender expression. Richard C. Friedman, for example, writes, "the distinction between nonconformists and people with psychopathology is usually clear enough during childhood. Extremely and chronically effeminate boys, for example, should be understood as falling into the latter category."[7] But whom does this pathologizing serve? In *The Normal and the Pathological*, Georges Canguilhem holds that we can speak of that which is *pathological* only against a background of a pre-established *normal*: "Every conception of pathology must be based on prior knowledge of the corresponding normal state, which is, inevitably, value-laden."[8] If our conception of gender were more fluid, would not the very notion of gender "nonconformity" be nonsensical?

Canguilhem suggests a return to the Hippocratic conceptualization of the normal, given in terms of harmony and equilibrium, both within an organism and between the organism and its environment: "It is *life itself* and not medical judgment which makes the biological normal a concept of value and not a concept of statistical reality."[9] If we begin with an affirmation of lesbian and gay life and an appreciation of gender diversity ("life itself"), then we will automatically expand our conceptualization of *the normal*. What will be *abnormal* will be the conflict, pain, and anxiety that follow from growing up homosexual and differently gendered in a traditional culture or conventional family. Construing "the normal" in terms of harmony or equilibrium distinguishes the well-being of an organism from its falling outside the majority; normal-as-internally-harmonious allows for aberrations, for difference. Canguilhem writes, "But diversity is not disease; the *anomalous* is not the pathological. Pathological implies *pathos*, the direct and concrete feeling of suffering and impotence, the feeling of life gone wrong."[10]

People live adult lives that are gender-unconventional and they can and do live them successfully and happily. But in a traditional culture such as ours, rarely do we come to live our lives without struggle—a struggle that often begins in childhood. In the best of circumstances, adults have the capacity and opportunity to articulate and work through these conflicts; children most often do not. We must move backward, then, from adult experience, memory, reflection, and theory to consider what might be the causes of children's intrapsychic conflict around gender. We must consider possible factors such as internalized disapproval or rejection from parents and society or self-consciousness about a developing sexual orientation that is different from those around him/her. If we allow for a wider spectrum of gender expression in childhood, then the way we think about children's conflicts and anxieties will be different—due not to their intrinsic characteristics or their ways of being in the world, but rather to how they are perceived and stigmatized by parents, siblings, teachers, and peers.

Differently gendered lives—their individual variation, their difference from the majority—constitute a *normal diversity* of gendered experience. But how can we acknowledge such diversity when diversity resists categorization?

> Though "pluralism" is commonly held to be a democratic value, pluralistic democracy is limited by its tolerance only for established social groups that it already recognizes as coherent, if somewhat odd, configurations. Tolerance does not extend to idiosyncratic individuals; neither does it extend to groups molded outside the master cultural template and which don't conform in some recognizable way to dominant social principles.[11]

It is the particularity of the individual human life that best resists the tyranny of generalization. And it is narrative that most effectively demonstrates both the previously unrecognized or unacknowledged suffering endured by others and the cruelty which we, as fellow human beings, are capable of inflicting on them:

> [Human solidarity] is to be achieved not by inquiry but by imagination, the imaginative ability to see strange people as fellow sufferers. Solidarity is not discovered by reflection but created. It is created by increasing our sensitivity to the particular details of the pain and humiliation of other, unfamiliar sorts of people.[12]

Personal narratives are perhaps the strongest testimony to the need for a richer conceptualization of gender across the board. The sissy and tomboy narratives included herein celebrate a variety of gender experiences, and demonstrate the conflict that arises when parents are embarrassed and peers threatened, and when society at large revolts against unconventional gender expression. These narratives also point to strategies to negotiate the psychic pain that results—strategies that are needed to carry one through a life. The richness and sophistication of these narratives work along with the theoretical papers in this volume to allow us to rethink models of gender development and begin to explore the unique experience of homosexual childhood.

NOTES

1. Statistically, the majority of cases presenting with gender dysphoria are boys.

2. Susan W. Coates, personal communication.

3. For the most part, the psychiatric discourse is about boyhood femininity: masculinized behavior in girls is not a clinical problem; effeminate behavior in boys is—in the extreme, the "sissy-boy complex."

4. For a fuller overview of the causal theories of GID, see Shannon Minter, this volume.

5. Eve Kosofsky Sedgwick, "How to Bring Your Kids Up Gay." *Social Text* 29 (1990): 26. Emphasis in original.

6. This volume grew out of a conference entitled "Sissies and Tomboys: Gender 'Nonconformity' and Homosexuality," sponsored by the Center for Lesbian and Gay Studies (CLAGS) of the City University of New York, in February 1995.

7. Richard C. Friedman, *Male Homosexuality: A Contemporary Psychoanalytic Perspective* (New Haven: Yale University Press, 1988), pp. 32–33.

8. Georges Canguilhem, *The Normal and the Pathological* (New York: Urzone, 1991), p. 51.

9. Ibid., p. 131. Emphasis added.

10. Ibid., p. 137. Emphasis in original.

11. Harriet Malinowitz, "Citizenship and Sexualities: Transcultural Constructions," a statement prepared for CLAGS as part of an application to the Rockefeller Foundation's Residency Fellowships in the Humanities Program, 1996.

12. Richard Rorty, *Contingency, Irony, and Solidarity* (New York: Cambridge University Press, 1996), p. xvi.

Part I

Gender Identity Disorder (GID) and the Normal

Diagnosis and Treatment of Gender Identity Disorder in Children

Shannon Minter

The purpose of this information sheet is (1) to provide a representative overview of the published clinical literature on the diagnosis and treatment of Gender Identity Disorder (GID) in children; and (2) to summarize and comment on the controversy over current clinical approaches to gender-variant children.

Gender Identity Disorder (GID) is a diagnosis in the Diagnostic and Statistical Manual of Mental Disorders (DSM), the American Psychiatric Association's official nomenclature of psychiatric disorders. As defined in DSM-IV (1994), GID includes a broad spectrum of people. Those diagnosed with GID range from transsexual and transgendered adults to children as young as two years old. ("For clinically referred children, onset of cross-gender interests and activities is usually between ages 2 and 4 years" APA 1994, p. 536). As psychiatrist Richard Green has observed, "Both the diagnosis and the treatment of gender identity disorder in children remain controversial. Not only is there dispute over what constitutes each, but debate continues over whether either is justified" (Green 1995, p. 2002).

The diagnosis of GID in children has two components: (1) "a strong and persistent cross-gender identification"; (2) "persistent discomfort about one's assigned sex or a sense of inappropriateness in the gender role of that sex" (APA 1994, pp. 532–33). *DSM-IV* notes that GID in children "can be distinguished from simple nonconformity to stereotypical sex role behavior by the extent and pervasiveness of the cross-gender wishes, interests, and activities" (p. 536). As this statement suggests, the diagnostic criteria focus mainly on cross-gender interests and behaviors (see listing below).

Both components of the diagnosis (cross-gender identification and discomfort with assigned sex or gender role) may be evidenced solely by cross-gender interests and behaviors. A child need not verbalize any unhappiness with his or her body or state that he or she desires to be the other sex to receive the diagnosis, nor does the diagnosis require the child to verbalize any subjective distress over his or her condition. *DSM III-R* (APA 1987) observed that "[m]ost children with this disorder deny being disturbed by it, except that it brings them into conflict with the expectations of their family or peers" (p. 72). *DSM-IV* omits this observation but specifies that a child's subjective "discomfort" may be inferred from "aversion toward rough-and-tumble play and rejection of male stereotypical toys, games, and activities" in boys, and by "marked aversion toward normative feminine clothing" in girls (p. 537).

GID in Boys

According to *DSM-IV*, boys with GID have a "marked preoccupation with traditionally feminine activities," including:

- "dressing in girls' or womens' clothes,"
- "drawing pictures of beautiful girls and princesses,"
- playing with "[s]tereotypical female-type dolls, such as Barbie,"
- preferring girls as playmates,
- assuming a "mother role" when playing house,
- avoiding "rough-and-tumble play and competitive sports,"
- showing "little interest in cars and trucks."

GID in Girls

According to *DSM-IV*, GID in girls is manifested by:

- "intense negative reactions to parental expectations or attempts to have them wear dresses or other feminine attire,"
- preference for "boy's clothing and short hair,"

- identification with "powerful male figures, such as Batman or Superman,"
- preference for boys as playmates, "with whom they share interests in contact sports, rough-and-tumble play, and traditional boyhood games,"
- a lack of interest in "dolls or any form of feminine dress up or role-play activity."

(For a complete description of diagnostic criteria, see APA 1994, pp. 532–38.)

Minors and adults have very different legal and practical relationships to the diagnosis of GID. As minors, children and youth are under the legal control of parents or other adults. As a result, children and youth diagnosed with GID have little or no control over whether to enter treatment or over the objectives of their treatment, and may be placed in an inpatient facility without the due process protections afforded adults. *The great majority of children treated for GID grow up to be lesbian, gay, or bisexual.* A small percentage grow up to be transsexual. Treatment of GID in children and youth is typically designed to eliminate or minimize cross-gender behavior and/or identification, with the short-term goal of alleviating social ostracism and the long-term goals of preventing adulthood transsexualism or homosexuality.

In contrast, *the vast majority of adults diagnosed with GID are self-identified transsexuals who usually must seek out and receive a diagnosis of GID in order to obtain hormones and/or sex reassignment surgeries.* As the trans community has gained more political power and visibility in recent years, there has been a growing movement to challenge the characterization of transsexualism as a psychiatric disorder and to advocate for recognition of transsexualism as a nonpsychiatric medical condition. For a more detailed discussion of the complex issues raised by the definition of transsexualism as a mental disorder, see "Joint Statement on GID and the Transgender Movement" (issued by the National Center for Lesbian Rights and the International Conference on Transgender Law and Employment Policy in 1996).

As Kenneth Zucker has observed, the introduction of GID in 1980 "followed 20 years of clinical research" on gender-atypical children (Zucker 1990a, p. 4). Much of this research was touted as a means to identify "prehomosexual" and "pretranssexual" children and to prevent them from growing up to be gay or transsexual (see, e.g., Rosen et al. 1978; Rekers et al. 1977). Clinical interest in gender-atypical children dates to the social conservatism and virulent homophobia of the post World War II era, when many mental health professionals joined the chorus of voices urging women to give up their wartime jobs and return to the roles of wife and mother (see, e.g., Griswold 1993). In particular, many child and family specialists became preoccupied with identifying the type of parenting that would perpetuate "appropriate" sex roles in children and prevent children, especially boys, from growing up to be homosexual (see, e.g., Fontaine 1950; Kolb and Johnson 1955; Berg 1956, 1957; Brown 1957; Gershman 1957; West 1959; Mussen and Distler 1960).

The American Psychiatric Association eliminated homosexuality as a mental disorder in 1973. (For an account of the political battles around this decision, see Bayer 1981.) Published in 1980, *DSM-III* was the first edition of the *DSM* that did not list homosexuality as a mental disorder. *DSM-III* was also the first edition to include the "new" diagnosis of Gender Identity Disorder. Commenting on the coincidence between the elimination of homosexuality as a psychiatric disorder and the creation of GID in children as a newly recognized disorder, Eve Sedgwick has argued that GID of childhood provided a new conceptual framework for pathologizing homosexuality. By yoking "the depathologization of an atypical sexual object choice . . . to the new pathologization of an atypical gender identification," GID allowed psychiatrists to reconcile the declassification of adult homosexuality as a mental disorder with redoubled efforts to prevent the development of homosexuality in gender-variant children and youth (Sedgwick 1990, p. 21). Lawrence Mass has also suggested that "American psychiatry is . . . engaged in a long, subtle process of reconceptualizing homosexuality as a mental illness with another name— the 'gender identity disorder of childhood'" (Mass 1990, p. 214). Heino Meyer-Bahlburg, one of the leading clinicians in this area, has stated that GID in children is "to some extent related to but not identical with development to homosexuality. . . . The big question is whether we should call it a disorder" (Meyer-Bahlburg 1993, pp. 13– 15).

There are several reasons that treating children for GID in order to prevent homosexuality has become controversial. First, follow-up studies of children who were treated for GID have found that treatment has no impact on adult sexual orientation—most of the children grow up to be lesbian, gay, or bisexual (Money and Russo 1979; Green 1985, 1987). Second, it is difficult to reconcile attempts to prevent homosexuality with the removal of homosexuality as a psychiatric disorder. Some therapists believe the decision to remove homosexuality from the *DSM* was wrong and continue to view homosexuality as a disorder (Rekers 1987; Siegel 1988; Silverman 1990; Niccolosi 1991). Others have sidestepped this conflict by suggesting that such attempts might be justified on the grounds that "a homosexual lifestyle, in a basically unaccepting culture, simply creates unnecessary social difficulties" (Zucker 1990b, pp. 29–30). A third factor contributing to the controversy surrounding treatment of GID in children to prevent homosexuality is the desire on the part of many mainstream therapists to distance themselves from George Rekers, an early proponent of the claim that treatment of GID in children can prevent homosexuality, after Rekers publicly endorsed treatment of GID in children based on religious and moral disapproval of homosexuality (Rekers 1982a, 1982b).

Currently, George Rekers is still the most vehement and forthright proponent of the view that treatment of GID in children can prevent homosexuality, a view he has promoted through his clinical and academic work at the University of South Carolina and his affiliation with the openly antigay Family Research Council. Richard Green is the leading proponent of the view that treatment has no impact on adult sexual orientation (Green 1987, 1995). Somewhat paradoxically, Green is also the most vocal and consistent proponent of the view that "parents have the legal right to seek treatment to modify their child's cross-gender behavior to standard boy and girl behavior even if their only motivation is to prevent homosexuality" (Green 1995, p. 2007). Susan Bradley and Kenneth Zucker have taken the position that "there is no strong evidence either way as to the effectiveness of treatment on later sexual orientation" (Bradley and Zucker 1990, p. 482). Susan Bradley has suggested that sexual orientation is highly resistant to change once a young person has consolidated a homosexual identity by engaging in same-gender sexual relationships, but may be redirected in some cases if GID is diagnosed and treated in childhood or early adolescence (Bradley 1985).

As the ethics and clinical validity of attempts to alter sexual orientation have been called into question, therapists have emphasized the alternative rationale of preventing adult transsexualism. Kenneth Zucker, for example, has argued that "[t]here is little controversy in this rationale, given the emotional distress experienced by gender-dysphoric adults and the physically and often socially painful measures required to align an adult's phenotypic sex with his or her subjective gender identity" (Zucker 1990b, p. 30; see also Green 1995, p. 2006). There is no direct evidence that gender identity is any more amenable to manipulation or alteration than sexual orientation. Nonetheless, therapists have suggested that the relatively small number of transsexual outcomes among children who are treated for GID, combined with the fact that few adults who seek sex reassignment were treated for GID as children, may indicate that the "natural history of transsexualism is disrupted by the child's contact with the mental health profession" (Zucker 1985, p. 150; see also Bradley and Zucker 1990; Green 1995).

Some psychoanalytic therapists have attempted to justify treatment of gender-variant children by arguing that extreme gender-atypicality in children is evidence of a global developmental psychopathology. Although the psychoanalytic approach is not new (see, e.g., Ovesey and Person 1973; Meyer 1980; Loeb and Shane 1982; Bleiberg et al. 1986; Lothstein 1987), it has gained new prominence through Susan Coates's research on GID boys at the Childhood Gender Identity Unit at St. Luke's-Roosevelt Hospital in New York City. Coates believes that "behavioral difficulties, depressions and separation anxiety" in boys with GID are "intrinsically associated with the gender confusion and may even be prerequisite to the development of effeminacy" (Coates 1987, p. 211). She has suggested that GID in boys may be caused by a disturbed mother-son relationship, reporting that "most of the mothers [of the feminine boys in her study] had character disorders. Most striking was their fear, anger, and devaluation of men" (Coates 1990, p. 423).

Coates's hypothesis that GID in boys is part of a pervasive underlying disorder is controversial (Green 1995, p. 2008–9). Richard Green has noted the absence of significant copathology in the GID boys he studied (Green 1987). Kenneth Zucker has reported a "moderate degree of associated psychopathology" in boys with GID, but found that at least "some of the behavioural [sic] problems observed in boys referred for assessment because of gender identity problems may be partly a function of age related difficulties in the peer group" (Zucker

1990c, p. 490; see also Zucker 1985, pp. 95–117). Elsewhere, Zucker has concluded that "the evidence linking general psychopathology and gender identity disorders in children is equivocal" (Zucker 1990b, p. 29). In Zucker's view, "this treatment rationale rests on a theory that, although possibly correct (at least in part), is not yet proven" (Zucker 1990b, p. 29).

Excerpts from Clinical Publications on the Diagnosis and Treatment of Gender Identity Disorder in Children

Methods of Treatment

Although parents' verbal and physical prohibition of cross-gender behavior will not terminate it in the G.I.D. child, their disapproval of it—in behavior and words—needs to be consistent. (Sugar 1995, p. 271).

Most children are responsive to the behaviorist messages from parents and peers that specific behaviors are undesirable. After a period of resistance to the curtailment of cross-gender activities that test the staying power of parents, children will begin to change. Some will go underground, cross-dressing when they think they are not being observed or playing with cross-gender toys only when visiting a female friend. Although cross-gender identity may not change, this decrease in overt cross-gender behaviors will reduce peer group stigmatization. (Green 1995, p. 2011)

With the advent of television talk shows, . . . male and female transsexuals parade regularly before the television cameras to be witnessed by children at home after school. . . . Formerly, I would tell gender-disgruntled youngsters that they could not change gender, so they might as well find the best of being the gender to which they were born. Now, children know that they "can get an operation." I tell them, however, that children cannot get the operation, and that when adults do they do not really change sex, and further that they cannot have any of their own children after the operation. (Green 1995, pp. 2009–10)

As the aetiology of gender identity disorder is unclear and probably multifactorial, at our clinic we have developed a model of management in which altering the gender identity disorder per se is not a primary therapeutic objective. Our primary therapeutic objectives are the developmental processes which, on clinical and research experience, seem to have been negatively affected in the child. (DiCeglie 1995, p. 254).

Several therapeutic strategies have been employed to treat children with GIDC, including behavior therapy, psychotherapy, family therapy, parental counseling, group therapy, and eclectic combinations of these approaches. (Bradley and Zucker 1990, p. 482)

Our clinic . . . suggests that parents disallow cross-dressing, discourage cross-gender role play and fantasy play, restrict playing with cross-sex toys, tell the child that they value him as a boy (or her as a girl), encourage same-sex peer relations, and help the child engage in more sex-appropriate or neutral activities. (Zucker 1990b, p. 38)

My position with him tonight in play was that I can understand that not everybody likes to play ball . . . but at the same time he doesn't have to do girlish things. That's something, doing sissy things, that people make fun of. . . . [H]e's going to be very unhappy doing sissy things. He heard me. He just sat there. He was playing with a doll while I was saying it. He got a little upset and put the doll away. . . . I told him that as he grows up, and if he continues to do sissy things, that he won't have many friends, and people will make fun of him, and that he'll be very unhappy. (Green 1987, p. 274)

The behavioral approach assumes that children learn sex-typed behaviors and that these behaviors can be shaped . . . by encouraging some and discouraging others. Therapy, accordingly, consists of systematically arranging that rewards follow sex-appropriate behaviors and that no rewards (or perhaps punishments) follow sex-inappropriate behaviors. The behavior targets of intervention have included a variety of cross-gender behaviors, including toy and dress-up play, role-playing, exclusive affiliation with the opposite sex, and mannerisms. (Zucker 1990b, pp. 30–31)

Treatment recommendations . . . would be focused on understanding and controlling the individual's anxiety, perhaps involving desensitization/conditioning techniques as well as promoting self-validation in the gender role. In addition, intervention with parents of gender-disturbed children should involve advice regarding discouragement of gender inappropriate behaviors and encouragement of same-sex activities and peer involvement. . . . With the gender-disturbed early adolescent, efforts to diminish cross-sex mannerisms and social skill training to allow better integration with same-sex peers seems critical. (Bradley 1985, p. 186)

The therapist . . . met with Kevin weekly for 1-hour sessions throughout the 15 weeks of treatment. During each treatment session, the therapist described the covert modeling sequence in detail and waited for Kevin to acknowledge that a sequence was clear in his mind by raising his index finger. . . . An example of a treatment sequence was as follows: You are walking out of school onto the playground. You imagine that Steve Austin, the Six Million Dollar Man, is walking ahead of you. You look at how he walks and you want to walk just like him. You see that he takes long smooth steps and his hips don't swish or move from side to side as he walks. His arms hang loosely at his side. He doesn't move his hands very much when walking and his wrist isn't limp or loose. (Hay and Barlow 1981, pp. 390–91)

Becky's mother explained to her that treatment would be undertaken because Becky "acted too much like a boy" and because she didn't want her to "be like a boy" when she grew up. . . . Becky was observed and treated in a clinic playroom. . . . The research assistant gave Becky a wrist counter and gave her these instructions: "You may play with any of the toys that you like, but you can only press the wrist counter when playing with girls' toys." (Rekers and Mead 1979, pp. 408, 411)

When he was five, Kyle entered a behavior modification program . . . in a laboratory setting and at home. At home, a token reinforcement program was instituted. Kyle received blue tokens for "desirable" behaviors, such as play with boys' toys or with boys, and red ones for "undesirable" behaviors, such as doll-play, "feminine" gestures, or playing with girls. Blue tokens were redeemable for treats, such as ice cream. Red tokens resulted in a loss of blue tokens, periods of isolation, or spanking by father. The treatment program lasted ten months. (Green 1987, p. 295)

Rationales for Treating GID in Children

Perhaps if Western culture accommodated gender-deviant children in the manner of the Native-American berdache or the native Hawaiian mahu, intervention would be unwarranted. But our culture has not moved toward accommodating these children, notwithstanding the pronouncements of androgyny trumpeted so audibly decades ago. (Green 1995, p. 2014)

A rationale for treating this gender dysphoria component in children is its relationship to later life distress. Not only is the continuing of a cross-gender identity problematic when expressed as transsexualism (now called gender identity disorder of adulthood), but for male homosexuals, elevated levels of depressions and anxiety are correlated with persistence of gender dysphoria (Wienrich et al., in press). (Green 1995, p. 2010)

A young person's natural instinct might be to just eat salty or sugary food. But every parent knows that's bad for them. They'll have a healthier life if they have a balanced diet. And emotionally they'll have an easier life if they're heterosexual. (Rothenberg 1995)

I treat them, so I know why I consider it treatworthy. I tell the parents we have no idea what it will do to their sexual orientation, and that sexual orientation is not the aim of treatment. These kids are getting a lot of flak from their peers, and that causes a lot of stress. . . . We don't know how to change society, but we can change their gender identity problems so they can live in their peer group with less distress. (Meyer-Bahlburg 1993, pp. 13–15).

Two short term goals have been discussed in the literature: the reduction or elimination of social ostracism and conflict and the alleviation of underlying or associated psychopathology. Longer term goals have focused on the prevention of transsexualism and/or homosexuality. (Bradley and Zucker 1990, p. 482)

There are . . . various rationales for intervening in the gender identity development of highly feminine boys or masculine girls. Some of these rationales rest on firmer empirical or medical-ethical grounds than others. At least two goals—elimination of peer ostracism in childhood and prevention of transsexualism in adulthood—are so obviously clinically valid and consistent with the medical ethics of our time that either, by itself, would constitute sufficient justification for therapeutic intervention. The primary goal of avoiding adult homosexuality is considerably more problematic, especially if this is attempted for religious rather than clinical reasons. (Zucker 1990b, p. 30)

It is not presently possible to differentiate the pretranssexual from the pretransvestite or prehomosexual child, but nevertheless there are clinical rationales offered for the prevention of all 3 of these conditions. (Rekers 1988, p. 44)

After a thorough behavioral assessment has documented a pattern of cross-gender behavior, professional ethics would require informing the child's parents or guardian regarding (a) the possibility of transsexualism, transvestism, or homosexual orientation, and (b) the behavioral treatment interventions that have been demonstrated to reverse these cross-gender behavior patterns. (Rekers 1988, pp. 43–44)

There are numerous interrelated reasons for intervening in the life of a boy diagnosed with a gender disturbance. The first reason for treatment is the psychosocial maladjustment of gender disturbed children. The second reason for intervention is to prevent severe sexual problems of adulthood such as transsexualism and homosexuality . . . that are highly resistant to treatment in later phases of development. The third reason is to prevent the serious emotional, social and economic maladjustments secondary to severe adulthood sexual problems. And the fourth main reason is to cooperate with appropriate parental concern over gender deviance. (Rekers 1987, p. 24)

I have not been impressed by the pervasiveness of peer ostracism during early childhood, though by late childhood its presence is more obvious. Thus, unless one wishes to advocate treatment in order to avoid subsequent peer ostracism, I am not convinced that this rationale is a compelling one. Moreover, to advocate treatment simply because others do not "like" one's behavior can only be taken so far as a general principle. (Zucker 1985, p. 117)

In my view, offering treatment to a child (either on his or her own or through parental consent) can be justified for a relatively simple reason. Cross-gender identification constitutes a potentially problematic developmental condition. Taken to its extreme, the outcome appears to be transsexualism. (Zucker 1985, p. 117)

In general it would seem that preventing either transsexualism or transvestism is a goal that will never gather systematic opposition, but to make the same claim for homosexuality is highly unlikely . . . the prevention (or encouragement) of homosexuality in its own right is, at present, primarily an ideological issue. (Zucker 1985, p. 116)

[A]t least for many "homosexual" adolescents, object choice may be less fixed than is sometimes believed. . . . For many adolescents and their families, the key issue is whether one can or should change what appears to be a developing homosexual orientation. . . . [E]fforts to promote heterosexual functioning should focus on those individuals who have not yet had extensive homosexual experiences. (Bradley 1985, pp. 185–86)

Relationship of GID in Children to Adult Homosexuality and/ or Transsexualism

[C]hildhood cross-gender behavior is the age-specific presentation of a homosexual male or female. (Green 1995, p. 2008)

The empirical evidence linking childhood gender identity and adult homosexuality is clear and consistent. (Zucker 1990a, p. 19)

Green's prospective study of extremely feminine boys found that 75% to 80% were either bisexual or homosexual at the time of their follow-up in adolescence or young adulthood. Other follow-up studies by Money and Russo, Zuger, and Davenport have also yielded high rates of homosexuality—100% in the series reported by Money! Transsexualism, or at least intense gender dysphoria, has occurred at a rate much lower than would be predicted from retrospective studies, but at a rate higher than would be expected based on general population prevalence rates. (Bradley and Zucker 1990, p. 479)

[T]he risk for post-pubertal gender dysphoria is greatest among those children living in families in which their [sic] has been a high tolerance for the continuation of the cross-gender behavior. This often results in the child not being referred (among our adolescent transsexual cases, almost none were seen clinically during childhood). . . . The lack of intervention or limit-setting on the part of the parents facilitates, in part, the development of a fixed fantasy of the self as of the opposite sex. When this continues into the adolescent years, request for hormonal and surgical sex reassignment is seen by the adolescent as the only solution to his or her gender dysphoria. Gay adolescents with a history of GIDC are also at risk for gender dysphoria. If they move into the "drag queen" subculture or are unable to find a niche in the more conventional parts of the gay community, then the fantasy of changing sex becomes more prominent. (Bradley and Zucker 1990, p. 479)

[E]arly effeminate behavior is not merely a forerunner of homosexuality in that it forecasts homosexuality, it is in fact the earliest stage of homosexuality itself. (Zuger 1988)

If the psychopathology of "Gender Identity Disorder of Childhood" is one of the major etiological precursors to adulthood homosexual orientation disturbance (as the research indicates at present), it would now appear logical that homosexuality per se be re-examined as a mental disorder. (Rekers 1987, pp. 28–29)

[T]he psychosexual outcome in males is predominantly atypical. Of 94 cases, 5 are transsexual (5.3%), 43 are homosexual or bisexual (45.7%), 1 is a heterosexual transvestite (1.1%), 21 are heterosexual (22.3%), and 24 are uncertain (25.5%). If the uncertain cases are excluded, then 70% of the cases are either transsexual, homosexual or bisexual, or transvestite, and 30% are heterosexual. (Zucker 1985, p. 150)

The gender-disturbed child moving into adolescence is a sensitive individual with reduced anxiety tolerance, a rather weak sense of himself or herself, and a degree of gender insecurity. These factors may make it very difficult for this individual to contemplate heterosexual involvement. . . . The choice of a same sex partner may reduce that anxiety and may also coincide with that individual's need to reinforce his or her self-value through identification with another biologically similar but stronger individual. . . . Once begun, . . . sexual activity in itself is reinforcing because of the pleasure involved and the self-validation, both from other partners and from a group. This produces . . . a homosexual identity. (Bradley 1985, pp. 184–85)

It is clear from the data that boyhood femininity is correlated with an increased incidence of homosexual object choice in later life, atypical gender behavior, or both. However, we are presently unable to predict the development of heterosexuality, homosexuality, transvestism or transsexuality as these boys, treated or untreated, reach adulthood. (Coates 1987, p. 199)

[T]he . . . data point to a strong association between childhood cross-gender behavior and subsequent homosexuality. . . . This finding is probably, at present, the best validational data for considering childhood cross-gender identification a meaningful "syndrome" of behavior. . . . (Zucker 1985, p. 152)

Motivation of Parents Seeking Treatment for GID in Children

The principal long-range concern by parents with cross-gender children is later homosexuality or transsexuality. The public has long identified what was only demonstrated in Green's (1987) prospective research recently—the association between childhood gender nonconformity and adulthood homosexuality. (Green 1995, p. 2006)

Do parents have the right to request or demand treatment for gender identity disorder children? Under the United States legal system, parents have considerable latitude in raising their children. The U.S. Supreme Court held that Amish parents had the right to withdraw their children from mainstream American schools and continue their education in a traditionally ethnoreligious manner that could preclude their integration into the larger society. (Wisconsin v. Yoder 1972.) In this age of human immunodeficiency virus-related diseases, parents have the right to refuse to have their children receive condoms in school (In re matter of Alfonso v. Fernandez 1993). Parents can decide to have or not have their children take formal religious training. Thus, parents have the legal right to seek treatment to modify their child's cross-gender behavior to standard boy and girl behavior even if their only motivation is to prevent homosexuality. (Green 1995, p. 2007)

Not surprisingly, . . . the development of a heterosexual orientation is probably preferred by most parents of children with GIDC. It is important, therefore, that clinicians point out that, as of yet, there is no strong evidence either way as to the effectiveness of treatment on later sexual orientation. Both authors . . . have preferred to emphasize the merits of reducing childhood gender identity conflict per se and to orient the parents to the short term goals of intervention. (Bradley and Zucker 1990, p. 482)

Suppose that boys who play with dolls rather than trucks, who role-play as mother rather than as father, and who play only with girls tend disproportionately to evolve as homosexual men. Suppose that parents know this, or suspect this. The rights of parents to oversee the development of children is a long-established principle. Who is to dictate that parents may not try to raise their children in a manner that maximizes the possibility of a heterosexual outcome? (Green 1987, p. 260)

Reported Impact of Treatment

It is possible that by targeting and improving the developmental processes which may underpin gender development, the gender identity disorder itself will be affected in a secondary way and will not lead to an atypical gender identity development in adulthood. (DiCeglie 1995, p. 254)

There is no convincing data that anything the therapist does can modify the direction of sexual orientation (typically the parents' primary concern). (Green 1995, p. 2014)

Toward the end of therapy he . . . had ceased cross-dressing, dramatic narcissistic displays and acting the vamp. Instead, he now manifested mostly masculine interests, play and behavior, and complementary play. . . . Whether he was able to continue along this developmental path is unknown since he still needed treatment for his narcissistic personality, and gender identity disorders. (Sugar 1995, pp. 278–79)

[P]rospective studies of gender identity disorder children reveal few transsexuals at follow-up. One reason may be that parents who bring gender atypical children for clinical evaluation interrupt the transsexual developmental process. Treatment is directed toward facilitating acceptance by the child of the gender assigned at birth and developing effective same-gender social skills. This may abort the development of the compelling need to be a person of the other gender. (Green 1995, p. 2013)

There is suggestive evidence that therapy might have had a beneficial effect on adult gender identity, in that none of the patients who ended up transsexual had received treatment during childhood. . . . My own clinical experience suggests that treatment is most effective before puberty and that the desire to change sex becomes much more difficult to shift in adolescence. (Zucker 1990b, p. 39)

From the result of my research studies, it now appears that a preventive treatment for transvestism, transsexualism, and some forms of homosexuality has indeed been isolated in these techniques of early identification and early intervention in the childhood years. (Rekers 1987, p. 28)

Cross-dressing ceased very quickly after admission to hospital. Many of the other cross-gender behaviours, which had been present for years, vanished after several weeks. . . . The treatment of cross-gender behaviour by means of inpatient therapy seems effective. . . . These results may correct some previous pessimistic views about outcome. (Kosky 1987, pp. 567, 568)

Estimated Incidence of GID in Children

The incidence of gender identity disorders is not known. A rough estimate can be made from studies linking childhood cross-gender behavior and adulthood homosexuality. Rates of predominant homosexuality appear to be 2% to 5% for males and 1% to 3% for females (Diamond 1993). Three-fourths of the gender identity disorder children from my prospective study . . . emerged as homosexual or bisexual. Thus, the incidence of gender identity disorder could be 1.5% to just over 3% for males and about half that for females. (Green 1995, p. 2005)

Conservative estimates of prevalence might be inferred from data regarding the prevalence of transsexualism. . . . The prevalence rate . . . might also be derived from data regarding the prevalence of homosexuality. . . . [O]ne could argue that GIDC, or its subclinical variants, may occur in two percent to five percent of children in the general population. (Bradley and Zucker 1990, pp. 477–78)

Theories about the Etiology of GID in Children

No single cause has yet been found with certainty for the development of a gender identity disorder. (DiCeglie 1995, p. 253)

A number of authors, e.g., Money (1992) and Coates et al. (1991), would agree that many of these factors [hereditary, hormonal, family, and psychosocial] need to be present at the same time and work together during a critical period to produce a full-blown gender identity disorder. (DiCeglie 1995, p. 254)

Evidence from other cultures of the association between childhood cross-gender behavior and adulthood homosexual behavior is substantial. . . . This cross-cultural research, and the evidence for biological origins of sexual orientation, suggest that childhood cross-gender behavior is the age-specific presentation of a homosexual male or female. (Green 1995, p. 2008)

[Susan Coates] speculates that temperament may be a predisposing factor for GID in boys, but neither offers data to support this nor addresses the issue of how temperament applies in GID girls. Instead of temperament, may I suggest that the constant proximity of the GID boy to his mother with imitation of, and identification with, her instead of his father serves as a predisposition; the same would then apply to the GID girl and her father. (Sugar 1995, p. 265)

Temperament, family traits and state, and severe stress must lead to a common pathway in which massive anxiety occurs in the child during a developmentally sensitive and vulnerable period. . . . [D]evelopmental, biological, psychosocial, and psychodynamic components . . . interact to produce a gender identity disorder. (Coates 1990, pp. 434–35)

The predisposing role of biological factors in psychosexual development is accepted by the majority of contemporary sex researchers. Psychosocial factors have also been the subject of study and it is the integration of biological and psychological factors that has become the subject of diverse enquiry. (Bradley and Zucker 1990, p. 480)

Parental tolerance, or even encouragement, of the nascent cross-gender behaviour also appears to be an extremely important part of the clinical picture. (Bradley and Zucker 1990, p. 481)

The common denominator of psychoanalytic theories of cross-gender identity is the assumption that pathogenic early parenting is the root cause of this disorder. There is a great deal of variation beyond that, however, and in some instances, precisely opposite causes are asserted for the same disorder. (Zucker 1990b, p. 34)

If there is a biological contributor to the etiology to childhood cross-gender behavior, the evidence at this point is quite weak and indirect. At the present time, we must tentatively conclude that the main source for gender deviance is found in social learning and psychological development variables in the family environment. (Rekers 1988, p. 39)

An overemphasis on a biological model of gender disorder may . . . lead to therapeutic pessimism. (Kosky 1987, p. 568)

The etiology of childhood cross-gender behavior remains a subject of great debate. (Zucker 1985, p. 153)

Children Referred for Diagnosis and Treatment

The following excerpts from clinical reports describe children referred for diagnosis and treatment for GID:

The mother of a 5-year-old boy telephoned me to say that her son might have a gender identity problem. From about the time of his second birthday, the boy had shown considerable interest in his mother's clothing and accessories. He walked about in her high-heeled shoes but showed no interest in his dad's shoes. He was fascinated by female figures in cartoons and storybooks and would imitate them, often while improvising feminine costumes. . . . During preschool years, the boy made friends more easily with girls. When other children played with cars or trucks, he was more interested in dolls. At toy stores, he would insist on buying toys from the girls' section. On more than one occasion he had said that he wanted to be a girl. (Green 1995, pp. 2001, 2003–4)

Toni, a 6-year-old girl with an IQ of 123, was . . . referred because of increasing parental concern over her gender identity development. . . .

At times, she displayed exaggerated masculine motoric movements and would lower her voice. She was adamantly opposed to wearing stereotypically feminine clothes and dressed almost exclusively in pants. Her only concession was wearing a dress to church. She stated that she dressed "like a gentleman" during the week but for church she dressed "like a lady."

Toni was quite outspoken in her desire to be a boy. At school, she began to call herself a boy and to spell her name as "Tony," which greatly alarmed her teacher. Toni had heard from neighborhood boys about "sex change" and subsequently asked her parents more about this. Toni's mother, perhaps because of her "liberal" or "permissive" child-rearing style, explained the mechanics of sex-reassignment surgery to her; after that, she became, in her parents' words, "obsessed" with the idea.

Toni was persistent in claiming that she had male genitalia "hidden inside." . . . If hit in the stomach with a hockey puck, she would clutch herself and exclaim, "Oh, my balls!" Information from interviews and psychological testing indicated that Toni knew that she was a girl but was struggling with intense desires that this not be so. For example, Toni stated that she knew she didn't really have a penis and testicles hidden inside of her, but that she said so "just to be like a boy." At a later point, she tried to explain her feelings thus: "I am a girl but I'm not."

During formal psychological testing, Toni was asked directly if she were a boy or a girl. Toni replied, "A girl," and also correctly answered the counterquestion, "Are you a boy?" When asked if she would grow up to be a mommy or a daddy, she replied, "I don't know! I don't know, I might have a sex change, I might not." (Zucker 1990a, pp. 1, 7)

Kevin [aged 10 years and 7 months] was referred for treatment of severe gender identity confusion following an independent evaluation at a local child guidance clinic. Kevin stated that he preferred to play with girls and with toys usually given to female children, such as dolls. Kevin's favorite television show was "The Bionic Woman," and his favorite game consisted of playing with a camper and a family of dolls. (In this game, Kevin fantasized that he was the mother). When asked if he would rather be a boy or a girl, Kevin vacillated between the two responses, feeling that it might be fun to be a girl but concluding that he would rather be a boy. Kevin also stated that in school other children called him names such as "sissy" and "fag" and that he was afraid to respond for fear of getting physically hurt. During this interview, Kevin's voice inflection and mannerisms were judged to be an exaggeration of feminine sex-type behaviors. (Hay and Barlow 1981, pp. 389)

Becky was referred for treatment at the age of 7 years 11 months by a psychiatric nurse specialist at the request of her mother. Throughout her childhood history, Becky dressed exclusively in boys' pants and often wore cowboy boots, while consistently rejecting feminine clothing (e.g., dresses) and jewelry. Her only use of feminine cosmetic articles was to draw a moustache and/or a beard on her face. She appeared masculine in her gestures, mannerisms, and walk. (Rekers and Mead 1979, pp. 407)

Conclusion

If GID in children was not strongly associated with homosexuality in adulthood, it is unlikely that "feminine" behavior in boys and "masculine" behavior in girls would have been designated psychiatric disorders or become the focus of an entire clinical field devoted to analyzing and "correcting" cross-gender behaviors and identifications (see, e.g., Zucker 1985, p. 152). Although some therapists have tried to promote recognition and understanding of gender-atypical children, these efforts have been undermined by clinicians' preoccupation with how and whether treatment can disrupt the association between gender atypicality in children and homosexuality and transsexualism in adults. There is no evidence that treatment of GID in children has any impact on the child's later sexual or gender identity. More importantly, attempts to alter or manipulate a child's future sexual orientation and/or gender identity raise serious ethical and legal concerns.

Some clinicians have tried to resolve these concerns by maintaining that homosexuality is either a mental disorder or so fraught with social difficulties that treatment of children who are known to be "at risk" of adult homosexuality is a compelling rationale (Rekers 1987; Zucker 1990b). Others have acknowledged that while the prevention of homosexuality may be dubious, treatment to prevent adult transsexualism is presumptively valid, even though few children with GID will grow up to be transsexual and even in the absence of any direct evidence that transsexualism is any more amenable to prevention— or any less compatible with psychological health—than homosexuality (Zucker 1985, 1990b). Others have acknowledged that gender-atypical children and transgendered adults have existed throughout human history and have participated as fully integrated members of many cultures. They have concluded, however, that clinicians are justified in attempting to change gender-atypical children to conform to contemporary social norms (Stoller 1985, pp. 171–80; Green 1995, pp. 2013–14). Still others have sought to justify treatment by adopting a developmental model that defines early acquisition of an unambiguously male or female "core gender identity" as the linchpin of normal development. Not surprisingly, this model can only interpret a gender-variant child as a developmental anomaly (Money 1994; Coates 1990). In the long run, as Meyer-Bahlburg has suggested, it is doubtful that any of these rationales for attempting to alter the development of gender atypical children will survive (Meyer-Bahlburg 1993).

The dramatic change in clinical perspectives on lesbian, gay, and bisexual youth in the past two decades provides a useful example of the direction that future research on gender-atypical children might take. As researchers have examined lesbian, gay, and bisexual youth without the preconception of inherent pathology, they have found (1) that sexual minority youth who have adequate social support are no more likely to experience mental health problems than their heterosexual peers; (2) that sexual minority youth who do not have adequate support are at heightened risk for depression and other mental health problems as a result of isolation and/or rejection from family and peers; and (3) that the most effective interventions for these youth are those that focus on alleviating isolation and other external stressors, including referrals to support groups and other community resources (Savin-Williams 1994; American Academy of Pediatrics 1993; Boxer 1993; Futterman and Casper 1992; Bidwell and Deisher 1991; Remafedi 1987; Gonsiorek 1988).

John Gonsiorek has stressed that "many of the problems that are experienced by gay and lesbian youth appear to be psychologic or intrapsychic in nature, but actually stem from external stress and lack of support." Thus, "[i]n the absence of obvious, severe psychopathology, a practical approach is to refer the client to a support group while a thorough mental health evaluation is being conducted. More often than not, improvement will ensue, and the need for mental health services will diminish" (Gonsiorek 1988, pp. 116, 120). Robert Bidwell and Robert Deisher have also emphasized that:

> It is not the role of the pediatrician to make a "diagnosis" of heterosexuality or homosexuality. Only the adolescent, provided with objective information, supportive resources, and an ongoing accepting relationship with the physician will be able to decide who he or she really is. These adolescents should be told that if they are, in fact, lesbian or gay, they are not alone and that their future personal, sexual, and professional lives can be as productive and fulfilling as those of other people. (Bidwell and Deisher 1991, pp. 298–99)

In a policy statement on "Homosexuality and Adolescence," the American Academy of Pediatrics has concluded that "[t]herapy directed specifically at changing sexual orientation is contraindicated, since it can provoke guilt and anxiety while having little or no potential for achieving changes in orientation" (American Academy of Pediatrics 1993, p. 633).

If research and treatment of gender-atypical children were not confined to a pathological model, clinicians might well find that gender-atypical children, whatever their later sexual orientation and gender identity, would also benefit from an approach focused on providing the child with family and social support and with reassurance that gender atypicality does not preclude a productive and fulfilling life. There is an important difference between defining gender atypicality in children as a disorder and identifying gender-variant children as a distinct group who may be at heightened risk for depression and other mental health problems because of social stigma and rejection. Although clinicians have shown little willingness to question their approach to gender-variant children in the past, the increasingly vocal concerns of lesbian, gay, bisexual, and transgendered people (including individuals who were damaged by treatment for GID as children) may encourage therapists and researchers to redirect the energies and research monies that continue to be spent on the dubious and futile quest to eliminate gender atypicality in children. Instead of generating new techniques and new rationales for conforming gender-variant children to "standard boy and girl behavior" (Green 1995), clinicians may finally focus on the far more rational, ethical, and achievable goal of how to help gender-variant children develop the emotional and social resources needed by every child who is at risk for stigma and isolation. In the meantime, there is little doubt that current clinical approaches to GID in children reinforce the larger society's rejection and disapproval of gender-variant children, or that current treatments have damaged children who already confront formidable obstacles to developing and maintaining self-esteem.

REFERENCES

Alfonso V. Fernandez, 195 A.D. 2d 46, 606 N.Y.S. 2d 259 (2d Dept. 1993).

American Academy of Pediatrics, Committee on Adolescence. "Homosexuality and Adolescence," *Pediatrics* 92 (4): 631–33. (1993).

American Psychiatric Association (APA). *Diagnostic and Statistical Manual of Mental Disorders*, 3d ed., rev. (1987). Referred to as *DSM III-R*.

————. *Diagnostic and Statistical Manual of Mental Disorders*, 4th ed. (1994). Referred to as *DSM-IV*.

Bayer, Ronald. *Homosexuality and American Psychiatry: The Politics of Diagnosis* (1981).

Berg, Charles. "The Problem of Homosexuality (I)," *American Journal of Psychotherapy* 10: 696–708 (1956) (cited in Griswold, infra, at 210).

————. "The Problem of Homosexuality (II)," *American Journal of Psychotherapy* 11: 65–79 (1957) (cited in Griswold, infra, at 210).

Bidwell, Robert J., and Robert W. Deisher. "Adolescent Sexuality: Current Issues," *Pediatric Annals* 20(6): 293–302 (June 1991).

Bleiberg, E., et al. "Gender Identity Disorder and Object Loss," *Journal of the American Academy of Child Psychiatry* 25: 58–67 (1986).

Boxer, Andrew. *The Children of Horizons* (1993).

Bradley, Susan. "Gender Disorders in Childhood," in *Gender Dysphoria* (Steiner ed., 1985).

Bradley, Susan, and Kenneth Zucker. "Gender Identity Disorder and Psychosexual Problems in Children and Adolescents," *Canadian Journal of Psychiatry* 35: 477–86 (1990).

Brown, Daniel, "The Development of Sex-Role Inversion and Homosexuality," *Journal of Pediatrics* 50: 616 (1957) (cited in Griswold, infra, at 210).

Coates, Susan. "Extreme Boyhood Femininity: Isolated Behavior or Pervasive Disorder?" in *Annual Progress in Child Psychiatry and Child Development* 197–213 (1987).

————. "Ontogenesis of Boyhood Gender Identity Disorder," *Journal of the American Academy of Psychoanalysis* 18(3): 414–38 (1990).

Coates, S., R. Friedman, and S. Wolfe. "The Aetiology of Boyhood Gender Identity Disorder: A Model for Integrating Temperament, Development and Psychodynamics," *Psychoanalytic Dialogues* 1: 481–523 (1991).

Diamond, M. "Homosexuality and Bisexuality in Different Populations," *Archives of Sexual Behavior* 22: 291–310 (1993).

DiCeglie, Domenico. "Gender Identity Disorders in Children and Adolescents," *British Journal of Hospital Medicine* 53(6): 251–56 (1995).

Fontaine, Andre. "Are We Staking Our Future on a Crop of Sissies?" *Better Homes and Gardens* 29: 154–56 (December 1950) (cited in Griswold, infra, at 207).

Futterman Donna, and Virginia Casper. "Homosexuality: Challenges of Treating Lesbian and Gay Adolescents," in *Primary Pediatric Care* (Hoeckelman ed., 1992).

Gershman, Harry. "Psychopathology of Compulsive Homosexuality," *American Journal of Psychoanalysis* 17: 58–72 (1957) (cited in Griswold, infra, at 210).

Gonsiorek, John. "Mental Health Issues of Gay and Lesbian Adolescents," *Journal of Adolescent Health Care* 9: 114–22 (1988).

Green, Richard. "Gender Identity in Childhood and Later Sexual Orientation: Follow-Up of 78 Males," *American Journal of Psychiatry* 142(3): 339–41 (1985).

———. *The Sissy Boy Syndrome and the Development of Homosexuality* (1987).

———. "Gender Identity Disorder in Children," in *Treatments of Psychiatric Disorders* (Gabbard ed., 1995).

Griswold, Robert L. *Fatherhood in America: A History* (1993).

Hay, William, and David Barlow. "Treatment of Stereotypic Cross-Gender Motor Behavior Using Covert Modeling in a Boy with Gender Identity Confusion," *Journal of Consulting and Clinical Psychology* 49(3): 388–94 (1981).

Kolb, Lawrence, and Adelaide Johnson. "Etiology and Therapy of Overt Homosexuality," *Psychoanalytic Quarterly* 24: 508 (1955) (cited in Griswold, supra, at 210).

Kosky, Robert J. "Gender-Disordered Children: Does Inpatient Treatment Help?" *Medical Journal of Australia* 146: 565–69 (June 1, 1987).

Loeb, L. and M. Shane. "The Resolution of a Transsexual Wish in a Five Year Old Boy," *Journal of the American Psychoanalytic Association* 30: 419–34 (1982).

Lothstein, Leslie. "The Adolescent Gender Dysphoria Patient: An Approach to Treatment and Management," *Journal of Pediatric Psychology* 5: 93–109 (1987).

Mass, Lawrence. *Dialogues of the Sexual Revolution*, Vol. (1990).

Meyer, J. K. "Body Ego, Selfness, and Gender Sense: The Development of Gender Identity," *Psychiatric Clinics of North America* 3: 21–36 (1980).

Meyer-Bahlburg, Heino. "Psychiatrists Set to Approve DSM-IV," *Journal of the American Medical Association* 270: 13–15 (1993).

Money, John. "The Concept of Gender Identity Disorder in Childhood and Adolescence after 39 Years," *Journal of Sex and Marital Therapy* 20(3): 163–77 (1994).

———. "The Concept of Gender Identity Disorder in Childhood and Adolescence after 37 Years." Proceedings of the Conference on Gender Identity and Development in Childhood and Adolescence, The Conference Unit, St. George's Hospital Medical School, London, 1992.

Money, John, and A. J. Russo. "Homosexual Outcomes of Discordant Gender Identity/Role: Longitudinal Follow-Up," *Journal of Pediatric Psychology* 4: 29–41 (1979).

Mussen, Paul, and Luther Distler. "Child-Rearing Antecedents of Masculine Identification in Kindergarten Boys," *Child Development* 31: 93–95 (1960) (cited in Griswold, supra, at 207).

Niccolosi, Joseph. *Reparative Therapy of Male Homosexuality* (1991).

Ovesey, L., and E. S. Person. "Gender Identity and Sexual Psychopathology in Men: A Psychodynamic Analysis of Homosexuality, Transsexualism and Transvestism," *Journal of the American Academy of Psychoanalysis* 1: 53–72 (1973).

Rekers, George. *Growing Up Straight: What Every Family Should Know about Homosexuality* (1982a).

———. *Shaping Your Child's Sexual Identity* (1982b).

———. "Inadequate Sex Role Differentiation in Childhood: The Family and Gender Identity Disorders," *Journal of Family and Culture* 2(7): 8–37 (1987).

———. "Psychosexual Assessment of Gender Identity Disorders," *Advances in Behavioral Assessment of Children and Families* 4: 33–71 (1988).

Rekers, George, and Shasta Mead. "Early Intervention for Female Sexual Identity Disturbance," *Journal of Abnormal Child Psychology* 7(4): 405–23 (1979).

Rekers, George, et al. "Child Gender Disturbances: A Clinical Rationale for Intervention," *Psychotherapy: Theory, Research and Practice* 14: 2–11 (1977).

Remafedi, Gary. "Adolescent Homosexuality: Psychosocial and Medical Implications," *Pediatrics* 79(3): 331–37 (1987).

Rosen, A. C., et al. "Ethical Issues in the Treatment of Children," *Journal of Social Issues* 34: 122–36 (1978).

Rothenberg, Annye (Children's Health Council of Palo Alto), quoted in Carole Rafferty. "Homosexuality Or 'Disorder'?" *Chicago Tribune*, Aug. 1, 1995 at Section 5.

Savin-Williams, Rich. "Verbal and Physical Abuse as Stressors in the Lives of Lesbian, Gay Male, and Bisexual Youths: Associations with School Problems, Running Away, Substance Abuse, Prostitution, and Suicide," *Journal of Consulting and Clinical Psychology* 62(2): 1–9 (1994).

Sedgwick, Eve Kosofsky. "How to Bring Your Kids Up Gay," *Social Text* 29: 18–27 (1990).

Siegel, Elaine. *Female Homosexuality: Choice without Volition* (1988).

Silverman, Martin. "The Prehomosexual Boy in Treatment," in *The Homosexualities: Reality, Fantasy, and the Arts* (Socarides ed., 1990).

Stoller, Robert. *Presentations of Gender* (1985).

Sugar, Max. "A Clinical Approach to Childhood Gender Identity Disorder," *American Journal of Psychotherapy* 49(2): 260–81 (1995).

West, D. J. "Parental Figures in the Genesis of Male Homosexuality," *International Journal of Social Psychiatry* 5: 85 (1959) (cited in Griswold, supra, at 210).

Wisconsin V. Yoder, 406 U.S. 205 (1972).

Zucker, Kenneth. "Cross-Gender-Identified Children," in *Gender Dysphoria* (Steiner ed., 1985).

———. "Gender Identity Disorders in Children: Clinical Descriptions and

Natural History," in *Clinical Management of Gender Identity Disorders in Children and Adults* (Blanchard and Steiner eds., 1990a).

———. "Treatment of Gender Identity Disorders in Children," in *Clinical Management of Gender Identity Disorders in Children and Adults* (Blanchard and Steiner eds., 1990b).

———. "Psychosocial and Erotic Development in Cross-Gender Identified Children," *Canadian Journal of Psychiatry* 35: 487–95 (1990c).

Zuger, B. "Is Early Effeminate Behavior in Boys Early Homosexuality?" *Comprehensive Psychiatry* 29(5): 509–19 (1988).

Two

Ethical Issues in Diagnosing and Treating Gender-Dysphoric Children and Adolescents

Richard R. Pleak

Back in the early 1980s, during my psychiatry residency in Pittsburgh, I evaluated an eleven-year-old girl who wanted to be a boy and only wore boys' clothes and did boy things. When our highly skilled and trained assessment team conferred about this patient, I learned there was no one in Pittsburgh who knew much about the evaluation or treatment of gender dysphoria, even though several of my supervisors and mentors were gay. Since the girl's family had the means, they were sent off to New York to see a gender dysphoria expert. I soon learned that very few people, and extremely few psychiatrists, across the country knew much about gender dysphoria in kids, and the professional literature was very sparse. Subsequently I took advantage of my child psychiatry residency at Columbia University in New York to work closely with psychologists Heino Meyer-Bahlburg and Anke Ehrhardt, both world renowned and respected specialists in gender identity who became my "gender mentors." In this essay, I review various psychiatric diagnostic issues and treatment approaches to gender dysphoria in childhood and adolescence, drawing attention to the inherent ethical pitfalls and potential remedies thereof. My focus will be on boys, as I see many more boys with gender dysphoria than girls, and very little information is available on girls.

Children with gender dysphoria can be labeled by others as being "sissies" or "tomboys," but generally have more extensive and overt cross-gender identification and behavior. Those who are very extensively cross-gendered would generally be diagnosed as having gender identity disorder.

The official American classification of psychiatric disorders is found in the American Psychiatric Association's *Diagnostic and Statistical Manual of Mental Disorders*, now in its fourth edition (APA, 1994). The DSM list of diagnoses and their codes closely correspond to the World Health Organization's *International Classification of Diseases*, now in its tenth edition (World Health Organization, 1992). These coded diagnoses are primarily used for communication purposes, such as for research agreement and for billing (third-party payers will not reimburse for treatment without these codes, and may limit treatment for certain codes). With *DSM-IV*, the previous diagnosis (in *DSM-IIIR*, APA, 1987) of transsexualism was changed and lumped together with the diagnoses of gender identity disorder of childhood (GIDC) and gender identity disorder of adolescence or adulthood, nontranssexual type (GIDAANT) into one diagnosis, gender identity disorder (GID), with specification as to "in children" or "in adolescents or adults." This was done despite the protest of some professionals (myself included) and many parents of gender dysphoric children. This lumping implies complete or substantial continuity of GID from childhood into adulthood, which follow-up studies of children show is not the case. Although most transsexual adults report histories of gender dysphoria and cross-gender behavior going back to early childhood, most children with gender dysphoria do not grow up to be transsexual (see below). Parents I have worked with do not want their children to be labeled with a diagnosis which equates them with being transsexual later; similarly, most parents do not want their children seen as being "pretransgendered" or "prehomosexual."

The *DSM-IV* diagnostic criteria for GID in children include the "repeatedly stated desire to be, or insistence that he or she is, the other sex, strong and persistent preferences for cross-sex roles in make-believe play or persistent fantasies of being the other sex, intense desire to participate in the stereotypical games and pastimes of the other sex, and strong preference for playmates of the other sex" (APA, 1994, p. 537). For boys, there is "preference for cross-dressing or simulating female attire . . . assertion that his penis or testes are disgusting or will disappear or assertion that it would be better not to have a penis, or aversion toward rough-and-tumble play and rejection of male stereotypical toys, games and activities" (p. 537). The criteria for girls include "insistence on wearing only stereotypical masculine clothing . . . rejection of urinating in a sitting position, assertion that she has or will grow a penis, or assertion that she does not want to grow breasts or menstruate, or marked aversion toward normative feminine clothing" (p. 537). Previous to *DSM-III* in 1980, there was no official diagnosis for children with extensive cross-gender behavior and fantasies: in studies done prior to *DSM-III*, terms such as "gender-disturbed" or "gender disordered" or descriptors such as "feminine" or "effeminate" boys and "masculine" girls were used. I now tend to favor "gender dysphoric" as a descriptor (not a diagnosis) for the patients referred to me, as it is less pejorative. Although a few of these children do not report dysphoria about their gender, many are confused about it and may evidence distress in their fantasies, play, and relationships.

Whether or not GID should even be a diagnosis has come under considerable debate in the past several years, in part due to its relationship to homosexuality. Charles Socarides, a prominent New York psychoanalyst, has argued for decades for the treatment of homosexuality itself as a disorder. Further, the organization Socarides cofounded and of which he has been president, the National Association for Research and Treatment of Homosexuality (NARTH), has advocated for the treatment of "prehomosexual" children, by which they mean children with atypical gender behaviors. Socarides believes homosexuality results in dysfunction and pathology, and is in part caused by a disturbed father-son relationship. Interestingly, his son Richard Socarides is a very successful gay man, currently a high-level aide to President Clinton, who has served as the White House liaison to the gay and lesbian community. Another prominent New York psychoanalyst, Richard Isay, has argued against the diagnosis of GID and for its deletion from *DSM* (1997). Isay has described atypical gender behavior as one early manifestation of homosexuality, which as a normal variation of sexuality should not be labeled as psychopathology and thus not be subjected to treatment. His argument has been met with angry opposition by some psychiatrists, most of whom continue to view homosexuality as a disorder in need of treatment.

The adult transgendered/transsexual communities have been very divided on the diagnosis of GID, which was seriously debated at the 1997 Vancouver meeting of the Harry Benjamin International Gender Dysphoria Association (HBIGDA). Some argued against the labeling and pathologizing of atypical gender identity and behavior, while others argued that the diagnosis is necessary for insurance reimbursement of medications (e.g., hormones), surgical procedures, and psychotherapy (necessary prior to sex reassignment surgery, according to HBIGDA guidelines and most professionals in gender work). Good recent discussions of these diagnostic issues can be found in articles by White and Townsend (1998) and Wilson (1998). Similarly, some in the transgendered/transsexual communities have sanctioned the GID diagnosis in children and support its treatment to prevent continued gender dysphoria and the need for hormonal treatment or surgery; others adamantly oppose this.

One compromise would be to eliminate the GID diagnosis as it relates to children, and retain it only for those transgendered adolescents and adults who wish to alter their bodies and are requesting therapy, hormones, and/or surgery. I do not use the diagnosis of GID for my child or adolescent patients, and I always have a thorough discussion of the relevant issues and possible consequences of this diagnosis with the parents. Diagnoses written in clinical reports and on insurance (billing) forms may find their way into the child's school records or be found by potential employers. For example, the FBI once called me for preemployment clearance of a nineteen-year-old patient I saw when he was a young adolescent: the FBI had learned of his treatment and diagnosis of attention deficit/hyperactivity disorder (ADHD: not GID listed!) from his parents' insurance company. The diagnosis of GID could result in discrimination against the child even later in life. Almost always, when a gender-dysphoric child is brought in to see a psychiatrist or other therapist, there are other issues or problems which can be diagnosed on record. If such a child has ADHD or a parent-child relational problem, either will suffice as the diagnosis of record.

Gender-typical and atypical behaviors should not be seen as dichotomies, but rather as being on a continuum or spectrum, with the majority of the population having gender-typical behavior, and a smaller proportion having some gender-typical and atypical behaviors. A small minority has extensive cross-gender behavior, and would generally be diagnosed in *DSM-IV* as having GID. There could be some uncertainty about the spectrum of the population with some to much (but not extensive) atypical gender behavior, in terms of whether and where such behavior may become clinically or diagnostically relevant. This illustrates what Meyer-Bahlburg (1985) has described as the "zone of transition between clinically significant cross-gender behavior and mere statistical deviations from the gender norm," or what others have described as the "gray area." Research done in the past few decades has shown that the future of children with gender identity disorders is not what it once seemed. In the 1960s, when Richard Green (1987) began recruiting a sample of boys with "gender identity disturbance," his assumption, and that of most investigators in the field, was that these children were pretranssexual: that is, in their teens and young adulthoods they would continue to have gender dysphoria of such a degree as to be transsexual. However, the long-term follow-up study done by Green (1987) and evidence by other investigators (e.g., Davenport, 1986; Zuger, 1988; Zucker and Bradley, 1995) has shown trannssexualism to be a rare outcome for these boys when grown up. In the natural history of childhood gender dysphoria, cross-gender behavior appears to diminish and may virtually disappear in the majority of boys around ages eight to ten. Instead of continued cross-gender behavior and transsexualism, they appear to have a much greater propensity to be homosexual or bisexual (and primarily gender-typical) in young adulthood than the general population.

Green's famous follow-up study of forty-four "feminine" boys showed that about three-quarters (73 percent) of them were homosexually or bisexually oriented by their later teens and early adulthood, while about one-quarter (27 percent) were heterosexually oriented (Green, 1987). All his thirty-five control boys were heterosexual. Only one boy later exhibited gender dysphoria. John Money and Anthony Russo (1979) followed nine boys with "gender disorder" into adulthood and found all of them to be homosexual. Bernard Zuger (1978) followed sixteen boys with "extensive effeminate behavior" into adolescence and young adulthood, and found that ten of the sixteen (63 percent) were homosexual and two (13 percent) were heterosexual. Phil Lebovitz (1972) found the opposite with sixteen boys with lesser degrees of cross-gender behavior: two (13 percent) were later homosexual and ten (63 percent) were heterosexual. Somewhat similar results were reported by Charles Davenport (1986), who followed up on ten feminine boys: two (20 percent) were homosexual and six (60 percent) were heterosexual. Kenneth Zucker and Susan Bradley (1995) reported that of the forty-five gender-dysphoric children (including five girls) they followed into adolescence and adulthood, 20 percent were later still gender-dysphoric, 60 percent were heterosexual, and 31 percent were bisexual or homosexual.

Looking at this association in reverse, one finds that retrospective reports of the childhood behaviors of gay men and lesbians show a higher propensity toward cross-gender behavior than the general population. For example, Saghir and Robins (1973), in retrospective reports of homosexual adults, found that 67 percent of men and 70 percent of women reported cross-gender behavior in childhood. However, these reports of "cross-gender behavior" included just being called sissy or tomboy: in childhood, only 16 percent of the men and 48 percent of the women had cross-dressed, and only 3 percent of the men and 6 percent of the women had expressed the desire to change sex. The predisposition to be homosexual thus appears to be positively correlated with the presence of childhood cross-gender behaviors: it is present with childhood gender-*typical* behavior, and increases with increasing degrees of cross-gender behavior. Likewise, the propensity to be heterosexual is present with childhood gender-*atypical* behavior, and increases with increasing degrees of same-gender behavior. The homosexual adult population can have a continuum of cross-gender histories, from none to extensive, with the majority probably having minor to moderate degrees of childhood gender-atypical behavior, such as disinterest (boys) or more interest (girls) in contact sports and aggression, as shown by the observations of Isay (1989) and others.

Despite (or perhaps even because of) these recent findings on the adult outcomes of gender-dysphoric boys, as well as the continued small number of professionals involved in this area, there has been a paucity of discussion of the justification and ethical issues involved in the treatment of children with gender dysphoria, both in the literature and at professional conferences over the past decade (notable exceptions are recent papers by Zucker, 1990b, 1995; and Pleak 1994, 1997; Pleak et al., 1991; Pleak and Anderson, 1998).

Debate on these treatment issues occurred with some frequency in the literature in the late 1970s, centering at that time on the behavior modification treatment of gender-dysphoric children. The treatment reports were primarily by psychologist George Rekers and his colleagues. The first such report, by Rekers and Lovaas (1974), described treatment focusing on reinforcing masculine behaviors and extinguishing feminine behaviors. There was quick criticism of this approach, which actively punished cross-gender behavior, as androgynous rearing practices were then being advocated by some as a way of eliminating later sexism (e.g., Nordyke et al., 1977; Winkler, 1977; Wolfe, 1979). In response, Reker and colleagues modified their descriptions of their treatment, stressing the reinforcement of masculine behaviors in an attempt to widen the child's repertoire of behaviors (Rekers et al., 1978; Rosen, Rekers, and Bentler, 1978; Rekers, 1980). Such debates abated around the time it began to be suspected that Rekers, the major proponent of behavior modification for gender dysphoria, was also using religious persuasion in "treating" these children, and that he had (and still has) an extremist religious bias against homosexuality (Rekers and Lovaas, 1974; Rekers, 1977, 1982a, 1982b, 1995).

Rekers, in his books *Shaping Your Child's Sexual Identity* (1982b) and *Growing Up Straight* (1982a), has called homosexuality "an unfortunate perversion . . . promiscuous and perverted sexual behavior . . . a sinful yielding to temptation," and he revealed that the goal behind his treatment was to promote "real masculinity, which should be affirmed in every young man in order to prevent them from being strongly tempted by the sexual perversions." Indeed, prevention of homosexuality was a stated goal of treatment in each of Rekers' early papers. In 1974, he and Lovaas wrote: "Only follow-up evaluations on these children at 15 to 20 yr of age . . . will allow us to claim a preventative treatment for extreme adult sexual deviations of transvestism, transsexualism, and some forms of homosexuality" (Rekers and Lovaas, 1974). In 1978, Rekers et al. (1978) wrote: "Professional intervention for [gender-dysphoric] children is appropriate because the early identification and prevention of male homosexual conflict . . . is preferable to all other clinical options." All these goals were established in the continued absence of any cases or data to substantiate Rekers's claims to "prevent" homosexuality. One must also recall that these goals were stated well after the depathologicalization in 1973 of homosexuality by the American Psychiatric Association and American Psychological Association. Morin and Schultz (1978) took early and vociferous exception to such goals in an early professional declaration of gay pride:

> It's a question not of the rights of children but of the rights of the adults that children become. That is, we regard a gay identity and life style as a positive option for adults, an outcome with certain developmental requirements. Unless and until these developmental needs are met, the

rights of adults to be gay is a hollow right. . . . From the perspective which values gay identity as a positive outcome for adults, the welfare of the adult requires that the child not be maimed, and the welfare of the child is best served by facilitating the child's growth toward any positive identity.

Now, twenty years later, their words are still pertinent.

Rekers's religious bias continues to be evident in his most recent book, *Handbook of Child and Adolescent Sexual Problems* (1995). A carefully written exercise in obfuscation, it contains extensive and biased discussion of homosexuality and gender dysphoria as pathology (with nineteen chapters, three are on homosexuality, two on GID). But it does so in very discrete ways. For example, although Rekers does not even reference his own two books from 1982, he does not repudiate or contradict them or his other homophobic/heterosexist writings either. Instead, his remarks, while gently criticizing "opponents of adolescent homosexuality . . . guilty of trying to bolster preexisting beliefs with data of convenience" (p. 309) are couched in terms of "life-threatening health risks . . . behavior proscribed by the Ten Commandments . . . comfortable heterosexual potential . . . postponement of *all* forms of overt interpersonal sexual involvement" (pp. 308–9) as he builds toward prevention of homosexual behavior at the least and homosexuality itself in general. It is remarkable that a major medical publishing house actually published this atrocious book. For a more balanced, contemporary review of adolescent homosexuality, see Pleak and Anderson (1998).

Rekers and colleagues have not been the only therapists advocating for the prevention of homosexuality. Judd Marmor (1980), in a reexamination of homosexuality, raised the issue as follows:

Is is legitimate for a psychotherapist to try to prevent the development of a homosexual life-style if it appears that a child is moving in that direction? . . . Until . . . our societal mores develop to a point at which homosexual behavior is no longer regarded with prejudice, the issue of preventing its development, where possible, is a legitimate one. . . . [E]ffeminate boys . . . should be considered as potentially susceptible to homosexual development and preventive treatment should be instituted as soon as possible. . . . With appropriate family therapy and guidance, many of these children can be helped to achieve more appropriate gender-role patterns, and presumably, in some of them at least, a homosexual life-pattern may be forestalled.

Once again, this goal is stated in the clear absence of any data or reports to support this presumption. More recently, the psychoanalyst Martin Silverman (1990) wrote:

> The complexity . . . of the path leading to adult male homosexuality or bisexuality make it difficult to predict . . . that any given child will ultimately develop such an orientation. . . . [H]owever, . . . the presence of certain factors . . . signals so high a risk that vigorous intervention should be given serious consideration. . . . A successful result from psychoanalytic treatment of a preschool boy apparently headed toward homosexuality . . . [is to] stem the tide toward homosexuality.

Calvin Haber (1991), another analyst, has written about a three-year-old boy whom he saw in analysis for several years:

> Mother feared Stanley might become a homosexual. . . . Without analysis, it seems that gender development would have moved toward a homosexual orientation. Followup during adolescence and early adulthood is required to validate the tentative conclusion that psychoanalysis during prelatency can be effective in gender identity disorders, and offers an alternative in some cases to a brittle sense of masculinity and/ or homosexual orientation in the future adult.

Haber has informed several parents of my patients (personal communications in 1993 and 1998) that his individual four to six days a week psychoanalytic treatment would reduce the chance of the boys being homosexual.

These claims assume that atypicality of gender identity (or some common underlying pathology) *causes* homosexuality. Just the opposite has been postulated by Isay (1989): that homosexual feelings, especially toward the father, can lead to the development of feminine characteristics. Another view (cf. Zucker, 1990a; Zuger, 1988) is that cross-gender behavior and homosexuality are different age-dependent manifestations of an underlying genetic or neural predisposition. This latter model would seem to be operative if the genetic marker findings of Dean Hamer et al. (1993) and/or the findings by Simon LeVay (1991) of size differences between heterosexual and homosexual men in an anterior hypothalamic nucleus are replicated, and if the size difference is found to be related to gender role behavior.

Although behavioral and some psychotherapeutic treatments have been reported to alter gender-role behaviors in children, evidence for treatment altering the course of sexual orientation is absent. Green (1987) spoke of the "powerlessness of treatment to interrupt the progression from feminine boy to homosexual or bisexual man." Of the twelve boys in his sample who entered various sorts of therapy, nine were later found to be homosexual or bisexual—the same proportion as for those without treatment (Green, 1987). The two boys in psychoanalytic therapy were both later homosexual. Two other boys had been treated in Rekers's program, and despite the goal of heterosexuality, both were later bisexual. The Rekers group has never published any information on the later sexual orientation or gender identity of their own patients. In Charles Davenport's (1986) study on ten feminine boys, six had received psychoanalytically oriented psychotherapy once to twice weekly for nine months to a year and a half, with the parents seen separately. On follow-up, when evaluated in their teens and twenties, three of the six treated men were heterosexual, while three of the four untreated men were heterosexual; two of the six treated men were homosexual, while none of the untreated men were. Thus, the two existing studies, while not at all treatment studies, do not give any credence to the idea that treatment of gender dysphoria can affect future sexual orientation. No studies have yet been designed to address this question specifically, and probably none will due to the ethical implications.

Parents who bring their atypical child to a therapist for treatment often make the assumption that their child is prehomosexual, and believe or hope that alteration of the child's gender-role behavior will diminish the likelihood of later homosexuality. Their open or hidden goal for treatment is that their child will not grow up to be homosexual, which they may view as a very negative future. Some therapists (such as Haber, above) claim, often to the parents' relief, that their treatment will not only eradicate cross-gender behavior but also result in later heterosexuality, or at least the goal of future heterosexuality is stipulated. Rosen, Rekers, and Bentler (1978) asked, "If a parent brings a child to a psychologist and asks that the possibility of homosexual development be prevented, is this not an ethical and professionally proper goal for the psychologist? We conclude yes . . . it need not be a goal that every psychologist would endorse, but it would seem appropriate nonetheless." Such claims and goals, it can now be seen, are unethical and unsupportable. Should future research show an effect of early psychological treatment on later sexual orientation, which is highly unlikely given the anecdotal evidence and according to widely accepted theories of sexual orientation (e.g., Friedman, 1988), then the debate will be focused upon the rights of the parents, society, professionals, and/or the government to attempt to alter the varieties of gender identity/behavior and sexual orientation in order to increase the possibility of heterosexual outcome (Green raised some of these issues back in 1987).

Some therapists, such as Zucker (1990b; Zucker and Bradley, 1995), make no claims as to treatment altering later sexual orientation, but justify treatment on the grounds of the social ostracism and peer rejection the child may endure if cross-gender behavior persists, especially as the child enters school and early sex-segregated play ensues. Treatment foci here are addressed to shorter-term alterations in behavior and comfort with assigned gender identity rather than to long-term outcome modification. While some therapists attempt to reverse cross-gender identification by actively extinguishing or even punishing cross-gender behavior (cf. Zucker, 1990b; Zucker and Bradley, 1995), others focus on increasing the child's abilities and skills in activities typical of their own sex, as well as increasing comfort and time spent with same-sex peers and adults. Focusing on reversing cross-gender behaviors via active disapproval or punishment may force these behaviors underground or "into the closet," and again raises the issues of sexism as well as how much the individual's behavior should be modified to fit the social norms of the time. Certainly, a therapist working with a black child who is having adjustment difficulties living in a predominately white society, should not treat the child to be "unblack." Rather he or she should focus on ways the minority child can effectively respond to and defend against the majority's biases, which may include broadening his repertoire of behaviors to sometimes adapt to societal expectations, as necessary for safety or when advantageous to the child. Instead of condoning parental disapproval or punishment of gender-atypical behaviors, I and my colleagues advise neutrality toward gender-atypical behaviors and positive redirection to gender-neutral or typical behaviors to expand what can be rigid preoccupations. We often find it necessary to intervene in the parents' extremely negative responses and overreactions to their child's cross-gender behavior, which draw inordinate attention to these behaviors and are a set-up for increased gender-atypical behaviors due more to the child's oppositionalism than to gender identification. My work is thus primarily done with and through the parents/caregivers, with initial education and clarification of goals followed by correction of the disturbed parent-child relationships and longer-term support and reinforcement of positive acceptance of the child.

The importance of this therapeutic method was seen in a supportive/educational therapy group for parent of boys with gender dysphoria. Dennis Anderson and I ran this group, the first described since Green's group in 1973, for about eighteen months with ten to twelve parents (Pleak and Anderson, 1993). The freedom of the parents in being able to talk openly about their children was one early benefit, and as the therapy progressed there was more overt acceptance of their children and the variety of adults they would become.

Although five to fifteen years ago the presenting complaint of most parents of gender-dysphoric boys was fear of later homosexuality, this has been less prominent in my practice recently. Nowadays, most parents worry that their child will not be happy, that they will be teased and rejected by their peers, and that they will be at risk for social and school failure. These parents are more accepting at the start that their child may be gay/lesbian later in life. A six-year-old boy I evaluated has three gay maternal uncles, two very successful, and his eventual sexual orientation in adulthood was not a concern for the parents: they were upset that his schoolmates and other adults were already castigating him. There is also much more appreciation by parents of the special temperament and creativity many gender-atypical boys have (a love or preference of certain colors and textures, particular interests in drawing and styling; see Coates, Friedman, and Wolfe, 1991) and a concern that with treatment some of these special and positive qualities may be lost. It is important to identify and address such concerns, and to find ways the parents can nurture their children's talents. A five-year-old boy patient would fashion dresses for his Barbie doll out of rags and yarn, and a fifteen-year-old designs and makes dresses for his mother and avant-garde androgynous or feminine clothes for himself. Both boys' parents see the potential for fashion careers for them, and have been able to encourage these interests to a greater extent with therapy.

Zucker (1990a, 1990b) has addressed another rationale for treating gender-disturbed children: to prevent or treat its underlying and/or associated psychopathology. Investigators such as Susan Coates and others (e.g., Coates and Person, 1985; Zucker, 1985) have reported high rates of separation anxiety, depression, and other behavioral problems in these boys. I and my colleagues (Pleak et al., 1989; Pleak et al., 1991) have reported our observation that less extensive gender-atypical behavior may not be associated with separation anxiety or other "internalizing" disorders, but rather may be associated with more disruptive, "externalizing" types of behavior. We have found that many of the children with gender dysphoria whom we have evaluated also have symptoms or a diagnosis of attention deficit/hyperactivity disorder and/or oppositional defiant disorder. As Zucker points out, the evidence for other types of psychopathology being related to gender dysphoria is not definitive, and using this as a rationale for treatment of gender dysphoria is tenuous. If these disorders are found to be of importance in gender dysphoria, when present, the focus of treatment should be on these pathologies rather than on the cross-gender behavior. If, however, the other pathologies are sequelae of the gender dysphoria (e.g., the child becomes depressed due to peer ostracism because of cross-gender preferences), the focus should be on managing the cross-gender identification and behavior in the light of societal genderism and sexism.

For adolescents, the discussion of diagnosis and treatment is even less enlightened. There is a general consensus among professionals who are experts in childhood gender dysphoria that various treatments do little to alter gender-role behavior or gender identity in the over-twelve-year-old or postpubertal youth (Pleak, 1997; Zucker and Bradley, 1995). An adolescent's strong sense and expression of cross-gender identity can pose many difficulties at home, school, and in other settings. A thirteen-year-old admitted to a day hospital I directed had been born male, but from age three to four identified as female and was fully cross-dressed and living as a girl by age eleven to twelve. Her mother did not fully support this identification, but did not dissuade it either, buying the girl feminine clothes and makeup. After discussion with the treatment team, the girl and her mother decided that prior to admission, the team would inform the other adolescent patients of the girl's situation, including the team's decision that she would attend the girls' psychotherapy group and use the girls' restroom. After much debate and open hostility by many of the adolescents, they soon came to accept her after meeting her and learning of her feelings, the girls going so far as to discuss and give advice on bras with her. Therapy with gender-dysphoric adolescents can focus on such issues, and can also be directed toward forestalling or preventing inappropriate, premature, and potentially harmful behavior by the adolescent, such as suicidality, self-castration, taking street or mail-order hormones, and sharing needles to inject hormones. Therapy with the family can help improve their relationships and prevent negative outcomes such as rejection of the teen ("throwaways" or runaways) or violence in the household (see Pleak and Anderson, 1998).

Ethical issues concerning treatment deserve more discussion as our knowledge about gender identity and behavior increases. For now, I propose eight guidelines for evaluating and treating children with gender dysphoria. The child with gender dysphoria and his or her family may best be served by the evaluating and/or treating clinician if there is:

1. Clear identification of the parents' stated and unstated goals for treatment. The therapist must ask for these goals up-front and concretely to establish the parents' wishes. It may take several sessions to fully evaluate this, and the risk is that the therapist may not share the parents' goals and they may go elsewhere for treatment.

2. Parent education about the natural history of extensive childhood cross-gender behaviors. The scant data should be reviewed with the parents to inform them that we know quite little at this stage.

3. Parent education about the known associations between childhood gender identity and adulthood transsexualism, bisexuality, homosexuality, and heterosexuality. Statistics and their meaning for an individual child should be clearly delineated, as should the chances of other children in the family who are gender typical to be gay or lesbian or transgendered later in life.

4. Open discussion of the therapist's treatment approach, biases, theoretical orientation, and goals (short-and long-term). This is essential to establish a working relationship with the family, just as are the therapist's qualifications and experience with gender issues.

5. Open discussion of the evidence for the proposed treatment modality to affect cross-gender behavior and identification, and what they may or may not see in their child.

6. Parent education about the lack of evidence for any treatment effect on later sexual orientation, despite claims they may hear to the contrary.

7. Parent education about homosexuality and bisexuality, including their nonpathology status. This is often in opposition to the parents' ideas, homophobia, heterosexism, and genderism, and that of their family members and support groups (school, religion). It can become difficult for the parent to deal with more overt hostility from the child's peers and from other adults as the child gets older in a way that is positive toward a possible gay or lesbian orientation.

8. Support of the parents' acceptance and love for their child as he or she grows up regardless of future sexual orientation and gender identification. Many parents see this as a given, but it should still be articulated clearly. Some parents will openly reject this initially, using epithets and derogation against gays, lesbians, and transgendered people, but may change their feelings and thinking with appropriate therapy. For most parents this obvious goal becomes primary, and they work constructively in therapy to maintain and improve this goal. This becomes for me a sine qua non of successful treatment.

REFERENCES

American Psychiatric Association (APA) (1987). *Diagnostic and Statistical Manual of Mental Disorders*, 3d ed., Revised. Washington, D.C.: American Psychiatric Association Press.

———. (1994). *Diagnostic and Statistical Manual of Mental Disorders*, 4th ed. Washington, D.C.: American Psychiatric Association Press.

Bradley, S. J., Blanchard, R., Coates, S., Green, R., Levine, S. B., Meyer-Bahlburg, H. F. L., Pauly, I. B., and Zucker, K. J. (1991). Interim report of the DSM-IV subcommittee on gender identity disorders. *Arch. Sex. Beh.*, 20: 333–343.

Coates, S., Friedman, R. C., and Wolfe, S. (1991). The etiology of boyhood gender identity disorder: a model for integrating temperament, development, and psychodynamics. *Psychoanal. Dialogues*, 1:481–523.

Coates, S., and Person, E. S. (1985). Extreme boyhood femininity: isolated behavior or pervasive disorder? *J. Amer. Acad. Child Adoles. Psychiatry*, 24: 702–709.

Davenport, C. W. (1986). A follow-up study of 10 feminine boys. *Arch. Sex. Beh.*, 15:511–517.

Friedman, R. C. (1988). *Male Homosexuality: A Contemporary Psychoanalytic Perspective.* New Haven, CT: Yale University Press.

Green, R. (1987). *The "Sissy Boy Syndrome" and the Development of Homosexuality.* New Haven, CT: Yale University Press.

Haber, C. H. (1991). The psychoanalytic treatment of a preschool boy with a gender identity disorder. *J. Amer. Psychoanalytic Assoc.*, 39:107–130.

Hamer, D. H., Hu, S., Magnuson, V. L., Hu, N., and Pattatucci. A. M. L. (1993). A linkage between DNA markers on the X chromosome and male sexual orientation. *Science* 261:321–327.

Isay, R. A. (1989). *Being Homosexual: Gay Men and Their Development.* New York: Farrar Straus Giroux.

———. (1997). Letter to ed. *Psychiatric News*, 21 November.

Lebovitz, P. S. (1972). Feminine behavior in boys: Aspects of its outcome. *Amer. J. Psychiat.*, 128:103–109.

LeVay, S. (1991). A difference in hypothalamic structure between heterosexual and homosexual men. *Science*, 253:1034–1037.

Marmor, J. (1980). Clinical aspects of male homosexuality. In: *Homosexual Behavior: A Modern Reappraisal*, ed. J. Marmor. New York: Basic Books.

Meyer-Bahlburg, H. F. L. (1985). Gender identity disorder of childhood: introduction. *J. Amer. Acad. Child Adoles. Psychiat.*, 24:681–683.

Money, J., and Russo, A. J. (1979). Homosexual outcome of discordant gen der identity/role in childhood: longitudinal follow-up. *J. Ped. Psychol.* 4:29–41.

Morin, S. F., and Schultz, S. J. (1978). The gay movement and the rights of children. *J. Soc. Iss.*, 34:137–148.

Nordyke, N. S., Baer, D. M., Etzel, B. C., and LeBlanc, J. M. (1977). Implications of the stereotyping and modification of sex role. *J. Appl. Beh. Anal.*, 10:553–557.

Pleak, R. R. (1994). Transgendered children and adolescents. Paper presented at the American Association of Physicians for Human Rights annual meeting, New York.

———. (1997). Transgendered, transsexual, cross-gendered, gender-dysphoric adolescents: what's it all about? Paper presented at the 44th Annual Meeting of the American Academy of Child and Adolescent Psychiatry, October, San Francisco.

Pleak, R. R., and Anderson, D. A. (1993). A parent's group for boys with gender identity disorders. Paper presented at the 19th annual meeting of the International Academy of Sex Research, Pacific Grove, CA.

———. (1998). Observation, interview, and mental status assessment (OIM): homosexual. In Noshpitz, J. D. (ed.) *Handbook of Child and Adolescent Psychi-*

atry, Volume Five: Clinical Assessment and Intervention Planning. New York: John Wiley and Sons.

Pleak, R. R., Meyer-Bahlburg, H. F. L., O'Brien, J. D., Bowen, H., and Morgan-stein, A., (1989). Cross-gender behavior and psychopathology in boy psychiatric outpatients. *J. Am. Acad. Child Adoles. Psychiatr.,* 28(3):385–393.

Pleak, R. R., Sandberg, D. E., Hirsch, G. S., and Anderson, D. A. (1991). Cross-gender behavior in boy psychiatric outpatients: replication and reinterpretation. Paper presented at the 38th Annual Meeting of the American Academy of Child and Adolescent Psychiatry, October, San Francisco.

Rekers, G. A. (1977). Atypical gender development and psychosocial adjustment. *J. Appl. Behav. Anal.,* 10:559–571.

———. (1980). The purpose of treatment for gender disturbed boys. *Personnel & Guidance J.,* 58:4550–4552.

———. (1982a). *Growing Up Straight: What Every Family Should Know about Homosexuality.* Chicago: Moody Press.

———. (1982b). *Shaping Your Child's Sexual Identity.* Grand Rapids, MI: Baker Book House.

———. (1995). *Handbook of Child and Adolescent Sexual Problems.* New York: Lexington Books.

Rekers, G. A., Bentler, P. M., Rosen, A. C., and Lovaas, O. I. (1977). Child gender disturbances: a clinical rationale for intervention. *Psychotherapy: Theory, Res. Practice,* 14:2–11.

Rekers, G. A., and Lovaas, O. I. (1974). Behavioral treatment of deviant sex-role behaviors in a male child. *J. Appl. Behav. Anal.,* 7:173–190.

Rekers, G. A., Rosen, A. C., Lovaas, O. I., and Bentler, P. M. (1978). Sex-role stereotypy and professional intervention for childhood gender disturbance. *Prof. Psychol.,* XXX:127–136.

Rosen, A. C., Rekers, G. A., and Bentler, P. M. (1978). Ethical issues in the treatment of children. *J. Soc. Iss.,* 34:122–136.

Saghir, M. T., and Robins, E. (1973). *Male and Female Homosexuality: A Comprehensive Investigation.* Baltimore: Williams and Wilkins.

Silverman, M. A. (1990). The prehomosexual boy in treatment. In: *The Homosexualities: Reality, Fantasy, and the Arts,* ed. C. W. Socarides and V. D. Volkan. Madison, CT: International Universities Press.

White, J. C., and Townsend, M. H. (1998). Transgender medicine: issues and definitions. *J. Gay and Lesbian Med. Assoc.* 2(1):1–3.

Wilson, K. K. (1998). The disparate classification of gender and sexual orientation in American psychiatry. Paper presented at the 151st annual meeting of the American Psychiatric Association, June, Toronto; also available online at www.priory.com/psych/disparat.htm.

Winkler, R. C. (1977). What types of sex-role behavior should behavior modifiers promote? *J. Appl. Beh. Anal.,* 10:549–552.

Wolfe, B. E. (1979). Behavioral treatment of childhood gender disorders: a conceptual and empirical critique. *Beh. Modif.*, 3:550–575.

World Health Organization (1992). *International Classification of Diseases*, 10th edition. Geneva.

Zucker, K. J. (1985). Cross-gender-identified children. In: *Gender Dysphoria: Development, Research, Management*, ed. B. W. Steiner. New York: Plenum.

———. (1990a). Gender identity disorders in children: clinical descriptions and natural history. In: *Clinical Management of Children and Adults with Gender Identity Disorders*, ed. R. Blanchard and B. W. Steiner. Washington, D.C.: American Psychiatric Press.

———. (1990b). Treatment of gender identity disorders in children. In: *Clinical Management of Children and Adults with Gender Identity Disorders*, ed. R. Blanchard and B. W. Steiner. Washington, D.C.: American Psychiatric Press.

Zucker, K. J., and Bradley, S. J. (1995). *Gender Identity Disorder and Psychosexual Problems in Children and Adolescents*. New York: Guilford Press.

Zuger, B., (1978). Effeminate behavior present in boys from childhood: ten additional years of follow-up. *Comp. Psychiat.*, 19:363–369.

———. (1988). Is early effeminate behavior in boys early homosexuality? *Compr. Psychiat.*, 29:509–519.

Three

Is Gender Essential?

Anne Fausto-Sterling

Gender

Webster's dictionary offers three definitions. (1) "Gender, race, kind or kin" offers us a system of classification. Many people think of gender as a kind of classification that divides things into binary categories, although binarism is certainly not inherent in this use of the word. So when we ask, "Is gender essential?" we might be asking whether we think binary gender classifications are essential. (2) A second dictionary definition equates "gender" with "sex." "Sex" in turn has multiple meanings. One thesaurus list I perused for synonyms for sex included, sexuality, male, masculinity, maleness, female, femininity, as well as activities such as sexual intercourse, copulation, and the like. (3) A third dictionary definition of gender refers to the grammar of languages that divide words into masculine, feminine, or neuter, and finally, an inflectional form, again grammatically showing membership in such a subclass.

Most dictionary definitions of gender ignore a totally different use of the word, one which came into being twice—from apparently independent sources. In the 1950s some sexologists—John Money foremost among them—developed a scheme to describe the development of "normal" adult males and females. In this scheme he separated elements of development into two major categories: one essentially physical (involving anatomy and hormones), and the other essentially psychological (involving acculturation and the psychological fixation of a gendered self-identity). He referred to the physical, as "sex," and the mental as "gender." In the 1970s, apparently with little knowledge of Money's earlier work, feminists reinvented "gender" in a way that differed to some degree from both Money (and subsequent use in the field of sexology) and the standard dictionary definition. It interests me that neither Money's definition nor the feminist reinventions of this word have made it into the dictionary.

The feminist and the sexological reinventions of gender have been both enormously helpful and deeply problematic. Early feminists distinguished the physical body, which they called "sex," from culturally constructed ideology, which they called "gender." They defined gender as a collection of attributes that a particular culture found appropriate for individuals who inhabited a particular body (or sex). This definitional move had a very specific set of political objectives—to make more flexible those behavioral traits and social roles that had traditionally been tied to the body. This move to separate culture from body created room for cultural change with regard to sex roles.

While there were positive political results from the separation of sex and gender, this rhetorical move was also deeply problematic, because to a great extent our bodies' physical appearance (i.e., their physical sex) locates us in our gendered culture. The separation of sex from gender is never clean, which means that there is always messiness and difficulty around deciding what we mean by "gender." More recently gay men and lesbians, people in the transgender movement, transvestites and intersexuals have formed political movements which continue to push up against sexual boundaries in ways that build upon, but differ from, the original feminist-inspired sex/gender divide. They have waged active warfare against a binary definition of gender. Somewhat tongue in cheek, in an article on intersexuality I came up with the idea that there are five physical sexes and by implication at least that many genders. Some people have taken my focus on the number five a little too seriously. Rhetorically, I used it to push on the number two. But in context, my own view is that a discrete (as opposed to a continuous) classification system is completely unsatisfactory.

Within the gay/transsexual/transgender movements there are different understandings and belief systems about the relationship between sex and gender (or the body and culture). Some want to completely sever the tie between the body and some definition of gender, while others wish to say that their version of gender, that is, what has happened to them personally and other people like them, must in some way be caused by their body. So the problem remains: trying to separate sex and gender in order to take a look at these two components, but never quite being able to uncouple gender from the body.

Essential

The word essential turns out to be even more complicated than gender. Perusing Webster's and the thesaurus, we find that among other things "essential" might mean "inherent," or "relating to or constituting essence," or "containing or constituting a volatile essence that imparts a characteristic odor, as in of a plant or oil." It might be something that is important or indispensable, or "something that is fundamental or applies to something that is a foundation without which an entire system or complex whole would collapse." It might be something that is vital, as necessary to a thing's continued existence or operation as air, food, and water are to living things. Clearly, in order to profitably answer the question, "Is gender essential?" we need to articulate which definition of essential we intend.

By combining different definitions of "gender" and "essential," we come up with several questions. If we take gender to mean "classification in binary categories," we can then ask: Must they be in the body? Is it some sort of human requirement that we classify? Is classification important or intrinsic to the way the human brain works? These are questions, I think, of speculation. There are theories of grammar, for example, that talk about the need for the human mind to classify. All sorts of cross-cultural data can be brought in to talk about how the mind classifies or whether the mind must classify into twos, fours, or fives.

But I think we are more interested in the questions of gender as "sex" meaning "biology" and "sex" meaning "culture." If by "essential" we mean that it is part of the body and has materiality, then is "gender" meaning "sex" (or the biological body) essential? The answer to this question seems to me to be "yes," in the sense that we are all sexual beings, or at least we are all born with the potential to be sexual beings. Is sex a requirement of the biological body? Well, in an evolutionary sense, the answer is yes. That is, if there were no reproductive sex from time to time, the human race couldn't continue, and obviously the human race is doing just fine in that regard. But the answer wouldn't be yes if we asked whether it is a requirement or a necessity in any one individual human's life.

Is gender/sex biologically important or intrinsic? Again, my answer to that is probably yes, especially if one takes an evolutionary point of view. But if one asks, does "gender"—meaning "sex" or "biology"—define the whole human organism? My answer is certainly no. If we move on to "gender" as sex in terms of culture, I have a number of question marks. Do the various kinds of genders that we define in our culture necessarily emanate from our bodies? I don't know. Is it a requirement of all cultures that there be genders at the cultural level? The answer to that too is, I don't know. Some cultures seem to have very little sex differentiation, gender differentiation, but the vast majority certainly differentiate at least between male and female. The specifics of such differentiations, however, vary from culture to culture.

Is sex/gender differentiation important? In our culture, clearly yes. It obsesses us, and we bring out huge audiences to discuss the matter. Culturally, in the United States in 1995, gender is clearly important. Is it the sole organizing principle of our culture? The answer to that is obviously no. In short, only by asking these kinds of questions can we carefully define what it is we want to argue about. We cannot have a fruitful discussion until we clarify the terms of the debate.

Permeability/Interpenetrations: How Bodies Work

One difficulty inherent in the rhetorical move to separate the concept of an embodied sex from that of a culturally constructed gender is that it forces us to think of the body as something that is fixed, a vehicle that changes very little, at least after puberty. We all recognize that the body grows and changes shape until sometime after puberty. We are born with bodies that are, in one sense of the word (i.e., a groundwork, framework, a structure on which other things are built or layered), essential. But as a biologist I don't find this to be a very accurate account of what bodies are and how they work. And although I'm not fond of giving examples from rodents and then saying, "Well, this should apply to humans" (in fact I spent a lot of time saying that that was a silly thing to do), in this case rodents might shed light on how bodies and environments interact and change one another, often mutually.

In a recent study, researchers looked at a particular set of neurons in the brains of female rats who were lactating and behaving maternally. (These could either have been rats who actually gave birth, or rats who were induced to lactate by hormonal injection.) They found that the actual structure of the brain changed when animals were exhibiting maternal behavior. Suckling not only nourished baby rats, but also provided feedback to the lactating rat's brain that changed the brain's structure. In this case something that we usually think of as essential, the brain, is not essential in the sense that it is a permanent, unchangeable framework; the same can be said for genes or various other physical attributes which we envision as foundational or unalterably structural.

It's becoming clear that structures like the brain, down to their very anatomy, change throughout one's lifetime. And here I am talking about humans as well as rodents. So we have to stop thinking of the body as something prior that is unchanging and that becomes the base on which some sort of cultural framework is built. We can't begin to develop decent theories about the appearance of gendered behaviors and gendered belief systems about our own individual bodies without understanding that our bodies are part of the process, that our bodies change in very profound ways in response to our behaviors. Not only do they generate behaviors, but they in turn are generated by behaviors.

If we now again ask, "Is gender essential?" and if by this question we mean to ask, "Does the body precede or form the basis for gender?" we find that we have framed a nonsensical question. The same conclusion emerges from variations on the theme, questions such as, "Are there genes for homosexuality?" or "Are people born gay or transgendered?" The body is not merely born and then enlarged as a framework upon which culture hangs a few signifying baubles. Rather, the body is continuously being born and remodeled in an environment that starts before birth and continues until death.

In the end, then, I have rejected the original question with which I began. Instead, I would like to pose some different queries. Why, for example, in our culture right now, are we witnessing a proliferation of genders? Can we sensibly define the terms "heterosexual," "homosexual," "masculine," "feminine," "male," and "female"? If we can't sensibly define them, why not? Are these unitary categories? If not, how can we discuss their embodied nature? Can we find ways to talk about all the elements of the body, from genes to anatomy, the brain and the psyche, as inherently or essentially malleable or permeable? Only when we begin to address these questions will we have developed a theory of gender and sexuality that adequately takes into account both the body and culture.

Four

Queering the Center by Centering the Queer

Reflections on Transsexuals and Secular Jews

Naomi Scheman

"Confusing yourself is a way to stay honest"
—Jenny Holzer

Twentieth-century liberatory activism and theorizing have lived with and on the tension between two visions: for one the goal is to secure for the marginalized and oppressed the relief from burdens and the access to benefits reserved for the privileged, including the benefits of being thought by others and oneself to be at the center of one's society's views of what it is to be fully human. For the other the goal is to disrupt those views and the models of privileged selfhood they underwrite—to claim not the right to be fully human in those terms, but rather the right to be free of a stigmatizing, normalizing apparatus to which one would not choose to conform even if one were allowed and encouraged to do so. Struggles in the arenas of race, colonialism and imperialism, gender, class, and sexuality have all, in varying ways and to differing degrees, in different times and places, been pushed and pulled, shaped and molded, formed and deformed by the tensions between these two visions.

Among the perquisites of modern Eurocentric privilege are socially supported expectations that one can and will conform to certain norms of selfhood: one will be a person of integrity—whole and of a piece, someone to be counted on, stable and steady; one's beliefs, attitudes, and feelings will be explicable and coherent; one's actions will follow straightforwardly from one's intentions; one will be simultaneously solid and transparent—a block of unclouded substance.[1] (That the very wealthy and powerful are often allowed, or even expected, to be creatures of unpredictable caprice and inexplicable temperament is the exception that proves the rule: the acquisition and in most cases the maintenance of privilege is a matter of discipline, so that flamboyant flouting can be a sign that, by one's own efforts or by the inheritance of the efforts of one's ancestors, one is so securely privileged as to be able to let the discipline go: part of the way one flaunts one's privilege is to act as though one need do nothing to continue to earn it.)

As María Lugones has argued (in a talk at the University of Minnesota), such an ideal of integrity is not as straightforward as it may seem. The direct, unmediated route from intention to action that is one of its hallmarks is typically more apparent than real: we are taught not to see the elaborate collaboration provided to the privileged by a compliant social structure. By contrast, the necessary survival strategies of the oppressed make these marks of a full, moral humanity unobtainable: manipulation, deviousness, fickleness, and other stigmata of less than fully straightforward, solidly transparent subjectivity can be the signs not of defects of character but of the only available ways of getting by in a hostile world. If the straight roads are ones that require tolls one cannot afford to pay, and if they are laid out not to go where one needs to, then one has no choice but to find alternative routes, routes that snake around the roadblocks thrown up by those who have no interest in your getting where you want to go.[2]

Among the coherencies that philosophers from John Locke to Derek Parfit have put at the criterial heart of personal identity is the continuity of memory. Such continuity marks what it is to be the same person throughout time, thus to be the bearer of responsibility, the maker and receiver of promises, the recipient of trust. From a wide range of causes—notably including childhood abuse—memory is subject to distortion and even erasure, making it difficult for those who have suffered such a loss to fashion a sufficiently coherent narrative of themselves to be credible. (At the extreme, such abuse can lead to the literal fracturing of the self: one of the distinguishing features of multiple personality disorder is the failure of memory across at least some of the different personalities—A has no recollection of doing what B did.)

Insufficiently noted by philosophical theorists of personal identity is the role of the memory of others in constituting selfhood. It is not just that we are the persons we remember ourselves as being: we are equally, for better or worse, the persons others remember us as being. The others around us may be loving or arrogant,[3] thoughtful or careless, with their memories of us; and we can be grateful or resentful or both for being held in their memories, for being continuous with the persons they remember us as being. Persons who are forgotten or not well remembered—if those in whose memories they might have been held are dead or gone, absent minded or uncaring—are seen and often see themselves as diminished. And some, in order to be the persons they are becoming, or believe themselves always to have been, need to detach themselves from the memories of those who would hold them too firmly in mind, trapping them in selves that no longer, if they ever did, fit. They need to reinvent themselves, to live without the coherence of a shared, remembered past.

One could argue at this point (especially with regard to the role of memory), as the adherents of the first vision would, that the picture of privileged subjectivity is not in itself a problematic one: the problem is in its exclusivity. Nor are wily survival strategies inherently admirable, much as we may admire those who manage by these means to survive: surely people often have to do things to survive that they would far rather not have to do. We need, on this view, to be careful not to romanticize oppression by celebrating the character traits it breeds.

Adherents of the second vision would counter that equally we ought not to celebrate ideals of humanity that have been realized literally on the bodies of others to whom those ideals have been denied. Privileged subjectivity is not some neutral good that just so happens to have been scarfed up by an unscrupulous few. Rather, it is a form of subjectivity well suited to unscrupulous scarfing up, that is, to a view of oneself as naturally meriting a far larger than average share of the world's benefits and a far smaller than average share of its burdens—as having, in Marilyn Frye's terms, the right to graft onto oneself another's substance (1983). The privileged self, on this view, is not only engorged but also diminished: it has split off and projected onto those same others the parts of itself deemed too messy or embarrassing to acknowledge: its seamless integrity is achieved by throwing out all the parts that don't quite fit, secure in the knowledge that one can count on commandeering sufficient social resources not to need a fully stocked, even if incongruously jumbled, internal toolkit.[4] Even memory works like this in some ways: the coherent remembered narrative, shared with others who hold us in mind, is an artifact of privilege both in what it contains and in what it omits. No one remembers everything that happens to them, and culturally available story lines help give shape to the stuff of some lives (make them "memorable"), while leaving others gappy and jerky. Narrativity *per se* may be humanly important, but we have no access to narrativity *per se*: what we have are culturally specific narratives, which facilitate the smooth telling of some lives and straitjacket, distort, or fracture others.

Resistance to the disciplining apparatus that defines privilege (even the "privilege" of full humanity) can take a romantic outlaw form, lived on what are taken explicitly, defiantly, to be the margins, shunning, insofar as possible, what is acknowledged as the center. Alternatively, in ways that will be the focus of this essay, resistance can take the form of challenge to the stable cartographies of center and margin. Such resistance aims to cloud the transparency of privileged subjectivity, making it visible, and visibly "queer," by revealing the apparatus that goes into normalizing it. The status of the "normal" can, that is, be problematized,[5] rather than either aspired to or rejected—or replaced by some competing normalizing picture.[6] I want to explore the possibilities for what I call "queering the center" by looking at two specific normalizing apparatuses: heteronormativity and what I call "Christianormativity."

I

As David Halperin argues in a discussion of Foucault (1995),[7] heteronormativity is productively slippery: a large part of its power comes from its deployment of two mutually incompatible discourses—that of (biological) normality and that of virtue. Heterosexuality, as both unremarkedly normal and markedly virtuous, is privileged indirectly: not itself a site of inquiry, it is constructed by implicit contrast with the mutually incompatible characterizations of homosexuality—as sickness and as crime or sin. Arguments against one mode of stigmatization tend notoriously, in the maze of heterosexist (il)logic, to buttress the other: so, for example, arguing that gay men and lesbians don't choose their sexuality reinforces the view of that sexuality as sick, while arguing that gay men and lesbians show no more signs of psychopathology than do straight people reinforces the view of their sexuality as chosen and culpable.

Heteronormativity constructs not only sexual identity but also gender identity: in order properly to regulate desire it must divide the human world unambiguously into males and females. The discourses of queerness are marked specifically by gender transgressiveness, by a refusal to allow gender to remain unproblematized in a struggle for the rights of same-gendered sexual partners. Such transgressiveness can also be found in some feminist, especially lesbian feminist, attempts to redefine women (or "wimmin" or "womyn"), as something other than not-men. That is, the feminist attempts recognize both that the gender divide is predicated on the sexuality of heterosexual men ("women" = sexual objects for heterosexual male subjects), and that the male/female gender dichotomy is actually a male/not-male dichotomy (see Frye forthcoming).

There is a striking similarity between the heteronormative representation of the homosexual and the representation of the Jew in what I call "Christianormative" discourse. Analogously to the androcentrism of heteronormative gender, Christianormativity purports to divide the world into religions, resembling Christianity except for being mistaken, while really having only two categories: Christian and not (yet) Christian. The Christian model of religion misrepresents many of the indigenous cultures Christians have evangelized, as heteronormativity misrepresents what it is to be a woman. Like homosexuals, Jews are not only misrepresented but abjected by the normative scheme, not properly caught in its classifications. Since the start of the Christian era Jews have been defined by their closeness to and knowledge of Christianity, as homosexuals are defined by their closeness to and knowledge of gender difference: in both cases there is a perverse refusal or inability to act on the knowledge they all too clearly have.

On the one hand, the Jew is the quintessential (potential) Christian: Christianity is a matter not of birth but of choice; the paradigmatic Christian is a convert—originally, and most naturally, from Judaism.[8]

On the other hand, the Jew is indelibly marked on her or his body: an extraordinary range of body parts have been taken in anti-Semitic discourse to mark Jews (Gilman 1991). Jews are both profoundly culpable for continuing to deny the divinity of Jesus and unable, no matter what we do, to shed the racial heritage of Jewishness.[9] This contradictoriness, as in the case of heteronormative discourse, is productive: it grants to Christians the simultaneous statuses of natural (the way humans are meant to be, the default state for humanity) and especially virtuous.[10] Literally, of course, Christianity is not supposed to be biologically natural, as heterosexuality is, but it is part of most Christian orthodoxy to believe that everyone is loved by Jesus in the way he loves Christians: what is called for is acknowledgment of that love, not the earning of it. Similarly, heterosexuality can be seen as part of essential human nature, so that homosexuality counts as the willful denial of one's true self, as Jewishness counts as the willful denial of God's love.

In addition to their dichotomizing aspect, both heteronormativity and Christianormativity have a universalizing aspect: they both imagine a world of sameness, even as they continue to require both objects of desire (proselytizing or sexual) and abjected others. The emphases, on maintaining difference or striving toward sameness, may differ, but the tensions between the two animate both discourses. Although Christianity is officially universally proselytizing, there is reason to believe that Jews play a sufficiently important role in the Christian imaginary that if we didn't exist, they would have to invent us; and certainly assimilating Jews have met with less than full cultural acceptance, often being stigmatized precisely for conforming to the norms of Christian society (see Prell 1992). Heteronormativity officially envisions a world of only heterosexuals, while similarly requiring the homosexual as a negative definition of normality. And, as Daniel Boyarin and Natalie Kampen have persuaded me, even the gender dichotomy itself contains a universalizing moment alongside the more obvious, official emphasis on ineluctable difference. Although men don't typically proselytize women into sex change (that women are important to the male imaginary seems clear), there is a strong current of mono(male)-gender utopianism, both in Pauline Christianity (see Boyarin 1994) and in Enlightenment thought. Notably, in both cases, the body is meant to be transcended: it is in our minds, or our souls, that we are all really men.

II

The inconsistent conjunction of sin and sickness, nature and virtue that characterizes heteronormativity and Christianormativity strikingly (but unsurprisingly) characterizes modern Western conceptions of subjectivity. The clearest statement is perhaps Kant's (1969, Sec. 2). The rationale for the categorical imperative—the answer to the question of why it ought to motivate us—is that only by seeing ourselves as bound by it can we see ourselves as free. Our noumenal identities, if expressible at all, are expressed through duty; the alternative is to be determined by inclination—that is, by natural forces no more expressive of our freedom than are any other causal determinations. Virtue may be impossibly difficult, but it is in an important sense natural, not an imposition from outside. Kant is left with the problem of accounting for culpable wrongdoing: if acting freely is always acting morally, how can we hold someone responsible for acting badly? The problem is at the heart of Kant's account of the nature of morality and agency: if he allowed for the possibility of acting freely in a way that didn't accord with the categorical imperative, he would have to answer the moral skeptic, who challenges the motivational charge behind the categorical imperative. The question of why we should do what duty commands would be a real one and, in Kant's terms, unanswerable, if freely, rationally, we could do otherwise. So the person who heeds not duty but inclination (who might be all of us, all of the time) is not only immoral but (contradictorily) unfree.

Epistemologically, as well, the emphasis has been less on the positive difficulty of obtaining knowledge than on the negative challenge of avoiding error—from Descartes's emphasis on resisting assent when ideas are less than fully clear and distinct, to the positivists' emphasis on the error-producing dangers of subjectivity. Both morally and epistemologically the knowing subject is characterized as both generic (normal, universal) and as especially virtuous. The connection is in a sense unpuzzling: as a matter of fact most people most of the time won't be thinking in the manner argued to be the correct one, which inescapably raises the question of what makes such thinking correct. What is it about those who do think in the privileged ways that makes their thought right for all the rest of us? The distinctively modern—that is, liberal—answer to that question cannot be that those people are in some way special, that they have the authority to do the important thinking for the rest of us. Rather, they have to be seen as us—all of us—at our best, where "best" means simultaneously most natural (uncorrupted, healthy) and normatively most excellent. The two have to go together in the absence of anything other than "natural" to which normative excellence refers.

One can, therefore, see the naturalizing moves of much of twentieth-century analytic philosophy, with its characteristic problems of theoretically justifying normativity claims, as rooted in the fundamental project of liberalism—what I have elsewhere referred to as "democratizing privilege" (Scheman 1993, 77). That oxymoron reflects the tension between the universalistic theories and the inegalitarian practices of modernity, with the attendant need to explain the inequalities that theoretically ought not to exist, especially those that are uncomfortably correlated with the supposed irrelevancies of race and gender or the supposed anachronism of class. In the absence of anything to account for inequality other than what people actually do—and can properly be held responsible for doing—the accounting has to be in terms of the wrong—or at least the less than optimally right—behavior of those who fail to prosper, without there being any independent, non-question-begging way of characterizing "wrong" or "right." The coupling of the apparently contradictory discourses of nature and virtue (or sickness and sin) are the inevitable result of the need to maintain a normativity that cannot speak its name.[11]

In the work of many philosophers, notably Descartes, there is nothing to mark those who exemplify the norms—in his case by thinking properly—from those who don't: we are all equally capable of careful and of sloppy thought. Other philosophers, notoriously Kant—who thought duty and obligation meant nothing to women (1960, 81)—have been less egalitarian: it is only some among us who actually have the capacity to reason in the ways supposed to be generically human. The rest of us have been marked by the odd conjunction of moral turpitude and natural incapacity that are taken to characterize the homosexual and the Jew. We have, that is, been characterized as constitutionally incapable of instantiating what is nonetheless supposed to be the essence we share with more privileged humans. The latters' generic status and the privileges that go with that status require that we be essentially like them, while the terms of our exclusion, resting as it does on what we are, not on anything we may do, requires that we be essentially different from them.

Those of us so marked have variously struggled against such stigmatization, most often using the tools of liberalism: we have denied our alleged natural incapacity and claimed an equal share in humanity's essential attributes. Thus, for example, Jews have sought civil emancipation, gays and lesbians have sought civil rights, and women have sought equal rights: in all cases the argument has been made that however members of these groups differed from the already fully enfranchised, such differences were of no importance when it came to the status in question, typically that of citizen. Given the distressing hardiness of racism, anti-Semitism, sexism, and homophobia, it has been easy for liberals to argue that to do otherwise—to assert the relevance of difference, however socially constructed; to resist offers, however genuinely goodwilled, of acceptance into the ranks of the same—is political suicide.

I do not want to minimize the truth in this argument, nor dispute the goodwill of those who make it, but it does have the logic of a protection racket, as Peterson (1977) noted in relation to the discourse around male violence toward women: there are very bad people afoot who will do you grave harm, and your safety lies in availing yourselves of the protection we offer. What makes the offer suspicious, no matter how sincere and empirically grounded, are the connections between the protectors and those who pose the danger. Protection is problematic when one's protectors benefit from one's acceptance of the terms on which that protection is offered—feminine docility in the case of protection from male violence, and acceptance of the paradigmatic status of the privileged in the case of protection from racism, anti-Semitism, sexism, and homophobia. As women are supposed to acknowledge needing men, those who are "different" are supposed to acknowledge the "honor" of being regarded as essentially the same as straight white middle-class Christian men.

The disputes concerning "multiculturalism" currently roiling college campuses illustrate the normativity of the paradigmatic. The deepest challenge of multiculturalism is to the paradigmatic centrality of the privileged: from whose vantage point is the world most accurately seen? Whose art and literature set the standards of aesthetic excellence? Whose experiences represent generically human encounters with life, death, the natural and social worlds? Shifting the center with respect to questions such as these—shifting which work is taken as most interesting, innovative, significant, worth supporting and encouraging—by those who set curricula, give grants, and make decisions about hiring, tenure, and promotion—has nothing to do with freedom of speech or academic freedom, but it is so profoundly threatening to those whose placement at the center has seemed to them a fact of nature that, faced with such shifts (which are, to date, minuscule) they are convinced, I suspect in some cases sincerely, that their rights *must* be being violated. Similarly, one finds the conviction, probably also in some cases sincere, that the shifting of norms means the abandonment of the true ones, those that can seem to come from nowhere only so long as they come from an unchallenged center, at once privileged and universal.

The liberal strategy is to leave unchallenged the paradigmatic status of the privileged, but to argue that it does not in theory, and ought not in practice, entail the exclusion or even the marginalization of others: the others are, in all the respects that ought to matter, essentially the same as the privileged. If this argument were a good one, then shifting in the other direction ought not to matter: it ought to be unproblematic to put at the center some groups previously relegated to the margins, to say not that black people are just like white people except that their skin is darker, but that white people are just like black people except that their skin is lighter.[12] But, as the near hysteria around "political correctness" indicates, such shifts are hardly unproblematic: being the standard of comparison is a very big deal, no matter how liberally others are deemed to measure up to it.[13]

For the remainder of this essay I want to work at "queering the centers" of heteronormativity and Christianormativity by juxtaposing two subject positions, neither of which makes sense in the respective normative terms: the transsexual and the secular Jew. The juxtaposition is in part fortuitous: I am a secular Jew, and I have for some time been trying to figure out what that means; and, as a born-female feminist, I have been pressed to understand the experiences and perspectives of those whose attempts to deconstruct gender have an embodied literalness absent in my own life. Furthermore, living outside the norms exacts disruptions of memory and integrity for transsexuals and secular Jews significantly more than for homosexuals and religious Jews. With such experiences at the center, I want to ask what it is to live an intelligible and admirable life—what the structures of subjectivity look like from perspectives other than those of normalizing privilege. The question is an explicitly transcendental one: it starts from what I take as the fact that such lives are lived, hence livable, and asks about the conditions of that possibility.[14]

My hope is that starting from the intelligibility of the normatively unintelligible can serve to uncover the problematic assumptions that make secular Jews and transsexuals incoherent, assumptions that sustain both the status of the normatively coherent (including, in the case of gender, me), and the larger hierarchies in which those identities are embedded. I want to argue that placement at the intelligible center is always a matter of history, of the playing out of privilege and power, and is always contestable. One reason for the contestation is to lead us beyond the impasse between the two visions with which I began—both of which as usually understood tacitly accept the structures of normalization, whether by claiming one's rightful, central place in them or by defining oneself as outside or marginal to them. Relocating the gaze to a place of normative incoherence can help to destabilize the center, upsetting the claims of those who reside there to that combination of naturalness and virtue that characterizes normativity.

III

As our (modern Western) world is now, failure to conform to the norms of gender is socially stigmatizing to an unbearable extent: to be human just *is* to be male or female, a girl or a boy, or a man or a woman. Those who cannot be readily classified by everyone they encounter are not only subject to physically violent assaults, but, perhaps even more wounding, are taken to be impossible to relate to humanly, as though one cannot use the pronoun "you" with anyone to whom one cannot with total assurance apply either "she" or "he." Those who are not stably, unambiguously one or the other are, as Susan Stryker puts it (1994, 240), "monsters."[15] In such a world boundary-blurring carries psychic costs no one can be asked to pay, and the apparently conservative gender-boundary-preserving choices (surgical, hormonal, and behavioral) of many transsexuals have to be read in full appreciation of what the real options are.

One need not downplay the oppression of women to acknowledge that a certain sort of privilege, one essential for social validation as human, attaches to being located squarely on one side or the other of the gender divide.[16] Those of us who, as stably female-gendered feminists, would choose to see that boundary blurred to oblivion need to learn how to see and be seen as allies by those whose lives it slices through. The work of blurring that boundary is being taken on by a growing number of theorists and activists who are variously resisting the imperatives of gender conformity, including the imperative that transsexuals move decisively from one side to the other. (See, for example, Bornstein 1994; Feinberg 1993; Gabriel 1995; Stone 1991; and Stryker 1994.) To the extent that the social construction of gender is against the interests of all feminists, it ought to fall to those of us who occupy positions of relative safety and privilege to complicate our own locations, to explore the costs of our comfort, and to help imagine a world in which it would be safe to be non-, ambiguously, or multiply gendered.[17]

My own gender identity has never been a source of confusion, nor have I puzzled over what it means to say that I am a woman, and this certainty has been untouched by my increasing inability to define gender.[18] My certainty has its original grounding in my relatively easy conformity with heteronormativity: as theorists as diverse as Catharine MacKinnon (1990) and Judith Butler (1990) have argued, sexual identity, in particular the structures of compulsory heterosexuality, ground, rather than depend upon, gender difference. My questioning of heterosexuality (including my own) along with the other norms of gender, came rather late in my life (after adolescence) and in communities that tended toward an empirical stability (if not essentialism) concerning who women were: lesbians, for example, were woman-identified and woman-loving, not "not-women."[19]

I was, therefore, initially puzzled as to how to understand the claim of (most) male-to-female (MTF) transsexuals to be women—how, that is, to make their claims (their lives and experiences) intelligible.[20] My inability to understand seemed to come from the fact that, despite my own unshakeable sense of being a woman, there was nothing I could point to as constituting my gender identity when I abstracted from a lifetime of unambiguous gender ascription on the part of others and an unambiguously female body. Surely, it seemed to me, if there was something independent of social role and body that male-to-female transsexuals could recognize as their gender identity, I should be able to find whatever it was in my own sense of identity—but there simply didn't seem to be anything like that there. (I was reminded of Hume's inability to find in himself a substantial Cartesian self.) Whatever they meant when they said they were women, it didn't seem to be what I meant. What, then, did they mean? And how, to put a Wittgensteinian spin on the question, were they able to mean it?

For various reasons, reinforced by Leslie Feinberg's eloquent politics of solidarity, I found myself moving away from the feminist suspicion that lay behind that puzzlement, a suspicion that tended to see male-to-female transsexuals as men, with typical male arrogance, claiming female identity; and female-to-male transsexuals as self-hating, male-identified women. Those analyses singularly failed to fit the people whose voices I was hearing and reading, especially those who were seriously concerned about being allies in feminist struggles. Nor did those analyses fit with a commitment I thought I had to the deconstruction of gender (in reality, not just in theory).

But even with the motivation of solidarity, I still just did not understand. But that motivation—and the political thinking it engendered—did lead me to what it ought not have taken me so long to see: I was keeping to myself the position of unproblematized, paradigmatic subject, puzzling over how to understand some especially recalcitrant object. To put it in Wittgensteinian terms, I was finding one sort of phenomenon to be maddeningly opaque because I was taking another sort of phenomenon to be transparent. I couldn't understand the gender identity of transsexuals in part because I thought I understood my own—or, more accurately, could take it for granted, as not in need of understanding. (Wittgenstein suggested that part of why we were hopelessly puzzled about how it was possible to figure out what other people were thinking and feeling was because we thought there was nothing to figure out in our own case.)

The very overdetermination of my gender identity, the congruence of body, socialization, desire, and sense of self—the fact that everything pointed the same way—was what made it hard to see what was going on, hard, in fact, to see that anything was "going on" at all.[21] I am (unlike very many diverse nontranssexual women, who for all sorts of reasons do not conform in so many particulars to the norms of femaleness) so close to the paradigmatic center that I am in a very bad position to see how the apparatus works, to get a feel for how diverse forces could push and pull one in different directions. I may not like the forces that construct gender identity, but their tugs on my body and psyche tend more to hold me in place than to unbalance me: I don't know them, as others do, by the strains they exact in the attempt to stand erect. Clearly what I needed to do was to problematize my own gender identity.

Easier said than done.

IV

By contrast, I don't have to work at problematizing my Jewish identity. Unlike my gender identity, my Jewishness, while a central and unquestionable part of who I am, is a puzzle to me. Not only, as with gender, can't I define it, but I can't figure out what it means to say of myself that I am a Jew, nor what I might be conforming to to count as one. While I have no doubt about it, or about its centrality to who I am, I am genuinely puzzled about how to understand it—and, unlike my gender, it does seem to need to be understood. That is, while the ways I live gender make its operations unproblematically transparent to me, as invisible as the air, the ways I live Jewishness are maddeningly opaque. But opacity, of course, is also visibility: again, in Wittgensteinian terms, what seems to get in the way of seeing clearly is what we need to be looking at, and recognizing as what we need to know. In my case there is a rich set of mostly familial experiences that inform my sense of Jewishness, in ways that link it with my rationalism, my respect for science, my judgmentalism, my sense of humor and irony, and (most centrally) my passionately internationalist, socialist sense of justice. But my awareness of how less-than-fully shared these commitments are among Jews, along with the absence in my life of a community that takes these as constitutive even of one way of being Jewish, makes such experiences, and the identity they ground, seem not to be an answer to the question of what I know about myself when I know myself to be, specifically, Jewish.[22]

Nowadays in the United States, the questions to which "Jewish" is the correct answer are almost always questions about religion. Being Jewish here and now is one identity in a contrastive set that includes Christian (with all the subsets thereof), Buddhist, Muslim, and the like. Forms of Christianity, most centrally forms of mainstream Protestantism, are the paradigm cases of religions in the United States So Judaism is distinguished by its most noteworthy distinguishing features from a Christian perspective: its adherents go not to church but to synagogue or temple, and they go not on Sunday but on Saturday or on Friday night. If you're in the hospital (one place you're likely to be asked your religion) and take a turn for the worse, they'll send for a rabbi, not for a priest, minister, or pastor. For some Jews this religious way of thinking about what sort of identity Jewish identity is may work reasonably well (though I think even for observant Jews there has been a problematic "Christianizing" of identity, for example, in the moving of religious observance for all family members from the home to the synagogue). But it makes no sense at all to secular Jews like me (as, for different reasons, I suspect it makes no sense to Buddhists, among others).

I don't have a religion: I'm a lifelong atheist on increasingly principled moral grounds; I know very little about Jewish religious observance and feel comfortable with less; and though I know I had religious ancestors, among them my paternal grandparents, what I share with them, as with other Jews, does not feel to me to be a religion. Religion is rather what estranges me from many other Jews, for much the same reason as it estranges me from Christians and others: I am nonreligious, even antireligious, about as deeply as I am Jewish.

But I am Jewish. No one, actually, would dispute this, even though many people would insist on misrepresenting it. So far as anyone knows (albeit, as is the case for most European Jews, this is not very far) I have only Jewish ancestors, and that settles it. Were I to deny that I was Jewish, I would be accused (rightly, I think) of self-hatred, of internalized anti-Semitism. As I was growing up I was told (apocryphally, perhaps) that Einstein had said that he would consider himself Jewish as long as there was anti-Semitism in the world, and certainly by the definitions of anti-Semites I am Jewish. That is surely part of it: disaffiliation is dishonorable.

But that isn't—or shouldn't be—all there is to Jewish identity, even for the most secular. Surely, it seems, the Nazis and their ilk ought not to be the arbiters of our identity. What is it I know about myself when I know that I am a Jew?

As with questions about gender identity, part of my questioning comes from trying to understand someone who claims to share this identity with me but who seems clearly not to have it in the same way that I do. In the case of Jewish identity my questions have concerned converts, in particular converts to Judaism.[23] In Christianormative terms individual faith and knowledge are at the heart of identity, and conversion to Judaism is a religious process, governed by rabbis and requiring large amounts of religious instruction. The consequence is that converts to Judaism are intelligible as Jews in a way that I am not. Christianity is quintessentially a religion for converts: being born a Christian may make you one in the sense that you are part of a Christian community, but to be a "real" Christian you have to acknowledge for yourself the place of Christ in your life, and being born to a Christian family merely makes that more likely. Similarly, converts to Judaism know a lot more about Judaism as a religion than I do, which also makes them more intelligible on Christian terms: one can't be a real Christian if one is ignorant of creedally appropriate interpretations of scripture, for example. If it is hard for me to understand how one can be a woman other than by being born female, it is all too easy to understand how one can be a Jew having been born something else. But that's not how I am a Jew.

Problematically, the Jewishness of converts is intelligible, even to me, in a way that my own is not, since theirs, unlike mine, fits the conceptual framework of Christianormativity. Part of that framework is that there be a definite "there" out there, typically involving confirmation (as it is called) by a designated authority. And part of my problem is that, were I required to submit to such confirmation, I would surely fail. The rabbinical authorities charged with deciding who will get to become a Jew decide on grounds that have no connection to my own Jewishness. I am not, of course, required to be so confirmed: those same authorities, specifically as they interpret the Israeli Law of Return, would unquestionably include me: having a Jewish mother is sufficient. But even so, their authority feels irrelevant to me. Rabbis are religious authorities, and my Jewishness is not a religious identity.

Contemporary Jewish thinking is deeply concerned with what it is to be an authentic Jew: in particular, there are those who deny the possibilities of authentic nonreligious identity after the Holocaust, or of authentic diasporic Jewish identity after the founding of the state of Israel[24] (Goldberg and Krausz 1993). And while no one would deny that I am a Jew, there are many who would question the authenticity of my Jewish identity, who would claim that as a Jew I have obligations I am turning my back on. I, too, am tempted to make similar claims on others: it seems to me profoundly un-Jewish to be a Republican or to oppose affirmative action or, for that matter, to oppose the rights of Palestinians to self-determination. Unlike the rabbis, I have no power to enforce my claims, but what is it that grounds my making them: what do I mean by them? What am I doing in attempting to police the boundaries of an identity I find unintelligible? And how might figuring that out help me to understand my temptations to police the boundaries of an identity I find all too intelligible?[25]

V

When I bring the murkiness of my Jewish identity together with the suspicious transparency of my gender identity, one question that suggests itself is: Who cares? To whom does it matter, and why, that I have the identities that I do, and that I do or do not share them with certain others? Another, related question is: Who gets to decide, and on what grounds? How are some people counted in and others out? These are, I think, better—more useful, more practically pressing— questions than the ones I started out with, namely: What can a transsexual mean when she says she is a woman, and what can I mean when I say I am a Jew?

One way of framing the shift from the earlier questions to the later ones is by way of a Wittgensteinian account of why the earlier ones seem so intractable. The focus on what we mean (rather than on what we do and why, as though we can answer the one without the other) usually leads to one of three possibilities, or to an oscillation between them. The first is some form of privileged access essentialism: femaleness or Jewishness is just there, an abstractable part of one's overall identity, a definite, discernible something. Aside from the well-known problems both with privileged access and with essentialism, a serious problem with this approach, from my perspective, is that it leaves me out: if being a woman or a Jew consists in a particular inner state, knowable independently of the body or the history one happens to have or of how one is regarded by others, then I fail to be one. And though I am willing to consider forgoing paradigmatic status, I do think any definition of either women or Jews that simply leaves me out is quite likely to be wrong.

The second possibility is expert essentialism. On this view, such identities are complex and not necessarily introspectively accessible, but, exercising some combination of scientific and legislative authority, experts can make determinations. This view does in fact capture much about current practice. There are in both cases experts who are in the business of making such determinations, though, as I've argued above about Jewishness, they do so in ways that I and many others find troubling. The situation is even clearer when we look at the experts who determine gender, especially as this is done in the case of transsexuals.[26] The physicians and psychiatrists who have had the authority to decide who is "really" gendered differently than they are biologically sexed have tended (though this is changing, as transsexual activists are gaining some influence with the medical establishment) to reinforce precisely the gender stereotypes feminists have attempted to undermine: to be a woman in their terms has meant to be feminine. There has also been (though this too is changing) a conflation of gender and sexual identity: a real woman is supposed to be hetero-sexual.

Also, curiously, in the case of gender though not in the case of Jewishness, the experts insist on the inbornness of gender identity, even when it is discordant with biological sex. Those who would convert to Judaism do not have to demonstrate to the rabbis that they have "really" been Jewish all along—one can quite openly be a con-vert. But, as Kate Bornstein sardonically notes (1994, 62), the only way to be a "certified" transsexual is to deny that you are one, that is, to convince the doctors (and agree to try to convince the rest of the world) that you are and always have been what you clearly are not, namely simply and straightforwardly a woman (or a man). Since you cannot have had a history that is congruent with such an identity, you are left without a past (Feinberg 1993). As I argued above, it is not only in our own memories but in the memories of others that our selves take shape, and the institutionalization of transsexuality func-tions as a theft of selfhood, in making a transsexual life not only closeted but literally untellable, incoherent.

The theft is premeditated, carried out with malicious forethought. The illusion of the naturalness of sex and gender requires that we not see what the magician is up to before the impossible being—a newly born adult man or woman—emerges from beneath the surgical drape. Our (nontranssexual) comfort requires that we fail to acknowledge transsexuals as such, seeing what the surgery and the hormones and the scripted behavior intend to have us see: a "natural" man or woman. If the illusion fails—perhaps because those who "rise up from the operating tables of [their] rebirth . . . are something more, and something other, than the creatures [their] makers intended [them] to be" (Stryker 1994, 242)—we respond to the affront to that comfort by seeing the transsexual as, in the term Stryker uses and appropriates, a "monster."

"The transsexual body is an unnatural body. It is the product of medical science. It is a technological construction. It is flesh torn apart and sewn together again in a shape other than that in which it was born" (Stryker 1994, 238). But so are the bodies of women who attempt to stave off aging by multiple plastic surgeries. So, especially since my hysterectomy, is my body. And none of us, for reasons as natural and unnatural as the full complexities of our lives, is the shape we were when we were born. We are all, as Stryker reminds us we are unwilling to remember, "creatures" (1994, 240), not just in our mortal corporeality but in the constructedness of our psyches and our bodies. The illusion of the naturalness of bodies and psyches that conform to the dictates of heteronormativity is maintained when identity boundaries are policed by experts committed to keeping their work under wraps. Even when the experts are facilitating the crossing of sex and gender boundaries, they do so in ways that attempt to do as little damage as possible to the clarity of the lines: they may be crossed, but they are not to be blurred.

A third way an identity can be claimed—privileged access voluntarism—has, in the face of the inadequacies of the other two, seemed very attractive, especially to some transgendered people. On a privileged access voluntarist account, one is a woman if one says one is, and the claim means whatever one takes it to mean: it is not up to anyone else to tell me whether or not I am a woman, nor is there some particular essential property I have to have in order to be one; being a woman might in fact mean something quite different to me from what it means to you. The problem with this picture is that, in appearing to give the individual everything, it in fact gives nothing at all. As Wittgenstein has argued, meaning cannot be a private matter: a word means what it does not because I have joined it in my mind to an idea or an image (as Locke would have it), but because there exists a set of social practices in which I participate, in terms of which I can get the meaning right or wrong. Allowing "woman" to mean whatever anyone who applies it to herself takes it to mean gives one the freedom of self-naming at the cost of there being any point to the activity, any content to the chosen name, any reason for saying that one is a woman, rather than a man—or, for that matter, a car or a chrysanthemum.[27]

In practice, of course, naming oneself a woman is neither capricious nor unconnected to cultural meaning, even if, for some people—as Kate Bornstein suggested in a radio interview—what is really intended is that one is not a man, in a world in which there are simply no other conceptually allowable alternatives. On this view at least some MTFs are—or would be, if conceptual space allowed—not women but something else altogether. It will also be true that for those transsexuals who do think of themselves as women, the associations with womanhood that seem especially resonant may well be idiosyncratic, and there is no reason why they cannot pick and choose among them—why, that is, transsexuals should not have the same freedom as born women to embrace some aspects of womanhood and vehemently reject others. But once we drop the idea that there is a specific something (knowable either internally or to experts) in which being a woman consists, while holding onto the idea that there has to be some substantive, shareable content to the assertion, we have moved toward my second set of questions, those concerning who cares and who gets to decide.

The shift to this latter set of questions hinges on seeing meaning as something that we do, not something that we discover, as the introspective essentialist would have it. Both the expert essentialist and the privileged access voluntarist seem to recognize this fact, but in different ways they obscure the practices involved—the latter by making those practices empty, and the former by granting to experts a problematically unquestionable authority. To take seriously the idea that meaning is something we do is to raise questions about who "we" are and why and how we do what we do; it holds us accountable for how we mean what we say.[28]

I know myself to be a woman and a Jew because of the way I was named at birth: neither of them seems to come from anything that I have done. But what do I now do when I take these identities to be in this way given, and what is my role in maintaining systems that identify people at birth? Such a role can seem quite troubling. Susan Stryker experiences rage at the moment of "nonconsensual gendering" (in which she sees herself as complicit) at the birth of her lover's daughter: "A gendering violence is the founding condition of human subjectivity; having a gender is the tribal tatoo that makes one's personhood cognizable. I stood for a moment between the pains of two violations, the mark of gender and the unlivability of its absence" (1994, 250). The complexity of her rage is in that dilemma: it is not as though, in the world we know, one would treat a child better by withholding gender, since, in the world we know, one would be withholding personhood.

Recognition of the oppressive nonconsensuality of natal gendering need not obviate the significance of the feminist insistence on the specific oppressiveness of female, in contrast to male, gendering, although emphasizing one rather than the other has led to political and conceptual conflict. Such conflict has emerged in the political antagonism between (some) transsexual women and men and (some) feminists, especially lesbian separatists, conflict that emerges in differing understandings of the meaning of "women only" spaces. As Sarah Hoagland has reminded me, separatists were concerned with the creation of new meaning within self-defined spaces, not with the boundaries that marked off those spaces: attention circulated within lesbian space, rather than being focused on those on the outside, following Marilyn Frye's definition (1983) of lesbians as women whose attention was drawn to other women. Furthermore, as Anne Leighton pointed out to me, many lesbians, especially separatists, were more than ready to acknowledge transsexuals as such, as (another species of) "impossible beings."[29] Nor, of course, is "woman" a category lesbian separatists have had any particular fondness for, let alone any desire to maintain the clarity and distinctness of. Self-identified women, I am told, have never been asked to submit to tests aimed at "proving" their womanhood as a condition of entry to "women only" spaces such as the Michigan Women's Music Festival. Why, then, the battles over the inclusion in such spaces of (those who identify as) MTF transsexuals?

The interpersonal politics of such encounters are complex and surely not to be resolved by an armchair observer. But, aside from echoing Kate Bornstein's admonition (1994) that lesbian separatists are hardly the most politically savvy choice of adversary for transsexuals (and vice versa), I would like to introduce a possibly helpful piece of terminology to get at what I think separatists have in mind in using such problematic terms as "womyn-born-womyn" to exclude MTF transsexuals. A major reason for the existence of separatist space is to engage in the activity of self-naming and self-creation, and it is clearly inconsistent with such an aim to allow the definitions of the hetero-patriarchy to determine who is to be allowed in. (The use of "womyn" indicates that the identity in question is specifically not the one one was labeled with at birth, while the people to whom it is intended to apply are precisely those who were so labeled.) But separatism exists against the recognition of the Adamistic assumption that men have a natural right to name anything they deem worth naming, and of the fact that wresting that supposed right from them requires vigilance. It also starts from the recognition of the specific harms that flow from the natal ascription of femaleness in a misogynist world.

To get at the importance of these concerns, I suggest the term "perinatally pinked," which refers to the condition of having been named female around the time of birth: beforehand by chromosome-testing or ultrasound visualization, by visual inspection at birth, or by surgical "correction" shortly after birth (see Kessler 1990).[30] Separatist space (and other feminist practices that recognize the separatist im-pulses that inform even nonseparatist-identified female self-assertion (see Frye 1983) can be seen as a space of healing from having been perinatally pinked, and from living in a world in which being so marked makes one a target for subordination and abuse. Being in the company of others who, like one, were perinatally pinked, and creat-ing collectively with them the affirmative identity of "womyn" is for many separatists of the utmost importance to their survival in such a world. That MTF transsexuals were not perinatally pinked is a simple statement of fact, and it in no way diminishes the oppressiveness of their experiences of gendering—nor, importantly, does it preclude separatists' support of their claim to inclusion in the category of women. That category is one that operates in heteropatriarchal space—the space that requires unambiguous gender ascription for intelligibility—and in such space many lesbians are natural allies in the struggle to fight the harrassment (or worse) that targets those who visibly fail to conform to gender norms.[31]

If heteronormativity requires natally ascribed gender as the sign of intelligibility, Christianormativity tends to make the natal ascription of identity unintelligible. Abstract individualism, a distinctively Chris-tian view of persons, views group identity as properly a matter of choice, and as subordinate to one's unmarked humanity in constitut-ing identity.[32] In practice, of course, individuals are hardly unmarked at birth, and not only by gender: the obvious additional natal mark is race, and, as argued above, all sorts of deviations from normality get labeled inborn. But identities thought of as inborn are seen not as a matter of group membership, but as traits inhering in individuals. Group membership is meant to come later, and to be chosen. So the only intelligible way to be born a Jew is if Jewishness can be seen as a "trait," or a cluster of traits—a ground of intelligibility anti-Semitic discourse has been only too happy to provide.

But what if we resist the dictates of Christianormativity on this point, and insist on the intelligibility of being born a member of the Jewish people? Can we find in such an exercise a way of thinking that makes better sense of what it is to be born a male or a female (see Boyarin 1994), where one criterion for "better sense" is the greater intelligibility of those who come later to dispute the gender membership into which they were born?

We should note that Jewishness would not be the sort of identity it is if some people were not born into it: in this sense it is not (or not just) a religious identity. Being born Jewish is not the only way to be Jewish, nor is it necessary for born Jews to be thought of as more authentic or "real" than converts (though often they are). What is true is that born Jews have certain histories that converts do not, though it is important to keep in mind just how diverse those histories are, including not only the wide range of different experiences of Jewishness, but also the possibility of not knowing for most of one's life that one is Jewish: discovering that one is means discovering something about one's own history. (You may, for example, have been born to Jewish parents and adopted by Christians and discover your Jewishness when discovering your birth parents. Note that in the reverse situation, it would be wrong to say that you were discovering that you were Christian.)

Part of what is difficult about thinking Jewishness is acknowledging the importance of history, along with group identity. Ignoring or theoretically deconstructing the role of history—of the given, the unchosen—leads to the sort of arrogating voluntarism I discussed above. The denial of the relevance of the body and of history (often, confusedly, in the name of antiessentialism) also seems to me to be both masculinist and Christian, insofar as both those discourses privilege the mind over the body, the chosen over the given.[33] That some of us confront some of our identities as ineluctable, as constitutive of who we are, as something about ourselves we cannot change, is to say something about how certain experiences are socially constructed; it is not to be committed to essentialism.

To speak of Jewishness as paradigmatically unchosen has, of course, an additional resonance, since to be Jewish is to be "chosen." That is, it is God who gets to do the choosing; one is chosen whether one chooses to be or not. Jewish atheists are in general a peculiar breed: we are given to having deeply disputatious relationships with the God we don't believe in, often centered on just what He had it in mind to choose us for. My own sense is that we were chosen to be canaries. Just as one sends canaries down mines to see if the air is safe to breathe—if it will kill anything, it will kill a canary—so Jews are, over the long run, a good test of the oppressiveness of a social environment (at least in those parts of the world where Jews have historically lived). Sooner or later those who are committed to ideologies of domination and subordination will reveal themselves as anti-Semites.

Thus, the quintessentially Jewish injunction that "none is free so long as any are oppressed," is for Jews a literal truth, no matter how hard individuals or groups may work at denying it, whether by assimilating within a Christian culture or by militarizing the state of Israel: a canary on steroids is ultimately still a canary. Affluent conservative American Jews may think that their interests lie in opposing affirmative action and other efforts to undo antiblack racism, but they are mistaken. The black-Jewish alliance of the civil rights era may have been romanticized, but it had its roots in a deep truth: racists are also anti-Semites, and Jews have no business consorting with them, even if they allow us into their subdivisions, universities, and country clubs. Our mortgages, degrees, and membership cards will not make us safe: the world will not be truly safe for the Jews until it is safe for everyone, and we forget that at our peril.

A consequence of this notion of chosenness is that power is a misguided and ultimately ineffective response to danger.[34] Precisely because one cares about an imperiled identity, one has to resist the temptation to protect it with fortified barricades. Thus, one can think of conversion to Judaism not in the context of Rabbinic law (though for those for whom religious faith is at the heart of their Jewishness, chosen or otherwise, Rabbinic law will be something to engage, perhaps, as it has always been engaged, disputatiously) or of the intricacies of the Israeli Law of Return, but in the terms Ruth used in following Naomi: "Thy people shall be my people."

Conversion to Judaism is more like marrying into a family than it is like conversion to Christianity, including analogous problems around the policing of families by, for example, the social and legal restrictions of marriage. A notion of family that broke free of such restrictions would function like the notion of "my people" that Daniel and Jonathan Boyarin (1993) call "diasporic"—nonpoliced, not shored up by apparatuses of institutionalized power. Belonging to such a family or a people would mean being related in some complex amalgam of chosen and unchosen bonds to a group some of whom are born members, others of whom are, we might say, "naturalized."[35]

The term is both precisely right and deeply wrong. It is deeply wrong in its association with citizenship, that most quintessentially state-regulated of identities.[36] Its very suggestive rightness lies in its making it evident that "natural" is something one can become (there is a process that produces it), and in its marking a contrast that distinguishes collectivities that at least some members are born into from those that are wholly chosen. Being a born member of such a collectivity is, importantly, a matter of genealogy—that is, of history, not of essential traits: there is no suggestion that the whole shebang (the *ganze megillah*) is anything other than a social construction. A further important feature of such collectivities is that one shares one's membership in them with others with whom one would not choose to be associated and whom one cannot expel.

What happens when we bring these reflections on Jewish identity to the questions about sex and gender identity as raised by, specifically, MTF transsexuals? If we push the analogy, the fact that there are born women is constitutive of the category "woman," as the fact that there are born Jews is constitutive of the category "Jew." What counts, of course, is not who one's parents (or mother) are but how one is enrolled into the sex/gender system at birth. The category "woman," however, can also include variously "naturalized" members, where naturalization has to do with a deeply felt identification with at least some (and almost certainly only some) earlier members, a feeling that one is in some sense "like them." (When identity is officially regulated, those who are not officially naturalized have the status, as it were, of undocumented aliens—an apt description of not-officially-certified transsexuals, caught in a position in which they are unable to acquire usable drivers' licences or other forms if identification [Feinberg 1993].) Such identification has to be acknowledged by at least some earlier members, as one cannot become a Jew without the acknowledgment of at least some already-Jews, though not necessarily by all of them, and not necessarily by born members.[37] Those who are "naturalized" women are no less women than those who are born female, though the category would not be what it is were no one born into it.

An important disanalogy is that conversion to Judaism tends to be much more a matter of choice than does sex or gender change, and conversion may well have been preceded by a long period of quite comfortable identification as, say, a Christian. The disanalogy marks a deep difference in how different identities work: one need not be recognized as Jewish or non-Jewish in order to be intelligible, and we have the conceptual space to narrate a history that goes between them.[38] But the disanalogy reflects aspects of gender practice that we might want to think about changing: that is, thinking about sex/gender identity as more analogous in these ways to Jewish identity might help us to imagine a less oppressive way of "doing gender." The experiences of transsexual people tend to be quite different from the experiences of converts to Judaism—but that may be because of aspects of our sex/gender system that could be imagined otherwise.

There are, I think, other advantages to pushing this analogy. It is less constraining of identity than are the operations of those who expertly police the gender divide: the significance of natal assignment is not to pick out the "real" women from the others, but rather to note that there would be no categories of the sort that genders are if some people were not assigned to them at birth—there would, that is, be no such thing as a woman to believe that one was if there were not people who were assigned female at birth, just as there would be no such thing as Jewishness to convert to if there were not people who were Jewish from birth. (Again, the same is not true of Christianity.) To deny this conceptual role to natal assignment—to think of gender as more like Christianity, as a system of categories that people sort themselves into based on their own self-identifications—is to ignore the ways in which, as a matter of historical fact, no less real for being contingent and alterable, gender is socially constructed and how it functions in people's lives. (Part of the quarrel of lesbian separatists with transsexuals is a disagreement about how gender works. For many separatists gender is a social imposition that places them in a threatened category: women are created as the objects of misogyny;

while for many transsexuals gender is an inner identity that needs to be asserted in the face of social mislabeling. I want to suggest that both these conceptualizations are too restrictive to get at all the complex ways in which gender works, though each captures an aspect of gender that is, for some purposes, especially salient.)

Whether or not, or to what extent, the sex/gender system is disrupted by the gender experiences of transsexuals depends on the extent to which those experiences are thought of as paradigmatic. The irony is that in order to support transsexual claims to clear, stable, and unambiguous gender identities, those identities have themselves to remain marginal. Only a system that takes natally gendered persons as paradigmatic—that maintains the illusion of the normality of "natural" gendering—can have the solidity to ground *anyone's* unambiguous gender claims. The more important it is for transsexuals to claim a stable and unproblematic gender, the more conceptually dependent they are on their own marginality, as rare exceptions to a fundamentally natural dichotomy. The extent of this importance varies enormously from person to person—as it does for nontranssexuals. But it is a feature, surely alterable, of present-day Western cultures that stable and unproblematic gender identities are expected of everyone—so that those who resist claiming and enacting one live the perilous lives of "outlaws." A sex/gender system in which, by contrast, not only natal members are paradigmatic, in which paradigm status can be shared with transsexuals, would be much more like the system that underwrites Jewish identity: full of ambiguity, unclarity, and vagueness. (In the *Philosophical Investigations* Wittgenstein tried to disabuse us of the Fregean conviction that ambiguous, unclear, vague concepts were no concepts at all: having been so disabused, we can contemplate the possibility that we might have reason in some cases not just to tolerate but to prefer ambiguity, unclarity, and vagueness.)

It is also, I would argue, an advantage to the analogy that it highlights the differences between the relationships of MTF and FTM transsexuals to the born members of their respective genders. Analogizing specifically womanness with Jewishness (something that has, of course, a long and exceedingly complicated history) draws attention to anti-Semitism and misogyny as parts of the social world in which those categories have meaning and in the light of which they are lived. It helps us make sense of the particular anxieties felt by some Jews and some women about the possibility that core definitions of those identities will shift if the boundaries are not policed; and it can help, if not to allay those anxieties, at least to suggest that they are counterproductive. So long as I have no say (and given the sort of category "woman" is, I can have no say) about whether Margaret Thatcher is a woman, it avails me nothing politically to try to keep Kate Bornstein or Sandy Stone or Susan Stryker from being one. Ironically, it is the fact that some people are born women that provides one of the strongest arguments against attempts to police the boundaries of womanhood.

The analogy also shifts the question: what is it to be a woman (or a Jew)?—as though there were something there, in me, to be discovered—to, instead: how did I get to be one? how was I claimed or assigned? how was I chosen—by whom and for what? and, having been chosen, to whom do I have what responsibilities, with whom is my fate tied and how? Conversion to Judaism is not, like conversion to Christianity, a matter between an individual and God or an individual and an institutionalized church. It is a matter of joining a "people," of coming to share their history, and their fate. An MTF transsexual may be no more a feminist than Phyllis Shlafly, but she is no more immune to sexism and no less accountable for her failure to identify with the struggle against it.

Such accountability will mean different things to different ones of us and different things to each of us at different times. One thing it always means is a recognition of and active resistance to the misogyny and anti-Semitism that are part of the inherited histories and contemporary realities of women and Jews. (And a failure of accountability is a moral failure, not an identity test: one has failed to be, in this instance a good person, not a "good Jew" or a "good woman," still less a "real" woman or Jew.) Resistance entails not just fighting the attacks but equally refusing the benefits that are advertised as coming with closeting, silence, collaboration, or disaffiliation. I would regard it as profoundly dishonorable to pass—as there is frequent occasion to do—as an "honorary" man or Christian. The emphasis is on the "honorary": it is no dishonor to be taken to be a man or a Christian; what is dishonorable is to let stand the implication that one is therefore more worth respecting than if one were a woman or a Jew. (As a woman currently monogamously involved with a man, I regard it as dishonorable to pass, in this sense, as a heterosexual, which is rather different from identifying as a bisexual.)[39]

Resistance is connected to solidarity, which is a matter of identifying *with*, rather than *as*.[40] As such, it can bind different groups rather
than divide them, but typically it does primarily bind groups, and
individuals insofar as they are members of groups. Daniel Boyarin, in
his deeply suggestive articulation of what he calls "diasporic identity," makes this point: such identity is particularist but not isolation-
ist. As nonhegemonic others (he has in mind primarily, of course,
diasporic Jews) we live in larger, diverse communities to which we
are deeply bound and to which we are responsible in part as a condition of our group identity (1994, 257). Solidarity, identifying with, is
at the heart of the Passover seder, and in some traditions, such as the
socialist ones of my family, the celebration of the liberation of "our
people" was inseparable from a rededication to solidarity with all the
continuing liberation struggles in the world. Similarly, I think, AIDS
has come to play a role in lesbian identity, not because lesbians are at
particular risk of HIV infection—which, course, they are not—but
because of solidarity with gay men who are, a solidarity that is at once
"natural" (grounded in shared resistance to homophobia) and conscientiously chosen: my sense is that AIDS-related politics has greatly
increased the numbers of lesbians who identify with gay men, and
that lesbian identity has been as a consequence reshaped. Who one
identifies with is inseparable from what one identifies as.

VI

I have (despite my recurrent temptations) no real interest in policing
the boundaries of either womanhood or Jewishness, nor is it a job I
want anyone else to do: both identities are better left undefined—or,
more strongly, incoherent and confused. If the meaning of identity,
like the meaning of anything else, is a matter of the practices that
shape it, then it would be both intellectually mistaken and politically
unwise to give either of these identities more clarity and coherence
than are warranted by their structuring practices. And those practices
are a mess—a jumble of oppression and resistance, history and imagination, drudgery and heroism: if meaning is use, "woman" and
"Jew" have been and continue to be put to such a dizzying variety of
contradictory uses that any coherent account of either would have to
be untrue. Furthermore, and importantly, it may well be incoherent

identities, those that do not fit into the available taxonomies, that bear particularly liberatory potential. María Lugones has been articulating this vision, for example, in arguing for the embracing of "multiplicitous" identities lived across worlds and in what, following Victor Turner, she refers to as "anti-structure—places of creative liminality" (Lugones 1990; see also Lugones 1994).

What does that leave us with as a way of finding identity intelligible? Family resemblances, for one: male-to-female transsexuals or Jewish converts see in my identity—or the identity of some other women or Jews, born or not, perhaps very different from me—a variation of what they feel or want themselves to be; they look at some of us and see kin. (Talk of family is notoriously dangerous, as white feminists were reminded with reference to the talk of "sisterhood," and as Jacob Hale has reminded me again. But, aside from its Wittgensteinian implications, I think it's worth engaging with—carefully. It helps to remember that family resemblance, like any other form of resemblance, is only very weakly transitive; and one thing we know about relatives is that they can cause us to be related to people we cannot imagine having as kin: but, imagine it or not, we are so related.) What I see when I look back is not a simple matter. I may look at an MTF transsexual and see not a woman but a man who, with typical male arrogance, claims both the right to define what it is to be a woman and the right to take anything he wants, even if it's my identity. Increasingly, this is not what I see, and the change has to do both with my looking more carefully—seeing, for example, the ways in which the oppressiveness of gender affects those who inhabit its unnameable borders at least as much as it affects those who live near the center of the female side—and with a growing feminist consciousness among transsexuals.

Part of being careful about the use of familial imagery involves displacing its role as a primary site of heteronormativity. Using the family in counternormative ways is one sort of response to the reactionary deployment of family rhetoric: rather than rejecting the family (as image or social arrangement), we can "queer" it. David Halperin (1995) proposes "queer" as a term not for a particular identity, constructed, as all identities are, by complex amalgams of normalizing and stigmatizing practices, but as positionality: as flexible strategies of resistance to the practices of heteronormativity.[41] Such flexibility is suggested, he argues, by the flexible illogic of heteronormativity: it is strategically better suited than any affirmation of, say, positive gay identity to slipping over, under, around, or through the stigmatizing net. Queer identity, so conceived, is a slap in the face to the alleged "straightness" of heterosexuality, an illusion maintained by diverting attention away from those who are supposed to be the unmarked "normals" and toward the crafty maneuvering of those who try to live lives they can respect in the face of contradictory imputations of sickness and sin.

The question of who is queer (along with the related question of whether queer is a useful and appropriate identity for gay men and, even more controversially, for lesbians) has taken on some of the controversy that surrounds questions about who is a woman or who is a Jew. With the ascendancy of queer theory in some parts of the academic and cultural worlds it has become chic to be queer, and many gay men and (perhaps) more lesbians have felt that their identities—and, more importantly, their histories and struggles— were being ripped off.[42] As Halperin puts it, in a caveat: "[l]esbians and gay men can now look forward to a new round of condescension and dismissal at the hands of the trendy and glamorously unspecified sexual outlaws who call themselves 'queer' and who can claim the radical chic attached to a sexually transgressive identity without, of course, having to do anything icky with their bodies in order to earn it" (1995, 65).

I want to argue for the claiming of queer identity as an important liberatory strategy in part because of the challenge it poses to the paradigmatic status of privileged subjectivity. Simultaneously it maintains the tension between the boundary-shiftiness of queerness and respect for the historically and personally specific experiences of those who have found themselves (with the mix of activity and passivity that term implies) in identities whose boundaries they encountered as given and fixed, whether as a matter of internal certainty or of unyielding social decree.[43]

The symbolic appropriation of marginalized, oppressed, or stigmatized identities is the flip side of the expert policing of identity boundaries. The policing of boundaries results in definitive statements about who is or is not a "real" Jew or woman or homosexual, whether in the name of valorizing and defending the category or of keeping those in it from getting out. Symbolic appropriation often displaces those who have been thus defined—who may, in part because of such policing, regard those identities as central to their senses of self—in favor of others whose nonliteral (i.e., nonbodily) identifications become what it is to be a "real" Jew or woman or queer. Some male Jungians talk this way about their anima, and it is the suspicion (no doubt in at least some, though I suspect not many, cases well-founded) that this attitude characterizes MTF transsexuals that is behind much of the feminist resistance to acknowledging MTFs as women. Daniel and Jonathan Boyarin (1993) have explored the phenomenon of the (lower case) "jew": the outsider and nonconformist in the European imagination—the *real* Jew, more real for not being confined by a limited and limiting history.[44] There are good reasons to resist this symbolic appropriation of identity, even as it seems to be made possible by—and positively to further—the breaking down of confining definitions.

But there are equally good reasons for encouraging creatively playful, politically serious border transgressions on the part of those who could, given what seem to be the facts about them, safely reside on the more privileged side.[45] Adrienne Rich, writing in the seventies, articulated a conception of lesbian identity that has affinities with queerness, and it met with similar resistance (see Zita 1981 and discussion in Rich 1986). Rather than focusing on the specificities of the experiences of some women, Rich wrote about—and to—the lesbian in every woman: "It is the lesbian in us who is creative, for the dutiful daughter of the fathers in us is only a hack" (Rich 1979, 201). The "lesbian continuum" encouraged women to find and identify with their own rebelliousness against heteropatriarchy (Rich 1986). The concern of Rich's critics was that such expansiveness drew attention away from the radical core of lesbian identity—an embodied erotic connection to other women. Rich wasn't advocating the position I referred to above as privileged access voluntarism, so the problem isn't that "lesbian" becomes contentless; rather it's that the specific transgressiveness of lesbianism is lost if the sexual is downplayed. The dispute is over which practices will be taken as constituting the language game, and, consequently, which family resemblances will emerge as salient.

It was Rich's strategy—as it is the strategy of queer theorists—to be expansive about the practices that constitute lesbian identity, in part as a means of destabilizing those that constitute heterosexual identity. Such destabilization is not just conceptual: heteronormativity (akin to Rich's notion of compulsory heterosexuality) functions in part through the quotidian complicity of those who cannot imagine—or desire—an alternative. Similarly, in poems such as "Transcendental Etude" and "Sibling Mysteries" (1978) Rich reminds women of mother/child eroticism and of the unnaturalness of abandoning a woman's body for a man's: she is "queering" (women's) heterosexuality, in a way similar to Michael Warner's discussion in the introduction to *Fear of a Queer Planet* (1993). Queerness is not meant to contrast with straightness so much as to displace it, to reveal its inherent contradictions and instabilities. Thus, queer readings of canonical texts are not attempts to demonstrate that some author hitherto believed to be straight was really gay, but are, rather, subversions of our reading practices, disruptions of our imputations to authors of the sort of straightforward, transparent integrity that characterizes privileged subjectivity.

Other theorists have urged the privileged to find in themselves the shreds and patches of transgressive identities. María Lugones (1987) suggests that "world"-travel—the movement into a social world in which one is marked as other, something the oppressed and marginalized have to do for survival—can be embarked on "playfully" by those among the privileged who have the courage and the loving commitment to learn how they are seen by those in whose eyes their privilege marks them as other. Sandra Harding (1991, 288) urges those who are privileged to learn to think out of "traitorous" identities, conscientiously disloyal to their privilege. Daniel and Jonathan Boyarin (1993) suggest diasporic identity as an alternative to nationalist identity: a history-and body-laden sense of identity—a sense that these particular others are "my people"—is viable (nonracist) only when it is uncoupled from state power.

Strategies for "queering the center" will vary as the identities in question are variously constructed, policed, and transgressively lived—in particular as one or the other side of the oxymoronic natural incapacity/willful refusal construction is dominant. Womanhood and Jewishness are illustrative of these differences. Part of heteronormativity is the assumption that gender is not chosen but "natural": given and immutable, either inscribed on the body or, even if in some "deviant" cases at odds with it, set one way or the other at a very early age. As I noted above, the medical control of transsexual experience has served to reinforce, rather than to undermine, the fixity of gender. In the face of this rigidity, it can be liberatory to blur the boundary (both by straddling and by crossing it), to argue for the ways in which gender is neither definite nor fixed. Doing so need not, as many feminists have worried, undermine the intelligibility and efficacy of feminist politics, for which the undeniable reality and oppressiveness of sex/gender systems, however historically mutable or even arbitrary, are grounds enough. It can also be important to claim the power of self-naming, including the power of boundary setting. But the "selves" that do the naming need not be confined to those who in the dominant view of things count as women: a politics of solidarity can underwrite transgressive boundary *marking*, as well as blurring or straddling.

Jewishness, on the other hand, is aberrant in a Christianormative culture in being paradigmatically a matter not of choice, but, as Daniel Boyarin puts it, of "genealogy" (1994, 236–46). From a Jewish perspective postmodern antiessentialist arguments can sound suspiciously Protestant, resting, as they often do, on the idea that any identity at all is "nothing but" a social construction, and that taking oneself to be anything as a matter of birth is bad faith. Furthermore, the conflation of givenness (i.e., the denial of voluntarism) and essentialism is a mistake, as is the opposition between givenness and social construction: Jewishness is no less socially constructed for being heritable.[46]

It is important, I think, to assert Jewishness specifically as an identity that is paradigmatically not a matter of choice, that is, to resist not only the assimilation of individual Jews into Christian culture, but the assimilation of Jewish identity itself. (The term "Judeo-Christian" is an example of such assimilation: not only does it amalgamate Jewishness with Christianity, but it makes Jewishness out to be the larval form, important not in its own right but as a precursor to Christianity.) Concerning gender and sexual identity, I would argue that although a case can be made for more body-based, less voluntaristic conceptions than are currently popular in gender studies, given the fit between such a view and that of heteropatriarchy, the dangers probably outweigh the benefits. But I have tentatively, suggested that some ways of thinking about Jewish identity can provide a helpful model for breaking the hold on us of the rigidities of gender identity, by providing a middle way between the supposed dichotomy of either unproblematically natural or ungrounded and arbitrary. [47]

There is no single answer to the question of whether an explicitly, flexibly constructionist or a historically given, body-based view of identity is more politically progressive. (I am assuming, of course, that in some sense there is no "fact of the matter," that questions concerning categorization do not admit of nonstrategic answers: that is, on the metaphysical level, I am assuming some version of social constructionism.) It depends on who is asserting what sort of identity when and where and why, in the face of what other sorts of assertions, especially those that have authoritative standing. My suggestion is that here and now there are good reasons to queer the centers of both heteronormative and Christianormative discursive practices and that such queering can proceed by way of exploring the ways in which some of us live as impossible beings, emphasizing those aspects of our lives that render us impossible: the shape shifting of the transsexual and the unchosen givenness of the secular Jew. Against the normative backgrounds of essentialized gender and chosen religion, such emphases move the two identities onto a shared middle ground of complex—and normatively unintelligible—mixtures of givenness and choice.

In these ways and others—in articulations of *mestizaje* (see Anzaldúa 1987) or exhortations to become "world"-travelers (Lugones 1987), and in diverse invocations of trickster subjectivities (see Haraway 1991, 199; Gates 1988)—the experiences of variously marginalized people provide alternative models of subjectivity, less seamless and transparent, less coherent and solid, than those of privilege. Each of them is grounded in the specificities of the experiences of historically particular groups, but all suggest that taking such experiences as paradigmatic of the human can both shatter the illusions of the naturalness of privilege and offer ways out of the constraints of its normativities. The point is not to generate legions of chic lesbian or mestiza or black or American Indian or Jewish wannabes, but to offer alternative, variously queer, provisional paradigms in relation to which each of us tells our own, shifting stories. The issue, then, is not who is or is not really whatever, but who can be counted on when they come for any one of us: the solid ground is not identity, but loyalty and solidarity.[48]

NOTES

1. I am deeply indebted in my thinking about issues of identity, subjectivity, and integrity by reading, listening to, and talking with María Lugones for fifteen years.

2. See also Hoagland (forthcoming) for the related argument that what is read as incompetence or unreliability on the part of subordinated people is often, in fact, sabotage.

3. See Frye (1983) for the distinction between loving and arrogant perception.

4. See Anzaldúa (1987), Sherover-Marcuse (1986), and Miller (1984).

5. "Problematize" is a word that has gotten something of a reputation as a piece of theory-jargon. I think the reputation is undeserved: I know of no other noncumbersome way of referring to just this activity, which is a crucial one for any liberatory theorizing: the rendering problematic (questionable, in need of explanation) some phenomenon taken to be transparent, natural, in need of neither explanation nor justification.

6. The norm-flouting I have in mind here has a political meaning at odds with that of privileged eccentricity, but the two are not always easy to distinguish, especially when class privilege accompanies, for example, a stigmatized sexual identity. The risks and costs of being "out" vary enormously, and some forms of politically progressive trangression can be more easily available to those who are otherwise comfortable and safe. Alliances between those who do not have the choice to pass, for whom strategic inventiveness is required for bare survival, and those whose trangressions are more a matter of choice, are precarious—at risk on one side from the need for protective coloration that can be read as overconformity, and on the other from the possibility of playfulness that can be read as unseriousness. The responsibility for establishing trusting alliances is not, however, equally shared: Nancy Potter (1994) has argued that the burdens of creating trust properly fall disproportonately on the relatively privileged.

7. Halperin also draws on Eve Sedgwick's discussion (1990) of the productive incoherence of heteronormative and homophobic discourses.

8. In a liberal Christian society, such as the present day United States, there is a presumption of Christian identity that works much like the presumption of heterosexuality: people are given the "benefit" of the doubt and assigned, in the absence of positive counterevidence, to the privileged category. Nor, as Jacob Hale has pointed out (1996), is the privilege that comes of being born to Christian parents easily shed, especially since the alternatives to it that occupy the American imaginary are racialized: even if the question "Are you a Christian?" is typically about faith, the presumption of Christian identity is usually not.

9. As Lisa Heldke has reminded me, there is a common way of resolving this tension, by dividing Jewish identity in two—the religious component and the racial or cultural component. The resolution doesn't work, in part because it simply pushes the problem back one step: what is the relationship between the two "components," and how are we to characterize the second—since on

any plausible notion of race or culture, Jews belong not to one but to several or many races and cultures. The problem was literally "pushed back" by the Nuremberg Laws, by which the Nazis sought to racially classify the Jews: Jewishness was defined in terms of religious observance in the grandparental generation (Pascale Bos, personal communication).

10. Putting the matter this way highlights the fact that Christianormativity and Christianity are no more the same thing than are heteronormativity and heterosexuality: in both cases there are particular histories of ascendancy to centrality, which histories need to be told in tandem with the complementary histories of the corresponding stigmatized identities.

11. For reasons much like these, David Halperin (1995) has called heterosexuality "the love that dare not speak its name," that is, that dare not name itself as one sexuality among others, needing like them to explain itself. Thanks to Diana Tietjens Meyers for pointing out that the discourses of normality and of virtue are not contradictory if normality is read in a normative way. The contradictoriness comes in when that normativity is occluded, camouflaging undefended, possibly indefensible, claims about excellence—when, that is, we are not supposed to be able to ask: "Says who?" Or if we do, the answer is: "Nature."

12. The specific example is Elizabeth V. Spelman's, and she makes the general point especially well (1988, 12). See also Sarah Hoagland's (forthcoming) refusal to take up the question of whether or not women ought to have equal rights, since it presupposes the rights of men as the unquestionable norm against which women need to stake a claim.

13. For an excellent discussion of paradigm case reasoning and its role in the maintenance of privilege (as well as its difference from "essentialism"), see Marilyn Frye, forthcoming.

14. Marsha Hagen (conversation) drew my attention to the historical specificity of the unintelligibility of secular Jewish identity, by pointing out the persistence in Canada for one generation more than in the United States of a vibrant secular Yiddish culture. My discussion is grounded in post-World War II U.S. culture, where the terms that governed assimilationist possibilities joined with the memory of the Holocaust to make impossible the thinking of Jewishness in anything like racial terms. And, in the American imaginary, religion was the only remaining possibility. (I wonder if the centrality of distinct Québecois identity to Canadian thinking, however problematic, helps to provide conceptual space lacking in the United States.)

15. Thanks to Jacob Hale for stressing the importance of this point. The monster Stryker has most particularly in mind is Frankenstein's, but the figure of the monster—as "unnatural" because created, a "creature"—is central to her discussion of what she calls "transgender rage" (1994). See Feinberg (1983) for a harrowing and moving portrayal of the experiences of a "he-she," and

Frye (1983) for a discussion of the extent to which gender ascription shapes our responses to each other.

16. Analogous work is being done around race and the experiences of those who are not readily racially classifiable, in particular, those of mixed race (see, for example, Camper 1994; Zack 1995). There are, of course, enormous differences: miscegenation provides an all too easily imagined answer to the question of how someone "came to look like that," and looking and otherwise seeming more white is more a matter of privilege for people of color than looking and otherwise seeming more male is for women (though in some circumstances the former can be more problematic and the latter more privileging than is usually acknowledged).

17. Being "stably female-gendered" is not an all-or-nothing thing: the dividing line of gender slices through at least the edges of many lives. In our culture's terms, as a feminist and a philosopher I may not be a best paradigm case, and certainly many others are even less so—notably lesbians, who are routinely told, and often, especially as children believe, that they are not "real women." And certainly not all feminists share the desire to eliminate gender— one may, for example, be more concerned to fight for the recognition of one's identity as a woman despite one's gender-role nonconformity or one's less than stereotypical appearance. My appeal here is to those feminists who do share the desire to eliminate gender and who have the privilege of at least suffcent gender conformity to, for example, use a women's restroom without being hassled. Obviously, the challenge will be different depending on one's circumstances: I'm addressing most directly those who, like me, have lived close enough to the center never to have directly experienced the knife-edge of the gender divide.

18. I share this confusion with many if not most feminist theorists. Kessler and McKenna's book (1978) played an important role in moving us away from the premature sense of intelligibility expressed in the sex/gender distinction of most seventies' feminist theory. As I will argue, this confusion is entirely appropriate at this point in history: we have good reason to distrust *any* conceptually coherent account of gender.

19. Jacob Hale (1996), in a discussion of Monique Wittig's claim that lesbians are not women, provides a subtle and complex (Austinian) analysis of the diverse meanings of "real woman," along with a persuasive argument that any understanding of gender or sexuality has to proceed by way of an understanding of the margins: it is in the experiences and perspectives of those who inhabit the boundaries that the contours of a contested conceptual space are articulated. I have, of course, been surrounded by sophisticated discussions about the ways in which women are not born but made, and made specifically by patriarchy for its ends—but underlying those discussions has been a virtually untouched dualism concerning exactly who did, and who did not, get

made into a woman, and the centrality of that identity even for those who in many ways rejected it.

The impetus to explore these issues came largely from an invitation to a conference on "Sissies and Tomboys," Center for Gay and Lesbian Studies, City University of New York Graduate Center, 10 February 1995. I was invited by the organizer, Matt Rottnek, whose confidence that I did, despite my skepticism, have something to say about these questions, led me to begin to pull these thoughts together. I was enormously helped, in preparing for the conference, by several of the programs in "Differently Gendered Lives: A Week of Programs about Transgender and Transsexual Experiences" sponsored by the University of Minnesota Office of Lesbian, Gay, Bisexual, and Transsexual Programs, 28 January–3 February 1995, including Leslie Feinberg's plenary address.

20. Sarah Hoagland (1988) and Jan Binder (personal communication) have helped me to see the political implications lurking in questions of intelligibility: who has to make themselves intelligible to whom, in what terms, for what reasons, against what forms of resistance, with what resources? Heteronormativity requires for intelligibility that one be one gender or the other: some transsexuals are beginning to resist this requirement, in particular as enforced by "medical, psychotherapeutic, and juridical institutions" that police the gender boundary (Stryker 1994, 252), and hence no longer to identify as women (or men), plain and simple (Bornstein 1994; Stone in Gabriel 1995; Stryker 1994; Jacob Hale, personal communication; Susan Kimberley, in discussion at the University of Minnesota conference).

21. Aside from being a feminist, a philosopher, and an adult-onset bisexual (and having loved math and logic), my only major failure to conform to the norms of femaleness is that I have never been pregnant and I am not a mother. But I managed to leave those options at least hypothetically open until this summer, so never confronted the implications for my inclusion as a "real woman." I am writing the final draft of this essay while recuperating from a total hysterectomy, surgery that removed not only the possibility of pregnancy but the internal organs most definitive of my femaleness. The timing is coincidental, but suggestive.

22. Irena Klepfisz's account (1990) of her experience of a vanishing Yiddish culture in New York helped give me a sense of what it would be like to have a community-based sense of secular Jewish identity.

23. As in the case of gender, I respond differently to people who "go the other way," who give up the identity they share with me for another— female-to-male transsexuals and Jewish converts, especially to Christianity. I feel abandoned, as though someone I thought was "on my side" had gone over, if not exactly to the enemy, then to the class of others who historically have oppressed us. I'm learning, largely through listening to and reading

Leslie Feinberg and, more recently, reading and corresponding with Jacob Hale, to think and feel differently about FTM transsexuals, but it is harder to accept Jews who convert to Christianity. The difference, I think, is that although it is no part of sexism to get women to defect and become men (not, at least, in this world and in bodily form: see Boyarin [1994] for an argument that Pauline Christianity does envision women's becoming spiritually men), it is at the heart of orthodox Christianity to get others, most especially Jews, to defect and become Christians. If there is anything I think is essential to Jewish identity in Christian cultures, it is the resistance to Christian proselytizing. At the very least, a convert can be held accountable by Jews, as an FTM transsexual can be held accountable by women, for conscientiously dealing with newly acquired Christian—or male—privilege.

24. Natalie Kampen has pointed out to me the importance of the idea of authenticity to Jewish identity, and the relation to similar discussions concerning, for example, Black or Chicano identity. The concern is centrally around a subordinated community's fears in relation to the dominant community: for example, that those members most acceptable to the white or Christian world will be assimilated, while the others are increasingly stigmatized. It is an understandable response to such (realistic) fears to accuse the more "acceptable" of being inauthentic but, as María Lugones argued in a talk at a PIC conference at Binghamton University (April 1994)—it's misguided and self-defeating, reinforcing the oppressor's logic.

25. Thanks to Diana Tietjens Meyers, Lisa Heldke, and Jacob Hale for pointing out to me that in earlier versions I had (repeatedly, even after being warned) succumbed to these temptations. Rather than claim finally to have overcome them, I would note here that such lapsing into the perquisites of privileged subjectivity is not only a demographic but an occupational hazard, and the effort to give up identity policing needs to be an ongoing one. (This paper may be finished, but its author is a work in progress.)

26. For a discussion of sex assignment at birth in cases of genital ambiguity, see Kessler (1990): feminist suspicions about the phallocentrism of the sex/gender system are reinforced by her argument that the determining factor for sex assignment is the presence or absence of a "good enough" penis.

27. See Lindemann-Nelson, forthcoming. Also Leon J. Goldstein's essay, "Thoughts on Jewish identity," esp. p. 81, in Goldberg and Krausz (1993), similarly rejects the coherence of the idea of Jews as simply self-identifying.

28. The metaphysical underpinnings of the idea that social classifications (such as race and gender) are the real products of social actions—that is, that constructivism is compatible with realism—are being developed in detail by Michael Root.

29. One of the best articulations of what it is to be an "impossible being" is, in fact, Marilyn Frye's (1983), in her *tour de force* essay ("To be and be

seen,"): in the logic of patriarchy, it must, she demonstrates, be impossible to see women as lesbians see them. That she starts this essay by quoting Sarah Hoagland on the conceptual impossibility of lesbians further reinforces the point that lesbian separatist suspicion of MTF transsexuals need not rest on an essentialist or biologistic account of who women are. Both Frye (1983) and Hoagland (1988) are clear on the constructedness of female identity and on the inextricability of that construction from the subordinating projects of male domination. Both also insist that the focus of lesbian attention is on other lesbians, not on the borders that might be taken to define either "lesbian" or "woman." See especially Hoagland's (1988, 7) refusal to define "lesbian" in part because of a refusal to engage in what she takes to be the diversionary activity of boundary marking.

30. "Perinatally pinked" has, of course, another meaning, one that in this context demands at least acknowledgment: as a description of the circumcised penis of the Jewish male. For discussion of the ramifications of this way of inscribing Jewishness on the male body—that is, in a way that can be read (cannot but be read?) as feminizing—see D. Boyarin (1997), who quotes Geller (1993) quoting Spinoza to this effect.

31. Many thanks to separatists at the fall 1995 meeting of the Midwest Society for Women in Philosophy—especially Marilyn Frye, Sarah Hoagland, and Anne Leighton—for helping me to understand a separatist point of view on the dispute between MTF transsexuals and separatists, particularly focusing on admission to the Michigan Women's Music Festival. They are not responsible for "perinatally pinked," nor am I certain whether they would agree as to its usefulness. I've been helped in understanding transsexual womyn's arguments against their exclusion from the Michigan festival by reading letters and articles in several issues of *TransSisters*, especially Issue #7 (1995), and of *Transsexual News Telegraph*.

It was also helpful to read in both publications about the controversy over the exclusion from the New Woman's Conference of pre-or nonoperative MTF transsexuals: the argument is made that it is a conference for those who share a very specific experience: that of having "lived socially as a man at some time, . . . currently living socially as a woman, and [having] had genital surgery that resulted in making her genitals appear more female than they originally were" (*TransSisters* 7:11). In that same issue, both a letter writer, Riawa Smith, and the editor, Davina Anne Gabriel, suggest, what was apparently decided on, that the conference should change its name to better reflect just whom it is intended for, rather than using a name ("new woman") that others feel an equal need and right to claim.

As with my suggestion about "perinatally pinked," the idea here is that different people will find different parts of their complex identities and histories to be especially salient and, in particular, to define a space of safety and refuge—of home, in one of the senses of that loaded word; and that such identities and spaces are vitally important. But, as Riawa Smith echoes Bernice Johnson Reagon (1983), such spaces are not to be confused with the space of activist politics, even as they make such politics possible, by providing a space both of refuge and of wild imagining.

32. See Gordon Lafer, "Universalism and particularism in Jewish law: Making sense of political loyalties," in Goldberg and Krausz (1993).

33. Having had these thoughts rather inchoately for a long time, I was excited to find them developed in scholarly detail in Boyarin (1994), in which he discusses in detail the implications of Paul's proclaiming in Galatians that "There is neither Jew nor Greek; there is neither slave nor freeman; there is no male and female. For you are all one in Christ Jesus."

34. See Boyarin and Boyarin (1993) to which, along with conversations with Daniel Boyarin, I am deeply indebted for pulling together these ideas.

35. Thanks to Michael Root for suggesting the use of "naturalized citizen" for thinking about transsexual identity change.

36. See Boyarin and Boyarin (1993) for an argument that the particularism of Jewish identity is morally defensible only if *not* coupled with state power.

37. See Asa Kasher, "Jewish collective identity," in Goldberg and Krausz (1993).

38. See Lafer's essay (n28) in Goldberg and Krausz (1993) for the suggestion that traditionally Jewishness was much "deeper" and more connected to what made one socially intelligible. Also, as Diana Tietjens Meyers has reminded me, it is Judaism, the religion, to which converts convert, leaving that murky identity—"Jewishness"—still murky. It is both unclear and, in some communities and families, a matter of real dispute, whether or not one can "become Jewish," and, if so, just what that means.

39. Thanks to Jacob Hale for pressing me on the need to think about passing as a man from the perspective of an FTM transsexual. What is important, as he pointed out, is grappling seriously with the male privilege that one acquires.

What counts as the avoidance of "honorary" status is not always clear: for example, if I teach my classes and attend meetings on the high holy days, I am in effect setting myself apart from those "other" Jews who won't conform to the "normal," that is, Christian, calendar. But it feels dishonest to stay home, since neither synagogue attendance nor any other way of specifically marking the new year has any place in my life. Is it a matter of solidarity not to treat those days like any others in support of those faculty, staff, and students who—in the face of lack of cooperation or understanding—do observe the holidays?

40. See Cora Diamond, "Sahibs and Jews," in Goldberg and Krausz (1993).

41. For a related discussion of positionality as a way of thinking about identity that escapes essentialism without becoming empty, see Alcoff (1988).

42. For discussions of related phenomena, see Zita (1992) on "male lesbians," Boyarin and Boyarin (1993) on "the jew," and Kaminsky (1993) on exile.

43. The arguments here are related to those concerning how to think about racial identity: there are both scientific and political reasons to argue that race is unreal, but doing so obscures the histories and in many cases the antiracist politics of those whose lived experience of race is very real indeed. See, for example, DuBois (1966), Appiah (1986), and Outlaw (1992).

44. Daniel Boyarin (1994, 224f) is explicit about the parallels between this erasure of the specificity of Jews and "the post-structuralist deconstruction of the sign 'woman'."

45. In a video performance piece entitled "Cornered," Adrian Piper confronts presumptively white viewers with the challenge to acknowledge that, at least by the terms of the "one drop rule," many of them are actually black, and to consider claiming that identity.

46. These are among the clarifications being developed by Michael Root.

47. After completing this essay I encountered a paper of Jonathan Boyarin's (1995) in which he makes a similar argument, by way of a specifically Jewish intervention into a dispute he stages between Charles Taylor and Judith Butler concerning identity. I have also just begun to learn, from Laura Levitt among others, about the emerging conversation among Jewish feminists concerning the nature of Jewish identity: as with other identities, it is helpfully articulated from its own, in this case gendered, margins.

48. Many thanks to the challenging audiences for earlier drafts at the University of Minnesota and at meetings of the Canadian and Midwest Societies for Women in Philosophy, and especially to Lisa Heldke, Diana Tietjens Meyers, and Michael Root for extensive comments on an earlier draft. Unfortunately, those comments were interesting and provocative, and the result is a denser, more complex paper and not, as they intended, a clearer one. The largest portion of the blame for the density and complexity, however, lies with Daniel Boyarin and Jacob Hale, who have between them done a wonderful job of confusing me.

REFERENCES

Alcoff, Linda. 1988. Cultural feminism versus post-structuralism: The identity crisis in feminist theory. *Signs* 13(3):405–36.

Anzaldúa, Gloria. 1987. *Borderlands/la frontera: The new mestiza.* San Francisco: Spinsters/Aunt Lute.

Appiah, Anthony. 1986. The uncompleted argument: DuBois and the illusion of race. In *Race, writing, and difference*, ed. Henry Louis Gates, Jr. Chicago: University of Chicago Press.

Bornstein, Kate. 1994. *Gender outlaw: On men, women and the rest of us*. New York: Routledge.

Boyarin, Daniel. 1994. *A radical Jew: Paul and the politics of identity*. Berkeley: University of California Press.

———. 1997. *Unheroic conduct: The rise of heterosexuality and the invention of the Jewish man*. Berkeley: University of California Press.

Boyarin, Daniel, and Jonathan Boyarin. 1993. Diaspora: Generation and the ground of Jewish identity. *Critical Inquiry* 19(4): 693–725.

Boyarin, Jonathan. 1995. Before the law there stands a woman: *In re Taylor v. Butler* (with court-appointed Yiddish translator). *Cardozo Law Review* 16(3–4): 1303–23.

Butler, Judith. 1990. *Gender trouble: Feminism and the subverson of identity*. New York: Routledge.

Camper, Carol, ed. 1994. Miscegenation blues: Voices of mixed-race women. Toronto: Sister Vision.

DuBois, W. E. B. 1966. The conservation of races. *Negro social and political thought 1850–1920*, ed. Howard Brotz. New York: Basic Books.

Feinberg, Leslie. 1993. *Stone Butch Blues*. Ithaca, N.Y.: Firebrand Books.

Frye, Marilyn. 1983. *The politics of reality*. Trumansburg, N.Y.: Crossing Press.

———. forthcoming. Ethnocentrism/essentialism: The failure of the ontological cure. In *Social justice and the future of feminisms* (working title), ed. Center for Advanced Feminist Studies collective, University of Minnesota.

Gabriel, Davina Anne. 1995. Interview with the transsexual vampire: Sandy Stone's dark gift. *TransSisters: The journal of transsexual feminism* 8:14–27.

Gates, Henry Louis, Jr.. 1988. *The signifying monkey: A theory of African-American literary criticism*. New York: Oxford University Press.

Geller, Jay. 1993. A paleontological view of Freud's study of religion: Unearthing the Leitfossil circumcision. *Modern Judaism* 13:49–70.

Gilman, Sander. 1991. *The Jew's body*. New York: Routledge.

Goldberg, David Theo, and Michael Krausz, eds. 1993. *Jewish identity*. Philadelphia: Temple University Press.

Hale, Jacob. 1996. Are lesbians women? Worries about Monique Wittig. *Hypatia* 11(2): 94–121.

Halperin, David. 1995. The queer politics of Michel Foucault. In *Saint Foucault: Two essays in gay hagiography*. New York: Oxford University Press.

Haraway, Donna. 1991. Situated knowledges: The science question in feminism and the privilege of partial perspective. In *Simians, cyborgs, and women: The reinvention of nature*. New York: Routledge.

Harding, Sandra. 1991. *Whose science? Whose knowledge? Thinking from women's lives*. Ithaca, N.Y.: Cornell University Press.

Hoagland, Sarah Lucia. 1988. *Lesbian ethics: Toward new value*. Palo Alto, Calif.: Institute of Lesbian Studies.

――――. forthcoming. Moving toward uncertainty. In *Re-reading the canon: Feminist interpretations of Wittgenstein*, ed. Naomi Scheman. University Park: University of Pennsylvania Press.

Kaminsky, Amy Katz. 1993. Issues for an international literary criticism. *Signs* 19(1): 213–27.

Kant, Immanuel. 1960. *Observations on the Beautiful and Sublime*, trans. John T. Goldthwait. Berkeley: University of California Press.

――――. 1969. *Foundations of the Metaphysics of Morals*, trans. Lewis White Beck, ed. Robert Paul Wolff. Indianapolis: Bobbs Merrill.

Kessler, Suzanne J. 1990. The medical construction of gender: Case management of intersexed infants. *Signs* 16(1): 3–26.

Kessler, Suzanne J., and Wendy McKenna. 1978. *Gender: An ethnomethodological approach*. Chicago: University of Chicago Press.

Klepfisz, Irena. 1990. *Dreams of an insomniac: Jewish Feminist Essays, Speeches and Diatribes*. Portland, Oreg.: The Eighth Mountain Press.

Lindemann-Nelson, Hilde. forthcoming. Wittgenstein meets "woman" in the language game of theorizing feminism. In *Re-reading the canon: Feminist interpretations of Wittgenstein*, ed. Naomi Scheman. University Park: University of Pennsylvania Press.

Lugones, María. 1987. Playfulness, "world-travel," and loving perception. *Hypatia* 2(2): 3–19.

――――. 1990. Structure/antistructure and agency under oppression. *Journal of Philosophy* 87(10): 500–507.

――――. 1994. Purity, impurity, and separation. *Signs* 19(2):458–79.

MacKinnon, Catharine A. Sexuality, pornography, and method: Pleasure under patriarchy. 1990. In *Feminism and Political Theory*, ed. Cass R. Sunstein. Chicago: University of Chicago Press.

Miller, Alice. 1984. *For your own good: Hidden cruelty in child-rearing and the roots of violence*, trans. Hildegarde Hannum and Hunter Hannum. New York: Farrar, Straus, and Giroux.

Outlaw, Lucius. 1992. Against the grain of modernity: The politics of difference and the conservation of "race." *Man and world* 25(4): 443–68.

Peterson, Susan Rae. 1977. Coercion and rape: The state as a male protection racket. In *Feminism and philosophy*, eds. Mary Vetterling-Braggin, Frederick A. Elliston, and Jane English. Totowa, N.J.: Littlefield, Adams.

Potter, Nancy. 1994. "Trustworthiness: An Aristotelian analysis of a virtue." PhD dissertation, University of Minnesota.

Prell, Riv-Ellen. 1992. Why Jewish princesses don't sweat: Desire and consumption in postwar American Jewish culture. In *People of the body: Jews and Judaism from an embodied perspective*, ed. Howard Eilberg-Schwartz. Albany: SUNY Press.

Reagon, Bernice Johnson. 1983. Coalition politics: Turning the century. In *Home girls: A Black feminist anthology*, ed. Barbara Smith. New York: Kitchen Table Women of Color Press.

Rich, Adrienne. 1978. *The dream of a common language: Poems 1974–1977*. New York: W. W. Norton.

———. 1979. "It is the lesbian in us . . ." In *On lies, secrets, and silence: Selected prose 1966–1978*. New York: W. W. Norton.

———. 1986. Compulsory heterosexuality and lesbian existence. In *Blood, bread, and poetry: Selected Prose 1979–1985*. New York: W. W. Norton.

Scheman, Naomi. 1993. Though this be method, yet, there is madness in it: Paranoia and liberal epistemology. In *Engenderings: Constructions of knowledge, authority, and privilege*. New York: Routledge.

Sedgwick, Eve Kosofsky. 1990. *Epistemology of the closet*. Berkeley: University of California Press.

Shapiro, Judith. 1991. Transsexualism: Reflections on the persistence of gender and the mutability of sex. In *Body guards: The cultural politics of gender ambiguity*, eds. Julia Epstein and Kristina Straub. New York: Routledge.

Sherover-Marcuse, Erica. 1986. *Emancipation and consciousness: Dogmatic and dialectical perspectives in the early Marx*. Oxford: Basil Blackwell.

Spelman, Elizabeth V. 1988. *Inessential woman: Problems of exclusion in feminist thought*. Boston: Beacon Press.

Stone, Sandy. 1991. The *Empire* strikes back: A posttranssexual manifesto. In *Body guards: The cultural politics of gender ambiguity*, eds. Julia Epstein and Kristina Straub. New York: Routledge.

Stryker, Susan. 1994. My words to Victor Frankenstein above the village of Chamonix: Performing transgender rage. *GLQ: A journal of lesbian and gay studies* 1(3): 237–54.

Warner, Michael. 1993. *Fear of a queer planet: Queer politics and social theory*. Minneapolis: University of Minnesota Press.

Zack, Naomi, ed. 1995. *American Mixed Race: The Culture of Microdiversity*. Lanham, Maryland: Rowman and Littlefield.

Zita, Jacquelyn. 1981. Lesbian continuum and historical amnesia. *Signs* 7(1): 172–81.

———. 1992. The male lesbian and the post-modern body. *Hypatia* 7(4): 106–27.

Part II

Theorizing Gender Nonconformity

Five

Homosexual Boyhood
Notes on Girlyboys

Ken Corbett

The women in my family have a way with needles, and my closet is full of the evidence. Pillowcases bordered with yellow roses patiently crocheted, unfurled, and arranged by my great-aunt, Idie. A quilt pieced by my grandmother, Linnie, using cotton fabric I imagine to have come from summer dresses and kitchen curtains. Embroidered tea towels—one a coolie, his black braid swinging freely, the other a Dutch girl, her blond pageboy tight and precise. I don't imagine my mother, Laura, intended them as a couple, but I like to think of them deep in my closet in the grip of untold colonial transgressions. To bear witness, I add an entranced voyeuristic chorus of flannel gingerbread men, snow fairies, and bearded eggshell Santas, Christmas ornaments held together by the most miniscule of my Aunt Margaret's stitches.

In packing for a recent move, I came across some evidence of my own participation in this matrilineal craft. At the bottom of an underwear drawer I found a handkerchief. In the lower right-hand corner of the white child-size square, at a jaunty angle in navy blue, I had embroidered "Kenny." I immediately looked upon the handkerchief as symbolic: A femme ghost repressed by a brace of butch boxers. A defiant bottom spread out and proud, tempting those "Calvinists." I laughed at my preciosity as I recalled the role of the hanky in the elaborate gay coding schemes of the 1970s. I laughed again when I remembered that Tom in *Tea and Sympathy* earned the moniker "sister boy" when caught in the act of sewing with a group of faculty wives. As my thoughts circled around this artifact, I began to recall making the handkerchief, and with those thoughts, I began to contemplate my boyhood, or more precisely, my girlyboyhood as it threaded its way through my homosexual boyhood.

I embroidered the handkerchief sitting between Idie and Linnie on the porch of my grandparents' farmhouse. They cross- and chain-stitched, while my seven-year-old fingers fumbled with the most basic running stitch. Along with the handkerchief, I seem to remember something about embroidering a tea cosy, though no one in my family drank tea. But then again none of the other boys took up needles. What was it that I was looking for as I sat sewing with my grand-mother? Or at a later date as I embraced candle making with my mother? (The snowball variety made with whipped paraffin were our personal favorites.) After all, domestic craft was not supposed to be the realm of boys.

Sitting amid the rubble of packing, not unlike the rubble of a dream, my thoughts turned to where I more often sit as a psychologist listening to patients tell me about their homosexual boyhoods. While contemplating various aspects of their experience, I began to consider what the psychological canon has to say about homosexual boyhood. It was then that I realized there is no "homosexual boyhood."

Homosexual boyhood as a conceptual category does not exist. The existence of homosexual boys has until now either been silenced or stigmatized. Bullies identify sissies. Psychiatrists identify sissy-boy syndromes. There has been virtually no effort to speak of the boyhood experience of homosexuals other than to characterize their youth as a disordered and/or nonconforming realm from which it is hoped they will break free. The fate of these boys is contemplated with the kind of hushed charity that obscures antipathy.

My wish is to break through the hush, reject the charity, and begin to conceive of homosexual boyhood. I wish to be generous and to appreciate rather than judge the "peculiar ideality" of girlyboys (to borrow a phrase from William James). To that end I hope to use Nick, a ten-year-old participant in Green's longitudinal study of sissies, as my fanciful guide. When asked if he knew why he had been brought to a doctor, Nick proclaimed he had "a big, fat, girly problem" (1987: 277). His sass is a welcome moment of turbulence within the smooth "discursive orthopedics" (Foucault 1978: 29) that has accumulated around and through psychologists' scrutiny of boyhood cross-gender identification. This sissy-boy discourse has, in turn, produced a theory of homosexuality wherein adult homosexuality is infused by a path-ologized gendered past (Green 1987; Friedman 1988).

I am using "sissy-boy discourse" to refer both to the literature on sissies and the literature on Gender Identity Disorder (GID), including the work of Coates (1992, 1994), Coates, Friedman, and Wolfe (1991), Stoller (1968, 1985), Zucker (1990), Zucker and Green (1989), and Zucker and Bradley (1995). I have chosen to bring together the litera-ture on sissies with that on GID because about two-thirds of the boys who are diagnosed with GID develop into adult homosexuals (Green 1987; Money and Russo 1979; Zuger 1988). Clearly, there is not a complete concordance between GID and adult homosexuality, and one cannot predict any given child's adult sexual orientation based on that child's gender behavior; however, as I argue, I find the diagnostic category of GID problematic, as homosexual boyhoods are at times mistaken for GID. I have also taken this step because I believe that in this culture anxiety and resistance to the possibility of a protogay subjectivity discourages one from even imagining (much less attempt-ing to document) such subjectivities.

Guided by Nick, and by the spirit of parodically reclaiming oppres-sive signifiers, I would like to add "girlyboy" to the queer nomencla-ture. It is nearly impossible to locate a signifier for male homosexual-ity that does not either scapegoat women, flowers, or fruit. Consider the following list: swish, nelly, fruit, fruitcake, pussy, pansy, fluff, sissy, Nancy, Molly, Mary, and Mary Ann. Perhaps it would make more sense to rebelliously appropriate "sissy," and repeatedly and defiantly invoke its linkage with pathology, indictment, and scorn. But "sissy" carries the implication of weakness, unbecoming delicacy, and enervation, devoid of the possibilities born of resistance, agency, and action. Moreover, "girlyboy" captures the category problem that is essential to the boys I am attempting to describe. As a patient of mine commented, "I never believed I was a girl, but I had trouble believing I was a boy. You only have two options, after all. So how do you decide?"

A girlyboy's gender experience does not just reverse the traditional feminine/masculine binary, it goes further to destabilize these familiar gender signs (Garber 1992). The oxymoronic coupling of girl and boy in "girlyboy" captures the possibility that there may be forms of gender within homosexuality that contradict and move beyond the conventional categories of masculinity and femininity. The manner in which gender's necessity may give way within homosexuality prompted Freud, as early as 1920, to characterize the relation between a homosexual's gender attitude and mode of sexual satisfaction as the "mystery of homosexuality" (1920: 170). For homosexuals, according to Freud, maleness did not necessarily correspond to the activity analysts associated with masculinity, and femaleness did not necessarily correspond to the passivity that was linked with femininity.

But rather than draw on the mystery of homosexuality to open up the categories of gender, Freud and successive analysts have repeatedly restricted the possibilities of gender to the conventional heterosexual masculine/feminine binary. Homosexuals have thereby been repeatedly (dis)located within a theory of gender that rests on essential distinctions between the feminine and the masculine. Through this categorizing, analysts uphold the inevitability of a cultural order established through such reasoning. But as the homosexual's experience exemplifies, such logic results in a sanctioned cultural order that does not sufficiently problematize the experience of gender. This so-called logic has effectively silenced any consideration of homosexual boyhood outside the realm of pathology. Nick's cross-gendered identifications and gender variance become a "big, fat, girly problem," as opposed to a manifestation of gender's vicissitudes.

I have argued elsewhere that, due to countertransference difficulties with male homosexuality, analysts have often neither comprehended nor tolerated the gay man's experience of gender (Corbett 1993a). A similar lack of recognition and comprehension can be noted in the sissy-boy discourse. In the presumed service of mental health, analysts have been so eager to bring girlyboys back into the masculine fold that they have often lost sight of them. Furthermore, they have also lost sight of the actuality of gender variance and cross-gendered identifications within the domain of mental health. As my starting point, I argue that this analytic blind spot is fostered by a failure to adequately appreciate the complex and mysterious relationship between gender and psychic structure. I argue that gender conformity and psychic structure have been blurred into what I call "gender health."[1]

This blurring of psychic structure and gender is further promoted by an undertheorized notion of masculinity. Within the sissy-boy discourse, gender is as gender was; virtually no effort has been made to critically theorize gender. As such, this discourse bears the mark of a kind of generation gap—an old auntie tuning out the queer rap of postmodernism, feminism, and gay studies. To advance my argument I employ feminist, queer, and postmodern critiques of gender. But I also question whether such contemporary thinking does not at times overlook life beyond the pleasure principle and in so doing underestimate the human potential for both psychic pain and psychic growth.

In recognition of the preliminary nature of my efforts to conceive of homosexual boyhood, I have organized the latter half of this paper as notes on girlyboys. The note form—unfettered by an essay's demand for sequence and reason—seems more in keeping with the subjectivity I am attempting to capture. It is witless to be completely solemn about girlyboys, for solemnity runs counter to the extravagance and liberty that imbue girlyboy play. The note form also encourages (through the creation of an experimental and inventive space) a queer voice, a queer inflection. Through this queer inflection, I employ parody and irony as a form of cultural resistance and a means toward social critique. There is a long queer tradition, perhaps best embodied by Wilde's conscious ideological aestheticism (Sontag 1964), of queering the narrative through irony, parody, and theatricalization. There is, in short, a long tradition of being extravagant and silly.[2]

Gender Health

I want to make it clear at the outset that I am not proposing a causal developmental sequence from cross-gendered experience to adult homosexuality (Zuger 1988). Moreover, there are multiple homosexual boyhoods and I am not speaking about all homosexual boys. I am attempting here to describe a pattern and a common developmental narrative. In a sense, I am working a contradiction, because while I wish to describe a protoexperience, I do not wish to hold forth a prototype. I am not suggesting that these cross-gendered patterns are necessarily predictive or determining of adult homosexuality. Further, I am not claiming to put forth a developmental line, nor do I wish to set out a coherent narrative that forecloses the complex interimplication of gender, sexuality, and psychic structure. My assertion is more modest: I wish simply to propose that early cross-gendered experience is interimplicated with later developing homosexuality in complex ways that remain unaccounted for within current developmental theories.

I have chosen within this essay to focus on girlyboys—a frequent set of experiences and fantasies shared by many homosexual boys, but not exclusively and not only by them. Many, if not most, gay adults recall the significant role of cross-gendered identifications during their childhoods (Bell, Weinberg, and Hammersmith 1981). Many gay men have femme ghosts in their closets. Many do not. And for those who do, the vigor of the ghost varies between these men and within any given man. This pattern of experiences and fantasies is open (as are all patterns) to considerable inter-and intrasubjective variance. Gender appears to play a more important role in some lives than in others. As Sedgwick has put it, "Some people are just plain more gender-y than others" (1995: 16). Along similar lines, some theories are more gender-y than others. I want to emphasize that my effort to examine cross-gendered identification is one way to think about homosexuality, not the only way, and not necessarily the exemplary paradigm for thinking about homosexuality.

Queer people can feel unnamed within a gender matrix that is founded on certain ideals of heterosexual masculinity and femininity. Recognizing the inherent dilemma in trying to classify himself, a gay male patient commented, "There was this sense of otherness. You know, not being the norm—not the normal boy. But I don't know, I feel like civilization has robbed me of the words to describe this." Such sentiment illustrates that neither a masculine nor a feminine categorization sufficiently captures the experience of gender otherness these men and boys describe.

The category problem reasserts itself with regard to the relationship between gender and sexuality. A hallmark of gay politics has been the effort to resist and deconstruct the long tradition of looking upon gender and sexuality as continuous categories. Gay activists and theorists alike have labored to reject developmental theories of sexuality, especially those that position gender as the causal determinant of sexuality.

The political efficacy of such resistance notwithstanding, I have long wondered about the psychological efficacy of this tactic. I fear that in our quest to freely question and deconstruct sexuality we have thrown the queer baby out with the utopian bath water. Gay theorists have long ignored the link between boyhood femininity and adult homosexuality, thereby dislodging childhood gender experience from adult sexual identity, closeting the feminine boy, and creating a "haunting abject" (Sedgwick 1993: 157) of our gendered past.

I do not believe that queer hope and resistance need to be radically divorced from what may be developmental aspects of gender and sexuality. It is no longer enough to deconstruct developmental paradigms and prescriptive norms. As Butler (1993) has suggested, we must now begin to construct models that theorize the complex inter-implication, as opposed to causal implication, that unites gender and sexuality. Indeed, there may be aspects of homosexual development that call for a theorization that moves beyond the developmental paradigms analysts now employ.

We need to recognize the multilinearity and interimplication of psychological process that is born of the intertwining of gender and sexuality (Butler 1993; Chodorow 1995; Dimen 1995; Goldner 1991; Harris 1991). As Chodorow suggests, we need to recognize the ways in which "the 'solution' of gender problems involves the solution of general problems of personal subjectivity and capacities for intersubjectivity" (1995: 297). Likewise, Goldner has argued that "personhood, gender identity, and relationship structures develop together, coevolving and codetermining each other" (1991: 261–62). Hence the extreme difficulty in making generalized statements about gender, because genders are as infinite as subjectivities. Yet our psychological needs for ego coherence and stability push toward such generalizing and sense making, pushing in consort with (while simultaneously constructing) cultural injunctions.

I strive to conceive of my patients as intricate beings, beset by contradiction and paradox. I like to believe that we are capable of complex fates that are too often underestimated by the developmental parameters set forth by traditional ego psychology. However, I also strive to understand my patients' needs for stable self-representations and bounded subjective coherence—including their quest for stable gender and sexual identities. This need for stability does not preclude underlying contradictions. Likewise, the underlying contradictions do not preclude the need for stability. Recognizing the ego's stabilizing function should not be confused with a reification of convention; indeed, convention can be defensively employed to impersonate stability.

The Problem of Effeminacy

While I argue that all boyhood femininity is not the same, I do not wish to reify the manner in which male femininity has been looked at from the perspective of a continuum—from more to less femme—with the more femme end of the continuum linked with greater ego deficits and character pathology. This notion of a continuum is made explicit by Friedman's assertion that the number of "homosexual men who are entirely masculine (by usual cultural standards) increases as the level of global character pathology decreases" (1988: 93). In other words, according to Friedman, the more a man is like a woman (the more a boy is like a girl) the more pathological he is likely to be.[3]

Another expression of this femme continuum is the separation of gender identity disorder from what is termed "gender nonconformity." Boys who are identified as having a gender identity disorder are depicted as extremely feminine and severely distressed. Boys who are identified as nonconforming are seen as less problematic both with regard to their femininity and their mental health. One could look at the manifest behavior of GID boys as opposed to the manifest behavior of gender nonconformers as signaling some manner of continuum. I would argue that we are looking not at a continuum of femininity, but rather a continuum of ego-integration and psychic structure. So-called nonconforming boys can be just as feminine as GID boys, but the femininity is contained within a more stable psychic structure. The femininity of GID boys is looked upon as extreme because of the affect that surrounds their gender performances—at times nearly hysterical performances that simultaneously mask and unveil chaotic states of regression and psychic pain.

Consider the play behavior of two four-year-old boys I have seen in consultation within the past year. Both boys were brought for consultation following concern about their manifest gender behavior. Jerry spent much of the hour dressing Barbie and setting up various domestic scenarios, such as cooking breakfast. The domestic scenarios, however, seemed secondary to Barbie's many costume changes, and her apparent wish for admiration. These costume changes were undertaken with an eye toward detail, and considerable care was exercised to insure that Barbie looked "just right." At first, I was not given a role within the play, but Jerry did frequently look toward me, through Barbie, for admiration. Barbie often inquired as to whether I liked what she was wearing, or whether I liked what she had done with her hair. As I indicated my willingness to play as Jerry wished, I was given the role of Barbie's husband and the domestic scenarios became more central. These prosaic scenarios were played out in a rather inert manner that struck me as constricted and lacking in the pleasure of play. My impression that such constriction may have been the result of being observed was confirmed by Jerry's parents and preschool teachers, who indicated that in more familiar contexts Jerry was often to be found pleasurably absorbed in domestic play.

The second boy, Donald, spent the entire hour enacting a scene with Barbie that centered around being menaced. Barbie was elaborately dressed, then stripped, tied to a tree, and repeatedly threatened with the possibility of violence. At first a male doll approached, struck Barbie and, as she struggled, pushed himself up against her. Further into the play, the same menacing behaviors were enacted by a dog. Chaos followed these threats. Barbie would thrash about, scream, break free, and run to me. I was charged with offering her protection and safety. Eventually, though, she would be wrenched from her safe haven and the drama would be reenacted.

I would suggest that what distinguishes these two play scenarios is not the femininity but the expression of psychic pain. Moreover, these interactions are distinguished by the nature and quality of the boys' defenses and object relations. Jerry's constriction, which suggested the pain of shame, contrasted with Donald's ritualized and nearly hysterical expression of traumatic pain. Donald's play of menace was rigidly and compulsively repeated. Each repetition resulted in such chaotic escalation that I found it necessary to redirect the play so that Donald would not injure himself. Behavior that is compulsive and rigid is often employed to effect a shutdown of affective life. But Donald's efforts along these lines failed him as fear and anxiety overwhelmed his defensive organization, leaving him dependent on adult assistance and care. Jerry cautiously looked toward the adult for assurance, but on the level of self-esteem, not ego-integration. The obsessive and narcissistic features that characterized Jerry's play did not bespeak the sense of urgency and need that characterized Donald's play. Aside from the variance in Jerry's gender play and the narcissistic conflict such variance invokes (Can I have this fantasy? Can I wish as a boy to play as a girl looking toward a boy for admiration? Can I wish to be beautiful?), he did not present any clinical symptoms that called into question his emotional development. Aside from his gender variance, neither his parents nor his teachers had other concerns. Likewise, his history was clinically unremarkable. Donald's early history, on the other hand, was replete with indications of developmental strain and early trauma, including the loss of his mother and brother, that could account for the disruption in his psychic growth. In turn, Donald's daily life, both at home and at school, was beset by disorganization and distress.

The contemplation of psychic growth takes us into the realm of health. In keeping with postmodern trends in contemporary psychoanalytic thought, mental health is no longer equated with equilibrium and self-possession but rather with some faculty to contain fragmentation. We introduce more and more violent and unresolvable subject matter, making only fragments possible (Flax 1990). Health raises the specter of hierarchies, quantities, and virtue. "Health" has too often been bestowed by authorized doctors upon unauthorized patients, and developmental hierarchies that are advanced in the name of health have too often been misused in the name of conformity. The conflation of conformity with health has perhaps been nowhere more evident than in developmental theories of gender.

Pointing toward the conflation of health and conformity has been a central tactic of feminist and queer theorists as they have set about retheorizing gender. Such contemporary reconsiderations have led to the question, Does gender have a place at all in a postmodern discussion of health? It is that question that underscores my dilemma in thinking about children who have been identified as suffering from a Gender Identity Disorder. I find myself thinking, Isn't a Gender Identity Disorder the apotheosis of postmodernism? Do these children pose an irresolvable conflict that destabilizes the binary categories of male and female, and in so doing promotes a crisis of category itself (Garber 1992)? What could be more postmodern?

We are left to ask, Are these children constructed as disordered because we have no other category for them? And further, Does such categorization result in additional psychic pain? I think we have to answer, Yes and yes. Gender Identity Disorder is the constructed category within which these boys are placed. I feel all such classificatory practices should be rigorously questioned and challenged for the manner in which they are constructed. I could call a number of aspects of this category into question. I have chosen here to focus on one—

throughout this essay I have and will continue to focus on the problem of effeminacy. Boys and men who exhibit cross-gender behaviors are always at odds with the culture, and their oddity is met with contempt and hostility. Such antipathy often takes the form of comparing such boys to girls, as though placing a boy in the category "girl" is an act of devaluation. As Garber has pointed out, "in expressing condemnation of various types of men, it is always women who are scapegoated" (1992: 138).

Indeed, within the sissy-boy discourse, femininity becomes a symptom. Friedman actually employs the diagnostic phrase "femalelike symptoms," (1988: 199) as if to suggest that one could fall ill with the disease of femininity. And for those boys who escape this feminine illness but do not traverse the gender spectrum all the way to the safety of masculinity, there awaits the "syndrome" of "juvenile unmasculinity" (Friedman 1988: 199), and/or a "subclinical manifestation" of Gender Identity Disorder (Zucker and Bradley 1995: 25). This manner of medicalized discursive intervention restrains gender as an either/or binary. Through medical sleight of hand, variance becomes "subclinical." Gender is fixed as a system of conformity; variance is erased.

The point here is that the diagnosis of Gender Identity Disorder takes place within a contested realm of human experience, namely, femininity. One could, therefore, reasonably ask, Can these boys be seen outside of the belief that femininity is intrinsically diseased? The invidious effects of such thinking with regard to the ways in which women and girls have been thought of and treated has by now been well documented by others. Similarly, the effects of what I have referred to elsewhere as the trauma equation of male homosexuality (male homosexuality=femininity=trauma) (Corbett 1993a) are increasingly being brought to light through the action of gay liberation politics and the burgeoning field of queer studies. For specific and insightful analyses of these issues relative to boyhood femininity, I direct you to Mass (1990) and Sedgwick (1993). I hope to add my voice to this as yet small chorus as I move forward in this essay.

But to stop here, and not to tangle with the psychic features of gender and its complex relationship with health and development, would be as problematic as conflating health with conformity. Anti-developmental discourse too often romanticizes pain, underestimates the profound impact of early parent-child relations, and undervalues the role of ego-integration in human development. Confining the debate about boyhood femininity to categories and the social construction of gender misses several features of the genderness of boys diagnosed as Gender Identity Disordered. Most importantly, such a vantage point misses the necessity, melancholy, abjection, and anxiety that surrounds these boys' gender performances. The affect that surrounds the femininity illustrates how gender is not only a constructed category, but also a psychic performance.

Pain can collect around gender. But how do we speak about that pain when the gender in question is in and of itself contested—when the gender itself is burdened with the pain of shame? How do we speak about pain and gender, when the pain is more acute and distressing than shame—when the pain speaks through symptoms indicative of a breakdown in psychic structure (splitting, dissociations, depersonalization, regression, and omnipotent dependencies)? And how do we speak about pain and gender when, if we have learned anything through the queer reappraisals of the psychoanalytic theory of homosexuality, it is that psychologists have a way of looking at variation and calling it illness. This dilemma, which is so well illustrated by the very notion of a Gender Identity Disorder, points to our need to find a way to approach the interimplication of the psyche, the soma, and the social.

In an effort to elucidate such interimplication, the three theorists who present the most comprehensive theories of Gender Identity Disorder, Coates (1992, 1994), Coates, Friedman, and Wolfe (1991), and Zucker and Bradley (1995) have recently introduced updated composite analyses of the multiple factors that contribute to gender's development. These theorists position themselves within the epistemological traditions of developmental psychiatry and psychology. They assemble the phenomenology of GID by employing the criteria set forth by psychiatric differential diagnosis, empirical evidence from biology and cognitive science, and "knowledge about normative psychosexual development" (Zucker and Bradley 1995: 1). Coates and Zucker describe similar phenomenological characteristics, and similar clinical models. Zucker and Bradley maintain that GID is a defensive solution that "develops from a state of inner insecurity that arises out of the interaction between a boy's temperamental vulnerability to high arousal and an insecure mother-child relationship" (1995: 262). Coates

(1992, 1994); Coates, Friedman, and Wolfe (1991) takes a similar position, proposing that for GID boys, cross-gendered fantasies and behaviors psychically perform as compromise formations to manage separation anxiety and aggression. Both Coates and Zucker have provided us with intricate analyses of how gender can be knit into psychic pain. They also succeed in drawing our attention to the way in which gender is knit into psychic growth.

But there is an aspect of gender's development that is conspicuously undertheorized within both Coates's and Zucker's work—namely, the social. Zucker and Bradley telescope the social into "social reinforcement," concentrating on "parental gender socialization," and a parent's ability to encourage "psychosocially appropriate gender identification" (1995: 223–24). The social construction of appropriate gender is dismissed; social normativity is uncritically heeded as the knowing voice of natural authority. In contrast, Coates has recently begun to incorporate ideas about the social construction of gender into her theorizing, and has endeavored to define gender as "a social-psychological construct that is shaped by societal norms and personal experience" (1994:3). Yet, along with Zucker, Coates does not make an effort to *specifically* address boyhood femininity as shaped or constructed by societal norms. These theorists do not adequately consider the fact that effeminacy is a contested realm of human experience. And their failure to directly address the social construction of effeminacy is both clinically and theoretically insufficient.

The clinical insufficiency that issues from not taking up the problem of effeminacy is that it leaves one inadequately prepared to address countertransference, and to recognize whether counterresistance or counteranxiety is being repeated in the treatment. For example, there is a nagging technical dilemma that haunts Coates's therapeutic technique. Although she maintains that "cross-gender behaviors *per se* are not the focus of treatment," they nevertheless "present a number of issues that constitute a complex challenge to the therapist" (1994: 17). One such challenge is the management of cross-gender behaviors. In general, Coates advocates neither passively accepting nor encouraging such behaviors, while at the same time not suppressing them. It appears that such a stance often results in a kind of ameliorating or modifying substitution for cross-gender behaviors. For example, Coates (1994) suggests to a father that his son may want fancy boy's clothes instead of a tutu. Several rationales are presented for such management, but their purpose is to foster better adaptive skills and thereby minimize scapegoating at the hands of peers.

Coates's redirection of cross-gender behavior may in many respects be clinically well reasoned. For instance, I think it is likely that feminine boys who present with a more intact psychic structure and better ego-integration are better able to read social cues, and thereby are at least partially better able to protect themselves. But to fail to ask at what cost such adaptation takes place misses a vital aspect of these boys' reality, and how that reality may contribute to their experience of psychic pain.

I am asking that we recognize the contingency of such instrumental reasoning and adaptation as it animates the pain of repression. These requests for adaptation amount to asking that these boys resolve an internal dilemma by subordinating their subjectivity (or an aspect of their subjectivity) to the desire to avoid cruelty and pain. Moreover, following on Rorty's (1989) examination of liberalism and solidarity, I am asking that we set such requests for adaptation against the possibility of providing a holding environment for these boys, and in so doing dedicate ourselves to creating a more varied culture infused by as yet unattained imaginative realms of tolerance.

I am also asking that we examine these requests for adaptation in relation to the social construction of effeminacy. The omission of the problem of the social construction of effeminacy within the GID and sissy-boy discourse has the effect of suggesting that all male femininity is symptomatic or pathological. For example, in what is by now a rather comprehensive body of work, neither Coates nor Zucker have presented examples of nonproblematic boyhood femininity, either in reference to a child in treatment or to a feminine boy who does not fit the criteria for GID. As a result, we are not given clinical or developmental data about a broad range of feminine boys, and this narrow focus helps sustain the view that all boyhood femininity is pathological.

We need to begin examining boyhood femininity across a spectrum of boyhood health. All manifest feminine behaviors do not flow from the same degree of psychic structure or level of ego-integration. All manifest feminine behaviors do not flow from the same latent fantasy. All manifest feminine identifications do not flow from the same internal world. Further, manifest feminine behaviors vary relative to the affect that they express; not all of them are an expression of pain. All boyhood femininity is not a compromise formation. By not examining boyhood femininity across a broader range of mental health, gender is sustained as a system of conformity as opposed to a system of variation. This emphasis on conformity sustains the shaming attribution of a nonconforming, damaged, or abjected gender to those boys who step over the normative line. It is with an eye toward those boys that I now turn.

Notes on Girlyboys

Girlyboys Defined

Feminine identifications for homosexual boys are not so much an expression of a wish to be a girl (although often that is the manifest behavior and, at times, the latent wish) but rather an avenue to passive experience and wish fulfillment.[4] Passive longings and feminine identifications reside alongside a masculine identification, often creating what one patient referred to as "mixed gender feelings" during boyhood. For example, a gay male patient stated, "I know that my father wanted me to be a man, and I knew that I was not being a man like him. I was not being a woman, but I was not being a man within his definition of it." He rather aptly expresses the paradox of the girlyboy's experience of gender: gender is not fixed, but mixed. Girlyboys do not feel themselves to be girls exactly, although they are aware of identifying with their mothers more than do most boys. They have girlfriends and enjoy participating in games and pastimes with girls more than do most boys. They do not feel themselves to be boys, exactly, at least as it is defined by their fathers and their male peers. They do not wish to grow up to be women nor to deny their male bodies. Many do, however, experience concern about the adequacy of their male bodies, worrying that perhaps they are too small, too weak, or that some aspect of their bodies is too much like that of a girl. While such concern is often experienced on the level of the body, many of these boys have an inchoate understanding that their identity is a matter of mind. For example, one patient said, "I just couldn't seem to get my mind to work like other boys, and then get my body to follow."

Girlyboys Do Not Fight

1. Simon's family moved in the middle of his sixth grade year. He recalled how his "junior-high angst" was magnified by both the loss of old friends and the familiarity of his old school. He took note of how the turmoil of the move paralleled a growing sense of turmoil regarding his sexual identity. During the first week at the new school, a classmate invited Simon to hang out after school. They spent a couple of hours in a neighborhood park, sharing a cigarette and talking. Simon recalled feeling some relief about his capacity to relate to this new boy, in that his prior relations with boys had often been strained. He indicated that he had never felt entirely comfortable in the company of other boys. In retrospect, Simon wondered if he did not find this boy attractive, but indicated that if he did, he "was busy repressing it." A few days after their afternoon in the park, the seemingly friendly boy attempted to provoke a fight with Simon in front of a group of other boys. Simon recalled feeling very anxious, frightened, and "utterly confused." He feared that he would begin to cry. As he backed away from the crowd, the inviting-boy taunted Simon, calling him a "pussy."

2. Arnie recalls that in sixth grade he had his first male teacher. This teacher seemed to take a special interest in Arnie, who, in turn, enjoyed the attention. During a parent conference, the teacher apparently told Arnie's parents that he felt Arnie needed to develop greater "masculine self-esteem," and advised them to encourage Arnie to join the school's wrestling team. Arnie recollected feeling "revealed" and "somehow betrayed" by his teacher, as well as "pushed" by his parents. He reluctantly joined the team and, to his surprise, found that he could "pass." But he began to grow increasingly uncomfortable with wrestling, not only due to the pressure of having to sustain a false adaptation to please his parents and teacher, but also because he began to be aware of sexual feelings that were stimulated by the physical contact with other boys. Fearful that he would not be able to "control [his] penis," he fashioned a hard plastic liner for his jock-support, hoping that the device would suppress his desire. His anxiety did not abate, and so he added another layer of plastic, and took to wearing two pairs of underpants over the device. Arnie eventually left the wrestling team and joined another after-school activity. But he

recalled how his teacher "made an example of [him] in front of the whole class" by labeling his withdrawal as a "failure of will."

3. Pointing out the conflicts that girlyboys have with aggression and rough-and-tumble play is a hallmark of the sissy-boy discourse. In fact, Friedman (1988) seizes on this aspect of girlyboy behavior as the queer common denominator. According to Friedman, the problem with girlyboys is that they do not fight. They do not occupy the privileged masculine domain of battle. They do not sport the vim of victory. They do not put up their dukes.

Traditionally, we have been told that such fear represents a retreat from oedipal rivalry and competition. Indeed, I believe that girlyboys may face a particular and complex oedipal conflict. However, modern retheorization of homosexuality would suggest possibilities beyond simple oedipal retreat. For example, Isay (1989) has retheorized male homosexual development through his consideration of a homosexual boy's oedipal desire for his father. And Silverman (1992) has pointed to the various ways in which male homosexual desire may be tethered to a boy's identification with his mother. Such oedipal configurations may, in part, account for a girlyboy's conflict with aggression. For example, it seems likely that a girlyboy's aggressive feelings may conflict with his wishes to be cared for by men.

Friedman unwittingly reflects this possibility in his description of Sam, whose "first memories were of feeling insecure and vulnerable." He recalled that at age five, he had been envious of girls because "they were taken care of by men when they grew up" (1988: 28). Instead of taking this opportunity to reflect on Sam's desire, Friedman contrasts Sam's vulnerability with his heterosexual twin brother's security and boyhood rowdiness. Friedman points out that while "unassertive" "mama's boy" Sam was "frightened of rough-and-tumble activities," his twin "never felt masculine or feminine," and "responded to challenge with attack and usually emerged the victor in fights with other boys" (1988: 28–29).

Friedman's reflections along these lines reveal his belief in the manner in which a boy must gain masculine identity and competency through aggression. Regarding this belief that aggression underlies masculine development, Person has pointed out that, "The fundamental sexual problem for boys is the struggle to achieve phallic strength and power vis-a-vis other men" (1986: 72). Phallic narcissism and activity must be maintained and passivity must be repudiated. In particular, passive desire for another man is to be denied. Elsewhere, I have taken up the limits of such a phallic narcissistic solution to serve as the foundation of masculinity (Corbett 1993b). Suffice it to say that if we accept phallic narcissism (along with the denial of the contribution of prephallic factors) as the foundation of masculinity, we are left also to accept the sadistic and narcissistic consequences of such masculinity.

4. As is well known, perhaps more in life than in theory, men and boys are often easily provoked into defending the honor of their masculinity via violent means. Yesterday's duels bleed into today's drive-by shootings. Needless to say, the ravages of such sadistic mastery have an ignominious history (Bersani 1989). But a part of this history that has not been so well documented is the hate and violence employed by men to defend the honor of their masculinity from the perceived threat of homosexuality. One of the reasons this history has gone undocumented is the belief that such hate is constitutive of masculinity. It is one of the ways in which boys will be boys.

An especially insidious example of the way in which this boys-will-be-boys defense is employed to ward off the threat of homosexuality is the way in which girlyboys are encouraged to join the masculine fold, lest they fall victim to masculine protest. Consider this material taken from a case reported by Green (1987). In meeting with a boy's parents following a consultation with their son, Green states,

> My position with him tonight in play was that I can understand that not everybody likes to play ball. . . . But at the same time he doesn't have to do girlish things. That's something, doing sissy things, that people make fun of. . . . He is going to be very unhappy doing sissy things. He heard me. He just sat there. . . . He got a little upset and put the doll away. I told him that as he grows up, and if he continues to do sissy things, that he won't have many friends, and people will make fun of him, and he will be very unhappy. (1987: 274)

Following this consultation with Green, the boy participated in a group with other boys. When one of the boys in the group initiated some cross-gender play, the boy Green had just seen in consultation said,

> He should be spanked. Or at least reminded. He probably wants to be a girl, because he can wear girls' dresses and have long hair. But he

shouldn't do this because children will make fun of him. Boys burn up dresses of boys. Boys can go places and have more fun. (1987: 271)

5. Deep in the Bible Belt, Wally kept a diary. He tells me that it mostly consisted of drawings that evolved from princesses to fashion models to classical Greek sculpture. He kept it hidden under the floorboards of his closet. After his first sexual experience with a boy, and in a state of great shame and anxiety, he burned the diary. He buried the charred object in a nearby field.

Girlyboys and the Penis

1. Girlyboys have a penis, want a penis, and often identify with those who do not have a penis. This having, desiring, and lacking contribute to a unique gender experience. One feature of this experience is a particular form of anxiety: girlyboys frequently feel their bodies to be inadequately phallic. Conflict over internal identifications and desires are expressed through the belief that their bodies are lacking in what they feel to be a masculine essentialism. And while this essentialist anxiety can be focused directly on the penis, it is more likely to be expressed with regard to overall body size and strength.

2. Zach tells me a joke with the following punch line: "Santa I want a lot of shit for Christmas—money, a baby and a penis." And then Zach exclaims, "What in the world do I want with two things that I already have, and one that I couldn't possibly have?" When I ask which two does he have, and which one couldn't he have, he impatiently says, "Well, it's obvious, isn't it? I'm a man, after all." Later in the same hour, he refers to his efforts to repress his homosexual desire during adolescence. Typical of adolescent boys, he was anxious about his ability to control his penis. His anxiety took a particular form. He says, "To get an erection in the locker room would be to be seen as a girl." This seemed a remarkable statement to me, and I said as much. I then reflected on how he might have felt there was no way to be seen as a homosexual boy. Zach then recalls his earlier statement about being an obvious man, and laughs as he says, "It's hardly been obvious."

After the session, I found myself wondering, What is it that makes manhood obvious? And while I considered a number of possibilities, I think that Zach was pointing out the privileged display of the heterosexual phallus in contrast to his struggle with his homosexual erection, his homosexual phallus. And I began to think of how the penis is invested with an identity. Some men even name their penises. I considered how it may be easier to name your penis if it behaves as convention dictates. Convention provides a ready-made category, unlike Zach's category crisis: Does his erection, the sine qua non of maleness, make him a girl?

The manner in which this category crisis takes place on the level of the body is a central conflict of girlyboyhood. A girlyboy is aware of his male body and the masculine gender identity that attends such a surface. However, as he grows more aware of his identifications with women and his desires for men, a conscious conflict ensues: Can he have such wishes and identifications and still have the body of a boy? Do such wishes somehow belie a male body?

3. An aspect of this phallic conflict that I have seen repeatedly in psychotherapy with gay men is the manner in which girlyboys idealize and envy the conventional heterosexual phallus. Consider the following memory Jack reports in the opening phase of his treatment. At around age nine, he was out riding his bike, and came upon a group of older boys playing baseball. He stopped to watch them, and became transfixed by the first baseman. Jack was especially taken with the older boy's arms, the way his muscles strained against his T-shirt, and the fact that this boy could drink a beer and play ball at the same time. Jack indicated that as he straddled his bike, he became aware of a wish to see the boy naked, and became aware of his own body as well. In contrast to the older boy, Jack felt "skinny," with "stick arms," and a small penis. Jack tagged this memory as his first conscious experience of homosexual desire. And while reflecting on the "maelstrom of feeling" provoked by this incident, he asked, "Did I want to be him, or be with him?" and answered, "I suppose it was both."

As Jack's treatment progressed we were able to see the ways in which his mixed wish of being and wanting was often defended against through envy—a kind of penis envy. Other men were consistently depicted as more active and phallic, while Jack forecasted a life of fundamental dissatisfaction following on his painful feelings of deficiency and lack. Jack's conflict was manifested in a variety of ways, most notably through his "slavish" attachments to men, who he enviously admired as more potent, and as having "natural" access to a world outside his reach. Jack also set about to fashion himself into the kind of man he desired. Through a strenuous program of working out, he produced an idealized phallic surface. The surface got results in the form of a lot of attention from other men. But Jack was perplexed by his lack of satisfaction. In time we were able to understand that while Jack had taken on a phallic surface, he did not necessarily desire to be phallic. Instead, he wanted to find a phallic other.

Principal to our analysis of Jack's wish for a phallic other was understanding how Jack's envy was a defensive move against possessing his own desire and his own body. As Torok has suggested in reference to penis envy, "The problem of analysis is precisely to bring back into the open the authentic but repressed desire which, disguised as envy, has remained hidden" (1985: 136). Slowly, we were able to see that the inhibitions and envious conflicts that repeatedly interrupted Jack's life served to repress (principally passive) desires that he found "shameful, unmanly, and unacceptable." We were able to trace one root of this repression to his childhood belief that his desires were flawed, and to further trace how this belief in deficiency was experienced on the level of his body.

In addition, we were also able to see the ways in which the cultural prohibition against the homosexual phallus contributes to such feelings of deficiency and envy. Following a weekend spent with his oft-envied younger brother, Jack complained about his feelings of inhibition in expressing his desire for men, in contrast to his brother's lusty exclamations about various women they encountered. Jack said of his brother, "It's like he had access to a font of sexuality that was off-limits to me." At another point, he reflected on how as adolescents, he saw his brother as being able to "project sexuality and potency" in a way that once again was not within his reach. Continuing, Jack said, "It's like he could advertise it, put it out there, but I couldn't wish to get it, couldn't even become aware of wanting it."

Girlyboys and Their Mothers

1. Peter says, "I was always in the kitchen with the women," and I think of Prior in *Angels in America* (Kushner 1992). When asked, "Would you say that you are a typical homosexual?" Prior replies, "Me, oh I'm *stereotypical*" (1992: 99).

Peter's in-the-kitchen-with-the-women sentiment embodies a stereotype of protogay boys. The kitchen is a girlyboy domain. A stereotypical domain. A stereo domain—that is, through two channels—for Peter intended to impart the manner in which he finds and refinds his mother in the kitchen and in himself. Mothers have a way of recurring, and one repeatedly finds them either in the self or in the other. Analysts would have us believe that girlyboys find too much mother in themselves, and not enough in others.

Peter's mother was everywhere. She was at the center of his childhood memories. She was the shy, loving mother with whom he shared a blissful childhood. She was the creative mother he found and refound in his work as an artist. She was the Christian mother he found and refound in his efforts to establish a center for the homeless with AIDS. She was the rural mother of nature, the mother of the woods he found and refound in his garden. Like the woods, her maternal body emerged, within Peter's dreams, as protective, yet wild and filled with undergrowth. She was both the phallic and containing mother. She was earnest and empathic. She was aggressive and threatening. She was the overprotective mother who seemed out of touch with her child's growth. She was the mother who repeatedly emerged as repressive and censorious. She was the mother he feared he damaged through his own separation and sexual development. She was the mother from whom he hid his phallic strivings. She was the mother who baked a cake on the occasion of his fifth anniversary with his lover. Such contradictory themes are to be found in every intensive psychotherapy. Such contradictory themes abound around those to whom one is deeply attached.

Peter struggled to sustain his deep attachment to and identification with his mother, while also attempting to move ahead to new attachments and an expanded sense of identity. It was a difficult struggle. But, importantly, a struggle within the neurotic spectrum of distress, not a struggle that revealed a fragmented self and distortions in mental functioning—the kind of distress analysts have so often prognosticated for boys who identify with their mothers.

2. Analysts have repeatedly posited a developmental course for boys who identify with their mothers that assumes early trauma, and forecasts poor ego development and maturational difficulties. In fact, the idea of development is incongruous within this model of arrest. Current psychoanalytic developmental theory does not afford the pos-

sibility that a feminine boy could have his own feminine identity. Rather he is seen as subsumed within his mother's identity. There has been no effort to entertain the ways in which a boy may identify with his mother as distinct from a regressive lack of separation.

This gap in our theorizing reveals at least two pernicious and dogged features of psychoanalytic theory:

(1) Mothers and women are consistently constructed as archaic and regressive. The mothers of girlyboys are viewed as especially dangerous. In fact, Green advises, "You've got to get these mothers out of the way. Feminine kids don't need their mothers around" (1987: 275).

(2) Ego-integration and character development are tethered to sex-linked parent-child identifications. According to psychoanalytic theory, one develops an integrated ego and a stable character through identification with one's parents. This identificatory process has consistently been theorized as sex-linked; boys are supposed to identify with their fathers, and girls are supposed to identify with their mothers. Through this so-called logic, ego development, character development, and gender development commingle. As I have argued elsewhere (Corbett 1993a), through this commingling of ego, character, and gender, analysts perpetuate the belief that masculine health is signaled by the reproduction of fathering. A healthy boy wishes to be a father. Those boys who wish to be a mother are seen not only as having stepped off their proper developmental ladder, but also as traumatically falling into the arms of an archaic mother. Mothers continue to be marginalized, or pathologized as overprotective, indulgent, seductive, overanxious, or unhappily married. There is no consideration of the possibility that a mother's and son's subjectivities may afford greater closeness and empathy.

3. Girlyboys face a special crisis in separating from their mothers. They do not wish to disidentify with their mothers. Rather, they strive to retain feminine identifications. Their wishes are greeted with denial as they attempt to move forward. There is no cultural support, no place of cultural malleability, for such a developmental wish. By not moving toward an identification with their father—the move that is expected and encouraged—girlyboys face a crisis of shame and nar-

cissistic injury that can lead to boyhood depression. However, the vestiges of this early crisis may not be solely traumatic. It appears that, at least for some girlyboys, the long struggle to overcome shame and depression (the long struggle to come out) may foster greater character flexibility and empathy.

Girlyboys Adorn

1. A mother of a boy in Green's group of girlyboys said of her son, "He loved beautiful things. There was just so much he could do with girls' hair and a girl's dress and her body. He just liked pretty things" (1987: 122). A patient described how he had a knack for dressing Barbie and doing her hair. He was not as interested in the play that would ensue as he was in the act of dressing. He enjoyed creating Barbie as an aesthetic object to be admired and desired. Another patient described how as a child he enjoyed having "mock weddings and mock children." He claimed that his interest in playing at marriage was not fostered by the wish to enact the role of groom, but rather, he said, "The impetus for all of that was to get dressed up and have a wedding. We borrowed all my aunt's prom dresses—that was undoubtedly the reason for it. So I could do the flowers and the hair!"

2. Girlyboys have a feeling for artifice, beauty, and style. The body often becomes the avenue for this mode of aestheticism. Girlyboys dress. They dress up. They accessorize. They delight in gender's masquerade. They do not simply throw clothes on; they put clothes together in an act of presentation. They love themselves as beautiful. They want others to love them as beautiful as well. But such narcissistic delight is policed as feminine. Girlyboys begin to equate such narcissistic delight with the shame of losing hold over their proper gender. In turn, they learn to defend against such narcissistic yearning through envy and repression.

3. Throughout the beginning of an hour, Paul repeatedly indicates that he is unhappy with a new shirt he is wearing. I find myself somewhat perplexed in that the shirt is in my eyes rather nondescript. But when I ask him to what he is referring, he replies, "You know." When I indicate that in fact "I am not sure that I do know," he becomes rather exasperated and maintains, "Yes, you do." Further into the hour, Paul recalls an incident from his childhood, a struggle with his mother over who would choose his school clothes. Appar-

ently she had chosen some items, including a pair of blue shoes, that he did not like, which led him to tell her they were ugly and he would not wear them. They left the store angry and empty-handed. When I inquire as to why his thoughts may have returned to this childhood scene, Paul cuts me short, saying, "I wanted the black shoes—Beatle boots, really." To which I reply, "I see," for in fact in a certain way I did. It is then that I realize the shirt is black.

He explains that later that evening he is to meet a date for dinner, and that is why he is wearing the new shirt. But now he fears the shirt is "too much." I question, Is the shirt too much, or something else, perhaps his wish to be admired and desired? He wearily entertains this inquiry, but indicates that he does not trust my analysis. "After all," he says, "look at how you dress." I have the urge to check to see if I am wearing Beatle boots. Instead I ask what it is about the way I dress. With much reluctance, he accuses me of dressing to attract the attention of men. I point out both his reluctance and accusatory tone— as though I should be ashamed of such a wish. He once again wearily entertains my interpretation, but we are to return to such material many times within this young man's treatment.

Girlyboys Flame

1. Stoller maintains that girlyboys show "precocious ability with paints and other coloring materials, not only in the flamboyant use of colors but also in imaginative, well-formed objects expansively placed on paper and telling an understandable story" (1968: 127). Then, without adequate explanation, he denounces such creativity and flamboyance as a "lovely sign nonetheless of psychopathology," which he believes either time or treatment will remove (1968: 128).

2. Bobby, who works as a designer, tells me, "I come to the world through my eyes. Mine is a totally visual world. I can look at a room, have a vision, and make it happen, and (he adds with a laugh) I can look at a room and know it's not happening." He goes ahead to detail how he works to suppress what he sees, lest he should be taken for an "effete snob." In the next hour, he comes back to his effort to hide what he sees, and blurts out that for two years he has held back on telling me that the carpeting in my office is "just dreadful." I comment that it seems he has been quite concerned about how I would react to what he sees. He replies, "You know, it's just all that sissy shit. Boys

are not supposed to notice carpeting—they just track mud on it." He paused, and then returned to a memory that had come up several times in the course of his treatment. When he was a young boy there was a playhouse on his family's property. The house had been used for many years by his older brothers as a neighborhood clubhouse. When his brothers moved on to other interests, the house fell into his hands. Laying claim to the house, Bobby set about redecorating, as he described it, "a la 'Bewitched,' a homage to Samantha, very 60s house-wife." He made curtains, he painted, he applied appliqué daisies to the walls, and his crowning achievement was wall-to-wall shag carpeting made from remnants he procured from the trash. He undertook this project in secret, wishing to unveil it to his family upon completion. Unveil it he did, and Bobby laughs as he says, "Can you imagine? They were horrified—amused, but horrified."

In the course of Bobby's treatment, he would frequently circle back to his efforts to hide his domestic visions, even as he built a successful career around creating such visions for others. This act of hiding, this wishing not to see, served as a gateway to his conflict with feminine identifications. Boys were not supposed to see the realm of the domestic, much less wish to be creative within that realm. He frequently insinuated that domestic creations were evidence of a faulty boy who was weak and mediocre. But as Bobby described some of his childhood projects, such as the clubhouse, they hardly struck me as mediocre or weak. As I pointed out, such projects, and the manner in which he conveyed them, seemed to be fueled by complete seriousness and passion. One does not stitch wall-to-wall carpeting without drive. Eventually we began to see Bobby's wish to look away from his visions as a defense against his love of extravagance and flamboyance. As Bobby put it, "You notice, I wasn't interested in June Cleaver, it was Samantha who did it for me."

It became important to understand that Bobby's visions were not solely domestic. In fact, he often set out to undomesticate the domestic. Along these lines, Bobby took on the job of creating the set for a charity drag ball. He brought in pictures to show me what he had created. He had never done this before, and I was mindful of the unveiling of the clubhouse. As I looked at the photos, I laughed over their outlandish aspect and the zany enthusiasm they seemed to convey. I noticed, though, that Bobby seemed eager for me to hand the photos back, as though we should not linger over the images. I brought this to his attention, and with some reflection he thought that was correct. As we worked to understand his response, he revealed that he was concerned that I was too permissive. But in addition, he feared that my permissiveness would implode and I would pull away from my enjoyment of his creations. It was in this way that we began to understand an important family dynamic. It seems that his parents and his brothers—his father in particular—often appeared to take great pleasure in Bobby's capacity to create larger-than-life spectacles. But after a while, Bobby became aware that they grew self-conscious over such enjoyment, and pulled away. In fact, I realized that what I was enjoying was the way in which the photographed images were extreme and irresponsible in their fantasy, and thereby more enjoyable than everyday fantasies. As Sontag (1964) has suggested, such visions are liberated from moral relevance, duty, and seriousness. Such pleasure calls forth policing, guilt, and shame.

Reclaiming the Girl in Girlyboy

1. Peter says, "The older you get, the more you understand what's going on. And the more you realize you shouldn't be . . . or that you should be opening up and you are just sort of shutting down."

2. Femininity in a person with a penis is a transgression. Denial of femininity in a person with a penis is conformity. Girlyboys develop through a dialectic of transgression and conformity. A crucial step in the treatment of any former girlyboy is the recognition of this dialectic and how his early experience is knit into the fabric of his subjectivity.

3. Holly Hughes, in *Clit Notes* (1996) reflects on being called "shameless" by a stranger, after he observed her kissing her girlfriend. She says, "I wish what he said were true. I wish I had no shame. Maybe there are shameless queers. But I know that I'm not one of them, and neither is my girlfriend. I know that buried deep in our bodies is the shrapnel of memory dripping a poison called shame" (1996: 205).

4. Hughes continues, "But we're the lucky ones. There's not enough shame in us to kill us. Just enough to feel when it rains" (1996: 205). My work as a psychologist has taught me many things. One is, that there is indeed luck in survival. Another is, there is growth toward survival. *Psychic growth is a protogay child's way out. And for those who have been wounded by the shrapnel of shame, who have felt the shame of being hated, or have suffered the deeper wounds of trauma, under-*

standing psychic pain may provide a way out. It is, therefore, crucial to develop a theoretical apparatus that will account for queer psychic growth and pain.

As I have endeavored to posit within this essay, I believe such a developmental theory can be constructed by retaining the concepts of psychic structure and ego-integration, and by moving them forward into revitalized conceptions of identification and relationality. I do not speak of the need for integration, internalization, and identification in human life naive to the postmodern deconstruction of the unity and stability of human subjectivity. Nor do I undertake such a course in opposition to postmodern theories. Rather I contend that a complex appreciation of human subjectivity rests not only on the reversing force of deconstruction (and the widened scope of reality such postmodern techniques achieve), but also on an equal and opposite forwarding force of construction. I believe a concept such as psychic structure can properly denote this multilinearity of psychological process. For example, following on Loewald (1980), I would suggest that early identifications (the linchpin of psychoanalytic developmental theory) through the process of internalization build structure and foster ego-integration. These early levels of psychic development are not simply outgrown and left behind, but continue to be active in our patients' lives, and come alive through the replenishing regression of an analysis through transference. A central feature of any analysis is the need to examine the ways in which early identifications are paradoxically stable and shifting, persistent and dynamic. It may be helpful here to imagine identification as functioning both as the boat and the anchor. Identifications go forward, shifting with the current and/ or the cargo, while at the same time holding fast, stabilizing, and thereby providing security—but also restricting mobility and transformation.

5. To know someone's gender identity is to know very little. You know one way in which they categorize themselves. You may know something about the identifications and misidentifications this identity is built on. You may know something about how they measure themselves against prevailing cultural norms, and how motivated they may be to adhere to such norms (Person 1995). You may know something about the ways in which identifications paradoxically construct and deconstruct identities at the same time. And for an analyst these are important things to know.

But not as important as knowing about a patient's experience of gender and their gender fantasies—as opposed to their gender identities. Analytic inquiry into gender experience and fantasy provides a very valuable way to understand what are generally persistent and organizing fantasies and experiences. As Ethel Person argues, such fantasies persist as they do because they "condense and incorporate in their scripts our early identifications, childhood sexual theories and fantasies, experiences, and solutions to important childhood conflicts" (1995: 75). In having the opportunity, as analysts, to examine such early fantasies and experiences, we have the opportunity to learn about our patients' psychic structures, and to understand the ways in which early identifications through internalization build structure and foster ego-integration.

6. I like to believe that psychic development is not simply a slow march toward reality. While it is the case that greater ego-integration, including the capacity to better adapt to reality, is a feature of development, another feature of development is the capacity to resist reality's adaptive pull. As Bollas has argued, "As we grow we become more complex, more mysterious to our self, and less adapted to reality" (1992: 50). Drawing on such complexity can allow for the resurfacing of gender's mystery and complexity within psychotherapy. Helping queer people recover their distinct gender mystery provides them with access to a new vantage point from which they can reassess and revalue their development. Similarly, such a vantage point may allow queer people to reassess and revalue cultural ideals with regard to gender and sexuality, and thereby begin to resist the real effects of homophobia and discrimination on queer development.

7. Jack reports being upset with his boyfriend. He tells me he was so upset he thought he was going to cry. He hastens to add, however, that he did not cry, because that would have been "too dramatic." When I ask, "Who cries dramatically?" Jack replies, "Girls." I add, "And the girl in you?" There is a period of silence. Then, bemused, Jack indicates that he is thinking about a red and yellow dress. Simultaneously we say, "Bright," referring to a former association. We laugh. Then Jack says, "You know, the more I stop trying not to be a girl, the easier it is for me to be a boy. Whatever the hell that is."

NOTES

1. Throughout this chapter, I employ the concepts of psychic structure and ego-integration to express various ideas about the need for integration in human life. My use of the concept of psychic structure follows on the work of Loewald (1980). My use of the concepts of ego-integration, emotional development, and health follow on the work of Winnicott (1965) and Masud Khan (1974). I maintain, in league with these theorists, that internal worlds are created and psychic structures are built through processes such as internalization, projection, introjection, and identification—these internal worlds are not simply inner worlds, schemata, or maps that represent the external world of objects and their relations. Further, following on Winnicott (1965), I correlate successful ego-integration with health, as opposed to disintegration which I link with dissociation, chaotic states of regression, splitting, and depersonalization.

The term "ego" has become something of a four-letter word in these postmodern times. As I see it, ego has earned its damned status through guilt by association—the manner in which the ego has been associated and implicated in psychoanalytic developmental theories that prescriptively enforce what Dimen (1995) has called "the regulatory force of the idea of the 'normal' " (p. 135). However, normal is not inherent in the concept of the ego. I believe we can and must revitalize concepts such as psychic structure and ego-integration, and apply them to our efforts to reimagine psychic developments that are free from the determinisms that psychoanalysts have so readily fallen back upon to account for human development.

2. The fact that "girlyboy" is a label is worthy of doubt in and of itself. Labels denote categories, and I am reluctant to advocate yet another category. Moreover, it is just the sort of category that implies yet another binarism. In other words, if there is a girlyboy, is there a boylyboy? I hope, however, that I have made it sufficiently clear that I chose girlyboy because I felt it succeeded in capturing the complex interimplication between masculinity and femininity that so many homosexual men describe. It is this interimplication that I hope to illuminate and explore in this essay; the label is in the service of that project. In this world, many things are named but few are described, and while this name will fail (as do all names) I hope the description, or at the very least the effort of the description, will in some measure succeed.

3. I hasten to add that this belief is held not only by Friedman; what is regarded as pathological by Friedman and many of his fellow analysts is frequently held as unattractive by gay men. One need only peruse the personals to note the ubiquitous disclaimer, "No fats, no femmes."

4. As with all conventional binaries, passivity can exist only in reference to its dialectical opposite, activity. Given the nature of this dialectic, one could

reasonably question whether passivity exists at all. However, opposites that are held in a dialectical tension are not negated through such tension. They may contradict one another. They may fold into one another, as passivity may fold into activity, and thereby be transformed. But contradiction and transformation do not neutralize the dialectical poles; rather, they hold them in a qualified tension. So long as one is aware of the manner in which activity and passivity are qualified through this dialectical tension, I believe that passive and active wishes can be identified. Moreover, I maintain that identifying these wishes is both clinically relevant and significant.

I am defining male homosexual passivity as manifested by a variety of wishes and behaviors, ranging from the object relational wish to be cared for by another man to the sexual wish to have one's erogenous zones touched or filled by another man. For example, passivity can be expressed through the wish to be held by another man. A gay male patient of mine speaks of his pleasure in "sleeping like spoons" cradled in his lover's arms. He especially enjoys the sense of his lover as being "bigger and stronger, and able to envelope" him. Passive desire is also expressed through the pleasure that gay men experience in anal intercourse. Describing a fantasy of loving merger, a gay male patient stated, "When Alex is in me, it's like I feel filled up with him. Like his cock reaches all the way through to mine, as though we are one." Both these examples serve to illustrate a central feature of passivity—a temporary losing sight of the self through a merging surrender with another.

REFERENCES

Bell, A., M., Weinberg, and S. Hammersmith (1981). *Sexual preference: Its development in men and women.* Bloomington: Indiana University Press.

Bersani, L. (1989). Is the rectum a grave? In D. Crimp (ed.), *AIDS: Cultural analysis/cultural activism* (pp. 197–222). Cambridge, Mass.: MIT Press.

Bollas, C. (1992). *Being a character.* New York: Hill and Wang.

Butler, J. (1993). Critically queer. *GLO* 1(1): 17–32.

Chodorow, N. (1995). Multiplicities and uncertainties of gender: Commentary on Ruth Stein's "Analysis of a case of transsexualism." *Psychoanalytic Dialogues* 5(2): 291–300.

Coates, S., R. C. Friedman, and S. Wolfe (1992). The etiology of boyhood gender identity disorder: A model for integrating temperament, development, and psychodynamics. *Psychoanalytic Dialogues* 1(4): 481–523.

Coates, S. (1992). The etiology of boyhood gender identity disorder: An integrative model. In J. Barron, M., Eagle, and D. Wolitzky (eds.), *Interface of psychoanalysis and psychology* (pp. 245–65). Washington, D.C.: American Psychological Association.

————. (1994). Psychotherapeutic intervention for boys with gender identity disorder and their families. Unpublished paper delivered at the 41st annual meeting of the American Academy of Child and Adolescent Psychiatry.

Corbett, K. (1993a). The mystery of homosexuality. *Psychoanalytic Psychology* 10(3): 345–57.

————. (1993b). Masculine protest: Opposition to lifting the ban on gays in the military. Unpublished paper presented at the 13th annual meeting of the Division of Psychoanalysis of the American Psychological Association.

Dimen, M. (1995). "On our nature": Prolegomenon to a relational perspective on sexuality. In R. Lesser and T. Domenici (eds.), *Disorienting sexualities* (pp. 129–52). New York: Routledge.

Flax, J. (1990). *Thinking fragments.* Berkeley: University of California Press.

Foucault, M. (1978). *The history of sexuality: An introduction.* New York: Random House.

Freud, S. (1920). The psychogenesis of a case of homosexuality in a woman. Standard Edition. London : Hogarth Press, 1963. 18: 145–72.

Friedman, R. C. (1988). *Male homosexuality.* New Haven: Yale University Press.

Garber, M. (1992). *Vested interests.* New York: Routledge.

Goldner, V. (1991). Toward a critical relational theory of gender. *Psychoanalytic Dialogues* 1(3): 249–72.

Green, R. (1987). *The "sissy boy syndrome" and the development of homosexuality.* New Haven: Yale University Press.

Harris, A. (1991). Gender as contradiction. *Psychoanalytic Dialogues*, 1(2): 197–224.

Hughes, H. (1996). *Clit notes.* New York: Grove/Atlantic Press.

Isay, R. (1989). *Being homosexual.* New York: Farrar, Straus and Giroux.

Kushner, T. (1992). *Angels in America, part two: Perestroika.* New York: Theatre Communication Group, Inc.

Loewald, H. (1980). *Papers on psychoanalysis.* New Haven: Yale University Press.

Mass, L. (1990). *Homosexuality and sexuality.* New York: Harrington Park Press.

Masud Khan, M. (1974). *The privacy of the self.* New York: International Universities Press.

Money, J., and A. J. Russo (1979). Homosexual outcome of discordant gender identity/role in childhood: Longitudinal follow up. *Journal of Pediatric Psychology* 4: 29–41.

Person, E. (1986). The omni-available woman and lesbian sex: Two fantasy themes and their relationship to male developmental experience. In G. Fogel, et al. (eds.) *The psychology of men* (pp. 71–94). New York: Basic Books.

————. (1995). *By force of fantasy.* New York: Basic Books.

Phillips, A. (1994). *On flirtation.* Cambridge, Mass.: Harvard University Press.

Rorty, R. (1989). *Contingency, irony, and solidarity.* Cambridge, Mass.: Harvard University Press.

Sedgwick, E. (1993). How to bring your kids up gay: The war on effeminate boys. In E. Sedgwick, *Tendencies* (pp. 154–66). Durham: Duke University Press.

———. (1995). Gosh, Boy George, you must be awfully secure in your masculinity! In Maurice Berger, et al. (eds.) *Constructing Masculinities* (pp. 11–20). New York: Routledge.

Silverman, K. (1992). *Male subjectivity at the margins.* New York: Routledge.

Sontag, S. (1964). Notes on camp. In *A Susan Sontag reader* (pp. 105–19). New York: Farrar, Straus and Giroux.

Stoller, R. (1968). *Sex and gender.* London: Karnac Books.

———. (1985). *Presentations of gender.* New Haven: Yale University Press.

Torok, M. (1985). The significance of penis envy in women. In C. Chasseguet-Smirgel (ed.), *Female sexuality: New psychoanalytic views* (pp. 135–70). London: Karnac Books.

Winnicott, D. W. (1965). *The maturational processes and the facilitating environment.* New York: International Universities Press.

Zucker, K. (1990). Gender identity disorders in children: Clinical descriptions and natural history. In R. Blanchard and B. Steiner (eds.), *Clinical management of gender identity disorders in children and adults* (pp. 1–23). Washington, D.C.: American Psychiatric Press.

Zucker, K., and S. Bradley (1995). *Gender identity disorder and psychosexual problems in children and adolescents.* New York: Guilford Press.

Zucker, K., and R. Green (1989). Gender identity disorder of childhood. In T. Karasu (ed.), *Treatments of psychiatitric disorders,* Vol. 1, (pp. 661–70). Washington, D.C.: American Psychiatric Association.

Zuger, B. (1988). Is early effeminate behavior in boys early homosexuality? *Comprehensive Psychiatry* 29: 509–19.

Six

Tomboys and Cowgirls
The Girl's Disidentification from the Mother

Dianne Elise

I have long been interested in the tomboy phenomenon in female development. This phenomenon is common enough almost to be considered a developmental stage. However, while occasional references to tomboys are scattered throughout the psychoanalytic literature on female psychology, no specific treatment of the subject has existed (see Harris 1996). In this essay I will consider how, given their theoretical framework, various authors might account for tomboyism. I propose that each of these hypothetical explanations includes, explicitly or implicitly, the issue of disidentification of the girl from the mother. My formulation is used in counterpoint to Greenson's (1968) classic paper on the special importance of disidentification from the mother for the *boy*.

In addition to discussion of various hypothetical accounts, I will raise a number of questions. As the tomboy phenomenon may start as early as age three and continue into—sometimes throughout—latency, I am curious about the relationship of preoedipal and oedipal themes in interaction with whatever contribution might be specific to latency. I also wonder: What does it mean when a girl is *not* a tomboy? Why is it that adolescence usually ends tomboy life; what significance does this ending have for female development? What is the need for a label—"tomboy"—that is redundantly masculine? Playfully using the image of the "cowgirl," I will speculate on the gender nuances of these two terms, each of which refers to a girl being "not like a girl" *and* not like "a mother."

Accounting for the Tomboy

The Masculinity Complex

Clearly, the concepts of penis envy and the masculinity complex would likely constitute Freud's overarching explanation for the existence of tomboys. In describing three developmental lines stemming from the girl's confrontation with castration, Freud stated that "the second possible reaction to the discovery of female castration [is] the development of a powerful masculinity complex. By this we mean that the girl refuses, as it were, to recognize the unwelcome fact and, defiantly rebellious, even exaggerates her previous masculinity, [and] clings to her clitoral activity" (1933: 129). Freud's reference to the girl's "previous masculinity" reminds us that he saw the girl as initially *masculine* in her development, both in the activity of her libidinal drives and in their direction toward the mother. Thus, the question for Freud regarding tomboys was not so much how they come to behave in a masculine fashion, but how it is that they have not followed the "circuitous path" toward femininity.

Freud states that, in the masculinity complex, the "wave of passivity is avoided" that would have paved the way toward femininity (1933: 130). In the feminine line of development, passivity is seen to gain the upper hand, clearing phallic activity out of the way and smoothing the ground for femininity. Freud concludes, "if too much is not lost in the course of it through repression, this femininity may turn out to be normal" (1933: 128).

Another aspect of Freud's thinking relevant to the topic of tomboys concerns object relations and the issue of identification. Since Freud believed that the libidinal desire for the mother would of necessity involve a masculine identification on the part of the girl, a continued focus on the mother as love object might also explain the tomboy's masculine identification. Alternatively, an intense, incestuous tie to the father could, out of guilt, promote a defensive identification with the father. Thus the masculine identification of the tomboy might be seen as an expression of taking *either* the mother or the father as love object. Curiously, in each case the girl seems to identify with the father and disidentify with the mother; the girl ends up with a masculine identification regardless of object choice. Horney's work on the masculinity complex attempts to explain why girls more generally might tend toward masculine identification.

Picking up one piece of Freud's theory, but arguing against the primacy of penis envy, Horney (1926) viewed "the flight from womanhood" as a defensive reaction to incestuous desires for the father. She understood the masculinity complex not as a direct continuation of any supposed initial masculinity, but as an identification with the father in guilty retreat from oedipal love for him. For Horney, penis envy does not begin the sequence of turning to and then identifying with the father, nor is it the primary source of the masculinity complex. Instead, an initial feminine sense of self leads the girl to her oedipal desire for the father, then out of frustration, guilt, and fear, the girl repudiates femininity and hides herself in a desexualized, masculine identification with the father.

Horney describes this oedipal outcome: "the girl now takes refuge in a fictitious male role"—this fantasy of being a boy "devised for the very purpose of securing the subject against libidinal wishes in connection with the father. The fiction of maleness enable[s] the girl to escape from the female [oedipal] role now burdened with guilt and anxiety" (1926:66, 67). Thus, Horney would likely explain the masculine identification of the tomboy as a displacement of oedipal love for the father. This hypothesis could account for the fairly common occurrence of tomboys given that most girls could be seen as needing a close but desexualized relation with the father during latency. Tomboyism, though still defensive, could then be viewed as less pathological and atypical than in Freud's account. What I find interesting in this early classical theory is the recognition by both Freud and Horney that the girl has some motive not found in the boy to seemingly repudiate or renounce her gender identification.

Horney also considered the cultural context, a contribution for which she is typically most well-known. She referred to the actual disadvantage that females experience in social life as reinforcing unconscious oedipal dynamics: "In actual fact a girl is exposed from birth onward to the suggestion—inevitable, whether conveyed brutally or delicately—of her inferiority, an experience that constantly stimulates her masculinity complex" (1926: 69). This point leads us to Clara Thompson, a sensible voice in the forties.

Writing in the midst of a three-decade lull in the literature on female development, Thompson's emphasis on the sociocultural realities in female development seemed to stimulate little response. However, I would like to give her her due: She predates by thirty years Grossman and Stewart's (1976) well-known paper on penis envy as developmental metaphor. In 1943, Thompson stated: "In a patriarchal culture the restricted opportunities afforded woman, the limitations placed on her development and independence, give real basis for envy of the male quite apart from any neurotic trends" (1943:56). "The position of underpriviledge [*sic*] might be symbolically expressed in the term penis envy using the penis as the symbol of the more priviledged [*sic*] sex" (1943:52).

Thompson emphasized the inferior evaluation placed on females and on the feminine role. She was critical of Freud's normative femininity: "Acceptance of the feminine role may not be an affirmative attitude at all but an expression of submission and resignation. It may mean choosing the path of least resistance with the sacrifice of important parts of the self for security" (1942:80). With regard to the tomboy, I imagine Thompson saying, "Good for her!" Far from exhibiting pathology, the tomboy, though still possibly atypical, might be expressing certain strengths.

The issue of disidentification from the mother for the girl has been implicit in the perspectives of Freud, Horney, and Thompson. Moving ahead several decades and to a developmentally earlier focus on the preoedipal period, one encounters a blend of theory on object relations, gender identity development, and separation-individuation, all leading to an *explicit* focus on disidentification from the mother— particularly for the *boy*.

Separation from the Mother

In complete reversal from Freud, Stoller (1976) viewed both the boy and the girl as similar in an initial *feminine* identification. Stoller posited that through the primitive identification with the mother, each sex would have a sense of self as female and that it would be the boy who needed to come to terms with a change in gendered sense of self. Stoller, following Greenson (1968), argued that masculine identification is achieved by disidentifying with the mother.

Greenson's and Stoller's work on gender disorder in boys points to the difficulties of too much symbiotic identification with the mother for the formation of masculine gender identity. The concern in much of this work on core gender centers on how detrimental feminine identification will be for the boy in developing his identity as a masculine person. The boy has, according to Greenson, "a special problem of dis-identifying from mother" (1968:372)—an "additional step of development from which girls are exempt" (1968:370). Greenson points out that this step concerns the boy's "sense of belonging to the male sex" (1968:370). Both Stoller and Greenson acknowledge that it is of course crucial for the girl to separate and individuate from the mother. However, in their work with gender-disordered children, the intricacies and difficulties of the girl's disidentification from the preoedipal mother-infant relation have been overlooked. She too has a special problem. The girl may be exempt from problems of core gender identity, but she definitely encounters difficulties regarding feminine identity and a unique sense of self. It is in Chodorow's work that we find a detailed focus on the girl's difficulty in separating and individuating from the mother, as well as on her possible envy of the boy's apparent ease in doing so.

Differences for the two genders within the preoedipal period have been highlighted by Chodorow (1978), strengthening the conviction that issues of gender identification intertwine with those of separation-individuation (Elise 1991). Feminine identification is typically thought of as a continuation and extension of the symbiotic relation to the mother and masculine identification as the break with the preoedipal mother and thus a route to separation-individuation.[1] From this line of thinking, tomboys could be seen to be "borrowing" masculinity as an aid to separation. The girl sees that this strategy seems to work quite well for the boy and for the father; it makes sense that she would try it as well, especially when, as Chodorow has argued, the same-sex identification between mother and daughter leads to a longer, more intense, less boundaried experience in the preoedipal period. In turning to the writing of Chasseguet-Smirgel, one sees a strong emphasis on disidentification from the mother for both the boy and the girl.

Chasseguet-Smirgel (1976) argues that idealization of the penis is an attempt to assuage the narcissistic injury caused by the child's sense of helplessness in the face of the omnipotent, maternal imago. Chasseguet-Smirgel states that it is this primary helplessness that has both the boy and girl narcissistically cathect the penis and masculinity in an effort to maintain an illusion: "The wish to break away from the primal mother drives children of both sexes to project her power on to the father and his penis, and to more or less decathect specifically maternal qualities and organs" (1976:283). Thus, scorn of the maternal and disdain of femininity can be seen as a reaction-formation to the "powerful maternal imago, envied and terrifying" (1976:283). The phallic phase is defensively overdeveloped by both the boy and the girl, as evidenced in penis envy and masculine identification. Each sex attempts to detach or escape from the omnipotent mother by an investment in the father which Chasseguet-Smirgel refers to as " 'gluing' oneself to the father and his penis" (1976:284).

It is not difficult to see in this formulation a probable motivation for the tomboy—one that could lead to masculine identification as early as the late preoedipal period and be carried on throughout the oedipal phase and well into latency. Referring specifically to the girl, Chasseguet-Smirgel states that the emphasis on the penis—the organ the mother lacks—represents a desire to triumph over the mother and "makes identification with the mother and the acceptance of femininity rather difficult" (1976:285). Instead, the possession of the penis seems to allow for opposition to the mother; girls envy a boy in this regard and "say that he can 'do everything' " (1970:115). Masculinity is idealized and femininity devalued. Chasseguet-Smirgel's work contains a very explicit statement of the need on the part of the girl (as well as the boy) to disidentify from the mother as a means of separating and moving out of the preoedipal phase.

In moving to Benjamin's conceptualization of identificatory love and father identification our attention is focused on the girl's use of masculine identification as a healthy developmental step in negotiating the rapprochement subphase. In Benjamin's (1988, 1991) work, father identification is the route, albeit problematic, that the preoedipal girl may take toward a sense of agency and subjectivity. Benjamin writes that, within the cultural institution of women's mothering, "men appear to have exclusive rights to sexual agency" (1988:91). The "phallus simultaneously signifies power, difference, and desire; and as bearer of the phallus, the father represents separation from the mother. . . . [T]he father's power and the male monopoly of desire" are viewed as "the only route to individuality" (1988:86).

Referring to the "partial truth of Freud's gloomy view," Benjamin (1988:90) states "we are. . . . obliged to confront the painful fact that even today, femininity continues to be identified with passivity, with being the object of someone else's desire, with having no active desire of one's own" (1988:87). Benjamin describes the mother's lack of sub-jectivity, both on a sexual and on a more general level, with which the girl identifies and the boy disidentifies. Any power that the mother is viewed as having is to be used in the service of her children. "Her power may include power over others, but not over her own destiny" (1988:88).

This picture emphasizes a very different view of the mother than the one described by Chasseguet-Smirgel: the child's maternal imago. Following from Chasseguet-Smirgel, I believe the mother is, in the child's experience, the *first* "subject"[2] of desire in her omnipotence; she has not only been what Benjamin refers to as a "source of good-ness" (1991:283). The mother's initial overwhelming control over the child (which appears to the child as the mother's ability to get what *she* wants) does not seem a promising model to emulate *especially in relation to her*. Any recollection of *her* omnipotent "subjectivity" recalls too strong a sense of helplessness on the part of the child.

As Benjamin indicates, we are not just dealing with maternal lack, but with maternal power as it is initially perceived by the child; the relation to the father can seem a solution to both problems. Benjamin states that "the boy now imagines himself to be the father, the subject of desire, in relation to the mother" (1991:283); this last phrase is key. The child chooses the father as the model for the subject of desire, not based solely on the father's power in relation to the outside world but, most importantly, in relation to the mother.

The originally omnipotent mother is transformed into the culturally devalued stereotype. Identification with the father is a way of estab-lishing subjectivity that, in the child's eyes, both is and is not repre-sented by the mother. The girl does and does not want to view the mother as powerful subject; she is in conflict with each view. While threatened by the mother of symbiosis, the girl, especially, is disillu-sioned and disappointed with the mother of rapprochement. As gen-der differences in general and between mother and father are begin-ning to be comprehended, the girl realizes that she does share a great lack with the mother: membership as the devalued and constrained sex. The phrase "she who desires" (Benjamin 1988:87), originally an all-encompassing truth in relation to the primal mother, becomes, at the point of rapprochement and beyond, a contradiction in terms.

If, as Chasseguet-Smirgel, Chodorow, and Benjamin have argued, the phallus—idealized masculinity—is the only way to separate and to represent oneself as a desiring subject, then clearly it would hold an appeal for the girl as well as the boy. The girl too will try to disidentify with this female lack of subjectivity. Some active striving for mastery and selfhood would, at least initially, be present in girls. Given that what is viewed as a masculine identification seems to be the only avenue forward, the girl is, as Benjamin has indicated, in a trap: she has to relinquish her gender identification, as it is understood in our culture, or her sense of subjectivity; she has no female agentic subject with which to identify. Her choice is that of a devalued feminine identification with a devalued mother, or an identification with her father as subject for which she then risks being pathologized as unfeminine.

In accounting for paternal identification on the part of the girl, Benjamin explicates a rapprochement phenomenon, Horney an oedipal resolution. Given that masculine identification is often continued throughout latency, it is important to understand how this identification evolves and persists through all three phases and to consider multiple influences in the patterning of these various strands of masculine identification.

Latency and the Female Ego Ideal

In the few empirical studies (Hyde, Rosenberg, and Behrman 1977; Burn, Nederend, and O'Neil 1994) on tomboys, 50 percent of adult heterosexual women subjects identify as having been tomboys in grammar school. What do we make of the prevalence of tomboyism in the girl's latency? Various theories considered above indicate that the girl can have many reasons to disidentify from the mother. Although her first identificatory love has been the mother, the overwhelming intensity of the preoedipal merger makes it difficult to use the mother as a figure of identification in subsequent phases. Direct identification with the omnipotent maternal imago is intimidating. If the girl does directly identify with the mother as a figure of power, analytic theory often describes this as an identification with the "phallic mother." Thus, it is still viewed as a masculine identification. In breaking away from the preoedipal dyad, paternal identification seems to be the ticket to separation-individuation.

As love for the mother evolves into an oedipal, triadic affair, the girl realizes that the object of mother's desire (most often) is masculine; in wanting mother, she may adopt masculinity as an attempt to win mother. Thus, this motive for maternal disidentification would not be to get away from, but "to get," the mother. If she "chooses" to opt for father instead, we find that *this* oedipal love is also likely to result in a masculine identification. Finally, as gender differences and inequities under patriarchy are comprehended and feminine lack of subjectivity is realized, identification with mother loses some appeal. Latency asks for a mastery not typically promoted in our culture by maternal identification.

It appears that disidentification with the mother has special significance for the girl, just as Greenson (1968) pointed out it does for the boy. A feminine identification based on the mother as ego ideal becomes a very complex, conflictual, and subtle layering of dynamic issues (Elise 1997). While separating and individuating from the mother and negotiating oedipal desires and then latency achievements, the girl is expected to simultaneously use the mother as ego ideal. Given the cultural image of "mother," this is often not easily accomplished. As Benjamin indicates, synthesizing subjectivity and femininity is a difficult task—one which frequently the mother has not been able to model. Feminine role adherence and a daughter's identification with her mother may result in a foreclosing of the development of a stronger sense of self.

Freud himself pointed out that when the little girl "represses her previous masculinity a considerable part of her general sexual life is permanently injured" (1931:238). Consideration is beginning to be given to a number of ways in which the girl's development may be injured when she is pressured into a caricature of femininity. The latency girl herself has little trouble maintaining a solid, female core gender identity *along with* masculine identifications; it is the rest of the population that is underinclusive (Fast 1984; Bassin 1996; Elise 1998, 1996) in maintaining cross-sex identifications. Latency reveals the girl as subject, labeled "tomboy."

What's in a Name?

A young, female, agentic subject has been such a contradiction in our culture that we doubly label her "male" with the redundant "tomboy." We want no female ownership of supposedly "masculine" turf, though we allow for occasional exceptions: for instance, in certain respects a "cowgirl" is a tomboy by another name. I would like to play with certain nuances regarding gender in these two labels.

In musing about children's games and costumes, it occurred to me that cowgirls are outfitted the same as cowboys in all but one respect—a skirt. Otherwise, she too has boots, holster and pistols, a hat and a lasso—all the requisite accoutrements. The existence of the skirt seems to be what allows the "cowgirl" to do everything a "cowboy" does without losing her identity as a female—an equal opportunity act where females, as well as males, can have ownership of the position. A cowgirl can do everything a cowboy can do, as Annie in *Annie Get Your Gun* bellows out in her song "I can do everything better than you can." Obviously she is addressing a man and she is not referring to domestic skills; the cowgirl is not in the home. Annie, the consummate cowgirl, is clearly the ultimate tomboy. She not only engages in "masculine" activities and rejects male superiority, but she is not particularly interested in her suitor. Tomboys (gender denied by the label) seem to be on a gender continuum with cowgirls (gender affirmed) with tricky implications regarding sexual orientation and orientation to sexuality. "Cowgirl" implies a "cowboy," thus presuming an opposite-gender pairing within what is likely a heterosexual structure. Tomboys themselves are not focused on, nor are they defined in terms of, a cross-gender, sexualized partnership with males.

Latency, for many girls, is a developmental period suspended between oedipal sexuality with the father and adolescent heterosexuality. A girl is allowed to be a full person, versus a feminine role inhabitant, between these two focal periods. Mastery equals competence and achievement, qualities associated with latency and some hint as to why latency promotes tomboyism. Latency has been the girl's chance to do things that are valued versus trivialized (such as tea parties and doll-play). The cowgirl/tomboy may actually not be disidentifying with her mother as a particular individual and as a female, but with the cultural stereotype of the limited feminine role. We have accepted "mother" as stereotype and girls are viewed as masculine when they do not prefer indoor games, dresses, and dolls. This leaves feminine identification defined by a very narrow sphere of activities, which, not surprisingly, parallels the social situation.

As we all know, *Even Cowgirls Get the Blues*. One gleans a lot from the provocative title. The emphasis on the word "even" implies that of all females, "cowgirls" should somehow be safeguarded from depression or have developed an immunity to this female affliction. However, the image of the cowgirl comes from a time when women were needed to perform out-of-role while the American frontier was being inhabited. When times change and the only range to roam becomes the one in the kitchen, depression is not a surprising result. Just as *Rosie the Riveter* was pulled back into the feminine mystique at the end of the war, the cowgirl or tomboy is pulled back into the heterosexual demand for femininity at adolescence.

Tomboyism may not be an unusual phase; possibly it is vigorous girlhood ended by typical, but somewhat debilitating, feminine adolescence. If tomboyism is the unfolding of a healthy girlhood, why don't all girls do it? Why do a higher proportion of lesbians than heterosexual women report having been tomboys as girls (Saghir and Robins 1973)? Lesbians may have skipped the adolescent induction into heterosexuality that seems to have a diminishing effect on many females. Perhaps the dive that girls are seen to take in adolescence with regard to many measures of self-esteem and self-respect reflects the possibility that heterosexuality as it is constituted under patriarchy isn't always good for girls.

Conclusion

Since a masculine identification is a "forbidden identification" (Bernstein 1993:33), labeling a girl who is out of the feminine role "tomboy" is a way of saying, "This is not yours, you as a female cannot keep it." Certain ways of being are considered *unusual* for a female, even though in reality they may be quite common. The actual process of labeling sets these traits and behaviors apart and denies *permanent* ownership to the girl; the traditional gender balance is maintained in the face of many girls acting out of role. The culture waits and bides its time, knowing that in adolescence it will reclaim the female and that these other expressions of self will be "just a phase," increasingly distant in the woman's personal history (Hancock 1989)—nothing to be taken seriously. That tomboys are not much written about may itself be a parallel process to the effect of the labeling. Being a "tomboy" becomes a short-lived, insignificant phase that we ignore or humor out of existence as merely a lapse in the ongoing stream of feminine development.

NOTES

1. See Person and Ovesey (1983) for a critique of this issue.
2. I put "subject" in quotes here because, as Benjamin (1995) articulates, the child's recognition of the mother's "omnipotence" is distinct from the later developmental ability to attribute true subjectivity to her.

REFERENCES

Bassin, D. (1996). Beyond the he and the she: Toward the reconciliation of masculinity and femininity in the post-oedipal female mind. *Journal of the American Psychoanalytic Association* 44 (Suppl.): 157–190.

Benjamin, J. (1988). *The bonds of love.* New York: Pantheon.

———(1991). Father and daughter: Identification with difference—a contribution to gender heterodoxy. *Psychoanalytic Dialogues* 1: 277–99.

———(1995). *Like subjects and love objects.* New Haven: Yale University Press.

Bernstein, D. (1993). *Female identity conflict in clinical practice.* Northvale, N.J.: Jason Aronson.

Burn, S. M., S., Nederend, and A. K. O'Neil (1994). Childhood tomboyism and adult androgyny. Unpublished paper, Cal Poly, San Luis Obispo.

Chasseguet-Smirgel, J. (1970). Feminine guilt and the oedipus complex. In J. Chasseguet-Smirgel (ed.), *Female sexuality: New psychoanalytic views* (pp. 94–134). London: Karnac.

———(1976). Freud and female sexuality: The consideration of some blind spots in the exploration of the 'Dark Continent.' *International Journal of Psychoanalysis* 57: 275–86.

Chodorow, N. (1978). *The reproduction of mothering.* Berkeley: University of California Press.

Elise, D. (1991). An analysis of gender differences in separation-individuation. *Psychoanalytic Study of the Child* 46: 51–67.

———(1996). Unlawful entry: Male fears of psychic penetration. Paper presented at Annual Spring Meeting, APA Division of Psychoanalysis (39), Denver, Colo.

———(1997). Primary femininity, bisexuality and the female ego ideal. *Psychoanalytic Quarterly* 66: 489–517.

—————(1998). Gender repertoire: Body, mind and bisexuality. *Psychoanalytic Dialogues* 8: 353–71.

Fast, I. (1984). *Gender identity: A differentiation model.* Hillsdale, N.J.: Analytic Press.

Freud, S. (1931). Female sexuality. Standard Edition. London: Hogarth Press, 1961. 21: 223–43.

—————(1933). Femininity. Standard Edition. London: Hogarth Press, 1964. 22: 112–35.

Greenson, R. (1968). Dis-identifying from the mother: Its special importance for the boy. *International Journal of Psychoanalysis* 49: 370–73.

Grossman, W., and W. Stewart, (1976). Penis envy: From childhood wish to developmental metaphor. *Journal of the American Psychoanalytic Association* 24 (Suppl.): 193–212.

Hancock, E. (1989). *The girl within.* New York: Fawcett Columbine.

Harris, A. (1996) "The Tomboys' Stories." To appear in A. Harris, *The Softly Assembled Self: Developmental Theory for Relational Psychoanalysis* (in preparation).

Horney, K. (1926). The flight from womanhood: The masculinity complex in women, as viewed by men and by women. In Harold Kelman (ed.), *Feminine psychology* (pp. 54–70). New York: W. W. Norton, 1967.

Hyde, J., B. G. Rosenberg, and J. A. Behrman (1977). Tomboyism. *Psychology of Women Quarterly* 2: 73–75.

Person, E., and L. Ovesey (1983). Psychoanalytic theories of gender identity. *Journal of the American Academy of Psychoanalysis* 11: 202–26.

Saghir, M. T., and E. Robins (1973). *Male and female homosexuality.* Baltimore: Williams-Wilkins.

Stoller, R. (1976). Primary femininity. *Journal of the American Psychoanalytic Association* 24 (Suppl.): 59–78.

Thompson, C. (1942). Cultural pressures in the psychology of women. In J. B. Miller (ed.), *Psychoanalysis and women* (pp. 69–84). Harmondsworth, Eng.: Penguin, 1973.

—————(1943). "Penis envy" in women. In J. B. Miller (ed.), *Psychoanalysis and women* (pp. 52–57). Harmondsworth, Eng.: Penguin, 1973.

Seven

Oh Bondage Up Yours!
Female Masculinity and the Tomboy

Judith Halberstam

In a 1977 punk rock classic, Poly Styrene, lead singer of X-Ray Spex, produced her classic wail of teen girl outrage: "Some people say little girls should be seen and not heard," she whispered, "but I say . . ." and here she went from a whisper to a scream, "oh bondage up yours!" In her music and in her personal style, Poly Styrene signaled her absolute refusal of the bondage she associated with "natural femininity"; she wore dayglo clothes in bright and unnatural colors and fabrics and her teeth were encased in heavy braces as if to signify her indifference to the injunction on girls to be pretty or nice, sugar and spice. X-Ray Spex's songs called for liberation from the bondage of gender and consumerism and they did so by making almost unbearable sounds. While few punk girls would ever lay claim to the label "feminist," the content of their assault on conventional femininity was often quite similar to feminist critiques of gender. However, punk allowed for a different trajectory of rebellion than feminism did. While feminism has been preoccupied with producing strong women out of strong girls, subcultural forms like punk and riot grrl have generated queer girls, often queer tomboys with queer futures. The 1970s was both the decade of punk and the decade of the tomboy film; this period witnessed the rise of feminism and the development of gay and lesbian pride; in the 1970s, we might say, great social change produced the hope that things could be different for girls. But the hope of the 1970s has not necessarily materialized into a better world for the cross-identified girl. In this essay I trace the evolution of two different models of rebellious girlhood: both have been labeled "tomboy" but one is linked securely to femininity and heterosexuality while the other is tied precariously to masculinity and queerness. Despite the rise of feminism and the recognition of the dangers posed by conventional femininity, I will argue, we still hesitate to cultivate female masculinity in young girls.

The subculture of 1970s punk rock, especially in England, offered girls like me a refuge from femininity. From about the age of fourteen until the end of my grammar school days four years later, I embraced punk rock culture as if it were a life raft in the high seas of adolescence. Punk allowed me to dance wildly, dress in scruffy hand-me-downs, mess up my hair, and scowl a lot. It provided a barrier between me and conventional girlhood and gave me a loud and rebellious language for my outrage. Although it was not completely clear to me at the time, my own brand of adolescent rage was fueled by the demands made upon me at school and out in the world to be a girl in conventional ways. Punk music and style countered those demands with an invitation to be different and to make sense of that difference. For many tomboys, punk was an opportunity to avoid the strictures of femininity that bound girlhood to the safety of domesticity; indeed, the ubiquitous safety pin which adorned many a punk outfit, for example, symbolized the misuse and indeed abuse of that household item. Within the outfits of punks, the safety pin was transformed from a marker of rational utility to a symbol of useless and totally unsafe fashion. Punk allowed tomboys to extend tomboyism into adolescence; punk gave us permission to be ambiguous about gender in our unisexual punk outfits, and, of course, in relation to the music, it allowed us to scream and shout and make noise and to finally be heard: "Some people say little girls should be seen and not heard, but I say . . ."

While "punk" tends to be the name we give to the rogue male who embodies a masculine refusal of socialization, when associated with girls it has a wholly different set of connotations. The punk girl marks her difference through indifference and she takes her rebellion seriously as a political statement rather than just an individualistic stand against adulthood. Although punk rock of the 1970s did not really sustain extended interest in gender politics or sexual politics, it did provide a subcultural context in which girls could be boys and femininity could be totally rejected. Cultural studies of punk have not generally paid too much attention to the participation of girls. This has much to do with the fact that, as Angela McRobbie and Jenny Garber note, the very term subculture "has acquired such strong masculine overtones."[1] Accordingly, girls tend to be viewed as girlfriends or fans within the subculture rather than as agents, participants, and performers. If it is true that the term subculture has acquired "strong masculine overtones," then it surely makes sense to look for masculinity within girl subcultures: when girls in punk are studied, however, it is never in the context of female masculinity. The masculine girl, moreover, often functions as a lone outsider rather than as part of an elaborate subcultural group. She may be the only girl in her group to ride a motorcycle, to play boys' sports, or to dress in male clothing. In this essay I want to extend the label of punk beyond its 1970s subcultural context and make it into a marker for a particular form of tomboyism, one marked by female masculinity, noisy political rebellion, and the refusal of compulsory heterosexuality. Punk, in this essay, signifies the affirmation of masculine tomboyism.

Tomboyism usually describes an extended childhood period of female masculinity. If we are to believe general accounts of childhood behavior, some degree of tomboy behavior is quite common for girls and does not give rise to parental fears. Because comparable cross-identification behaviors in boys do often give rise to quite hysterical responses, we tend to believe that female gender deviance is much more tolerated than male gender deviance.[2] I am not sure that tolerance in such matters can be measured, nor that responses to childhood gender behaviors necessarily tells us anything concrete about the permitted parameters of adult male and female gender deviance. Tomboyism tends to be associated with a "natural" desire for the greater freedoms and mobilities enjoyed by boys. Very often it is read as a sign of independence and self-motivation. It may even be encouraged to the extent that it remains comfortably linked to a stable sense of a girl identity. Tomboyism is punished, however, where and when it appears to be the sign of extreme male identification (taking a boy's name or refusing girl clothing of any type) and where and when it threatens to extend beyond childhood and into adolescence.[3]

Teenage tomboyism presents a problem and tends to be subject to the most severe efforts toward reorientation. We could say that there are at least two marked forms of tomboyism, feminine and masculine, and that tomboyism is tolerated as long as the child remains prepubescent; as soon as puberty begins, however, the full force of gender conformity descends upon the girl. Gender conformity is pressed onto all girls, not just tomboys. This is where it becomes hard to uphold the notion that male femininity presents a greater threat to social and familial stability than female masculinity. Female adolescence represents the crisis of coming of age as a girl in a male-dominated society. If adolescence for boys represents a rite of passage (much celebrated in Western literature in the form of the *bildungsroman*) and an ascension to some version (however attenuated) of social power, for girls adolescence is a lesson in restraint, punishment, and repression. It is in the context of female adolescence that the tomboy instincts of millions of girls are remodeled into compliant forms of femininity.

The fact that some girls do emerge at the end of adolescence as masculine women is quite amazing. The growing visibility and indeed respectability of lesbian communities to some degree facilitates the emergence of more masculine women. But as even a cursory survey of popular cinema and literature confirms, the image of the tomboy is only tolerated within a narrative of blossoming womanhood; within such a narrative, tomboyism represents a resistance to adulthood itself rather than to adult femininity. Tomboy identities are conveyed as benign forms of childhood identification as long as they evince acceptable degrees of femininity, appropriate female aspiration, and as long as they promise to result in marriage and motherhood.

Many tomboy narratives are about the coercion of the masculine girl and the process which transforms her from boy to woman. For example, in both the novel and film versions of the classic tomboy narrative, *The Member of the Wedding* by Carson McCullers, tomboy Frankie Addams fights a losing battle against womanhood and the text locates womanhood or femininity as a crisis of representation which confronts the heroine with unacceptable life options. While the film version, as I will discuss later, dramatizes Frankie's sense of her own freakishness in relation to the confining social relations of the American South, the novel weaves Frankie's tale quite clearly through multiple other narratives of belonging and membership. This novel is all the more remarkable for the fact that it emerges out of the repressive cultural climate of the American South in the 1950s. Carson McCullers was born Lula Carson in 1917 in Columbus, Georgia, and she grew up with a sense of her own freakishness and inability to fit the mold of conventional femininity. She was often called "weird," "freakish," and "queer" and she felt herself to be outlandish and different.[4] McCullers's girl hero Frankie Addams is similarly preoccupied with her own freakishness which is depicted most often as a lack of commonality with other girls and sometimes as a form of female masculinity.

In the novel, as her brother's wedding approaches Frankie Addams pronounces herself mired in a realm of unbelonging, outside the symbolic partnership of the wedding but also alienated from almost every category that might describe her. In a haunting description of tomboy alienation, McCullers writes: "It happened that green and crazy summer when Frankie was twelve years old. This was the summer when for a long time she had not been a member. She belonged to no club and was a member of nothing in the world. Frankie was an unjoined person who hung around in doorways and she was afraid."[5] McCullers positions Frankie on the verge of adolescence ("when Frankie was twelve years old") and in the midst of an enduring state of being "unjoined": "She belonged to no club and was a member of nothing in the world." While childhood in general may qualify as a period of "unbelonging," for the boyish girl arriving on the doorstep of womanhood, her status as "unjoined" marks her out for all manner of social violence and opprobrium. As she dawdles in the last light of childhood, Frankie Addams has become a tomboy who "hung around in doorways, and she was afraid."

As a genre, the tomboy film, as I will show later, suggests that the categories available to women and girls for gendered and sexual identification are simply inadequate. The tomboy film dramatizes the plight of both the masculine and the feminine tomboy. In her novel, McCullers shows that the inadequacy of gender categories is a direct result of the tyranny of language—a structure which fixes people and things in place artificially but securely. Frankie tries to change her identity by changing her name: "why is it against the law to change your name?" she asks Berenice (1973:107). Berenice answers: "Because things accumulate around your name." Without names, confusion would reign and "the whole world would go crazy." But Berenice also acknowledges that the fixity conferred by names traps people into many different identities, racial as well as gendered: "We all of us somehow caught ... And maybe we wants to widen and bust free. But no matter what we do we still caught" (1973:113). Frankie thinks that naming represents the power of definition, and name changing confers the power to reimagine identity, place, relation, and even

gender. "I wonder if it is against the law to change your name," says
Frankie, "Or add to it . . . Well I don't care . . . F. Jasmine Addams"
(1973:15).

Psychoanalysis posits a crucial relationship between language and
desire, such that language structures desire and expresses therefore
both the fullness and the futility of human desire—full because we
always desire, futile because we are never satisfied. Frankie in particular understands desire and sexuality to be the most regimented forms
of social conformity—we are supposed to desire only certain people
and only in certain ways. But her desire does not work that way and
she finds herself torn between longing and belonging. Because she
does not desire in conventional ways, Frankie seeks to avoid desire
altogether. Her struggle with language, her attempts to remake herself
through naming, and remake the world with a new order of being are
ultimately heroic but unsuccessful. McCullers's pessimism has to do
with a sense of the overwhelming "order of things," an order which
cannot be affected by the individual, which works through things as
basic as language and which forces nonmembers into memberships
which they cannot fulfill.

In this essay, unbelonging characterizes a queer girl identity, the
punk tomboy, which can successfully challenge hegemonic models of
gender conformity. I want to carefully produce here a model of youthful female masculinity which calls for new and self-conscious affir-
mations of different gender taxonomies, taxonomies flexible and varied enough to recognize the masculinity of young girls. The
affirmation of alternative girl masculinities may begin not by subvert-
ing masculine power or taking up a position against it but by turning
a blind eye to conventional masculinities and refusing to engage.
Frankie Addams, for example, constitutes her rebellion not in opposition to the law but through indifference to it: she recognizes that it
might be against the law to change one's name or add to it, but she
has a simple response to such illegal activity: "Well, I don't care." For
the tomboy, the girl with no real social power of her own, the preadult
with no access to the agency required to bring about social change,
power may inhere in different forms of refusal: "Well, I don't care."

I want to trace here the meanings that attach to preadult female
masculinities, the logics used to explain them, and the measures taken
to dispel all cross-identification during puberty. I also want to examine the ways in which youthful female masculinity articulates itself

over and against the many strategies used to silence it and the ways
in which a rogue or punk tomboyism might be cultivated among girls.
This punk tomboyism, I will argue, constitutes a pathologized form of
girl identification which parents, counselors, and psychologists find
aberrant and try to repress. Social science studies of tomboyism use
the feminist language of "androgyny" to refer to the versions of which
they approve. Androgyny within this literature represents a healthful
alternative to the excesses of gender polarization. But androgyny, I
will propose, does not really describe the gender identity of the punk
tomboy. By framing discussions of tomboyism in relation to androgyny, the masculinity of the young girl is once again discounted. While
much of the scholarly work on tomboyism has appeared in social
science journals, there are many different zones of representation to
which one might look for alternative images of the tomboy, including
children's literature, films, and TV specials. I will be drawing my
examples of alternative depictions of tomboyism from a set of films
made between 1953 and 1986 that constitute the genre of the tomboy
film. I also want to examine closely a TV special on tomboyism which
aired in 1995 and which proposed to examine boyish girls, their desires, and their potential futures. This program examined head on the
great anxiety generated by the prospect of lesbian futures for tomboy
girls. At the same time, the researchers and interviewers in the program were unable to identify any bad effects of early cross-
identification among girls. Ultimately, I will be asking questions about
how we might cultivate an aesthetic of masculinity among young
girls, how we might encourage punk tomboyism, and how we might
theorize the relations between preadult and adult female masculinity.

The Androgyny Trap

Tomboyism of a certain genre is far more common and far more
tolerated than one might think. Indeed, it has become almost com-
monplace nowadays for at least middle-class parents to point to their
frisky girl children and remark proudly upon their tomboy natures.
Tomboyism in such contexts usually means no more than a healthy
interest in active play and a disdain for gender-appropriate clothes
and toys. While a permissive attitude toward active little girls is a
positive change in the parenting of girls in general, the reduction of

the meaning of tomboyism to active play among girls suggests something more sinister. If tomboy simply means "active," then those forms of pronounced masculinity that many girls cultivate—complete male identification, lack of interest in girls and girls' activities, desire to dress in boys' clothes and play exclusively with boys as a boy—remain beyond the pale. This preadult female masculinity, in other words, is still very much outside the parameters of acceptable girl behavior. Tomboyism is tamed and domesticated when linked to non-masculine girls, and allows for a more harmful, fully pathologizing discourse to explain strong masculine identifications among preteen girls. Furthermore, excessively feminine little girls are also harmed by the generalization of the tomboy label because when tomboy becomes a normative standard, they look pathologically bound by their femininity to weakness and passivity.

Much of the feminist psychological and sociological research on tomboyism since the 1980s assumes that there is a nonpathological form of tomboyism that can lead to adult androgyny. Such research is founded on the recognition of the social construction of gender and assumes that gender polarization can be particularly bad for women. Articles with titles such as, "Is the Traditional Role Bad for Women?" and "Dismantling Gender Polarization," mark the ill-effects produced by excessive gender polarization for women.[6] Many of these studies even suggest that while gender conformity has its rewards for women early in life, women suffer from isolation and narrowed life ambitions as they grow older on account of their adoption of conventional female roles.

Androgyny in much of the psychological literature means some form of "mixing of masculinity and femininity," and signals flexibility in relation to gender conventions. The language of androgyny replaces an older pathologizing discourse of gender-appropriate and gender-inappropriate behaviors. One study suggests: "Research links androgyny to situational flexibility; high self-esteem; achievement motivation; parental effectiveness; subjective feelings of well-being and marital satisfaction."[7] When extended to tomboys the notion of androgyny is often used in such studies to determine whether childhood tomboyism is an accurate predictor of adult androgyny. While of course these studies maintain a strict sense of objectivity, there is no doubt that ideologically they are committed to the production and cultivation of androgyny in both children and adults. The concept of androgyny has mixed consequences for the tomboy.

One study on "destereotyping" used the notion of androgyny to suggest that tomboys do not simply "reject traditionally female activities." Instead they are flexible children who are able to "expand their repertoire to include both gender-traditional and nontraditional activities."[8] The authors of this article admit that earlier studies of tomboys had indeed linked the tomboy to an aversion for girls' games and female playmates and a preference for athletic activities and boys' clothing and toys. But they dismiss such data because "these defining criteria are based on atypical samples (homosexual females and genetic females masculinized in utero) compared to control samples" (1984: 704). Here we see clearly the ideological import of the emphasis on androgyny: because a high sample of women (as high as 50 percent in some studies) report childhood tomboy identification, much effort is made to deemphasize the link between tomboyism and active male identification or, more specifically, between tomboyism and adult lesbianism, transsexualism, or hermaphroditism. Instead the concept of adult androgyny becomes a reassurance that today's tomboy will not grow up to be tomorrow's bull dyke. This study on destereotyping concludes that "girls who are able to transcend gender-role behavior in childhood are the ones who will be most flexible and androgynous as adults" (1984: 711). There is no explanation as to how the authors arrived at the conclusion that androgyny is desirable and positively linked to flexibility. But such assumptions force a pathological label upon the child who eschews androgyny in favor of cross-identification. The tomboy who prefers boys' activities and clothes and rejects girls as playmates is constructed in articles such as this as an antitype for the destereotyped androgynous tomboy.

Earlier research on tomboys—research not committed to the concept of androgyny but nonetheless determined to depathologize tomboyism—also refused the notion that tomboyism is rare and abnormal. Hyde et al. at Bowling Green State University found that 63 percent of a sample of junior high girls and 51 percent of a sample of adult women reported having been tomboys in childhood.[9] The authors suggest that the reasons tomboyism has been conceived of as rare has to do with links made between tomboyism and adult transsexualism and lesbianism; however, they believe that tomboyism should be viewed as "a normal, active part of female development" (1977: 75). The unfortunate effect of the normalization of the tomboy role in this study is uncannily similar to the effects of placing tomboyism within a model of androgyny: in both cases, good and bad models of tomboy identification are produced in which good tomboyism corresponds to heterosexual female development and bad tomboyism corresponds to homo- or transsexual development. In their clearly feminist study, Hyde et al. reject an earlier definition of tomboyism as "preference for the company of boys and for boys' activities" and a "persistent aversion to girls' activities and girls as playmates" (1977: 75). Their definition of tomboy "is a girl who says she's a tomboy" (1977: 75). Hyde's research group also suggests that "the discrepancy between the high-percentages of self-reported tomboys we found and the low percentages found by Saghir and Robins (1973) may be accounted for by differences in definition" (1977: 75). They believe that particularly as regards the rejection of other girls as playmates, the earlier definitions of tomboyism forces it "a priori into being a reactive and maladaptive syndrome" (1977: 75).

While it sounds like a good idea to allow self-definition to determine who is and who is not a tomboy, it then becomes even more important to know what it means to the girls and women surveyed to say that they do or once did identify as tomboys. Hyde reports that she and her coresearchers used a sample of thirty-four females entering seventh, eighth, and ninth grades who were at a summer church camp and "63% reported being tomboys currently (in response to the following item on a questionnaire: Would you say that you are sort of a tomboy?)" (1977: 74). As the survey gets more specific we find out that tomboys differed from nontomboys in their preference for boys' games, but both tomboys and nontomboys reported their preference for trousers over dresses; the researchers downplay the differences between the two groups, noting: "Wishing to be a boy, hiding good grades, and clothes preference did not differentiate tomboys from nontomboys" (1977: 74). The researchers seem to feel heartened that the gap between tomboys and nontomboys has narrowed because it indicates a wide dispersion of the positive aspects of tomboy activity and perhaps also shows the nonperjorative meaning of tomboyism among girls. However, the study can also be read in a different way: we might adduce that in fact the label "tomboy" may not have meant very much to this group of girls because it refers only to a high degree of physical activity and self-expression but has been completely divorced from female masculinity. In relation to this last point, it is important to note that when and where tomboy becomes the general term for active girlhood, many young masculine girls may not feel comfortable expressing their desire to be boys or to play exclusively with boys. In fact the omission of any data about the girls' masculinity leaves out important information and produces a false image of tomboyism as just an active stage along the road to adult femininity.

By contrast, among the women interviewed about their childhoods, "51% reported having been tomboys in childhood" (1977: 74). Contrary to the girls' group, within the adult group "tomboys differed from nontomboys in terms of clothing preference, preferred sex of playmates, preferred games, wishing to be a boy, and the parent to whom they were closest in childhood in adolescence" (1977: 76). The researchers do not comment on the discrepancy between the women and the girls. While the girls would not admit to any desire to be boys, the women recalling their tomboy days did reference their desire to be a boy and strong clothing preferences. Obviously, questions must be asked about what the girls felt comfortable admitting to in the context of the study. The discrepancies between the women remembering their childhoods and the girls describing theirs may also be explained by a change in definitions of tomboyism over time. The high number of adult women recalling tomboy pasts could have to do with the increased acceptance of tomboyism in the present, or with changing conceptions of acceptable models of femininity. In fact, it is extremely difficult to interpret any of these results about tomboy identification without acknowledging that there may be a high degree of deception or misinformation in both the girls' self-definitions and the women's memories of self-definition. Girls have their own functional parameters for acceptable and unacceptable degrees of boy identification and it may well be that "tomboy" did not mean boy-identified among them.

Sandra L. Bem, one of the most important proponents of androgyny, returns to the concept of androgyny in her later work and expresses some dissatisfaction with it. In her 1993 book, *The Lenses of Gender*, Bem admits that androgyny did not live up to its early promise as a feminist challenge to gender polarization. She writes: "Androgyny inevitably focuses more on the individual's being both masculine and feminine than on the culture's having created the concepts of masculinity and femininity in the first place. Hence, androgyny can legitimately be said to reproduce precisely the gender polarization that it seeks to undercut, and to do so even in the most feminist of treatments."[10] While Bem is absolutely right that androgyny only confirms binary gender systems, she does not highlight the potentially homophobic and indeed transphobic effects of promoting androgyny. In fact, the literature on androgyny shows all too clearly that when it comes to cross-gender identifications, feminist recommendations may often actually produce homophobia and transphobia.[11] Proponents of androgyny seemed to think that gender polarization was responsible for sustaining male domination and that the appropriate response was therefore to soften the contours of gender difference and argue for gender sameness. While Bem no longer proposes androgyny as the feminist solution to the problem of gender polarization, she does still argue for "gender depolarization." Since it does not seem likely that conventional gender divisions will disappear anytime soon, I would personally argue less for gender depolarization and more for gender proliferation and what we might call the deregulation of masculinity, or the extension of masculinity to nonmale bodies. Since masculinity is a sign of privilege in our society, it is much more heavily guarded than femininity. Young boys who exhibit feminine behavior are punished, not to protect femininity from male incursions but to encourage masculinity in male bodies; young girls who exhibit masculine behavior, on the other hand, are punished not only because their femininity is in jeopardy, but also because masculinity has been reserved exclusively for male bodies. The fostering of youthful female masculinity, therefore, can constitute a powerful assault on male privilege.

We might expect, having examined some of the "androgyny" literature and the research on the widespread nature of tomboyism, that the sociobiological research which links tomboyism to prenatally androgenized girls would make a strong case for the link between tomboyism and adult lesbianism or adult transsexuality. John Money's much quoted study, *Man and Woman, Boy and Girl* (1972), surprisingly holds back from such conclusions even when the evidence seems to point toward strong links between tomboyism and adult gender and sexual variance. Money studied a group of girls whose mothers had taken steroids during pregnancy to prevent miscarriage and another group of girls with female andrenogenital syndrome.[12] Money distinguishes between these groups by noting that within the first group, the fetally androgenized genetic females, some "masculinization of the clitoris" occurred (meaning it was deemed too big).[13] Usually surgical alteration of the girls' genitals would be recommended and no further treatment would be needed. In the second group, that of girls with female andrenogenital syndrome, the girl is virilized when her adrenal glands secrete androgen instead of cortisol. While it is not completely clear what the dangers of androgenization might be for the girl's health, Money notes:

> Because the abnormality of adrenocortical function does not correct itself postnatally, it is necessary for children with this condition to be regulated on cortisone therapy throughout the growing period and, indeed, in adulthood also. The regulation is imperative to prevent growth and maturation in childhood which is too rapid, too early, and too masculine. Otherwise the physique would simulate that of normal male puberty, but eight to ten years ahead of the normal time of male puberty. Of course, masculine puberty in a child living as a girl is unsightly and wrong. In later years, a girl does not desire to be hairy, deep-voiced and masculine in appearance, for which hormonal regulation on cortisone must be maintained. (1972: 97)

We do not know from this paragraph what the effects of prolonged cortisone therapy might be upon the health of the girl.[14] Furthermore, while obviously one would not want a girl to go through puberty prematurely, Money's comments on the effects of virilization upon girl bodies are oddly unscientific. Masculine puberty for a girl is "unsightly and wrong," he tells us, and he further assumes that no woman would want to grow up to be "hairy, deep-voiced and masculine." Since we all know women who are hairy, women who are deep-voiced, and women who are masculine, or are all three, it becomes apparent that much of the impetus for this research is the maintenance of dimorphic gender despite the proliferation of hybrid genders in "nature."[15]

In his comments about the psychosexual development of these girls, Money examines them for "tomboyism," which he defines according to a list of activities and preferences like "clothing and adornment," "childhood sexuality," "maternalism," and the like. Money reports that most of the women in both groups had strong tomboy identifications in childhood. But he also notes in relation to the prenatally androgenized girls: "it is of considerable importance that there were no indications of lesbianism in the erotic interests of the fetally androgenized girls, nor in their controls" (1972: 102); and for the other group he reports some incidence of homosexual fantasy but no lesbian identification or transsexuality. As Ann Fausto-Sterling has argued convincingly, much of the reclassification effort directed at intersexuals has to do with the challenge they pose to binary gender systems and compulsory heterosexuality. It is quite clear that Money's scientific research on intersexuals uses tomboyism as a benign form of childhood virilization which the girl is expected to outgrow. He has no real investment in learning about potential cross-gender identifications made by the girls or homoerotic desires that they may actively cultivate.

There is a sense of the absurd in some of Money's analysis which underscores the effort made by scientists to force irrational and multigendered behaviors into binary gender systems. For example, Money provides an index of tomboy behavior designed to definitively summarize the category: he lists formulae like "the ratio of athletic to sedentary energy expenditure is weighted in favor of vigorous activity, especially outdoors" (1972: 10). In other words, tomboys tend to be sporty and like to play hard. Or, "rehearsal of maternalism in childhood dollplay is negligible" (1972: 10). Basically this means that tomboys have no interest in playing mommy. Money follows this up with the observation that tomboys do not rule out the prospect of motherhood in the future, they just do not become too excited about it. He gives us a precise prediction: "the preference, in anticipation, is for one or two children, not a large family." Finally, my favorite tomboy characteristic as summarized by Money falls within the category of self-adornment. He tells us first that the tomboy favors utility over adornment and prefer slacks and shorts as far as clothing goes; but then in relation to makeup, Money categorically asserts that the tomboy's "cosmetic of choice is perfume!" This attempt to produce a definitive index of tomboy behavior and to pinpoint tomboy likes and dislikes both homogenizes the category and makes the tomboy sound pathological in relation to this set of desires. It also creates a firm sense of the predictability of tomboy behavior and therefore lends credibility to Money's assertion that there were no traces of lesbian identification among the group. The production in the social scientific and scientific research on tomboyism of such things as "tomboy indexes," "sex role inventories,"[16] and "destereotyping measures" almost invites parody, if only because such behavioral models take themselves so seriously. One only has to refer back to one's own childhood in order to produce counterexamples. Clearly, the emphasis upon explaining tomboyism, and doing so in highly detailed ways, makes tomboyism into an abnormal model of child development because of the scrutiny it endures. Imagine, for example, a "macho index" that might be developed and applied to young boys who show early signs of antisocial behavior (fighting, dominating conversations, rudeness, bullying). If scientific researchers spent time and money trying to evaluate whether there were a "macho boy syndrome" that may serve as a predictor for adult sexually abusive behavior or violent personalities, boys who fight a lot or act out aggressively would grow up thinking there was something very wrong with them (and there may well be). In other words, scientific attention can produce self-censoring among kids and adult scrutiny of otherwise normal childhood behavior.

A TV special on tomboys which aired in 1995 made clear some of the dangers of scientific observation of active and masculine identified girls. In a surprisingly even-handed NBC production of *Dateline*, the topic of tomboyism was presented in relation to the vexed issue of its predictive value for adult sexuality.[17] The program, entitled "Sugar and Spice," focused upon a new long-term study of tomboys being carried out by behavioral scientists at Northwestern University. The researchers, Michael Bailey and Sherry Berenbaum, claimed to be collecting data on tomboy behavior by observing and videotaping a hundred girls ranging in age from four to nine "who do everything a typical boy does." The scientists wanted to find out, among other things, how many of these little girls would grow up to be lesbians, although no mention was made of their interest in how many might turn out to be transsexual. One of the scientists suggested that 10 percent of tomboys become lesbian-identified. The two girls featured in the program responded to the questions of an extremely feminine interviewer (Victoria Corderi), who also interviewed their parents. One girl, Simone, aged eight, only played with boys, wore boys' clothes, and told the interviewer that she really liked to wear ties "especially with my suit." Simone showed no signs of shame about her gender identity in the short interview segments but, when her mother spoke to the interviewer she gave clues as to how Simone had been subtly pushed away from certain forms of boy identification. The mother recalled that Simone used to like to refer to herself as a boy and for a while would only wear boys' underwear. Simone's mother admitted that this had disturbed her and that she had expressed her distress to her daughter. Simone no longer said she was a boy or expressed a strong preference for boys' underwear. This suggested that Simone had been trained out of certain extreme forms of male identification.

Both Simone and the other tomboy, Jackie, told the interviewer that they hated playing with dolls and both said they tore the heads off dolls if asked to play with them. Simone's masculinity seemed quite developed and she boldly told the interviewer to refer to her as "handsome" rather than "pretty." Both girls were articulate about their tomboy habits and seemed comfortable speaking about them; Jackie in particular seemed to take a certain pleasure in the attention her behavior had garnered. Again, it was unclear how much the experience of being observed played into the girls' ability to articulate their gender identities. In one interesting segment of the program, the interviewer brought the four parents of the girls together and asked them how they felt about their children being studied in a project on sexual preference. The parents admitted that this was the first time they had been made aware of the link made in the study between tomboyism and lesbianism and Jackie's parents admitted to being a bit disturbed. Simone's parents, on the other hand, were not perturbed at all. They admitted that they had considered the possibility that Simone might grow up to be lesbian and they articulated a high degree of tolerance in relation to this possibility. While it is encouraging that at least some parents of tomboys evince no real anxiety about possibly queer adulthoods for their children, the interview with the parents did suggest that the researchers themselves expected parents to resist connections between tomboyism and lesbianism. The researchers had apparently not told the parents that the study focused in part on the development of sexual preference. Nor had they shared the information about the high incidence of lesbianism among tomboys.

Potential problems arising from such a research project were predictably not articulated within the program as the danger of producing homophobia. Rather, in an interview with feminist Ann Roiphe, the program suggested that the research was most threatening to the development of a strong model of heterosexual womanhood. Roiphe said she worried that the information produced in the study could be used by future parents to "limit their girl children's lives" and to "intimidate women." Roiphe stated: "I think that the fact that there is such a study tells us that people are afraid that strong girls will make strong women and that strong women won't make good wives and mothers, they won't be heterosexual and of course this is completely absurd." While Roiphe may well have been correct in assuming that the study gave evidence of considerable cultural anxiety around the meanings of cross-identifications among girls, she took an oddly conservative line on the adult futures of these girls. Her fear was that people would disassociate female heterosexuality from tomboy behavior; but, rather than argue that we should welcome the possibility of lesbian futures for tomboys, Roiphe asserted that tomboyism should be seen as perfectly consistent with being a future wife and mother. Roiphe's strategy of encouraging us to see tomboyism as a normal part of female development, like the androgyny studies and the scientific studies, tried to depathologize tomboyism not by affirming girl masculinities and lesbianism but by making links between tomboyism and "normal" heterosexuality. By using Roiphe as the sole critic of the study and by not interviewing any adult lesbians, this program inadvertently turned the viewer's attention away from the crucial topic of sexual tolerance and gender variance and back to the issue of how to channel all childhood behavior into the safe havens of heterosexual domesticity. "Sugar and Spice" ended optimistically by claiming that neither the researchers nor the parents wanted to try to change the tomboys but it did leave us in doubt as to whether any of these masculine girls would be allowed to extend their boyish ways into adolescence.

Within the context of social psychology and behavioral science, the development of normalizing models of female development and the cultivation of models of androgyny are far preferable to the gender-polarized alternatives which associate men and masculinity with all things good and active and women and femininity with all things bad and passive. Psychological models of sex roles, for example, have tended to define masculinity and femininity along the lines of familial roles and have made a distinction on this basis between masculine instrumentality and feminine expressiveness.[18] Within such strict models of gender, girls in particular are likely to be punished for nonconformity because the rules of feminine behavior are so much more confining. But it is important not to replace one set of gender prescriptions with another. Basically, as long as we define gender in terms of a binary system there will be boys and girls who cross-identify. It seems important to find ways to depathologize cross-identification rather than simply promoting gender mixing as a healthful alternative. There most definitely are many young girls who identify as boys, enjoy boys' games, play with boys' toys, prefer boys' clothes, and who, as preadolescents at least, reject the company of other girls. If "tomboy" becomes a generalized term for an active girlhood, then these cross-identifying children are once again cast in the role of deviant and are viewed as abnormal and atypical. As I suggested earlier, since the literature makes a huge distinction between normal and abnormal tomboyism we might want to give this cross-identifying and indeed "rogue" form of tomboyism another name: I am calling it "punk tomboyism."

The Rogue Tomboy

There is a long literary and cinematic history which celebrates boys as rebel outsiders. James Dean (*Rebel without A Cause*), Matt Dillon (*The Outsiders*), Johnny Depp (*Edward Scissorhands*), Christian Slater (*Pump Up the Volume*) all represent the power of the sullen and recalcitrant white youth who says no to paternal authority. While James Dean pouted his way into the hearts of several generations of bad boys and girls, there is simply no cinematic girl equivalent for the rebel icon. When girls do rebel on film, it is usually by running off with a boy rather than by refusing heterosexual courtship or renouncing femininity altogether. Boy rebellion as exhibited by a Brando or a Brad Pitt is accompanied by motorbikes and guns, sexy indifference to authority, and a violent but maverick sensibility; girl rebellion as exhibited by a Sissy Spacek or a Juliet Lewis represents only precocious sexual knowledge, rejection of the father for the boyfriend, too much makeup, and other markers of dangerous femininity. Indeed, the recent spate of killer girl movies (*Heavenly Creatures, Fun*) might be seen as one alternative to the depiction of girls as helpless and passive and trapped within powerless models of femininity. These killer girl films represent girlhood as a tenuous balance between rage and hysteria which could erupt at any moment into violent outrage.

While few if any contemporary girl films focus upon the masculine tomboy, there was a set of tomboy films from the late 1950s to the early 1980s which examined the forms and contours of tomboy rebellion.[19] To a certain extent, the tomboy film is an offshoot or variation of another more mainstream genre, the boy film. Hollywood, as we know, loves stories about little boys. It doesn't really matter what the little boys are doing; they might be growing up or refusing to, bonding with a pet or torturing it; they could be playing with aliens, struggling to get by without a father or a mother or both; they might be good or evil, smart or impaired, left home alone or reunited with a family. The timeless popularity of the boy movie suggests that the transformation of boy into man is endlessly interesting to this culture. Predictably enough, there seems to be little or no interest in girls in Hollywood unless they are becoming the sexual objects of male desire. But this has not always been the case and indeed the girl movie has not always been such a debased category.

In *Hollywood Androgyny*, Rebecca Bell-Metereau suggests that "the popularity of the tomboy reached its peak in the years after the second World War" and she points to films like *National Velvet* (1945) and *Pat and Mike* (1952) as examples.[20] I think it is fair to say, however, that the heyday of the tomboy film was the 1970s and 1980s when a plethora of tomboy films were made featuring butch, wise-cracking, aggressive little tykes like Jodie Foster (*Foxes*, 1980 and *Alice Doesn't Live Here Anymore*, 1974), Tatum O'Neal (*Paper Moon*, 1973) and Kristie McNicholls (*Little Darlings*, 1980). These movies made girlhood interesting and exciting and even sexy. They also, of course, tended to imagine girlhood as tomboyhood.

In the 1970s and 1980s, the effect of the rise of feminism in the 1960s were finally beginning to affect child rearing. Tomboyism flourished in a climate of liberal parenting where parents were questioning sex role orientation and challenging the conventional wisdom about girls and boys. Within such a climate, feminists and others may well have thought that change begins at home and that the way to intervene most effectively in the seemingly concrete and rigid societal standards for female behavior (and misbehavior) was to bring up children differently. In the 1970s, moreover, there was finally a visible gay and lesbian community in the United States and in the wake of the Stonewall rebellion, many "gay power" groups sprang up across the country.[21] Of course, as gays and lesbians became more visible throughout the decade, the effects of that visibility changed. While at first queer visibility offered the promise of some kind of proliferation of sympathetic representations of gays and lesbians, as I showed earlier, the tomboy within a public psychologized discourse on homosexuality threatened to become the precursor to queer adulthood. The tomboy film featuring masculine girls faded from view by the end of the 1980s partly on account of the implicit link between tomboys and lesbians. Nowadays, the few tomboy films that appear (*Harriet the Spy*, 1996, for example) have to feature properly feminine girls. Indeed a 1997 remake of *The Member of the Wedding* as a made-for-TV movie featured the feminine actress Anna Paquin as Frankie Addams.

In the early 1970s child stars such as Tatum O'Neal, Kristy Mc-Nicholls, and Jodie Foster regularly played spunky tomboys with attitude and smarts; there were also, by the end of the decade, teen actresses such as Robin Johnson and Pamela Segall who portrayed the anguish of adolescence within an oddly gendered body. "They're gonna see who I am," shouts Robin Johnson as Nickie in the classic punk girl movie *Times Square* (1980). Her desire to be seen as something or someone other than a presexual woman propels her on a rocky search for fame that takes on heroic proportions. And, like the tragic hero, she suffers for her ambition. *Times Square* featured two girls on the run from parents, the law, and boys. To the accompaniment of a fine punk-influenced sound track, Nickie and Pammie very specifically aim their attack at the media. Their signature act of rebellion is to throw TVs off the top of buildings. This image of two wild girls—Thelma and Louise for juniors—destroying televisions is a perfect representation of girls bashing back loudly, angrily, and violently against their invisibility. It is also a perfect image of the two types of tomboyism that I have identified here and their different trajectories. Nickie is male identified, takes a male name, and aspires to be a rock star. Pammie is also rebellious and she struggles with the parameters of conventional femininity but she is not masculine. The two girls are involved in a beautifully nuanced teenage butch-femme dynamic but explicit lesbian content was edited out of the film.[22]

The original tragic hero of adolescent growing pains, as I mentioned earlier, was Frankie Addams as played by Julie Harris in *The Member of the Wedding* (1953). Fred Zinneman's adaptation of Carson McCullers's novel perfectly captures the balance between comedy and tragedy in this story. The set is sweaty and claustrophobic and the camera stays almost exclusively in the hot confines of the family kitchen. In one of the few outside scenes, Frankie runs onto the porch to greet the girls in the neighborhood girl club. "Am I the new member?" Frankie demands urgently as the girls march through her yard. The camera moves back and forth between the real girls, the emblems of true femininity and the ragtaggle tomboy Frankie who awaits their answer. "No," answers one particularly groomed girl, "you're not the new member." But of course Frankie has never been and will never be a member, has never belonged, and will never succumb to the pressure to be a heterosexual and feminine girl.

This film version of *The Member of the Wedding* draws attention to the clubby nature of gender: Esther Waters reminds Frankie of the definition of a club: "there must be members and non-members." Waters's character, Berenice, also articulates membership in relation to racial relations in the South in the 1950s, and the film and the book strenuously link racial oppression to gender oppression within the matrix of prejudices that characterized the South in the 1950s. While obviously unbelonging is a historical legacy for blacks in the South, the nonmembers of the club of white girls are the tomboys and pre-butches; the not-girls who struggle to make gender fit and who attempt to squash their angular and flat bodies into the curves of naturalized femininity. Failure to assimilate to the demands of femininity, of course, spells trouble for the tomboy by imagining a queer future for her butch body. *The Member of the Wedding* emphasizes the tragic nature of the tomboy quest and quietly confines the tomboy to a past better forgotten and left behind; the tomboy's tragedy is to be forced to blossom into a quiescent form of young adult femininity. In *The Member of the Wedding*, the tomboy is also paired up with a more feminine girl. While in *Times Square*, Nickie paired up with the little rich girl Pammie, in *The Member of the Wedding*, Frankie fantasizes about Mary Littlejohn. The novel suggests, however, that since Frankie cannot have Mary, she must become her. Thus the lesbian bond between the girls is transformed from desire into identification.

Thirty years after the release of *The Member of the Wedding*, the tomboy couple shows up again in *Little Darlings*, starring Tatum O'Neal and Kristy McNicholls. McNicholls and O'Neal play opposite ends of tomboyism in this film about a group of girls spending the summer together at Camp Little Wolf. McNicholls plays Angel Bright, a fatherless girl from the wrong side of the tracks whose mother smokes and wears sexy dresses and drives a big American car. Angel is a tomboy in an oedipally inflected relation to her mother who swaggers around the neighborhood in denims, beating up boys. O'Neal plays a motherless rich girl, Ferris Whitney, whose father is somewhat negligent and drives her to camp in a big Rolls Royce. The names of the girls suggest the archetypal opposition they represent. Angel Bright is the white trash devil child who turns out to have a heart of gold, and Ferris reveals an inner toughness (Ferris might refer etymologically to "iron") which is only superficially covered over by her rich and snotty exterior. McNicholls as Angel performs a truly butch tomboy, and while Ferris wears masculine clothing at the beginning of the film, her tomboyism develops as a wholly feminine form of rebelliousness.

Angel and Ferris are immediately linked by the other girls at camp as different kinds of outsiders. In a classic bathroom confrontation scene, the pretty girl of the group asks Angel and Ferris whether they are still virgins. "I think guys are a pain in the ass," intones Angel. Another girl snickers, "They are probably lezzies," and Ferris responds quickly: "*She* may be but I am straight!" Significantly, Angel does not deny the charge of lesbianism. Instead she defiantly makes a grab for the older girl's breasts and wrestles with her. Although the rest of the film degenerates into a competition between Angel and Ferris over who can lose her virginity first, the bond between Ferris and Angel is nicely established in this central bathroom scene. While in women's prison films the bathroom tends to be the scene of torture and sexual assault, in the tomboy film the bathroom, with its woman's sign on the door and its mirror-covered interior, becomes an active gender zone. Females are literally divided up here into women and girls, girls and not-girls, straights and dykes. Kristy McNicholls's tough stand in this bathroom scene echoes Julie Harris's outrage against the girls in her neighborhood club. And Tatum O'Neal's role as the nonmasculine tomboy reprises an earlier tomboy role she played in *Paper Moon* (1973).

In a comedic tomboy film, *Something Special* (1986, dir. Paul Schneider),[23] the tomboy narrative plays in and through a narrative of hermaphroditism. In this odd movie, a tomboy is granted her deepest and darkest wish one night when she wakes up with something very special—a penis. Millie Niceman changes her name appropriately to Willy and attempts to acclimate herself to boyhood. Gender trouble in this made-for-TV movie comes in the form of family pressures to be one of two available genders. Mr. and Mrs. Niceman confirm the doctor's opinion that Willy must choose a gender and stick with it. Willy asks pragmatically, "Can't I be both?" Mr. Niceman explodes with outrage and says, "There will be no girlish boys and no boyish girls in this house!" While this scene is humorous in the way it depicts a struggle between the parents as they try to convince their child that s/he must pick either his or her "side," it is troubling in the way it resolves the problem of intersexuality or transsexuality by abjecting gender ambiguity. It is in-betweenness (not androgyny but the active construction of new genders) here and elsewhere in the history of tomboys that inspires rage and terror in parents, coworkers, lovers, and bosses. As soon as the tomboy locates herself in another gender or in an affirmative relation to masculinity, trouble begins and science, psychology, family, and other social forces are all applied to reinforce binary gender laws. As Willy, Millie Niceman is at first lulled into the pleasures of boyhood: clothing, new freedoms, new privileges. However, the film reverses its originally transgressive premise by creating a rather predictable obstacle to the transition Willy seems to be making with no trouble from female to male. Suddenly, Willy is forced to confront the fact that his best male friend is also the object of his desire and while he may have changed sex, he has not escaped compulsory heterosexuality. With the specter of homosexuality looming in the not too distant future, Willy wishes to return to his girl self and gender normativity is restored.

The tomboy film has long since disappeared as a distinct genre and it is worth asking why. Where are the next generation of girl actors, sassy girls playing tough tomboys and pushing the limits of compulsory femininity? And what exactly is the threat of the little girl film and the tomboy aesthetic? One can only speculate, but it seems reasonable to suppose that the tomboy movie threatened an unresolved gender crisis and projected or predicted butch and transgender adulthoods. There is always the dread possibility, in other words, that the tomboy will not grow out of her butch stage and will never become a member of the wedding. Today we have only boy movies (think of *Free Willy*) and the girls are relegated to dumb sisters, silly crybabies, and weak playmates. Quite obviously, Hollywood sees tomboy films as a queer cinema for preteens. Boys can be shown bonding, hiking together, fighting, discovering dead bodies, killing people, killing each other; but even the suggestion that girls might be shown doing similar things raises the specter of the dyke. Girls in films tend to fight each other for boys (*Heathers*) or for older men (*Poison Ivy*) or just fight. They do not bond, they do not rebel, they do not learn, they do not like themselves, and perhaps most important, they do not like each other. In the rogue tomboy films, rebellious girls are locked into intense tomboy bonds and one girl often plays a butch role to the other girl's femme. Both these forms of queer tomboyism may threaten queer futures but it is the masculine tomboy who is singled out for the most severe forms of social reorientation.

Conclusion

Current research on tomboyism allows for the possibility that a high percentage of tomboys may well grow up to be lesbians. Much of the information circulating on tomboyism seems profoundly unclear about how researchers and parents should think about the relation between adult lesbianism and childhood tomboyism, and a variety of strategies have been used to temper the threat of queer adulthoods. The androgyny model presumes that gender polarization is counterproductive and sees tomboyism as a useful way of opposing social mandates to adhere to gender protocols. The androgyny literature, however, tries to downplay the possibility of strong tomboy cross-identification or masculinity. Scientific research on intersexed girls tends to channel all ambiguous bodies into binary genders and has no interest in promoting the gender variance and multisexuality made possible by such bodies. In cultural arenas, the tomboy narrative tells of the pain of tomboyism and the trials and tribulations of the tomboy who refuses to grow up and some films and novels offer alternative models of queer youth.

In this essay I have tried to offer an alternative model of the tomboy, one which rejects androgyny and binary gender systems, revels in girl masculinity, and encourages queer adulthoods (homo- or transsexual). The punk tomboy defies conventional gender paradigms and should be congratulated for her clear efforts to remake childhood gender. Punk tomboys like Nickie in *Times Square*, Frankie in *The Member of the Wedding*, Angel in *Little Darlings*, Willy in *Something Special*, and Simone and Jackie in the TV program "Sugar and Spice" all offer unique challenges to the Victorian notion that little girls should be seen and not heard and the current sense that little girls can be boys as long as they grow up to be heterosexual women. To such popular wisdom, the punk tomboy offers her own unique response: "Oh bondage! Up Yours!"

NOTES

Many thanks to Gayatri Gopinath who read and commented on many different drafts of this essay. Some of my discussions of tomboy movies are drawn from the clip show "Looking Butch: A Rough Guide to Butches on Film" which was cocurated with Jenni Olson and which also appears in my book *Female Masculinity* (Durham: Duke University Press, 1998).

1. Angela McRobbie and Jenny Garber, "Girls and Subcultures" (1975), in *The Subcultures Reader*, eds. Ken Gelder and Sarah Thornton (London and New York: Routledge, 1997), 114.

2. Most of the literature on tomboys and sissy boys makes this claim. The classic reference for the continued intolerance of sissy boys in Richard Green who claimed that the term "sissy boy" is always used as an insult while "tomboy" is not. He also argued that tomboyism is a common stage within female development and most women simply pass through it unscathed and then outgrow it. Green's argument was devised to argue for the "management" of the sissy-boy syndrome. See Richard Green, *The Sissy Boy Syndrome and the Development of Homosexuality* (New Haven: Yale University Press, 1987); also, *Human Sexuality: A Health Practitioner's Text* (Baltimore: Williams and Wilkins, 1975).

3. For more on the punishment of tomboys, see Phyllis Burke, *Gender Shock: Exploding the Myths of Male and Female* (New York: Anchor Books, 1996). Burke analyzes some recent case histories of so-called GID or Gender Identity Disorder in which little girls are carefully conditioned out of male behavior and into exceedingly constrictive forms of femininity.

4. Virginia Spencer Carr, *The Lonely Hunter: A Biography of Carson McCullers* (New York: Doubleday, 1975), 29–31.

5. Carson McCullers, *The Member of the Wedding* (1946; New York: Bantam, 1973), 1.

6. See R. Helson, "Is the Traditional Role Bad for Women?" *Journal of Personality and Social Psychology* 59 (1990):311–320; Sandra Lipsitz Bem, "Dismantling Gender Polarization and Compulsory Heterosexuality: Should We Turn the Volume Up or Down?" *Journal of Sex Research* 32, 4 (fall 1995):329.

7. Shawn Meaghan Burn, A. Kathleen, and Shirley Neverend, "Tomboyism and Adult Androgyny," *Sex Roles: A Journal of Research* 34, 5–6 (1996):419–29.

8. Pat Plumb and Gloria Cowan, "A Developmental Study of Destereotyping and Androgynous Activity Preferences of Tomboys, Nontomboys, and Males," *Sex Roles* 10, 9–10 (1984):703.

9. Janet S. Hyde, B. G. Rosenberg, and Jo Ann Behrman, "Tomboyism," *Psychology of Women Quarterly* 2, 1 (fall 1977):73–75.

10. Sandra L. Bem, *The Lenses of Gender: Transforming the Debate on Sexual Inequality* (New Haven and London: Yale University Press, 1993), 125.

11. Indeed, the feminist opposition to both gender polarization among lesbians (butch-femme) and transsexuality provides ample evidence of just such a historical conflict between feminists and queers over the cultural and political implications of extreme cross-identification. See Janice Raymond, *The Transsexual Empire: The Making of the She-Male* (Boston: Beacon Press, 1979); and Sandy Stone's critique of Raymond in "The 'Empire' Strikes Back: A Posttranssexual Manifesto" in *Body Guards: The Cultural Politics of Gender Ambiguity*, eds. Julia Epstein and Kristina Straub (New York: Routledge, 1993), 280–304.

12. John Money, *Man and Woman, Boy and Girl* (Baltimore: Johns Hopkins University Press, 1972).

13. It is important to know that the parameters for normal clitoral size are extremely narrow and many girls not exposed to steroids prenatally may also be deemed irregular in relation to large clitorises. Doctors have been quite comfortable until recently with cutting the clitoris to "normalize" its appearance. See Suzanne Kessler, *Lessons from the Intersexed* (New Brunswick, N.J.: Rutgers University Press, 1998).

14. Sandra Bem, in her analysis of Money's studies, suggests that "because of either their continuing cortisone therapy or both, all twenty-five of the fetally masculinized girls were, in a sense, chronically ill during some part of their childhood." Bem, *The Lenses of Gender*, 26.

15. See Ann Fausto-Sterling, "The Five Sexes: Why Male and Female Are Not Enough," *The Sciences* (March/April 1993):20–24. Fausto-Sterling examines the surgical interventions made by modern medicine upon the intersexed body and concludes: "Society mandates the control of intersexed bodies because they blur and bridge the great divide. inasmuch as hermaphrodites literally embody both sexes, they challenge traditional beliefs about sexual difference: they possess the irritating ability to live sometimes as one sex and sometimes as the other, and they raise the specter of homosexuality" (1993: 24).

16. See S. Bem, "The Measurement of Psychological Androgyny," *Journal of Consulting and Clinical Psychology* 42, 2 (1974):155–62.

17. Deborah Copaken (producer) and Billy Ray (editor), "Sugar and Spice," NBC *Dateline* (April 14, 1995). Thanks to Larry Gross for copying and sending me this tape.

18. For a discussion of such sex role definitions, see Ellen Piel Cook, *Psychological Androgyny* (New York: Pergamon, 1985).

19. In *Hollywood Androgyny*, Rebecca Bell-Metereau also creates a tomboy category but this is within a chapter on "male impersonation" and she links the tomboy to the "female cross-dresser who acts as a buddy" (1993:95). See Rebecca Bell-Metereau, *Hollywood Androgyny* (New York: Columbia University Press, 1993). I do not see the tomboy as either a male impersonator or a cross-dresser but as a preadolescent gender within which the adult imperatives of binary gender have not yet taken hold. Bell-Metereau also stopped her summary of tomboy movies with *The Member of the Wedding*, and many tomboy films were yet to come after this film was made in 1953.

20. Bell-Metereau, *Hollywood Androgyny*, 96.

21. See John D'Emilio and Estelle Freeman, *Intimate Matters: A History of Sexuality in America* (New York: Harper and Row, 1988), 319.

22. For more on the fascinating production history of *Times Square*, see Jenni Olson, *The Ultimate Guide to Lesbian and Gay Film and Video* (New York and London: Serpents Tail, 1996).

23. This film was also released as *Willie/Millie* and *I Was a Teenage Boy*.

Eight

Sexing the Tomboy

Lee Zevy

The following account describes a pivotal day in the life of a young lesbian tomboy which remained embedded in her memory as exemplifying the euphoria, risks, realizations, and actions which forced her sexuality underground.

It began one beautiful morning when my buddies (Jimmy, the leader; Tommy, Jimmy's sidekick, Boonsie, a black boy whose name was Daniel, Goofy, a large, slow, gangling kid, tolerated but not accepted) and I were going to explore the swampy hilly landfill behind the place we lived. This was a mysterious place of ponds, tall grasses and burning underground garbage that lead to the Bronx River where the older boys swam and did secret things.

I dressed carefully that day in clothing which I believed to have power, my leather Tyrolean shorts with the green and red suspenders worn without a shirt and red high top sneakers. I couldn't do anything with my hair which my mother made me wear in braids so I snuck out my father's fifteen inch navy knife. After I dressed I grabbed a quick breakfast and ran out to meet the guys, all of us punching each other and wrestling before we started out.

My buddies and I carried clothespin constructed match guns and as we hiked along through the tall grasses we each in turn fired a match setting the grass on fire and then quickly stamping it out before it got out of hand. As I shot my match and put out the fire they all swooped and shouted and pounded me on the back as one of the guys.

When we moved through a tunnel of tall grasses toward the river Goofy had to take a leak and disappeared into the grass. Jimmy looked at us with a knowing grin and said that Goofy had a thing that was so long that he had to tie it to his leg so it wouldn't swing around. I laughed along with the others but suddenly felt uneasy and separate, a feeling which grew as we arrived at the river and the guys made cracks about swimming naked and running into used condoms. I was glad when we started back.

Things were going well now, we were tired and relaxed and trudging through the reeds into a clearing when we ran into a group of big muscled teenagers. Jimmy and Tommy hitched up their pants and moved into the group. Boonsie, Goofy and I stayed on the periphery until the leader looked at me more closely, poked me in the chest and laughed to his guys that I was a girl. When he taunted my guys that they ran with a girl they all stepped away and I was alone. The leader was not done, he leaned toward me leering "Hey, you ever been laid?" I panicked and mumbled something about being late and ran back down the hill to home.

I was really shaken and scared but still needed to maintain my tough image. I couldn't tell my older sister who was standing in a circle of her friends watching the older boys haul themselves hand over hand across a rope strung between two trees. The girls would call out encouragement to the boys they liked and laughed among themselves as the boys strutted and responded with more risky maneuvers dangling over the excited girls.

I kept telling myself that I could probably pull myself across but realized with increasing despair that I might fail and who would care anyway. The boys would just laugh and none of the girls would be excited by my efforts. As I edged closer to my sister for comfort one of her friends commented that wasn't I really too old to be going around without a shirt. I felt humiliated. Although my sister came to my defense too much had happened throughout the day which taught me the meaning of being an outsider and I went in to put on a shirt and close down.[1]

The difficulty with using a socially constructed category like *tomboy*,[2] viewed as a presexual period, to explain a lesbian childhood is that it separates sexuality from childhood. This separation is incorrect and damaging.

All sexual development, including the lesbian, begins in infancy and continues throughout the life span. A theory which proposes that lesbian development begins at adolescence, where sexual identity is focused around object choice, fails to acknowledge the developmental continuum of lesbian sexuality. This continuum extends from infancy (maternal erotic desire) through childhood (pregenital sexuality) and into adolescence and adulthood (genital sexuality/object choice) *in one continuous developmental line,* which shares similarities with but is different from, heterosexual development. Although for some lesbians sexual preference is felt during early childhood, most lesbians experience early manifestations of sexuality within a matrix of desire, admiration, adoration, specialness, pleasure, understanding, reflection, excitement, longing, and fantasy which form the foundation for all sexual desire and activity. For many young lesbians unaware of their sexuality, the actual felt experience of sexuality is subsumed within tomboy behavior in sports, action, or fantasy (heroic rescue, best girlfriend/buddy, or caretaking) or manifested as a reaction formation in which they reject all association with girls. Hillary Mullins makes this point when she writes, "In the beginning, it had nothing to do with liking girls. In fact, being a tomboy was not about whom I liked at all: it was about what I liked. . . . I certainly never worried about being a lesbian."[3] Desire, as in Mullins's case, is often transformed into an inchoate longing or depression or a feeling that something is missing and one is not like other girls.

Sexual desire for women is at the core of the lesbian experience. It is the one thing which will carry them through the negative experiences and heterosexual inundation toward eventual relationships with women. The desire to be desired by someone one desires is a basic need originating in the childhood need to be desirable to one's parents, siblings, relatives, friends, and others. Maternal erotic desire forms the foundation for the experience of sexual desire and is a natural outgrowth of nurturing and caretaking.

> The beginning of relating is evident in babies as young as three days: they show distinct sensory preferences for their mothers and select by smell the breast pads of their own mothers. . . . Much attention has been given to the sensual bonding of feeding, bathing, cooing, and holding of the first year of life. . . . This sensual, erotic attachment proceeds developmentally and includes reciprocal visual, tactile, olfactory, taste and auditory behaviors, cues and fantasies.[4]

Wells and Wrye go on to stipulate that, "The early sensual bond between mother and baby . . . [t]hat love affair becomes the basis of loving relations and all eroticism after the separation-individuation phase."[5]

Yet Freudian theory, which codified societal norms into psychology, stipulates that in normal development by ages two or three girls are supposed to relinquish their own maternal desire and transfer their erotic needs to their fathers and eventually to other men. For heterosexual girls this shift away from the mother is often an inadequate substitute, and for the lesbian child it is a confusing and harmful process.

As with all children, lesbian psychological and emotional growth is fostered by the mirroring of desire by loving caretakers through carefully synchronized and acceptable forms of social and emotional expression. But for the lesbian girl, mirroring of desire toward women is rarely achieved. Mirroring occurs in all aspects of daily caretaking when the parental figures reflect approval, excitement, and love back to the child in linguistic, paralinguistic, and nonverbal ways for whatever the child expresses emotionally, verbalizes, and performs in activity. Mirroring begins at birth when the maternal figure looks at the child looking, smiles at the child smiling, and so forth until the child is old enough to have internalized the caretaker who then becomes part of the positive sense of self. Buloff and Osterman expound upon the damage which occurs when the mirroring of desire by parents is lacking:

> It is the attunement of early primary figures to the child's developing sense of self that enables her to consolidate that self. . . . Reflection of support, nurturance, pleasure and understanding to the child are essential to the growth of the authentic self. . . . Peering into the face of society, much as a child looks into the face of her parent, the lesbian looks for a reflection of her self. She does not see Kohut's "gleam in the mother's eye."[6]

This gleam is the essence of the mirroring function.[7] Communication takes place over a tightly braided pattern of linguistic, paralinguistic, and nonverbal (bodily) cues. Adults who fail to mirror appropriate approval cues ("the gleam in the mother's eye") for the behavior and personality of the lesbian child *teach that child to disengage from contact*.

Society at large does not respond well to sexual ambiguity, particularly in children. One father described how adults would become angry with him because his baby daughter was dressed in blue.[8] In addition to the negative responses from family and significant adults, social reinforcement for heterosexual behavior takes place on every level so that,

> [f]rom the time she is old enough to have access to the media, this child will be inundated by programs, commercials and cartoons devoid of lesbian images [author's note: and limited images that reflect positive relationships between women or girls] and filled with heterosexual implications. She will be read fairy tales where the aim is always to get the prince. If she shows more than an average interest in boys' activities and toys, she will be seen as a tomboy. Although this is hardly as pejorative a label as sissy, it still brands her as different.[9]

Lesbian emotional survival depends upon the control of desire so that the true object of that desire is not visible. The problem is that desire which is toxic first becomes constricted, then diminished, and finally denied. Erhenberg calls this process "a denial of desire" and describes individuals with this problem as presenting "themselves as walking zombies, living a living death, incapable of feeling, caring, wanting, and as a result unable to relate to others." She further explains that, "The experience of desire itself may come to be feared because desiring may be seen as being tantamount to opening oneself to the possibility of being hurt, disappointed, frustrated, exploited or betrayed."[10]

As I have illuminated elsewhere,[11] "in the 1940s from the age of two and a half, I behaved more like a boy, identifying with male characteristics and trying to wear male clothing. In nursery school, where other girls were generally neater, cleaner, more reserved, and more easily upset, I was active, aggressive and defiant, played more roughly, and took more risks than girls were typically permitted. And I would not nap without my football. My parents indulged this behavior at home but it angered and irritated my teachers and other adults, earning me the label of bad and disruptive. I began, at two-and-a-half, to deceive my teachers and hide my real feelings. Because I already identified with many male characteristics and was often responded to as a boy, I developed what would become lifelong problems. Because I was always engaged in a struggle with others who tried to force me into girl behavior I responded by communicating as if I were male, with the behavior, mannerisms, cues, signals, and responses of boys. Finally, in my effort to achieve what I saw as the epitome of maleness and to avoid the humiliation of being taken as female, I increasingly avoided emotional communication. Although this served to protect my internalized male image, I increasingly denied emotional and physical desires (including affection) to avoid being taken the wrong way. As I grew older this problem propelled me into a lifelong battle with invisibility.[12]

In such a homophobic, sexist, and misogynistic culture, practically all lesbians experience some degree of "denial of desire" during childhood from familial, psychological, cultural, or institutional pressures. This denial of desire is compounded when there are additional traumatic experiences of sexual and physical abuse. The seriousness of this problem cannot be underestimated when carried into lesbian adulthood. Left untreated, it is a major contributing factor in the development of eating disorders, alcoholism (an epidemic in the lesbian community), and other forms of addiction and self-harming behaviors.

Tomboyism as a fluid, creative physical/emotional construction has always been sandwiched between male/female social norms and relegated to a place of little significance. Because it is usually regarded as a "phase, a condition that girls pass through on their way to growing up and becoming women,"[13] it has been overlooked as a place of valuable learning for girls. During this period they not only learn the nurturing and social skills which will gain them acceptance into a female world, but also learn about behavior which will help them obtain power, mobility, and visibility. They will learn about adventure, activity, irreverence, fighting, competition, bonding, risk taking, and other tools from which they can gain confidence and self-esteem to be utilized later in life. In the nineties this play space has been extended, so that in animated action shows on children's television women are routinely portrayed as fighting alongside men and even transforming themselves into robots, cars, and planes along with their male buddies. However, they are still bound by sexuality, love, and loyalty to their male leaders and partners by a very male-defined viewpoint. Although the play space may have changed, so that women are now routinely on the field and in the professions and business, the boundary between acceptable behavior for men and women still exists and in some ways requires more vigilance because it is so variable.

Tomboys exists in a wonderfully fluid play space which signifies both excitement and praise for girls to leave the constriction of female behavior and a warning of potential sexual transgression if they encroach too far into the male domain. Although norms for men and women have become more congruent in some parts of the world, this

understanding of the tomboy remains attached to culturally determined boundary relaxations and constraints which control and
threaten girls who leave one sphere and transgress too far into another. Even where the expectations for women's behavior have
changed, being seen and labeled as a tomboy still means that a girl
leaves the safety and security of socially expected behavior (however
her culture determines it) and enters an exciting but potentially dangerous play space, wherein she can create herself as long as she is
careful not to approach the dangerous boundary separating her from
"all male territory." She can participate in boys' activities which seem
to be centered around physically active group or team games, singular
physical activities like climbing trees, getting dirty, taking risks, and
wearing male attire. Most, if not all, of the rationale for leaving a
space designated as feminine and moving toward one seen as masculine is to attain a sense of freedom and accomplishment, given that
tomboys always experience the feminine norm as a place of constriction and the male one as a place of action. Where a tomboy receives
familial and community support she can usually remain relatively free
of boundary problems until she approaches puberty, when sexual
pairing becomes an imperative. Although it is usually a given for
heterosexual women who wish to marry that they relinquish many
tomboy freedoms in adolescence, for lesbians it is precisely these traits
which will guide their sexuality. Latency or prepuberty—often considered a time for female bonding and a place to learn about sexuality
from girlfriends who help make the transition to heterosexual
relationships—is not a transitional place for lesbians but the reality of
what will be their eventual sexual relationships.

Tomboys have always been treated as an asexual entity, a phase, a
time of cuteness. This image completely belies the reality for tomboy
lesbians during childhood. Unlike their heterosexual counterparts, lesbian tomboys bring to this period of life an intensity and dedication
which will form the core of their future self-identification as lesbians.
As such they will utilize this relatively safe time to learn about asser-
tiveness, attachment, desire, and other aspects of sexuality which are
pregenital in nature.

In addition to describing themselves as "having been different"
from other children, lesbians frequently describe themselves as more
masculine than their heterosexual counterparts.[14] However, these
statements never indicate the range and variation of these masculine

identifications and the role they play in the adult sexual identities of lesbians. The broad spectrum of identification in the following accounts of early tomboy life attests to the influence of early behavior on adult sexual choice.

One woman, who is now living a lesbian life but considers herself to be bisexual, recounted, "I used to wheel my doll carriage to the ball field and park it so I could run over and play whatever games the boys were playing. Afterward, I would collect my doll and go home. Sometimes I would play with the girls, sometimes with the boys."[15] Another woman, who had been with men but is now exclusively with women, explained, "If you didn't wear pants and sneakers and run with the neighborhood pack playing boys' games then you didn't play at all. I had to tell the mother of a new girl that the reason no one would play with her is that she wore dresses and was too clean."[16] Then there were girls like the one in the opening narrative who wanted to run with the boys and be boylike, but at the same time allowed the adults to preserve her ability to partially fit in by keeping her hair in braids and wearing dresses to school or social events. She fit in externally even as her internal self resisted, and then withdrew.

Finally, there are children who incorporate masculinity in all aspects. In *Stone Butch Blues*, Leslie Feinberg writes,

> I didn't want to be different. I longed to be everything grownups wanted, so they would love me. But there was something about me that made them knit their eyebrows and frown. No one ever offered a name for what was wrong with me.... I only came to recognize its melody through this constant refrain, "Is that a boy or a girl?"[17]

Or in Julia Penelope's *Call Me Lesbian*,

> I decided that something I'd done in a past life (my karma) had dictated that I would spend my life as a male soul "trapped" in a female body, as punishment for some transgression.... I was uncomfortable with my femaleness (at least what I was told I was supposed to be as a "female") because I couldn't accept the weakness, passivity, and powerlessness that such "femaleness" required.
>
> Since I refused to be "female," as I understood it, I concluded I had to be "male."[18]

In each of these accounts these women's tomboy worlds had circumscribed boundaries which they understood and negotiated. They accomplished this negotiation successfully where the dangers and risks were manageable, or with tremendous difficulty and prejudice where the integrity of the developing core self ran counter to social role expectations.

Tomboys have always had to be allowed to be in their space. They are allowed by mothers, most of whom seem to have been tomboys themselves and who accept tomboyish behavior on the part of their daughters[19] and by fathers who favor daughters who identify with aspects of their maleness. In particular, they are allowed by the boys they wish to join and by the other parents and community. The degree to which a tomboy will be tolerated and liked or disliked depends on whether she attends to and keeps a distance from the boundary of all male behavior which is always bound up in sexuality and the male ownership of sexual difference.[20]

In a recent *New York Magazine* article (June 16, 1997), a teenager accused of murder was maligned by her peers for trying to be male.

> "She was a guy," says Sam 15. . . . "A friend of mine once grabbed her chest," says another boy, "to make sure she had breasts." Daphne turned around and walloped the kid." . . . "She was trying to be a thug," says Josh, 15. . . . "She'd walk along doing the homeboy roll, her fists clenched when she walked," says Will 17, "She was all 'yo' this and 'chillin' that. She was taking the hoodlum-guy thing to the extreme."[21]

The lesbian tomboy exists in a tenuous arena which can turn nasty or sexual at any time if the boundary of male sexuality is breached or shifts unexpectedly. For lesbian tomboys who did not feel "different" or identify themselves as lesbian until adulthood, the boundaries into dangerous "male territory" were never pushed too far. However, there are a substantial number of lesbian tomboys for whom excursion into "male territory" was a part of their core identity. This was true whether the tomboy was aware that her "difference" pertained to a sexual interest in girls or not. Mullins makes this point:

> an older boy playing with us while he waited for the high school bus took offense at my participation and warned me to clear out. When I tried to ignore him, hoping his hostility would blow over, he bullied me back of Town Hall and pummeled me, saying as he left me lying tear-streaked in the dust, "That'll teach you to try to be a boy."[22]

Such experiences are common among lesbian tomboys when a line has been trespassed. They are punished with violence associated with actual or threatened sexual domination. In writing about lesbian sexuality, Nicols quotes Apuzzo, who suggests that "incest may be perpetrated upon young tomboy girls [who are somewhat more likely to grow up to be lesbians, as reported by Bell, Weinberg, and Hammersmith] as a way of punishing them and 'keeping them in line.' "[23]

Mullins supports this theory when she continues to recount how the "boys closing ranks against me as a girl" turned into incest by an older cousin and, at his instigation, her brother. Her explanation organizes the lesbian tomboy experience into a perpetual outsider/objectified/sacrificial object relative to male desire. "All of them had to prove their budding manhood to the other boys or else, and in this dirty little game, a female body was the field on which to demonstrate it."[24]

An intrinsic problem for lesbian tomboys is that because they can only perceive and imitate boy behavior from an external vantage point they are caught unawares when that behavior reveals the internal physical/emotional/sexual male experience which dictates male behavior.

A more modern example of the risk involved in violating the boundaries of "normal" female behavior can be found in a new definition of transgression, which *DSM IV* labels Gender Identity Disorder. This diagnosis replaces the nomenclature which previously labeled lesbian or gay as pathological and which was debunked in 1974. In this new category,

> Girls with Gender Identity Disorder display intense negative reactions to parental expectations or attempts to have them wear dresses or other feminine attire. Some may refuse to attend school or social events where such clothes may be required. They prefer boy's clothing and short hair and are often misidentified as boys, and may ask to be called by a boy's name. Their fantasy heroes are most often powerful male figures, such as Batman or Superman.[25]

The list goes on but concentrates on girls who are "preoccupied" with their wish to live as boys. GID is a dangerous diagnosis because it labels as pathological what might be "normal" behavior for lesbian tomboys who are in the process of forming an identity which will fit their future self-identification and object choice. This process often includes shifts in the acquisition of male and female attributes and roles not only throughout childhood but also through the life span.

The danger is still quite real for lesbians who are diagnosed as "mentally ill" and treated psychiatrically because they are male identified. Leslie Feinberg, for example, describes her childhood ecstasy at trying on her father's clothes and her subsequent psychiatric hospitalization, which only ended when she forced herself to fit into girl behavior.[26]

These parental, social, and professional prohibitions prevent the kind of exploration young lesbians need to consolidate their identities, and damage the kind of gender flexibility they need to try on different aspects of maleness and femaleness. Their creative energy is overtly or covertly directed into resistance, and the process of lesbian identity formation is inhibited. Since lesbian tomboys rarely have role models for same-sex relationships they are forced to construct their own version of these relationships out of a heterosexual world, the only model available, and they need to be free of the sanctions which prevent experimentation. Julia Penelope, for example, writes poignantly about the damage which occurred because she only had male role models for her early relationships with females. Her subsequent teenage and adult "stone butch" identity, the only one she could construct, prevented her from participating in an adult sexuality with women, which could have been pleasurable to her as a woman.[27]

For lesbians the "tomboy" stage of development is an extremely important one in which they develop certain skills[28] which will help them hold on to their desires and resist adversity. First, they must accept and successfully negotiate an "outsider" position so that they hold on to their core identity and desires in spite of the pulls and pressures of competing groups, while at the same time keeping the boundaries between their own identity and others permeable so exchanges can take place. The outsider position can begin very early in life or it can come upon a woman when she decides to become involved with women.

At an early age, being the outsider is difficult because the skills needed to negotiate the boundaries are in their formative period. Although the lesbian child may feel that she can preserve her core identity only by remaining apart from all groups, she will eventually have to wend her way, when she comes out and seeks help, back to those feelings associated with females, that is, softness, tenderness, sadness, and the like. Lesbians who arrive at adulthood with only a masculinized persona find themselves with an emotional deficit and a diminished capacity for creativity and spontaneity. This can play havoc in relationships with women who want a fully developed woman.

Negotiating successfully as an "outsider" requires a complex and sophisticated form of communication, as I discussed in *Lesbian Psychologies*.

> When I entered adolescence, I encountered even greater risk of exposure, because adolescence is a time when knowing and following the rules of sexual interplay between boys and girls becomes increasingly important. . . . My particular problem . . . was to disguise the Italian male I had bred in myself successfully enough so that I could hang out with the girls and not be detected as a fraud by the boys; being seen as either a fraudulent male or fraudulent female would have been devastating. Sex-role invisibility was necessary to avoid isolation . . . [29]

Lesbian tomboys learn to negotiate this outsider position as they grow up so that by the time they "come out" they are at least familiar with the "outsider" aspect of gay life, although they still have to unlearn many of the deceptive communication patterns they have learned to be in sync with a world where they can now belong. Unlike the position of the "sissy" which is never positively reinforced by society, the tomboy as an outsider has certain positive aspects which are an aid to lesbian development.

Second, lesbian tomboys must find a role model or models whose own desire has been realized, so that they can observe the possibility of fulfilled desire. Children will imitate adults when they need to gain pleasure, power, property, or any one of a number of desired goals.[30]

In *Call Me Lesbian*, Julia Penelope writes,

> I was four or five when I heard the song "The Girl That I Marry." . . . [I]t was one of my favorites. I pondered what the girl I would marry would be like. One afternoon, when the song was playing on the radio, I informed my mother, solemnly, that the girl I married would be just like her.
>
> She was not flattered. In fact she seemed disturbed. She said: "Girls can't marry girls. Only boys can marry girls." I was puzzled. I was disturbed. "Why can't girls marry girls?" I asked, expecting a reasonable answer. Instead I was told, "That's the way it is." A most unsatisfactory answer!
>
> Well, if girls couldn't marry girls, if only boys could marry girls, I figured I must be a boy. I'd been given no alternatives.[31]

In this short account of her early experience with social role socialization Penelope provides us with a wealth of information. The role models she is imitating are men who marry and keep women. The song provides her with a description of the kind of girl she desires. She transfers that script onto her mother and needs to become like her father if she is to have the girl. The song also becomes symbolic of many meanings: romance, femininity, possession, and an emblem of family, community, and society.

The rejection does not curb Penelope's desire; instead, she transforms herself into a boy so as to keep the desire alive and continues to appropriate the male persona as she grows. "When I thought I was a homosexual at nine, I knew from what I'd read that this was not a good thing to be. Yet the description fit me perfectly: tomboy, likes to wear pants, has short hair, hates to sew. I was a happy *invert*."[32]

Third, lesbians must find emblems, scripts, and symbols which will help them project themselves beyond the anxieties of their own circumscribed heterosexually embedded environment into fantasies of a future where their dreams and longings (whether conscious or unconscious) of being desired by women can be realized. Lesbians appropriate symbolic gestures, clothing, attitudes, and styles which they feel will propel them into future fantasies of admiration and appeal. In "Stingrays," for example, Mooch is fixing her bike with wrench and pliers:

> It's a Stingray, a twenty-incher, same size as mine, only newer and a girl's. I run my fingers along the chain. Too much droop, gotta put more space between the back wheel and the sprocket up front. I comb my fingers through my brown hair, like Dad always does.[33]

And fourth, lesbian tomboys must create internal psychosexual gendered representations of themselves which incorporate femaleness and maleness in such an individual and creative way that they are able to push past all the prohibitions of same-sex love.

The lesbian tomboy is a very serious role for young lesbians, unlike their heterosexual counterparts. Climbing a tree for a heterosexual girl is a fun experience. But for the lesbian tomboy it is one of many such experiences which will be used to solidify her identity, self-esteem, and feelings of power and agency. She will need these strengths in order to withstand the hostility, disapproval, and rejection of others, as well as her own self-hatred, in the service of her own desire. By the time homosexual reality comes to consciousness with its accompanying feelings of desire and sexuality for another female, the lesbian's drives must be strong enough for her to believe she will be desired.

Many lesbians accomplish this by total absorption in their "tomboyishness" and the profound utilization of fantasy to create an image of themselves as sexually powerful. One woman described her early love and adoration of Michaelangelo's David. She would dream of being a boy like him and spent her time creating herself in that image because he seemed to possess an aesthetic, artistic persona. She did not believe women could possess those attributes and she needed to be aesthetic to be desired by women.[34]

Although these young lesbians know they are female, they push this awareness into the background and subsume it into a desire for maleness, the only way they believe their longings for power, agency, and connection can be realized. This process supports a growing internal structure and allows them room to grow and adapt until puberty when biological changes force them to recreate their inner representations to include themselves as females who want females. The process of consolidating a lesbian identity is psychologically long and arduous. It begins in early childhood and continues in a fluid, nonlinear pathway throughout life. The "tomboy" is not a phase which will vanish or be absorbed as the young lesbian grows. It is at the core of an identity which must continually resurface to resist pressures toward a "heterosexual imperative," and reaffirm its desire for a life with women. This process will continue to repeat itself as the lesbian renegotiates her desire throughout life when age and circumstance demand new creative adjustments. The tomboy, as she embodies desire and desirability, will empower the lesbian for the rest of her life.

NOTES

1. Anonymous report.

2. Tomboy originated in the late sixteenth century and originally meant a rude, boisterous boy, evolved into a "ramping, frolicsome, rude girl," then a "bold, immodest women" and "wild, romping girl." *The Compact Oxford English Dictionary*, 2d ed. Clarendon Press. From the beginning the word conjured up transgressive play and then moved toward sexual transgression.

3. Hillary Mullins, "Evolution of a Tomboy," in Lynne Yamaguchi Fletcher, *Tomboys! Tales of Dyke Derring-Do*, Lynn Yamaguchi and Karen Barber, eds. Los Angeles: Alyson, 1995, pp. 40, 41, 42, 43.

4. Harriet Kimble Wrye and Judith K. Welles, *The Narration of Desire: Erotic Transferences and Countertransferences*. Hillsdale, N.J.: Analytic Press, 1994, p. 37.

5. Wrye and Wells, *The Narration of Desire*, p. 34.

6. Barbara Buloff and Marie Osterman, "Queer Reflections: Mirroring and the Lesbian Experience of Self," in *Lesbians and Psychoanalysis: Revolutions in Theory and Practice*, Judith Glassgold and Suzanne Iasenza, eds. New York: Free Press, 1995, pp. 94–95.

7. Buloff and Osterman, p. 97.

8. Anonymous report.

9. Buloff and Osterman, "Queer Reflections," p. 97.

10. Darlene Bregman Ehrenberg, *The Intimate Edge: Extending the Reach of Psychoanalytic Interaction*, New York: W. W. Norton, 1992, pp. 1, 3.

11. Lee Zevy, with Sahli Cavallaro, "Invisibility, Fantasy and Intimacy: Princess Charming Is Not a Prince," in *Lesbian Psychologies: Explorations and Challenges*, The Boston Lesbian Psychologies Collective, ed. Urbana and Chicago: University of Illinois Press, 1987. pp. 83–84.

12. Zevy, "Invisibility, Fantasy and Intimacy," p. 84.

13. Yamaguchi and Barber, *Tomboys!* p. 13.

14. Alfred B. Heilbrun, Jr., and Norman C. Thompson, Jr., "Sex Role Identity and Male and Female Homosexuality," *Sex Roles* 3, 1 (1977): 65–79.

15. Anonymous report.

16. Anonymous report.

17. Leslie Feinberg, *Stone Butch Blues*. Ithaca, N.Y.: Firebrand Books, 1993, pp. 13, 20, 21.

18. Julia Penelope, *Call Me Lesbian: Lesbian Lives, Lesbian Theory*. Freedom, Calif.: Crossing Press, 1992, pp. 6, 5, 18, 19.

19. Katherine Williams, Marilyn Goodman, and Richard Green, "Parent-Child Factors in Gender Role Socialization in Girls," *Journal of the American Academy of Child Psychiatry* 24, 5 (November 1985): 720–31.

20. Historically the punishment for role transgression has ranged from admonition to death and has always been tied to genital differences between men and women. Up until the 1700s only a one-sex model was thought to exist, with the ovaries and vagina being thought of as undescended testicles and penis. "Given the conceptualization of woman's body as a thwarted male body . . . it is no wonder that desire was also thought of as masculine." Barbara Creed, "Lesbian Bodies: Tribades, Tomboys, and Tarts," in Elizabeth Groz and Elspeth Probyn, *Sexy Bodies: The Strange Carnalities of Feminism*. New York: Routledge, 1995, p. 90.

21. *New York Magazine,* June 16, 1997, p. 28.

22. Mullins, "Evolution of a Tomboy," p. 42.

23. Margaret Nicols, "Lesbian Sexuality: Issues and Developing Theory," in *Lesbian Psychologies: Explorations and Challenges,* The Boston Lesbian Psychologies Collective, ed. Urbana and Chicago: University of Illinois Press, 1987, p. 106.

24. Mullins, "Evolution of a Tomboy," p. 43.

25. *DSM-IV,* Diagnostic and Statistical Manual of Mental Disorders, 4th ed. Washington, D.C.: American Psychiatric Association, 1994, p. 533.

26. Feinberg, *Stone Butch Blues,* pp. 20, 21.

27. Penelope, *Call Me Lesbian,* pp. 5, 6.

28. Lesbians who will identify as femme also have to learn similar skills. However, their identification will be with a certain kind of powerful feminine sexuality which also serves to create a context for future lesbian relationships. In this culture, the perception of power is for the most part related to men. One has only to look at the continuum of masculinity as it relates to the identification of "butch," i.e., femmy butch (today soft butch), butch, dyke, bull-dyke/bull-dagger, diesel-dyke, truck driver, Mack truck driver, and the newer categories such as lipstick dyke and sports-dyke. Then there are femmes who constitute a single nondivisible category understood to represent a culturally stereotypic female. (Common usage.)

29. Zevy, "Invisibility, Fantasy and Intimacy," p. 86.

30. Paul Henry Mussen, John Janeway Conger, Jerome Kagen, and Aletha Carol Huston, *Child Development and Personality.* New York: Harper and Row, 1984.

31. Penelope, *Call Me Lesbian,* p. 18.

32. Penelope, *Call Me Lesbian,* p. 19.

33. (Janet) Capone Giovanna, "Stingrays" in *Tomboys!* p. 172.

34. Anonymous report.

Part III

Sissies and Tomboys Speak

Nine

My Life as a Boy

Kim Chernin

We are in the middle of a conversation. We have been talking for several hours and telling stories. It has grown late. The houses all over the neighborhood are dark. It is dark in our room too. When I reach over to turn on the lights I see that my listener has a heavy look about the eyes.

"It's a good thing this story is true," she says, "or no one would believe it."

"Would I believe it myself if it hadn't happened to me? I fall in love with a woman, I turn into a boy."

"It is hazardous to come of age," she agrees, "doubly so when you do it for the second time and into another gender."

"I thought I'd had all the coming of age anyone ever gets. But things didn't turn out exactly the way I imagined they might."

Our room is upstairs. A door is open onto a deck. Most people would close the door and turn up the heat, but we like it like this, especially on a wild, summer night, the moon still up and the clouds scuttling.

Our bed is an odd sight, now that I come to think of it. There is a clutter of German magazines, two identical plaid copies of a Jane Austen novel, a plate with bread crumbs and several dusty white crusts of goat Camembert, a map of Paris folded in half, slipped under a dictionary, an old recording of a famous opera set in Vienna. On the record jacket there is a photograph of two women, the younger dressed like a boy, in an ornate eighteenth-century room.

"Some risks are not for everyone," I say. "You can't know who will take them unless you drive things to an edge, or let yourself be driven.

At that time in my life I was looking for someone who would go the whole distance with me. Leave home, leave everything else behind, set out on the great adventure. The minute I met her, I knew with a strange kind of absolute certainty, yes, I've found her."

My listener leans back against the pillow.

"Do you know how many times I've had that feeling?"

"I see that you're trying very hard to stay awake. Shall I turn off the light?"

"Tell me about those women you met when you finally left everything behind and began your great adventure as a boy. I want to know how you went out into the world. I want something to come of all this turmoil and transformation you're always talking about. What did you do with your life as a boy? You talk and you talk but you're always evasive."

We had been planning to spend a quiet night reading in bed. But one thing led to another, then someone got hungry, someone else brought up the wine, I don't know who turned on the stereo, we briefly debated the location of a park in Paris, she got the map and she was right, of course, she had lived there for a long time before I met her. Then, she had to tell me about the first time she saw a black man, she saw him running after a bus in Berlin when she was a child and she never forgot it. I have heard this story before but that only makes it more exciting. I catch her out at every change in detail. How close did he get to the bus? Did it take off without him? What gesture did he make? At some point I must have started my story about becoming a boy. That story has to be told over and over, because there is always something left out, something I'm trying to say but can't yet manage. What do I mean by being a boy?

We have a view from the window next to our bed, down past the neighborhood, over the bay, across the bridge, and out to sea. No wonder we never want to get out of bed or fall asleep in it. But this time we have gone on a bit too long.

"It wasn't all that easy for me, you know." I was still thinking about the strange turn my life had taken.

"That's true, you were in a difficult position. You'd left your husband, you were in love with a woman, and you had, as you say, become a boy."

"I don't think you're in the right mood for this story. I had a hard time becoming a boy and I think that deserves to be taken seriously.

If it were as easy as you seem to think, why would you have all these women stuck in marriages they would rather leave? It is in the nature of women to be attached. The hardest thing in the world for a woman is to leave someone who needs her. Especially if it is her own desire that is impelling her. I know myself, I would never have left my marriage. Not as a woman. I'd have stayed right there, my whole life would have passed in fantasy. That's a serious problem and it deserves to be taken seriously."

"Don't I always take you seriously? I am taking you very seriously right now."

"Go back to your own side of the bed. Stop playing around and pay attention. You think you know where this story is going? You think you've heard it so many times before? Just wait, you might get more than you expect, you might end up with something you haven't heard before and wouldn't easily imagine."

I can tell she doesn't believe me from the way she laughs. It's the kind of laugh people have when they know each other very well, not scornful, not mocking, not really even ironic. She is laughing because she thinks I cannot tell these stories any other way and can't stop telling them once I get started.

"Let's see," she says, "how does it go? Alix Graham invited you to a women's retreat up in the hills. So you went and you all slept together every night in small groups under the trees. That would have been lovely. But you had become a boy. A highly unusual dilemma. Absolutely typical of you. But why become a boy in the first place? Why not go after women as a woman?"

"You don't know how to listen to a story. You always take things too literally. A woman who has always been a man's woman, who can't believe she can make it on her own, is going to have to invent some entirely new configuration of herself. I needed ruthlessness, a conviction about the rightness of going my own way, a refusal to be held back by any limitation. Those are good reasons for becoming a boy and I am certainly not the first woman to have found them compelling. Montaigne cites a case with which he, personally, was familiar."

"Haven't I heard this before?"

"Montaigne was traveling through a small French town, called Vitry-le-François and he was shown a man whom the Bishop of Soissons had confirmed under the name of Germain, but whom all the village's inhabitants had both known and seen to be a girl, and who had been called Marie up to the age of twenty-two. When Montaigne met him he was old, had a heavy growth of beard, and was unmarried. He told Montaigne that as he was straining to take a jump his male organs appeared. The girls of that neighborhood still sing a song in which they warn one another not to take long strides or they may turn into boys, like Marie Germain.

"What's the point? Marie the girl could never have been ordained by the Bishop of Soissons. So Marie found a solution. She turned in one set of genitals for another, changed her name to Germain and became a priest. Montaigne absolutely believes this story. In 1576, he had his motto, 'Que sais je?' inscribed on his famous medal. 'What [the hell] do I know?' he asked, in a radical skepticism that made him capable of questioning all received truths, including the fixed, immutable nature of gender. 'It is not very surprising,' he says, 'that this sort of accident happens frequently, for the imagination is so continually drawn to this subject that, supposing it has any power over such things, it would be better for it to incorporate the virile member in a girl once and for all, rather than subject her so often to the same thoughts and the same violence of desire.'

"That's it, that's my point, the violence of desire. But how touchingly Montaigne records the reluctance of the village girls to receive the male member—a hesitation which clearly suggests one reason so few girls, even in our day, take the long strides that would effect their transformation into a boy. I mean it.

"Montaigne talks about an intimate friend of his, a Count, who was afraid of the sorceries that might befall him on his wedding night, so that he would 'encounter the same bad luck as other men had . . .' This bad luck had also fallen upon Amasis, the king of Egypt, who had married a very beautiful Greek girl but was, Montaigne says, 'unable to enjoy her.' Montaigne and his fellows were similarly concerned about the 'untractable liberties taken by this member,' which would 'intrude so tiresomely when we do not require it,' and then fail 'so annoyingly when we need it most, imperiously pitting its authority against that of the will, and most proudly and obstinately refusing our solicitations both mental and manual.'

"I can only say, no wonder the girls of Marie Germain's village worried about taking long strides and turning into boys. Men don't have it easy in this life and women know that. Men are a burdened species, restless, never at peace, uneasy in their own skin, obsessed with women, the best of them always trying to be less violent than they have been taught to be. No woman would take on all that easily, believe me. But if that's the only way out, the only way forward, the only way into a sense of freedom, a natural ruthlessness, the ability to follow one's desires, hey, better become a boy than stay put as a woman.

"Of course, Marie Germain, who had lived twenty-two years as a woman before she acquired the male member, may have been a more literal person than I was, or she may have lived, simply, in a more literal time. When I say I became a boy, I'm not talking anything as simple as anatomy."

"No," she agrees, "you wouldn't be talking about anything blatant. You would have to get yourself into a dilemma in which you alone knew you were a boy, while everyone else went right on assuming you were a woman. Of course, women have their own troubles with the body. When my cousin Beate was nursing her first child her breasts would fill up with milk whenever her lover winked at her. She was constantly running out of the room to change her blouse. Nothing like that ever happened with her husband . . ."

"You really are not the best possible listener for this story. You get side-tracked. You can't keep to the point. There I was, at a woman's retreat and I, who had just become a lover of women, had just turned into a boy.

"At first I thought it was definitely odd. But after a while I got used to it and by the third day we were running around naked most of the time and I didn't give it two thoughts."

"Mmmm," she murmurs.

"We cooked our own vegetarian meals on Bunsen burners and open fires, told our dreams to one another when we woke up in the morning, learned how to chant the names of women who had been burned as witches during the middle ages, made masks, got into totem dances, chanted to the moon, chanted the thousand names of the goddess and probably left out a few."

"Mmm, just a few." She is looking nostalgically at an empty glass of wine. I had a glass of ginger tea, which spilled over onto the bedspread a few hours ago and is still drying.

"But Alix Graham, you know, I thought she was really eager to teach me everything I had to learn about women's lives when they are separated from the lives of men. I stayed longer than planned, met the women who would be my friends and companions for the next years of my life. Are you listening?"

She puts her head on my shoulder. She'll fall asleep and wake up and fall asleep again but she's content. She thinks she has managed to provoke me into telling my story in some new way.

"We were living mainly out of doors on the acres of land surrounding the house Alix used for retreats. The house was set in a valley thickly overgrown with pitchpine and cypress, a somewhat unusual landscape for Berkeley, even up in the hills. Some miles from where we camped out there was a natural rock cave, a sort of grotto, on the far side of the stream. It was known to the people in the neighborhood and was kept available only to them. This time, Alix had arranged to hold a ritual there and so we all had to promise to keep the grotto a secret.

"So, it took us about an hour to get there. We were walking barefoot along a path Alix knew well but which the rest of us found difficult to follow. As we walked, Alix pointed out the sound of falling water, then we had arrived and saw the shaded nook in which the clear water spread out into a wide pool with grassy banks.

"I don't know why but I'd hung back and had to run to catch up with the others. By the time I reached the little grotto, most of them had undressed and were dipping themselves very cautiously into the water. It was cold. There was a flicker of sunlight through the cypress trees, the impression of burnt pine or pitch, light roamed up and down across the naked bodies of the women and I felt a strange terror, as if I had blundered into a sacred site where a solitude of goddesses was bathing.

"Alix waved to me. The other women called me by name, but I stood rooted to the spot, as if trying to shake myself free from a certainty that if I were seen and went forward and were known to be there, I would be guilty of a transgression punished by savage laws. This is what I have been trying to explain to you. I was a boy. I felt the desire to gaze, to pursue them, to possess them, to take them to me, as was my right, my right, do you understand? To feel that you have a right to a woman's body? That is what I mean by being a boy.

"I think it was Alix who caught up a handful of water and threw it in my face; someone else laughed and told me to hurry up or I would grow horns like Acteon and be set upon by my own hounds and then everyone came running from the water to drag my clothes off and drag me in and that was the beginning of the ritual for me, my first immersion.

"Still, I just could not get used to the idea that these were women who lived with and loved women, when for so many years, for my whole life, I had known women who feared their closeness to other women and one way and another managed to avoid it. It was the sudden revelation of a female being in which I did not share, its comradely innocence, its erotic playfulness. I was dazed, but I was also troubled by a sense that I came from the outside, was a stranger not easily assimilated in this world, precisely because of my fascination with it.

"I was astonished to think what these women must know about love, the lessons they must have learned of woman's erotic self-sufficiency, during the slow, rich secret hours away from the eyes of men. All this would still have to be taught to me. You see what I mean? To become a woman like they were, I first had to become a boy. Don't you get it? How else could I have left my marriage? How else could I set out to find women who loved women? I, with all my fears? You think such women grow on trees?

"As a boy I desired these women, I tell you. It was this desire that had brought me out of my old life but once here, once having found them, my desire seemed to keep me apart from them, it kept me yearning for them, for their ease together, for their sunlit sexuality that seemed playful and sensual and collective, while mine was stormy, exclusionary, restless.

"It seemed to me that I had stumbled across the doorstep of myth and was coming upon them always as the disrupter, as if some violence of separation I always felt had not yet been hurled against them. They seemed at play on the fields of original oneness, Alix most of all and another called Rain, in a more ambiguous way.

"Rain spent the entire day, after our morning rituals, naked on a striped Indian blanket under a family of old, thick trunked oaks, which began their branching close to the ground and swept her in a freckling shadow. She lay in silence, staring at the piecemeal sky, under the speared grasses that bent over her conspiratorially to brush across her small, pointed breasts. Sooner or later someone was always sent out to gather her in and soon enough that someone was always I. I lay down next to her, the hawks consummated their murderous circles with the infinite patience of the prey bird. She drank red wine, smoked grass she grew to incredible potency in a hidden hillside garden a few miles down the road, called herself a witch, a word she and the other women used admiringly or simply as a description. I myself was afraid of her but that didn't seem a reason to keep away from her.

"She was a lean, tanned, muscular woman who sometimes reminded me of those wild, virgin girls who used to run with Artemis. I have seen her follow animal tracks no one else could see, vanish into the woods, where, with a single gesture, she became invisible. Wild animals would let her draw closer to them than I had ever been before, tugged along by her hand, silently treading behind her. One day we came upon a family of white deer in a remote woodland clearing, the young males leaping on all fours, butting heads, backing away from each other with their heads lowered, kicking their heels in a game they might have learned from Pan, rising up on their hind legs in a precocious, playful rutting, while the does lay in the grass paying no attention and the pale mothers took off after them when they raced suddenly just before sunset across the clearing.

"One dark, moonless night, I followed Rain through woods and heavy underbrush for hours it seemed, as she made her way without a flashlight, barefoot, on no path visible to me, from our encampment to a waterfall near her house, stoned out of her mind and perfectly steady, drawing me along by the hand. I was totally in the power of a stranger I did not trust, alone with her in a wilderness impenetrable to me, through which she made her way with a scornful, mocking arrogance I found irresistible.

"First nights come and go. Over time they tend to get confused with one another. That is why memory spears them with a wanton image. Rain used to dream of a snake making love to her, coiling around her arms and breast until its head came to rest in the hollow of her throat. She must have dreamt up the snake that night too, I tell you.

"At dawn, Rain and I were sitting at the edge of the pool, she was sitting on my lap, her arms flung around my neck, as if she were forgiving me for a slight inflicted many years ago, while I, who had met her a few days ago was grateful almost to tears for this reconciliation that had been so long in coming.

"Then, for a time, before I left the retreat, I thought I would have to choose between Rain and Alix, but they thought I should take them both for lovers, because they wanted to teach me detachment in love. Well, good luck to them. You can't blame them for trying.

"After a while the women started drifting off. Rain went first, to her cabin with the garden a few miles up the road; she invited me to visit, drew me a map and ran off barefoot in a golden cloud of dust. A few women stayed on to chop wood and clear a few overgrown paths, to thank the owner, for the use of the house and land. Finally Alix and I were alone, riding the horses to neighboring farms, riding bareback together back to the house.

"She asked if I was going to spend the night, as if there were nothing much at stake so I thought perhaps for her there wasn't.

"I didn't know if spend the night meant being lovers. I hoped it did. But if it did I thought I shouldn't because of Rain. A boy's idea.

"Alix was brushing the dried late summer leaves from the porch, where the boards were already coming loose which one day would require the owner to fix them.

"She walked me to my car, helped me load my sleeping bag and other gear, advising me to roll the window up or the dust would get me.

"I leaned out of the car to kiss her goodbye and she kissed me back. I drove off, because I was a boy and I had said I was going. I got to the road, turned around, drove back fast, took the steps two at a time. But I was too late, Alix had gone off somewhere . . ."

My listener seems to be nodding off. "Hey, are you listening? Are you falling asleep?"

"Why would I fall asleep? Do you think I've heard this story before?"

"If I were you, I'd listen. Alix had gone off somewhere, right? So, I think to myself, it must be to visit a neighbor. Or maybe she has gone off on her dappled horse along the dusty road . . . to spend the night with Rain?"

My listener sits straight up in bed. "You and Alix and Rain? That must have been quite a night," she says, doubtfully.

"They had a lot to teach me. I'd liked being a boy."

"It takes some people a long time to figure out how to love women. It took you so many lives before I met you anyone might have thought

you'd be old and exhausted by the time I got you. But you and Alix
and Rain. I suppose it would take two women to turn you back into a
woman. Are you sure? You never mentioned that before."

"You know how stories are . . ."

"Okay, I'm awake now."

"But the story has come to an end."

"Don't turn off the light."

"It's late. You look kind of sleepy."

"That look has nothing to do with fatigue."

"Shall I go on with the story?"

"Come here," she says, in that voice that always makes me want to
do whatever she wants.

Nevertheless I'm going to resist.

"You asked for it, you're going to get it. I have a story to tell about
why I liked being a boy and I'm going to tell it. What if there were a
new kind of woman, an entirely new strain, that creates itself by
passing through the transitional phase of the boy? You maybe are the
type of woman who loves women without becoming a boy. But maybe
that means you've missed out on a stage of erotic development from
which you still have something to learn?"

It has grown late. The houses all over the neighborhood are dark.
When I reach over to turn off the lights she put her arms around me.
"Okay," she says, dutifully now, with a languorous yawn, "I guess
it's time for you to teach me . . ."

Ten

Butch in a Tutu

Sara Cytron with Harriet Malinowitz

May 9, 1997, New York City

Last night, I dreamed I was looking in the mirror. First, I saw a lithe, delicate ballerina posing beautifully, gracefully, elegantly. (In real life, I am a butchy, thirty-pounds overweight, forty-five-year-old lesbian, whose walk and manner when lumbering lustily toward my partner have been likened by her to those of the Abominable Snowman.) In the dream, after an instant, the image of the ballerina melted into that of a statuesque, naked, Greek godlike man holding a towel to cover his genitals. And then the image melted back to the ballerina. End of dream.

Up until the last few years, despite the almost ubiquitous presence of psychotherapy in my life, I trivialized or ignored my dreams. Relieved to wake up and enter the world of palpability, I often called my dreams crazy, letting their images and emotional resonance float away from me. I didn't realize how much of my understanding of myself was floating away with them.

Now I feel quite different. I fight to hold on to these images and the feelings they produce in me because I have come to believe that, in dreaming, I am having a crucially important conversation with myself about my gender identification, my sexuality, the relationship between my adult self and my earliest memories, and what it meant to me to be Ethel and Izzy Cytron's youngest child—someone whose mother shrank from intimacy and whose father had a boundless need for love; someone who emerged with an anxious and complicated relationship to masculinity and femininity.

At this point in my life, I can't have the ballerina dream without being struck by the extremes of idealized masculinity and femininity represented there. As a lesbian who, for decades, has thought of herself as comfortably at home and well-adjusted in my butch self, having felt that all I ever really needed was the freedom to partake of the style and wardrobe of the opposite gender, I am shocked to find evidence buried in my psyche of identification not only with my own gender, but with a caricature of my own gender. It wasn't until my forties that, together with my therapist, I formulated a theory of my gender identification: I had anxiously submerged the feminine in myself—contrary to what I had always believed, I had done more than just fight a battle against rigid and sexist social norms in order to be able to express the masculine.

In many of my dreams, I am looking into a mirror searching for hidden parts of myself, some underlying essence. In my waking life, growing up in a large Jewish family where my appearance was a battleground, I would also turn to my reflection seeking the "real me" inside, the one who was sequestered from the war over whether I'd wear barrettes in my hair. I would look closely into my own eyes and face and find that contact with myself that was available nowhere else. There were moments in my life, both as a young child and as a young married woman in my twenties, when I would look in the mirror and secretly preen, knowing that the right eyes would find me attractive, handsome, and dashing, and the wrong eyes would find me wrong, too butchy, displeasing. Later on, the right eyes belonged to the lesbian women who became my lovers. In the beginning, however, the right eyes were only my own.

Summer 1958, Brooklyn, New York

I am in the bathroom of my home. I am about six years old. I have chosen to come in here for just this purpose: to take off my polo shirt and my T-shirt and gaze at myself in the mirror. I love the sight of myself in my sneakers, shorts, and dark hair; I love my bare chest. I smile at my reflection. I picture myself walking around like that, running on the beach like that, like I was a boy instead of a girl. I turn around, trying to catch my image at different angles, happily surveying my smooth back and sides.

The seconds pass and I know my time is up. I put on my T-shirt and polo shirt and then flush the toilet, run the water in the sink, wet the towel a little, and emerge to go back to living life as a little girl.

A little girl, however, who was described as a "tomboy." I was confused about whether I *really* wanted to be a little boy. I only knew that I felt sick and sad and panic-stricken about the pressure to wear a dress, carry a little purse, and play with dolls and tea sets. I felt completely undone by a visit to the beauty parlor and reacted to the news that my mother was going to take me there the way most children react to learning that they will be getting an injection in the doctor's office. I not only trembled when my own appearance was at issue; I would become hysterical when I had to make anything in school that had to look pretty. No one knew how to make sense of my terror and tears, especially not my mother who was baffled by her sobbing, shaking daughter, and who alternated between briefly trying to understand me (which mainly involved giving me a pep talk exhorting me to "rise to the occasion") and growing distressed at the way I found anything claiming aesthetic appeal so inexplicably disturbing.

Actually, I was terrified of all things feminine, though at the time I was incapable of explaining it as that to myself. I had come to associate my girlness with being invaded, flooded, and overwhelmed. If no one else was home, my father would ask me to lie down on him. He would hold me tightly, fervently, talking rapturously of how he loved me. I would feel his hot, close breath, the moistness of his lips, the faintly spicy smell of his skin. He would call me *medellah*, the Yiddish word for little girl, and then he'd intone in my ear, "Sarchkala, *medellah*, child-girl." Other times, as I played in the dining room where all the traffic of our six-member household would pass—right off the doorway so frequently opened by the aunt, uncle, and cousins who lived upstairs and the grandmother who lived in the basement—he'd pull down my shorts so he could tuck my shirt into my underwear. He did this often, sometimes numerous times a day—so it would be neat, he told me—in front of my mother, who said nothing. When he was at work he called on the phone to ask me how much I loved him. I had to give the expected answer: "Up to a million billion skies."

In contrast to my father's constant engulfment, my mother offered almost no physical contact. While my father would hold me in a vicelike embrace as he said, "I'm not going to let you go, I'm not going to let you go," my mother would stick out her cheek awkwardly to receive ritualized kisses from her children. She occasionally tickled me, allowing only her hands to touch my body. No feeling of her body against mine, no soft breast to lay my head on. My mother struggled to offer genuine connection, but it didn't come easily to her. More than a tiny bit of intimacy seemed unbearable. Rather than ask about what I thought or felt, or getting to know the details of my life of school, camp, and friends, my mother recited popular poems that she had memorized years earlier. While making me lunch of bananas and sour cream, she'd intone, "I think that I shall never see a poem as lovely as a tree." Sometimes on car trips she would sing the song "It's Delightful to be Married," and would make up verses about each child. I lived for the verse about me; the occasional burst of humor and warmth from my mother made me long for more. More often, though, she napped with one arm over her face while my father took us kids to the zoo, the Hayden Planetarium, or the park. If it was a weekday and my father was at work, I would be left to wander around the house aimlessly, waiting for her to get up and help me figure out what to do with myself.

Sometimes, hearing that I was annoyed at my father, she would emerge from the kitchen and playfully say to him in an exaggerated, indignant tone, "Are you bothering my child?" Even now it's hard for me to feel anger at the inadequacy of her responses rather than gratitude for the crumbs of her engagement.

These sharply disparate parental behaviors made me desperately want women to pay attention to me and violently want men to get away. I came to associate *my* being female with danger; but I wanted to be *near* femininity, though I dreaded inhabiting it. It was hard to forget that when my father threatened to devour me, the words he whispered were all about my being a girl. *Medellah*, child-girl. Girls, however, were who I lusted for. From second grade on, I picked the femmiest girls to love. The ones who were really pretty, graceful, with long silky hair and carefully chosen outfits. The ones who showed how femininity worked, how femaleness could be enchanting and intoxicating. And however much I loved girls my own age, any demonstration of affection from someone old enough to be my mother was even more potent. I remember once a very pretty, feminine woman my mother stopped to speak with on the street made a big fuss over me. I was about seven or eight. I flushed, I yearned, I couldn't sleep. I figured out how to masturbate as I relived her smiling at me.

I knew there was something very wrong with my feeling this way. Every time someone called my name, my heart began to race; it seemed a prelude to the moment of confrontation about my bizarre condition. And I thought God would punish me by making me grow a penis. I would check myself in the bathtub, thinking that my little clitoris was the first sign of my incipient condemnation. The sentence, apparently, was to actually *become* my father.

I also worried compulsively about most aspects of daily life. I would worry about talking to people, about being left on my own, about having to draw or sew something in school, about getting lost and not knowing where I was. By the age of eight, I had already begun to moan out loud when I was all alone, "Help me, God. Please help me!" But while I was full of desperation, my mother used palliative adjectives like "nervous" and "high-strung" to describe me. She called me "the absentminded professor" when I frequently lost, dropped, and banged into things.

Despite the obvious signs of my inner turmoil, I believed that I resisted all things girlish not because they terrified me, but because what was boyish beckoned so strongly. And I did envy the solidity and self-completion that boys seemed to have. Rather than going to a beauty parlor where the pressure was on to come out looking like a product, boys could go to a barber just because they were human beings who needed a haircut. Boys could be dressed up but still retain themselves and their dignity. They could be cleaned and combed out of respect for an occasion without serving as delicacies for the consumption of others. They could wear the things they needed and cared about *on them*, in their pockets. And it was taken for granted that when they found things in the earth they could keep them. I strongly suspected that, had I been a boy, when I showed people my rock collection they would just have examined the rocks instead of issuing me sharp looks of bemusement and surprise.

Male power and freedom had an earthy, sensual appeal. I wanted to come home with coins jingling in my trouser pockets. I wanted to drive a car with an arm leaning out the window, escorting the women (who were always just the passengers and who wouldn't open the window on their side because the wind would blow their hair). I wanted to register the end of a long, hot day at work with a simple tug at my tie knot. I wanted a sleek, sharp crease pressed into my slacks when they came back from the cleaners.

Of course, men did wield real privilege, and women's lives were dreary by comparison. My mother didn't drive, and for many years she didn't work. And men led the family Seders while the women cooked the meal, set the table, and walked around with a bowl of water so the men could wash their hands at the right moment. At all our many family parties and occasions it was the men who made the speeches and told the jokes, while the women laughed and applauded them.

But I wasn't just an early feminist. And I don't think I *only* wanted to find safety from men and intimacy with women. When I look at photographs from my childhood, I look handsome and happy and athletic in my little jeans, sad and awkward in my little dresses. The toys I picked out, lived with, and even slept with, the clothes I chose to wear gave me too much visceral, tactile pleasure for me to believe they represented only a position of default or retreat. On trips to the toy store, my sister Ellie (who is three years older than I) selected such items as a fake mink stole, fake pearls, fake China sets, and a diverse collection of dolls. I, despite my mother's best attempts to seduce me into choosing pop-bead jewelry sets or *Colorform* fashion dolls with different paste-on outfits, insisted on guns and holsters, caps, rubber knives and swords, astronaut helmets, Tinker Toys, and the only doll I could love—Popeye. I was enraptured by the smell of his plastic body and even tried spinach so I would grow muscles like his. I wore my astronaut helmet in the house despite the smell it acquired as my head sweated inside. Setting off caps produced the most aromatic perfume I could imagine; it was a tough choice whether to shoot them off in my gun or to experience the more immediate thrill of taking a sharp rock in my hand and scratching the cap until it exploded. Other little girls also played with caps, but it was counterbalanced by their involvement with Betsy Wetsy or Patty Playpal. I beheaded Ellie's Betsy Wetsy and exuded comradely rather than maternal feelings toward Popeye.

Early on, my behavior was only mildly disturbing to my parents. Tomboy was a concept that reassured them: this was a common enough phenomenon, harmless and temporary. I also understood the tomboy concept, and was grateful for the permission it gave me to wear my cowboy outfit (which my parents had to remind me to call my "cowgirl" outfit). I was happy to fit into a category that explained and permitted my breach from conventional girlhood, that gave me temporary license to act dangerously like a little boy without being one. What worried me, though, was the threat of postponement inherent in the concept: that, someday, this would all have to change. There was no such expression as "tom-man." Eventually I would be subject to all the expectations I was striving to avoid and would have to comply without "acting like Sarah Bernhardt," the phrase my mother sardonically used to characterize my complaints and tears as I was forced to make each foray into femininity.

The tomboy reprieve lasted until about age eleven. At that point, I developed large breasts. My mother made so many comments about how unacceptable my T-shirts were that I reluctantly started wearing the bra that had lain in my underwear drawer for months. The day I finally put it on I heard my mother triumphantly tell my married sister Bonnie on the phone, "She's wearing it." Around the same time, I started menstruating, and so pocketbooks became essential to carry spare sanitary napkins—although I tried valiantly to continue to stuff them into my pencil case.

My mother was the heavy in the battle over my gender nonconformity. My father didn't say anything about it at all up until my adolescence. Then, one night when my parents were practicing for their rumba class, he danced over to me and playfully tried to wrest me onto the living room dance floor. I felt awkward and uncomfortable, and responded as compliantly as a demonstrator being hauled off in a nonviolent civil disobedience action. Giving up, he asked me pointedly, "So when are you going to start to get interested in boys?" I was stunned, feeling a terrible sense of betrayal from the father who had always smiled distractedly or suddenly decided to peel an orange when my mother sarcastically threatened to send me to "finishing school." Now I saw they were united. They had let things go as far as they could; my mother had somehow recruited my father as extra reinforcement in the war. I would never win. My body had betrayed me and my fate was inevitable.

Their intractableness in this area was particularly surprising because my parents were strict about nothing else. As a young child, I could easily get around my bedtime by saying I couldn't sleep; I simply got up and watched another two hours of television. I could eat anything I wanted at any time or refuse anything I didn't want. I had no mandatory tasks or chores. They would have been content had I brought home scores in the eighties on school tests—I was the one who insisted on high nineties if not hundreds. Only in the realm of gender were they disciplinarians. For once there was something they cared about, fervently.

I know that my mother threatened me partly because she feared for the livelihood of a girl who refused to play her part. She wasn't educated and couldn't imagine that education or a career would play a significant part in her daughter's future. How would I get a boyfriend, get married, run a home, raise children? This was the fifties, then the early sixties. My parents, children of immigrants, had grown up in poverty and lived through the Depression. They valued security above all, and for a girl that meant finding a good husband. My mother took *The Hardy Boys* out of my hands in the bookstore and replaced it with *Nancy Drew*.

The pressure was reinforced everywhere else. Conversations among the girls at school and at camp had begun to have a lot to do with boys and clothes and makeup, and some girls were starting to have boyfriends. I was longing to be to them what they wanted a boy to be.

Then I met Roma. We found each other at Camp Wel-Met when we were twelve and were passionate lovers until we were sixteen. We reconnected at twenty-five and lived together until Roma died of cancer the month before she turned thirty-four. Warm, sweet, pretty, flirtatious, Roma played the stripper Adelaide, one of the two female leads in that summer's production of *Guys and Dolls* (I played Arvide, another character's grandfather). Roma seduced me, walking across to my side of the bunk each morning so I could hook her bra, sitting on my bed at lights out until I kissed her goodnight, and making fun of the quaint expressions that I had picked up from my parents and dispensed as if they were still in vogue.

As an adult, Roma recounted first spotting me at camp: she saw a tall, thin girl with absolutely straight, shiny, jet black shoulder-length hair, and concluded with adolescent logic that I must be a snob. But then she watched as one of the counselors walked over to me and complimented my hair; to her amazement, I jerked my head in disgust and shrank off in embarrassment.

With Roma, I discovered how much I loved having someone pay

attention to my appearance in a way that reflected the way I saw myself. Though my hair's market value in luring a boyfriend had initially caught her attention, it was my rough disavowal of that ostensible asset that drew her erotically to me. She admired my height, my strength, my low-timbred voice, the gallop into which I broke during group hikes in the woods. She said I had a half-smile that was like Elvis Presley's. The gaze that I had only been able to give myself in the mirror was finally coming from another female. Roma and I lingered behind when the others left the bunk, springing apart when a counselor reappeared to insist we participate in volleyball or arts and crafts. During sleepovers at each other's houses the rest of the year, we talked about folk music in front of our parents, then slipped away to the bedroom to make out.

But even in the midst of our secret love affair, Roma and I knew we had to publicly manifest the signs of normal development. We both obtained boyfriends—who did serve the redeeming function of affording mild jealousy pangs and opportunities for burning reassurances. Nevertheless, sustaining the role of a heterosexual teenage girl was stressful.

One way I coped with the public part of my life was to become my sister Ellie. Since I was instinctively theatrical and wore many of her old outfits, impersonating her came fairly easily to me. I grew used to taking on her bubbly manner and dramatic throaty voice, while at the same time dissociating from my body and feelings to escape how beaten and obliterated I felt.

Another way I managed to disown my panic and get the attention I craved was to act outrageously. I became a notorious conduct problem in most of my junior high school classes. The section sheet, used by teachers to mark down students who created a disturbance in their classes, was reviewed by the assistant principal. I was told I set a school record by being put on the section sheet seventeen times in one week. While I graduated with a 98 average, people around me were failing because they found it hard to concentrate near my jabberings and eruptions. I imitated a chicken, flapping my arms and clucking in the middle of science class. I gave gospel-type sermons in the middle of math class, and, since I had broken several sewing machines out of anxiety in my sewing class, was told by the teacher that she'd give me an 85 if I just sat there and didn't touch anything. On the final day of class, when we held a fashion show and all the other girls modeled the shifts they had made, I paraded around the class with a paper pattern pinned to my clothes.

In high school, my being "funny" continued. Some teachers found ways for me to get my moment of attention; in exchange, I would behave myself for the rest of the class. In English, I was always given a few minutes to read some monologue from *Macbeth* in a gum-chewing, Brooklyn accent. ("Out damned spot" worked particularly well.) In Spanish, where we were reading the book *La Nela* about a hunchback, I was permitted to walk around the room with my sweater under my blouse so everyone could feel my hump.

While I was considered funny and talented and was elected to be director of Sing (the huge annual musical theatrical production), I was also found strange, not like other girls, not someone easy to be friends with. I was anxious and compulsive. It became a great source of amusement for my classmates to notice me touching myself on the right side if someone happened to touch me on the left, or vice versa (a ritual I called "evening" myself). Eager to please my teachers, I carried every book for every class to school with me every day, counting them repeatedly to make sure the collection was intact. Instead of having conversations, I performed, injecting accents, impersonations, and jokes into every exchange. I found endless ways to avoid contact with myself. I used people narcissistically to reflect back to me how delightful I was as well as to avoid the quiet moment of awareness that threatened to reveal all that I wanted to suppress.

However neurotic I appeared, I still had some capacity to monitor my behavior in front of others at school. At home, I lost that control. I beat rhythms on my front teeth with my thumbs, which amazed and angered my mother. I sat in a chair by the dining room table, clutching my stomach before any social gathering. In the morning, I sometimes just stared into space with one sock in my hand. I kept Sominex in my drawer and fantasized on Monday about overdosing on Friday. But then I would find Monday through Friday too beautiful and poignant, as I bid silent goodbyes to everything and everyone around me. I didn't really want to die; I just didn't quite know how to live. Each day felt like an exhausting performance.

Then, when we were both sixteen, Roma started seriously sleeping with boys. The hopeful and resilient part of me collapsed, and an overwhelming passivity took over.

Despite my outstanding academic record and SAT scores high enough for a top school, I chose to go to Brooklyn College, a fifteen-minute bus ride from my house, and to continue to live at home. I told myself that my parents couldn't afford to send me out of town, but a part of me knew I was scared to death of people, of new situations, of heterosexual life, of growing up, of separating. My parents seemed relieved when I announced my decision, and only brought up the notion of applying for scholarships to other schools very briefly and unconvincingly.

But by the time I got to college, my mother was beside herself about my lackluster history with boyfriends. She exerted a lot of pressure on me to join a "houseplan" (a less snobby version of a sorority) so I would meet boys. I was still too dependent on her approval to resist her and so, very quickly, I found two boyfriends.

By that time, I had perfected being "Ellie" in order to survive on dates. But I started worrying about a Saturday night date on Thursday, and spent all day Saturday preparing myself for the show. I shaved my legs, my armpits, plucked my eyebrows, worked on my hair, and picked out my "Ellie" outfit. The last agonizing hour I sat in the dining room all dressed and ready, like a condemned person awaiting the moment of execution. When the bell rang, I donned Ellie's persona. I ended up going further sexually than I had ever planned to, and then felt used and frightened. The next day, Sunday, was glorious—I could return to my jeans, my shirts, my loafers, my grief over Roma, and my mild crushes on other girls. To myself.

By the time I was nineteen, I was crying much of the time. Friends would sit sympathetically but helplessly with me in my living room, as if we were sitting shiva for some unknown person. After founding a teen summer theater group and directing a few shows, I had to leave a show after casting it because I felt overwhelmed by the responsibility. One time, I lay draped over my bed, crying. The door to my room was open. My mother appeared in the doorway and said angrily, "What have you got to be crying about? You've gone to camp, had music lessons, you have four encyclopedias in the house. I had parents who didn't speak English. I could never buy a book for myself. Why don't you tell me what is wrong with you?"

I couldn't talk to her. Instead, she and my father offered to pay for psychotherapy when I told them I thought I needed it, despite their discomfort with the idea. I got a referral from a counselor on campus after I said I was thinking of killing myself. I saw the therapist for about eight months. When I told him I thought I was a lesbian, he said, "I don't think so." I submitted to his professional opinion, and soon had another boyfriend. This time the relationship worked for me: Lou was my perfect complement, a closet case like myself, a sweet, affectionate, theatrical, scared, and needy boy/man who performed musical comedy numbers on our dates and laughed at my comic antics. I no longer had to be Ellie. I quit therapy and at age twenty-two I married Lou.

September 1979, Great Neck, Long Island

I am twenty-seven years old. It is the afternoon of my nephew's bar mitzvah. I have been out as a lesbian to my family for two years. Roma (who is now known by them to be my lover, but has not been invited—though it has occurred to neither of us to question the predictable indignity) has driven me to Leonard's catering hall where the affair is being held. I am in my new three-piece tan wool pants suit, purchased especially for the occasion. I felt wonderful putting it on, buttoning the vest, seeing how the jacket lay to expose just the perfect amount of vest and blouse. Roma has complimented it and me in it many times in the few hours I've had it on. She tells me how great I look, how butch, how sexy, how really elegant. She drops me off at the Leonard's entrance. We kiss, make plans to talk later, and she pulls off.

While I am always nervous before entering any social gathering—especially a family gathering—Roma has filled me with the kind of confidence that makes me feel I can encounter my family on my own terms. With my butch haircut and my butch suit, I walk in. Within a few moments, I find all the women gathered together. They are all in skirts, dresses, makeup, coifed hair. They are all complimenting each others' outfits and hairdos. Although they greet me warmly, no one says a word to me about how I look or what I'm wearing. My mother walks over to a family friend and gestures to me. I overhear her saying, "So there's my daughter. That's what she looks like. What can I do?"

I want to run out of there, or just lie down and cry or throw up. Instead, I continue to smile and to insert myself into the conversations.

Conversations in my family are exclamatory and jokey, punctuated with frequent outbursts of hysterical laughter. This means that it is relatively easy to hide. After a few minutes, I am able to hide even from myself how violated I feel.

But what did I expect? How had I managed to manufacture the delusion that my family would reflect back to me that dashing self-image that I had found in the mirror and in Roma's eyes? Somewhere inside I must have known that I would end up feeling precisely the hurt that flickered through me for the moment before I narcotized myself. It was like choosing to pick a fight but then not having the courage to follow through. I had walked in to show myself to them, but when faced with the choice of claiming myself and, in so doing, losing them or of preserving the illusion of connection with them no matter what it cost me, I chose the illusion. I still needed to belong. Just as my mother had found an illusory comfort by eliding the complexities I had asked her to confront, it was now my turn to transform my actual family into an imaginary one, to pretend that our markedly divergent criteria for living in the world didn't exist, that the incredible gulf that faced us when we sought one another wasn't there.

July Fourth Weekend, 1995, Heath, Massachusetts

I am now almost forty-three years old. In an accelerated program of twice-weekly therapy sessions, I've lately been trying to figure out why I so often seem to be in a fog. I bump my head into the edge of the same kitchen cabinet at least thirty different times. I laugh at jokes in movies that I don't really find funny. I smell smoke but don't think of looking to see if something in the apartment is on fire. My therapist calls this "dissociation." Harriet, my lover of nine years, calls it being "zombified."

Harriet and I are spending the holiday weekend in our house in the country. I have the following dream:

The scene is a prison cell. A young girl, about eight years old, in a party dress, is swinging from a noose suspended from the ceiling. She is swinging in broad arcs, from one end of the cell to the other.

As in many of my dreams, a voice-over comes on to narrate. It says: "A young girl is being executed."

That same weekend, I have the dream again. But this time the voice-over says more. After "A young girl is being executed," I hear, "And now we get to the root of the problem." This is followed by the image of an erect penis coming out of a pubic mound.

In the weeks that follow I am barraged by other dreams. A dream about King Solomon has the voice-over: "What kind of father would split the baby?" A dream about a family celebration features my sister whispering to me, "So, do you know about Daddy?" A dream about returning to the house where I grew up has me finding a phallic-looking bottle labeled "CENTRAL" and me choking on it as I try to drink its contents which leave a terrible residue in my mouth. Another dream features a plate of cut-up sausage, with one of the slices being named "Sara" who is famous for having a "very notorious sexual history." A dream where I am trying desperately to first answer a phone and then hear the voice at the other end shows that I am failing in these efforts because I have a banana draped over my head. I dream repeatedly of spitting seeds or residue out of my mouth. One time, I look closely at what I have spit out, and find that they are tiny little penises. I dream of visiting a national park where men are naked, and their erections are called "Daddies." Everyone acts as if this is all perfectly normal. One naked man, who is the leader, the tour guide in charge, is acting especially nice and fatherly to me. We both ignore his big "Daddy" as he knowledgeably points out the features of the site.

In considering these dreams, I search my memory and cannot recall actual instances of the kind of sexual abuse suggested here. My therapist assures me that since I'm not suing anyone, I don't need to prove anything. Instead, we talk about the *young girl* who somehow, long ago, was executed. How did she die? What did she suffer? Where did she go?

Late July 1995, Heath, Massachusetts

I am driving on a country road back to our house. Too late, I see a squirrel dart in the path of our car, and I hear the thump. Within a second or two, I see an image in the rear view mirror: the squirrel literally flipping and flailing in the air, over and over again, in agony, until death releases it and it stops. A few nights later, I have a dream that replays this flailing and suffering. But instead of a squirrel, the casualty is a little girl of about six to eight years old in a party dress.

I have other dreams in which feminine objects such as lipstick, necklaces, and perfume rise up in the air and I salute them, or where I am on a wild search to find such objects buried in my home.

In my waking life I have enjoyed being the butch partner to far more feminine lovers. I have taken immense pleasure in watching Harriet, a great collector of earrings, make her selection for the day. My pleasure is in proportion to the degree to which I've submerged the desire for adornment of myself. Both Harriet, and before her, Roma, have remarked upon the virulence of my rejection of jewelry and scarves to accent my clothes. "What's the big deal?" they've asked. "Why are you so threatened?"

May 1997, Heath, Massachusetts

I've filled four dream logs in two years. I have gone through a brief period of feeling a bit like a transsexual—as if I am really a more feminine woman trapped in a butch's mind, body, and life, someone who can't quite bring to the surface a buried part of herself. I look at women on the subway platform and imagine my face under their hairstyles. I look at a coworker's skirtsuit at work and visualize myself in it.

But I cannot unloosen that part of me except in my dreams. A butch in a tutu in a dream is safely tucked away in the world of symbolism. A butch in a skirt in the office would look like a butch in a skirt. Furthermore, I know that my waking self could not cope with my own shock at such a transformation, much less the shock of those who have become so used to my particular brand of self-presentation. It's similar to the way I use sexual fantasies about men for occasional stimulation while knowing very deeply that I do not want actual contact with a male body. I derive a kind of release by daring to conjure up a different version of myself, as if I have always lived in a house with an attic that I was afraid to venture into, and finally understand that I will not die just from going in and turning on the light.

I don't know what my relationship to femininity would have been if my father had not filled that territory with land mines and if my mother had been able to meet my gaze and offer herself as the female mirror I kept searching for. I certainly don't think my tomboy childhood and butch lesbian life are simply the consequence of violation, abuse, and profound lacks. On the other hand, I do believe that my overwrought response to all things feminine (insofar as they applied to myself) must have had some wrenching origin, and my dreams offer the only clues I have as to what that might be. I also feel that the hysteria my parents brought to my developing femaleness made me respond with a kind of defensive hysteria about my butchness. There was panic and rigidity on both sides. Certainly we all lacked a sense of play and freedom; gender and sexuality were deadly serious matters.

As I removed myself from their hysteria, I was able to take a few steps back from my own. My dreams no longer invoked only horror and perplexity; instead, they challenged me with new ways of looking at myself. I began to relax. As a result, I discover lately that I want a different form of butchiness for myself. I find that I have lost interest in the very narrow range of clothing choices that fill my closet. I question my own self-enforced constraints. When I perform as a stand-up comic, I want to wear black silk slacks, not jeans. Rather than a man-tailored shirt and a vest, I choose silk blouses and more striking colors. I want my figure to show. Somewhat. I let my hair grow a little longer, find a more stylish haircut. For my office job, I wear blouses with rounded collars and like the way I look. Though I used to remain unperturbed when flight attendants and store clerks innocently called me "sir," now I want them to see—as I myself have come to see—that gender is more variegated than our narrow vocabulary allows. I want my own ambiguity to be recognized, accounted for. I want to be seen.

ACKNOWLEDGMENT

This piece was written with my partner of eleven years, Harriet Malinowitz. Harriet is a writer. I am not. While this is my story, Harriet used her knowledge of my life and my family to push me further and then still further. She offered her own clear insights and provocative ideas. She forced me to develop connections. She also pushed me to carefully craft the language and when I proved to be unpushable, she rescued me with multiple line edits, her own graceful language often covering up my clunkiness. With Harriet, who shares my life and is my greatest claim to happiness, I share the byline on this piece.

Eleven

Such a Polite Little Boy

Arnie Kantrowitz

Shades of the prison-house begin to close
  Upon the growing Boy . . .
                               —William Wordsworth

My parents were a Freudian classic. My father was withdrawn and
uncommunicative; my mother filled the household with fishwife ac-
cusations of failure. I don't know if he met her craving for romance,
but she had probably forsaken that for more practical priorities anyway. She was beautiful to me then, her long dark-blond hair done in
a pageboy, artful arches above her big Bette Davis green eyes, a
prominent Semitic nose fitting well above her Lana Turner lips,
painted in dark 1940s lipstick. Her square-shouldered, V-necked
dresses were covered with rosebuds and femininity. My father was
two inches shorter than she and squarely built. His body boasted a
heavy coat of hair, and he smoked cigars. He saw the world through
cool blue eyes set above his plain, even features, eyes that might
twinkle, but which did so only when he clowned in time-honored
Yiddish fashion for his own parents and siblings. "Jewish" would
have been no more than a label, but I was a child in World War II,
born at the end of 1940, growing to awareness just at the time when
the horrors of the Nazi concentration camps were whispered in uncertain tones, a time when it was puzzling to be both Jewish and alive.

  My father worked in a munitions plant during the war and then
took to the road to work for the state fairs with a game that consisted
of trying to cover a red circle painted on a white board by dropping

slate discs onto it. I never saw anyone do it successfully. My father's secret was probably quick hands and lots of double-talk. Mostly, though, he wasn't around for me. He would come back from his trips with a gift of a few comic books for me, and I was always too embarrassed to tell him that I had already read them.

Often my mother took me to the movies. On the way, she might point out a white-haired old couple helping each other along the sidewalk. She always noticed old people. Her eyes would mist instantly, and she would sigh, "After a long life together, to still love each other like that." She was in love with love. She saw herself as the suffering heroine in a love story, and exposure to her fantasies taught me to do the same. I developed that strange wish-frosted vision of love that novels of the nineteenth century had taught. My mother inherited most of them via Hollywood's versions, or more vulgarly from magazines like *True Romances* which, with mildly lurid suggestion, taught her everything her marriage had failed to be. Later she would abandon her pulp stories along with her pageboy, but she would never lose her secret belief that she had been cheated of her proper portion. She felt like a maiden in a tower, which is a far cry from the housewife in the third-floor walk-up.

We had moved to the third story of a modest two-and-a-half family house on the southernmost block of Newark. Our living room was unpretentious, decorated with blue-mirrored tabletops and a velveteen couch with palm-tree slipcovers. But my mother had taken me to the movies. Deep in both our hearts lurked the image of a vine-covered cottage, picket-fenced garden, gingham apron and all. It might be in Munchkinland modern, but that didn't matter. It had a kitchen where grease never spattered from the frying pans and dishes never broke; and it had a bedroom where you could lovingly remember last night's embraces while you tightened up the sheets. And of course it had him. Always about to come home. (We lived in eternal anticipation, never in plain reality.) His features would be more perfect than yesterday, his love more true. The final embrace would be perfect, and that's how it would stay forever when the gold brocade curtains swept closed across the screen and the houselights came up: frozen, under THE END.

Of course there was a minor hitch in my adopting those fantasies. I was a boy.

But what would I have given to be Merle Oberon, dying perfectly in Olivier's arms, in rerun after rerun? What wouldn't my mother have given? She wanted to be Scarlett O'Hara, carried up her ostentatious stairs. Those fantasies sustained us both through years when real emotions seemed lean. The escape into fiction and film provided exercise for an imagination that was starving, because lodged in its throat was the notion that life should imitate art, and that nothing of substance could pass, only perfection.

During my childhood I spent Saturday afternoons at the Mayfair Theater and the Park Theater, as we moved to different parts of Newark. Although I learned my multiplication tables and where the Nile River is from the texts of Maple Avenue School, I learned my feelings at the movies. And I learned my feelings well, in Technicolor with music and costumes and handsome leading men, with their trim moustaches and their devilish bedroom eyes, with their wind-blown hair and the aura of genius about them. I wanted Rhett Butler to sweep me away from Atlanta ablaze; I wanted Heathcliff sobbing on my grave.

My fantasies ... how dear they were to me! They were like old friends. They began to rule my life secretly from within. And all of it started at the movies—the Saturday matinees—and at the children's room in the library. The fairy tales, the dog stories, the comics, the serials, Tarzan, Flash Gordon, Clark Gable: they were all of a piece. My mind swallowed them whole. I was more than merely alive: because my images were larger than life, their heroism magnified into giant models on the screen. I wanted to swirl in the swirling gowns worn by the women; I wanted the men as my lovers, as I matured.

Imagining myself the pirate's captive in the ship whose sails billowed against a Technicolor blue sky ... knowing my hair was not Rita Hayworth's, but imagining it was, and my dimple—if only I had one, he would ... my dimple Lana Turner's and my Ava Gardner knowing eyes. I thought I wasn't beautiful enough; I was fat. He would never hold me; I would never look like her. Like my mommy, like a lady in the movies, with lipstick, who smells so pretty. (My daddy is away.) And this upturned table is a ship, and all my favorite things are on it, and I'm safe, and the blue, blue linoleum is a sea, and he is sailing toward me in a pirate ship, and he owns me. I am his, but I want him to want me, my pirate hero, my father. I would do anything. I tried to suffer. I suffered like Ida Lupino suffered. I suffered like Claire Trevor suffered. Like Barbara Stanwyck. I coped like

Susan Hayward. I ached like Judy Garland. I endured like Bette Davis. And it only took a little translating to make it gay. It only took defying everything I'd ever been told.

That wasn't me daydreaming in the folding cot with the metal frame and the yellow chenille bedspread, trimmed with the sporadic fringe that had survived the wash. It was Margaret O'Brien in ribbons and pinafore, sitting in the window seat of an English country manor house, and down the walk is a secret garden, and the seat is so snug and secure, the lawn so forever neat and green, and . . . your mother wants you to play baseball.

We lived on Grumman Avenue, a placid, pleasant neighborhood, full of children to play with. I liked jump rope. They bought me a cowboy outfit. The cap pistol was okay, but the arguments over whether you got me and I'm dead were boring. I much preferred playing house with the girls in the garage, even if they always made me the daddy. Tending to a family seemed so much nicer than score-keeping the dead. But it wasn't all right to play house. Little boys aren't supposed to. Almost every night when I came home for supper, I was interrogated about whom I had played with, what I had played, and for how long. It was easier to lie, so I could do what I wanted to do, but my inquisitor didn't believe me. Her cardinal rule was, "Just tell the truth, and you won't be punished." Now I live by it.

She bought me a baseball uniform and led me up to the other end of the street where the big boys played. Begging their indulgence, she planted me in the middle of their game. I didn't know them. I didn't know the game. No one had taught me. I cried. I didn't much like baseball anyway, and I liked wearing uniforms even less.

I escaped more deeply into my own fantasies. I passed through the usual stage of deciding I had been adopted by strangers and took it one step further. I imagined I was really the heir apparent of the King and Queen of Earth, and that I was being raised in humble circumstances to temper my understanding of my future subjects so that I would be a wise and compassionate ruler. I fantasized that whoever I encountered during the day was actually being rewarded for heroism— the more involved they were with my life, the greater their good deed. Rewards ranged from being seen on the street, to eye contact, to an exchange of words, or even feelings. I had been taken to the movies.

During the war years I was tucked into nursery schools, boarding farms, and day camps, but none of them worked. I always had to leave as soon as I arrived because I wanted to be near my mother. She was so beautiful. When the Zenith radio announced that Franklin Delano Roosevelt was dead, I remember she cried. (My mother went in for presidents in a big bipartisan way.) I wanted to join her out of sympathy, but I had been training myself not to cry. It wasn't manly to show emotions, not even for the European Holocaust which was mercifully rendered unreal by its distance. Europe was where children starved if I didn't finish my cereal. When the war ended, I was five years old.

I was six years old the first time I seduced a man. I even remember his name. It was Stuart. He was fourteen and lived up the street from me, and he was beautiful. He made me feel coy and flirtatious, which came out as hero worship and tagging along, the only means for expressing your lust when you're six. One summer day after watching him play ball, I walked home with him, hinting broadly that I would like him to take me down to his cellar.

"What for?" he wanted to know.

"Just to play," said I.

"Play what?" he persisted.

"Oh, whatever we think of," I said as suggestively as I could, though I scarcely knew what I was suggesting. I only knew I wanted him to protect and overpower me.

"Well," he conceded, "supper isn't for a while. Okay."

He was the pirate captain, and I was captured from another vessel. Inside the coal room, when I was caught, I managed to feel his embrace as he tied me up and "tortured" me by holding a lighted match far enough away so it could do no harm. Not quite Paulette Goddard, but respectable for openers.

The first time a man tried to seduce me was not long afterward. I was walking in my short shorts past the school playground when I passed the proverbial black sedan parked menacingly near the curb. The driver beckoned to me.

"Want to go for a ride?" he invited suggestively.

"My mother told me not to ride with strangers," I answered, obedient to the most stringent caution I had been taught.

"I've got what you want," he leered.

I was totally naive. "What do I want?"

"You know."

"No, I don't," I said, walking off firmly.

It was about that time that my mother first tried to counsel me about the evils of making love to someone of your own sex. The message wasn't specific, and I wouldn't have understood it if it were, but it was clear. My guts understood it all too well.

"Arnold," she began with import, "you know there are certain ways little boys are supposed to behave. You know what little boys who don't behave right are called? They're called sissies." I didn't know what she was talking about, yet I knew exactly what she meant. I was different from what she wanted me to be, and I was scared, scared there was something wrong with me, scared my mother didn't love me.

"When I was in high school," she continued, "there was a boy named Edward, and Edward didn't act the way he was supposed to. All the other kids called him a sissy and laughed at him. And one day a gang of them followed him home from school, and somebody threw a rock at him, and it hit him in the head and killed him. You don't want that to happen to you, do you?"

"No, Mommy."

"Then you'll behave the way you're supposed to, won't you?"

"Yes, Mommy."

Nonetheless, as the years went on, and she began to spend more and more nights away from home, I helped her to prepare for the soft-lit world of cocktail lounges she had discovered. As she dressed for her evenings out, she often asked my advice about whether to wear the shocking pink satin strapless with the fishtail pleat and the dyed-to-match shoes whose stiletto heels were ablaze with rhinestones, or the royal blue brocade with blue-tinted stockings, or the black dotted Swiss for simplicity's sake. I chose the pink. I began to draw pictures of pretty ladies in dresses, to design new ideas to win my mother's approval. She approved of the designs, but not of the fact that I was doing them.

I was doing everything wrong. Boys shouldn't talk with their hands. Boys don't sway their hips when they walk. (Remember what happened to Edward?) Boys don't laugh at such a high pitch. I shouldn't laugh the way that was natural to me. It didn't sound natural. Learned laughs don't come from the belly.

Now, except for an occasional foray into camping, my walk, my talk, and my laugh are all "acceptable." I learned well. I was always a good student, the teacher's pet, hugged with embarrassing approval in front of the whole class, bringing home honor certificates and report cards heavy with As. I was such a polite little boy. But I wasn't learning something right. I wasn't learning how to be a "man." More drastic measures were needed for that.

First she tried hormone shots. The excuse was that I was too short for my age, and I didn't want to grow up to be a runt like my father, did I? A year of weekly injections produced an excess of hormones that might have put a little more hair on my chest, but it didn't stop me from being attracted to hairy chests on other men. Maybe its main effect was to make me go bald earlier than anyone else in the family.

Next came the manly art of violence: boxing lessons. I had to go to a gym in downtown Newark once a week and grapple with heavy medicine balls and punching bags. Mainly I learned how to watch my eyes in the locker room. I couldn't seem to keep them on the locker. I was more interested in hugging my partners than in sparring with them anyway, but I wasn't completely aware of that yet. I didn't even know such things actually happened. Nor did I know there was a final exam in the self-defense course. Twice, on the street, coming home from Cub Scout meetings, friends stopped a perfectly amiable conversation and punched me in the mouth. I fought back the best I could—not the way I had been taught, but by hitting them with the pile of music I was carrying from my piano lesson, or trying to turn the attack into a wrestling match. Days went by with me still wondering what had provoked my friends into such outrages. Finally they explained that my mother had asked them to attack me for my own good. Thanks, Mom.

The guaranteed method was a summer of manly company for models and sports for training, with a little nature lore on the side. My mother made like Betsy Ross with the name tags and filled a trunk with shirts and socks and shorts all neatly labeled. I, meanwhile, went to the library and took out a pile of books for the summer, mainly animal adventure novels starring dogs with names like Lad or Awol and horses called Misty or Black Beauty. I carefully unpacked a third of the trunk and replaced my changes of athletic clothes with enough material to escape from my forced vacation, and off I went to the land of men: Kamp Kiamesha.

Sunday mornings we rose from our canvas-walled bunkhouses, where the bedwetters got the upper bunks as if by plan, and we were herded off to the canteen to draw a dime from our snack money to deposit as choiceless charity in the offering tray of the tidily nondenominational church. It seemed patently Protestant to me. The one denomination it was most definitely not was my forefathers' Judaism. Mother had dutifully warned me not to listen too hard, which was easy enough advice to follow, and so Sundays hardly fazed me. But she didn't warn me about the counselor who was always threatening to pin me down and make me smell his armpits and accept the used chewing gum from his mouth into mine. It was as close as I could get to nuzzling and kissing him, and I loved even the idea of it. In fact, I was probably the first to suggest it, and I did everything I could to encourage him. I don't remember a word of Sunday morning's sermons, but I remember exactly how good that chewing gum tasted.

Sunday afternoons my parents would be the very last to arrive after my father had put in half a day at his grocery and had chugged his father's old Packard convertible out to the wilds of northern New Jersey. By the time they got there it was almost time for them to go, and I barely had the opportunity to show them the plastic lanyard I had laboriously braided to hold my house key around my neck, or the leather belt I had looped for my father. But in the brief while they were there, my mother had a chance to nose around and discover that I had been sneaking off to read in the woods instead of playing baseball, and she instructed the counselor with a five-dollar bill that it was going to be baseball, not books.

Mainly I spent my baseball time trying to convince everybody that it was going to rain any second and we'd better put away our gloves and go inside, while hoping fervently that no fly ball would find its way to my part of the outfield. My mother had boasted enough of my professional boxing lessons to get me enrolled in the camp boxing contest, but I conceded that match by holding my bent elbows in front of my face and retreating. I have enough trouble hitting people I don't like, let alone people I don't even know. Also, I was scared.

Swimming wasn't much better. I nearly drowned because I was so entranced with the counselors' cocks bobbing blithely up and down as they tested the diving board. But hiking was the most trying: I was the last to reach the mountaintop where we camped out overnight amid grizzly bear campfire stories and marshmallows toasted on sticks, and then to sleep on the bare rock top which gave the mountain its name of "Old Baldy." In the morning I awoke surprised at its base, having slid there in my sleep. I trailed into camp an hour after everyone else that afternoon, my sneakers flopping because I had used their laces to tie my blanket together after I had lost the rope and my belt as well, causing my pants to droop around my hips, which were already beginning to itch from the poison ivy I had slept in. I lasted most of the summer. But even though I left early, I learned how to brew sassafras tea and what a salamander is, which contributed to a felt letter K for Kiamesha to sew on my sweater. I was proud of the K, and I don't mind at all knowing about salamanders, even if I've never met one in Manhattan. And that chewing gum was some of the best chewing gum I've ever chewed.

My relation to gender roles has never been very strong. As a boy, I remember thinking that the woman's social role was better than the man's because she could stay home to tend to house and family. I felt like a failure as the man that society wanted me to be, and I was ashamed of what made me different, which led to two suicide attempts in my twenties. Now most people don't perceive me as effeminate, nor do they seem to recognize my homosexuality until I declare it (which I do freely). According to my mother's dictates, I retrained myself to act in an acceptably male—but certainly not exaggeratedly butch—manner, and now it seems natural to me. My laughs do come from the belly. I don't talk with my hands or wiggle when I walk, but I don't feel repressed.

Since my childhood I have continued to seek solace in the movies and to identify with the women actors. I no longer want to be them. I simply see things through their eyes: love the men they love, use the same nonviolent verbal and emotional strategies they use to endure. With the exception of one or two Halloween costumes, which were my mother's idea, I have never experimented with cross-dressing nor had any desire to do so. This is not to say I in any way condemn cross-dressing; it's just not *my* thing.

I still play with the girls. I've always been close to women, both heterosexual and lesbian: an aunt, a cousin, colleagues at work, the mothers of friends. I have straight male friends too, but we talk more about public issues and less about intimate matters. It wasn't until I was nearly thirty that I formed a circle of gay male friends, and for twenty years I used to discuss my most personal feelings with them until I lost most of them to the AIDS epidemic. Now, in my fifties, the majority of the friends I share my intimate thoughts with are women.

My sensibility has a good measure of what I consider female traits, such as the satisfaction I get from nurturing, advising, and consoling, whether as a friend, a teacher, or a mate of fifteen years to writer and physician Larry Mass.

I am glad to be the particular mix of male and female that I am. I don't feel like a manly man or a womanly man or a woman trapped in a man's body. I feel like a person in a human being's body. The rest, such as clothing and mannerisms and artificially induced muscles, seems somehow superficial. It no longer matters to me what society thinks—although, with the exception of rabid homophobes, I usually meet with approval on a personal level. Perhaps it's because I like myself as I am.

Every once in a while I think back to that camp counselor with the musky armpits and the delicious chewing gum and I wonder what ever became of him. Wouldn't it be funny if he turned out to be a flaming queen?

Twelve

Las Nenas con las Nenas, los Nenes con los Nenes

Lawrence M. La Fountain-Stokes

There are times when everything seems divided, somewhat arbitrarily, by one of those fatal but decisive accidents, like the Pope's famous decree that split up the globe in 1494: everything west of the *Tordesillas* line in the "New" World for Spain, everything east for Portugal. The consequences of such historical arrogance and geopolitical might are astounding: Brazil and Africa joined by a stroke of the quill to half a continent extending across India through Macao and Timor. All this for the Lusitanians, leaving everything from the Philippines to Nueva España, Perú, and the Caribbean for the crown of Castille and Aragón.

When I was growing up, the world around me was similarly arranged in twos, some more understandable, other things just as random: two parents, two children, two languages, two countries, two sexes, two races. Everything set out in pairs, at times demanding my adherence to one side and not the other, a world of things I could or could not do, be or not be. I say two but I could say a thousand. Puerto Rico, where I am from, the result of a random act which split up the world, which set the stage for the effacement of the indigenous reality of an island and for the scarring of Africa through the violent transport of thousands of its displaced peoples to unknown lands as slaves. A world called Puerto Rico, firmly entrenched in Spain's former geographic dominion, reconstructed through a tragic history of migrations and invasions, including that of the United States in 1898. An island and culture divided by a line much less perceptible, not fixed in maps but in the imagination and bodies of all its members, a world which insistently reminded me of its dictum to keep to my side of the road, to behave like a little man was supposed to, an *hombrecito hecho y derecho*, the opposite of a girl.

Las nenas con las nenas, los nenes con los nenes. Girls with girls, boys with boys, not—mind you—in any delightfully perverse way, but as a code of conduct and socialization. Continuous repetition of this expression by both adults and children insisted on physical proximity as a controlling mechanism: girls were to do that which was proper for girls; boys that which boys do. And though I tried, this boy was always with girls (including many butch girls) and went about like one of them: fleeing from boys; avoiding sports and outdoor activities; wearing a shirt while others went shirtless; causing trouble for himself and others as a nonconformist in a sea of uniformity.

Those with Shirts and Those Without

An absurd and repressive *Tordesillas* line runs through my brain which says that men can go without shirts and women cannot, and for some reason I have always followed the latter. While emancipated women nowadays brave their unencumbered breasts to the sun and sky, I recall childhood school days of yore in which I precariously grasped onto my sweat-covered T-shirt, thinking of the possibility of my naked chest as a threat, my shame and utmost embarrassment. I cannot recall ever being on the team required to undress in this manner during gym class. The world divided in two: boys with shirts and boys without. How come girls got colorful little vests as markers of who was on what team, while boys had to show their naked flesh?

My father, an American, walks around without a shirt, fixes the car without a shirt, paints the house and putters in the garage and front yard without a shirt. Puerto Rico, land of eternal summer, allows for year-round shirtless behavior. I resist his sartorial liberty. I desperately grasp onto my cover. I am a fat, adopted, girlish boy who hated sports and other strenuous activities and preferred to eat or cook with my mother, or play in my room with blocks, or read or color or pretty much do absolutely anything else. Anything except climb a tree or throw *pepas* at other kids or play basketball or walk around shirtless.

Summer Camp

My worst nightmare occurs one day in summer camp, when I come out of the swimming pool and my T-shirt is gone. I sit in the bus that takes us back to school, where the camp usually meets, shirtless and embarrassed. I am convinced that someone has purposely stolen my shirt to humiliate me. I am seven years old, just out of first grade at *Academia del Perpetuo Socorro.*

That same summer, I remember walking down the side of the high school building where the tennis courts used to be, or maybe I was sitting in the bleachers of the basketball court. A group of boys approaches me and asks me if I would let one of them, Alberto, stroke my face. I see no problem in this and enjoy it when he touches my cheek. The boys ask me how I feel and burst out laughing when I respond that I liked it. I don't understand their reaction but I know right away that I have done something wrong, that I have somehow failed their test.

Puerto Rican Genealogies

My mother was born in the United States to an American father and a Puerto Rican mother and grew up going back and forth from the island to the continent, as family fortunes and luck determined. Most of her childhood was spent in the United States. This left my sister and me in a strange predicament. It is odd to be the children of Americans in Puerto Rico. Foreigners, and particularly those of our type, are always regarded with suspicion. Being from "over there" is perceived as a form of betrayal. Being from over there and over here at the same time unnerves people even more. Diasporic subjects are "troublesome," they refuse easy categorization, they defy common expectations. My maternal grandmother Carmen was born in Mayagüez. She was an educated woman, well traveled, a writer of children's stories and radio soap operas, who tried to instill in us an appreciation for culture and a curiosity for everything new and foreign. She had hundreds of cousins and other relatives, wore thick white makeup and too-white face powder, ate heavily salted food (especially *garbanzos con chorizo*), smoked cigarettes with long dangling ashes, had rosaries and beads for her Catholic church rituals, wore rose water perfume and, above all else, sat in wood and wicker rocking chairs moving slowly back and forth on the tiles of a balcony that faced the street.

The Maid

I am a middle-class kid, a strange middle class that sends its children to exclusive schools (mostly on scholarships or in exchange for my mom's "voluntary" service in the library) but really doesn't have that much money to spare. Yet there was enough money to allow for a maid to come occasionally, perhaps once a week or every other week, especially when my mother started to have back problems and needed help. The lady who cleaned our house was called Hilda, and she usually came with one of her three daughters, or one of her *ahijadas*, who would help her do her work that day.

Hilda would always make lunch for us, hot dogs and tuna fish and *arroz con salchichas con pegao* that my mother didn't know how to cook. She was black and working class, and her daughters followed meticulous hair practices which I did not quite understand. She would give my sister black dolls for Three Kings Day, and gave me yellow trucks. Most striking, however, was how Hilda glorified dominant, brutal masculinity, in the way she would inquire about my (nonexistent) love life, in her emphasis that she was raising her nephews to be real men, even if they were still only a couple of years old. I lived in terror of Hilda's interrogations and would feign impartial neutrality when listening to her stories of how she beat up boys found playing with dolls. I nevertheless loved her.

Los Libros de Titi Nacha y Tío John

When I was small, my sister and I would always get books from my *titi* Nacha and *tío* John, as well as horrible pinches on our cheeks that seemed to smart for hours. My aunt and uncle would always show up at those parties for which my grandmother made deviled eggs. *Titi* Nacha was really my grandmother's first cousin; she had met her Irish Argentinean husband in New York.

The reason why we always got books was because my uncle owned the *Librería Hispanoamericana* in Río Piedras, near the university. I mostly remember two: one that my sister got on how to organize little tea parties for her girlfriends, with recipes for cookies and the like, and one that I received about astronauts. Whatever made them think that I'd be more interested in outer space than in chamomile?

Big Jim Meets Barbie

There was a time when my Big Jim dolls would go visit my sister's Barbies. My parents never allowed me to have G.I. Joe, which they thought encouraged violence and militarism. This did not keep them from giving me cowboy guns. Since my sister always wanted me to play with her, I would oblige her by driving Big Jim's camper up to Barbie's town house. That's how I'd get to play with Barbie.

We especially loved to go on joint explorations of the cement back-yard patio and on simultaneous camping trips, in which little branches and twigs and leaves would become major obstacles. Our favorite hangouts included a big red bush nicknamed Clifford and a prickly green monster we referred to as Oscar the Grouch. The frequent spotting of random bugs and birds, or of tiny lizards called *lagartijos* and occasional iguanas would provide Big Jim and Barbie with Mutual of Omaha or prehistoric Godzilla terror scenes. Big Jim and Barbie always got along just fine. After all, Barbie had a little fully equipped kitchen, not to mention tons of outfits.

Swimming

When I was ten, I eagerly joined the Psi Sigma Alpha Fraternity swimming team along with the rest of my neighborhood friends. Perhaps it had to do with my father's past, with his having been a swimming champ in prep school, as he constantly reminded us. The problem wasn't sports; it was what to do while outside the pool.

Faced with the possibility of having to play with violent, mean boys, my task quickly became that of unofficial baby-sitter. What better job could there be for a twelve-year-old child allergic to boy's activities and rejected by boy-crazy girls in midpuberty? Mothers de-lightedly handed over their two- and three-year olds, whom I would accompany to the playground, while my peers beat each other up or played *gallitos* with stinky *algarrobo* seeds. Then the babies would grow and start to ignore me and I'd have to find younger ones to look after. I felt quite maternal in those days. I was convinced I had a special bond with kids and animals, and that we could communicate telepathically, in secret nonverbal ways.

Basketball Massacre

One Christmas, after my father had installed a basketball hoop in the backyard, our house was overrun by older boys from the neighborhood. No sooner had they started to play that they fatally knocked over and killed a succulent flowering plant with a big red flower, a flower akin to a big orange basketball, like the one that most probably crashed down on it. I cried inconsolably. It was a nice plant that had mysteriously poked through some rocks. It had a soft, feathery feel to its leaves and seemed special in my botanist-like perception of the world.

I don't really know what happened exactly. I'm not even sure if I tried to nurse that casualty of an unwanted and undesired sporting Armageddon back to life. I only remember crying in my mother's presence, while my father tried to get me to play ball with the guys. The only good thing that came out of that hoop was that my sister went on to play basketball in high school. She's now a sports announcer at ESPN.

Slow Dancing

When I was in junior high, I was friends mostly with girls. Dancing at backyard disco parties was always sort of complicated, especially when they played romantic boleros. I always tried to make sure I danced at least one song with each one of my many, many girlfriends. They all thought I was very nice. It amazes me how busy I kept myself.

While slow dancing, I never knew exactly where to place my hands or where to look. There is something to be said for the close proximity of two bodies, even if it's all decidedly unromantic. My girlfriends (and sister) always wanted me to dance salsa and merengue with them as well. I guess it was the closest thing to having two girls dance together without actually doing so.

La Casa Vieja (The Old White House)

I remember coming back home from school, one Halloween finding a big dead rat by the side of the house, and thinking that someone had left it there for me. I have blocked out most of the injurious insults and catcalls of my youth, but I will always remember that for many months there was a pencil-scribbled message in front of my house: *Larry es pato*, or gay. I kept to myself a lot when I was growing up, so much so that my mother would worry and try to send me off with my sister and her friends. After a certain age, however, the girls were not thrilled to have me around.

We lived in a big old house which is no longer standing. Its outer walls were cement but the insides were all wood, including the ceiling and floor. The roof was covered in zinc, and falling rain would make a funny noise as it hit the metal; during hurricane time, my sister and I would be spirited off to some neighbor's house whose more solid construction afforded greater safety. Our house was subject to periodic attacks by termites, or *polilla*, which my family would set out to kill, one by one. The little squiggly worms would run about, dropping their translucent wings as they tried to burrow into the walls or wood furniture or books before we got there and squashed them.

Public television was my salvation. Ballet and opera engrossed me, to the great chagrin of my family, who preferred baseball games and Star Trek and Magnum, PI. That was after we got cable TV. Before cable, my sister and I would sit entranced watching Puerto Rican programs such as "Sube, nene, sube!" and "Pa'rriba, papi, pa'rriba!" both hosted by Luis Vigoreaux and his family, in which grooms (in the first) and fathers (in the second) would compete to win furniture sets and electrodomestic appliances from Mueblerías Tar Tak. Our favorites, however, were the Iris Chacón and Charytín shows, which we watched in a hypnotized state, completely oblivious to the sexual double entendres and provocations the shows celebrated. Everyone knew that Iris Chacón's dancers were maricones (gays, or at least effeminate) but this didn't seem to be a problem; it was merely the source of many jokes.

My parents did not exactly appreciate my performative talents. On a certain late night evening I decided to dance naked in my room, draping my body with my red bedcover, using my night-light as source of illumination. My father, whom I awakened, thought the noise was caused by a burglar and burst into my room, catching me *in fraganti*. He was not thrilled to learn that the commotion had been caused by his prancing son, who was out of his pajamas wrapped in sheets.

Another time, on a day that the Miami windows in the front of the house were left open, I decided to dance around the living room and roll on the floor, pretending to be a modern dancer. To my great horror, a young friend of my sister's came over and spied me through the window. She didn't seem particularly phased by the spectacle, but I felt like it was the end of the world. Boys weren't supposed to dance around like that.

Cooking

While growing up, I was always most talented at the culinary art of "enhancement." I would take a can of generic brand spaghetti and meatballs or an assortment of leftovers and convert them into something slightly more edible. I usually had the kitchen all to myself for lunch, since my mother was a big advocate of no-cook alternatives such as sandwiches, and did not mind my invasion of what was usually her space. I suspect my willingness to cook might have had to do with the fact that in most Puerto Rican households, lunch was a very important meal; eating hot dogs with frozen corn on the cob American-style just didn't cut it with me.

I really don't know what my mother thought of my obsession with her cooking, of the hours I would spend watching her do whatever she had to do. She often conscripted me into peeling potatoes or doing some other unsavory task while she prepared dinner. My mother always enjoyed the results of my experiments except when I dirtied hundreds of pots and pans, which I usually forgot to wash. She would always say that I should open a restaurant. It was our little joke. My sister never learned to cook while we were growing up. She still doesn't cook very much today.

Tordesillas Revisited

Memories cross my thoughts in disparate and contradictory directions. I recall Mexican bodybuilder magazines the size of comic books purchased furtively in small neighborhood *supermercados*, transvestite prostitutes that I would see around Stop 18 in Santurce, effeminate men who everyone thought or knew or accused of being *patos*, distinctions which didn't really matter to me—how was I to know the difference? A very fit, hairy handyman who everyone knew was gay "betrayed" himself by the slightest actions, like carrying around one of those pocketbooks for men that became popular in Puerto Rico when I was growing up in the 1970s and 1980s. I remember a gay social columnist found murdered in his apartment, all tied up, with pornographic magazines strewn all about, in a building a couple of houses down from where I used to live. No wonder being like a girl caused such anxiety in me—if being like a girl meant that I was, or would become, like them. José Martí used to say that childhood was a golden age, the most wondrous one of all. How I would disagree! It's not as if I didn't have any fun when I was small. There was Barbie and cooking and dancing, after all. One makes do with what there is. And for me, that mostly had to do with hanging out with my mother and grandmother and sister, and with other girls and the maid, on the other side of the line.

Thirteen

Boys Don't Do That

Michael Lassell

As far as I can remember—and I spend more time in reverie (and playing computer solitaire) than I think is healthy, even if it's therapy that keeps stirring up the old witch's cauldron—I spent my childhood in the company of women.

Oh, there were boys around. I had more older cousins than I knew (and just found out about another). There were the male children of the neighborhood, even friends from time to time, like Little Michael (an epileptic who was born premature), Wayne (who grew up to father thirteen children before dying while still in his forties), Johnny (whose uncle was murdered in the parking lot of the local bowling alley by his Mafia cohorts and whose mother rode herd on our movie fare: *Bambi*, yes; *The World of Suzie Wong*, no).

But as an only child, my preschool years were passed almost exclusively in the company of my mother; my godmother / Aunt Helene (the oversized Polish wife of my mother's brother), my mother's life-long friend, the Swedish Tante Helen; and her daughter Linda, four years my elder, whom I called Didi when I was a toddler (Tante Helen was "Didi's Rara"). Aunt Helene's daughter Gloria, fourteen years older than me and my first baby-sitter, had already left the landscape by the time my consciousness kicked in.

My memory grows sketchy, of course, now that I have entered my official gay dotage, my fiftieth birthday having recently been visited upon me like an Old Testament plague. But my history was carefully recorded on reels of 8mm film and stacks of photographs that serve now as reminders. My earliest memories, which belong to the late 1940s, are actually quite pleasant.

Consider this dream I had once—an idyllic, soft-focus dream with feathery white dandelion seeds floating on the golden air above the field of our Catskills summer house backyard (kind of *Elvira Madigan* before this went bad). In this dream, a grasshopper jumped down Linda's cornflower-blue gingham dress. I dreamed her arm-flailing panic, the immediate attention of the three mother-women, all in dresses of bright floral cotton (the same attention I would have from them some years later when I ignited a pack of "safety" matches in my pocket one Fourth of July, the same attention I would offer Gloria's son Brian when he took a bite out of his first glass). I dreamed Tante Helen was pulling Linda's dress off and releasing the insect back to freedom, and I dreamed of the freedom of the two of us splashing in the creek in our underwear, and a trio of sweet bemused smiles.

And all this dream was true, Aunt Helene told me when I recounted it to her over breakfast one morning—so this must have been when I was still in high school (she died my freshman year in college). It was, in fact, a memory disguised as a dream. Whatever it was, I remember to this day these closest companions of my childhood, this complex love knot of three women and two children, only one of whom was male. And it serves as a talisman for me of how my memory works: in cinematic flashbacks that don't always cut into a coherent film. In fact, if you've ever seen an editing room piled with the spaghetti of discarded footage, that's what my life is like. Start with an idyllic scene from childhood and follow the celluloid strip, and you're as likely as not to find a dauntingly long Möbius strip that manages to loop back on itself revealing new images, new takes, new splicings each time.

When 1950 came, we sold the summer house where "the girls" would spend the summer, joined by "the men" only on weekends. The happiest times of my childhood, that little wedge between 1947 and the early 1950s, was about to be over. Our family of three moved to suburban New York, kissing bucolic summers and the extended Brooklyn family good-bye. Within a few years, the aunts and their husbands had moved to Long Island—along with all their relatives and my father's sisters and their families—but it was too late. I had already become somehow "different." I had already discovered shame—but I don't remember when or how.

How could I have felt shame if I don't remember learning transgression?

I felt it in my body. In debilitating headaches so severe I had to go to bed, where I would lie motionless with cold compresses over my eyes, all the Venetian blinds in the house closed and the curtains drawn, my parents walking around on tiptoe, each sound, each beam of light adding to the dull ache. The occasional migraine headache haunts me still, and in each nauseated spell I am brought back to childhood as vividly as the grasshopper dream.

This is when the great loneliness began, too.

Psyches are elusive, of course, elaborate constructions, the wires of cause and effect crossing in myriad ways that are difficult to untangle after the fact. What caused the loneliness? What caused the headaches? The unhappiness? I know now that some of it was doubtlessly related to the abortion my mother had when I was two, after she contracted German measles at a crucial moment in the gestation of her second child. But I didn't *know* about the abortion when I was a young child. In the tradition of our Anglo-Saxon forebears, no one ever mentioned it. But the secret lived with us as surely as if that fetal sibling of mine had been carried to term and occupied its own room. It is not an accident of introspection that I started to think of myself as a plural entity, a set of twins in a single body, or—like Thornton Wilder, I was to discover years later—the surviving half of a set of twins. I never had an imaginary friend: I *was* my imaginary friend; I spent my life in awe and in envy of any boy with brothers (even though my gay male friends tell me that having a brother could be unmitigated hell).

The other lesson my child self picked up from the ether of my home in those early years was this: If her children weren't perfect, my mother killed them. And perfection has been my standard ever since, the only condition I can comfortably tolerate in my own work and behavior. It's a burden.

My education in transgression began with school, I suspect, since it was not until school that I really understood there was such a thing as gender-appropriate behavior. My behavior was tolerated as long as it was sequestered within the confines of our five-room, G. I. Bill development house. The adults often segregated themselves along gender lines (card games where men played gin and women played canasta; holidays where women cooked and washed dishes while men watched football on TV). I was just a child, considered sexless, I suppose, or at least neuter. Eyewitnesses who were not related by blood, however, added the possibility of embarrassing my parents to the potential hazards of growing up gay—and I did, and they didn't like it.

In the rigid, preenlightened days of the 1950s, gender roles were even more strictly enforced than they are now. There was no G.I. Joe for boys who liked dolls to play with (although I would have had no interest in such a doll in any case; had there been a Barbie, I'd have been right there). There was no precedent for a boy who didn't like baseball. When forced to make art in grade school the boys put their crayons at the service of bloody battle scenes from World War II (or meticulously rendered bird's-eye views of baseball diamonds). If you didn't like baseball, you weren't a boy, not a "real boy," at least. And this was communicated, I must surmise, from the beginning of school. Just as the McCarthy goons were pronouncing that certain behaviors and certain people were un-American, so I was declared Not a Real Boy (much like Pinocchio, only far less accepted—although it's worth nothing that I later made alliances with the kind of bad 'uns Pinocchio found when he felt rejected and in just the same kind of nether world, mine being Times Square).

From the earliest days of kindergarten, to which I was escorted that first September day by my mother and Aunt Helene (I could reproduce the scene exactly on film), it was clear that I was not like the other children: I was smart, talented, precocious, responsible, strong-willed, high-strung. I wasn't like the other children in that I could be trusted to take care of another kid (usually Little Michael, who had physical as well as emotional problems); I wasn't like the other children because I absorbed information like a sponge and grasped nearly every lesson immediately. It wasn't long, however, before it became likewise clear that I was a sissy and a crybaby. The free-floating shame began to be attached not only to behavior, but to identity: It wasn't just that I never knew how to act (which meant, in parent parlance, I didn't know how to please adults), but there was something, I came to intuit, *wrong* with me. My mother and her Wednesday afternoon canasta friends may have thought it cute for me to play with them (and *adorable* that I kept winning—a word I had to be taught that boys don't use), but even then I knew it was not right. It was certainly not something Johnny or Wayne would have done, and *they* wouldn't have been allowed to. Of me it was expected.

Growing up as an only child, with Linda as my only real companion, I had come rather naturally to do and to enjoy the same things that appealed to her. As the closest thing either of us has ever had to a sibling, there has always been a deep attachment and a rivalry between us. Our mothers baked cookies together; our fathers built garages and back porches and turned attics into guest rooms and basements into family rooms. Linda and I designed dresses.

The dresses of the 1950s were glamorous, extravagant fantasies of silk, satin, and velvet yardage (much like the days of the Civil War, only *much* sexier). I loved drawing anything, but I particularly loved drawing dresses and spent whole days doing it. In fact, I loved every fantasy escape I could come by from the dull world of my parents' sweat-of-the-brow Protestant ethic, which involved a great deal of housecleaning and yard work and very little unscheduled time for reading or designing traveling ensemble for Brenda Starr (she had to have an *outfit* to go off to Brazil with her eye-patched mystery man, after all). I devoured comic books, not the superhero ones boys were supposed to like, but those cranked out by Disney (I loved the globetrotting adventures of Scrooge McDuck, Unca Donald, and the three nephews—identical brothers), those based on classic books (like *Ivanhoe*), and those aimed at teenage girls (the ones that featured hamburger-devouring Jughead and raven-haired Veronica, who was another of my high-fashion models).

I suppose it says a great deal that whenever my family divided along sex lines, I was assigned the women's hogan. That's why I sometimes say, sometimes think, that in some significant way I was raised to be a girl, but I was also being blamed for it.

The problem with nuclear families is that they are emotional ecosystems that frequently lack sufficient nutrients, sufficient psychic oxygen for the development of healthy offspring. Rather than healthy self-sufficient plants, they produce hothouse flowers, pale imitations of their parents. They are not just limiting, incestuous, and too self-congratulatory to admit the possibility of deficiency: they are frequently (more often than not?) toxic. I was forty when I first read Alice Miller's *The Drama of the Gifted Child*, and I wept all the way through it. Add sexual minority to gifted, and the die is cast for psychic disaster.

And here another memory splices itself into the epic hodgepodge of my life, another flush of shame:

"Are you a bride?" Mrs. Cosgrove asked. I can hear it to this day. Mrs. Cosgrove, our next-door neighbor, was the mother of two sons in those days, though she had more later. (One of them, Bobby, was a friend, and a boy I've lusted after in one way or another for nearly half a century.)

I had asked for and been given a torn white sheet to play with, and I ripped it into a costume. I meant to be the Mummy from the Boris Karloff movie of the same name.

"Go show it to Trudy," I can remember my mother saying. I can remember the heart-pounding anticipation too. And the shocking, stunning, red-faced disappointment when the mother of my friend mistook me for a bride!

"I'm a *mummy!*" I said, running away, somehow knowing that it was a hideous thing to have been taken for a would-be woman and that my secret confusions were a matter of public currency.

I assumed Bobby would never play with me again. But he did. We made log cabins with Lincoln Logs and I watched while he played stickball with his brother and the other Real Boys. He slipped into my libido early, and I'd peek between the blinds of my room for glimpses of him in his underwear. By junior high, his older brother was a tormentor; Bobby valiantly undertook a protector role with his brother and other would-be school bus bullies.

By the time I was eight years old, I was afraid of recess because of the humiliation meted out by the boys. By the time I was ten, I had made the transition from "Michael seems impervious to the opinions of his male peers" (which, at age eight, I had mistaken for a compliment) to "Michael does not play well with others." The boys wouldn't have me, and my close association with girls became a source of ridicule. To this day, I am more afraid of humiliation than I am of death. In third grade, I was granted special dispensation from recess by loving (female) teachers, who would let me stay indoors to draw scenes out of Mary Poppins or to write poems about brooks that somehow got to flow over the hills and beyond—just the place I wanted to be always. Later in life, when this feeling came over me, I just wanted to be dead.

All through school, everything I did seemed to be a source of amusement to my "peers," because everything I did was considered something girls did: art, music, even reading (which I did, voraciously). I was eight the first time I came to think my talent was shameful because it was associated with being perceived as a girl. It was a music class (or, rather, a music hour in our class). The music teacher—a woman with graying black hair piled on top of her head in a halolike braid and a necklace of beads the size of walnuts—heard something from the crowd she liked and singled me out to sing on my own. At church, where I was already singing in the choir, I would have relished the chance. But at school I was frozen in fear, not because I felt inadequate to perform, but because I anticipated that my performance would be condemned because it was good. I was dressed that day in my Cub Scout uniform (one of my many vain attempts to fit in with boys), and was placed in the hall as a punishment for refusing to sing by myself. Just as I was punished at age ten when, during a rehearsal for the fifth-grade play I realized that my facility at dancing was being made fun of by the boys *and* the girls. I felt betrayed (as usual). The rug was being pulled out from underneath me so relentlessly I never felt safe standing up.

My attempts to fit in with boys (and later to fit in with any peer group that would have me) were always failures. Of course, I was the last one chosen for every baseball team, but I wasn't actually physically inept. I just did not like contact sports (and had no idea where all the other boys had learned the complex rules they spouted with such authority). I didn't like pain. I didn't like roughhousing. I was, in the words of my mother—always eager to explain my unhappiness as the inevitable result of some defect of mine—"too sensitive." (I didn't have any friends because I always had to have everything my own way; no one would play with me because I had such a loud voice.)

My "gender identity" was not the only area of my life that was repressed, of course. I remember having a disagreement with an adult when I was perhaps twelve years old. My mother was livid.

"I was just expressing an opinion," I remember saying in self-defense, as she glowered at me from the front seat of the white Dodge Dart my father had bought instead of getting me braces for my crooked teeth.

"You have no right to express an opinion," she replied angrily, her love always absolutely conditional upon my pleasing her. "You have no right to *have* an opinion."

And I believed her. And somewhere inside the fen of my own highly ambivalent self-image, I still do.

My parents could not tolerate any behavior that deviated from their own, whether that deviation was positive or negative. They had inherited every idea they ever bothered to hold, and they assumed (with all the arrogant entitlement of the heterosexual world) that I would be some carbon copy of them, not a smart sissy kid who liked art. In the days of Eisenhower, *Father Knows Best*, and the Korean War, conformity was an American obsession, an addiction. I was one of its passive victims, poisoned by its vile fumes even though I wanted no part of it for myself.

My attempts at Real Boy behavior were really attempts to fit in, to escape the loneliness I felt everywhere I went (and especially at home). I tried to play baseball—glorying in each real or imagined success (a ball hit, a base run)—not because it was of any inherent value to me, but because I knew it should be. I was doing the right thing, the Real Boy thing. A caught ball would win me momentary camaraderie from the boys and approval from my father, who was, and is, even at eighty, entirely male in all the traditional senses of the word, even when he gets down on his hands and knees to scrub the kitchen floor (his husbandly contribution to the care and upkeep of his home). When I watch him now with my cousins and their sons watching football and baseball games on Thanksgiving or New Year's Day, all of them hooting and hollering and knowing all the players' names and statistics, I still feel like an aberration. I still think he likes them more than he likes me. And I'm still in the other room with the women and children.

In other times, perhaps, I might have discovered some kind of physical activity that did not pit me against other boys in competitions I was certain to lose. But my childhood was perpetrated in the days before individual sports, before dancing or gymnastics were even thought of as fit areas of physical education. So the strict male-female dichotomy of my upbringing robbed me of my body too. Soon I was a *fat* sissy crybaby who liked art. And this remains, at the core, my identity even now, even though I am not as an adult effeminate, even when I am not, as I usually am, appallingly overweight.

Only Aunt Helene loved me unconditionally, as we say now. She was a source of immeasurable and unstinting support, served up over coffee and crunchy cashew nut-butter sandwiches in a tiny tract house kitchen that was—let's admit it—a ludicrous Early American Reproduction cliché. She and I were insiders pitted frequently against my mother. If I asked my mother for a real adult 35mm camera for Christmas (as I did, year after year), I would get a kid's Kodak Brownie or a chemistry set. Aunt Helene would arrive at the door bearing shopping bags full of everything she could carry from the crafts store. She bought me a bulletin board one year when I was seven or eight, and I decorated it every holiday for years (my own personal display window). I still have the wooden box she gave me one day when I was too young by the normal standards to hold the oil paints we bought together at Long Island's first shopping mall, and it's been over thirty years now since she died and I used it last.

"Does your mother know you're reading that?" she asked me one day while we waited for a bus on Jerico Turnpike (dust underfoot, leafy trees *shushing* overhead). I was reading *Auntie Mame*. What was I? Thirteen?

"No," I answered, since I never felt I needed to lie to her.

"Well, for chrissake don't tell her," she said, taking a last pull of her Parliament before boarding the red and silver bus for Roosevelt Field.

In a way, she was my first sister, in the sense that gay men call their shopping, gossiping, doing-fun-things-together and crying-on-each-other's-shoulders friends their sisters. I still dream of her. I dream she is alive again and back in my life. I wake up in tears, but happy just to have been back in her company again.

Did she know I was gay? Did my parents? My sixth grade teacher, a patriarchal type named Waxenberg who had a seriously sadistic controlling personality, told my parents I would be gay at some parent-teacher conference in 1959. I found out about this conversation when, at twenty-four, I finally came out to them as gay. I was furious. How could they have kept so important a piece of information a secret? Didn't they know how much pain, how much deeply suicidal depression they might have prevented by telling me I was gay, by so much as a hint that my being gay was all right with them, even if it was not their first choice? What I got was silence and the torment I conjured for myself, so deep was my fear that I was gay and that they would find out. I wished them dead just to take the pressure off me.

In 1959, I had no idea I was homosexual, because I didn't know what a homosexual was. I knew that I was different. I knew I was despised. And I knew I was attracted in some mysterious way to what was going on inside the white Jockey shorts of my classmates as early as age ten. We were extremely untutored in those days in sexual matters. We found out what we did from our sexually active friends (and at least two of my classmates became parents before seventh grade). By the time I was fourteen and working in the public library after school, the only book on the subject was Kraft-Ebbing's wretchedly homophobic and outdated *Psychopathia Sexualis*. Not reassuring stuff. (The last time I walked into the place, a few years ago now, I noted that they not only stock my own books, but that Parents and Friends of Lesbians and Gays now meets in the same room I shelved books in all those decades ago.)

Oddly, and for this I am grateful, we just didn't have the word "queer" in our school yard vocabulary in the place and time that hosted my childhood. Whatever words we did have hurt me as much, I'm sure. But whatever they were, they weren't that one, although my ostracism, I fully knew, had something to do with this unspecified, gender-inappropriate otherness of mine.

I was just mystified all the time: mystified, terrified of exposure, horrified by the prospect of revelation, of humiliation. For me revelation *equals* humiliation. And that mistaken notion I have never shaken. Even now, intimacy is excruciating for me; writing is a muscular act of will. I spent my childhood trying to hide everything I was; in the words of my dear and sadly departed friend Kenny, I became an adult who would lie when telling the truth would do me more good. I started out hiding myself from others, but I hid myself so well, I am not sure that I've found me/him yet.

But did I actually or literally want to be a girl when I was a child? Yes. But only because if I had been a girl I could have done all the things I loved doing without constantly being told to be doing something else. "Get up off your fat ass and go do something useful!" my father would say when he came across me reading a book that had me so hypnotized I failed to hear his heavy (male) footfall. By "useful" he meant something he didn't want to do himself, like mowing the lawn. (When was the first time I dreamed of my father as a sharp fanged monster raging toward me down the hall of our cookie cutter Cape Cod home?)

Of all things I felt when I was a child, two were paramount: my mother loved me, my father did not (only after some years of therapy did I understand that my mother's "love" was something else entirely). My father had, I felt, abandoned all responsibility for me. Though we have managed to reach some state of graceful truce of late, he was a stranger to me when I was a child, a big, loud, angry stranger, with ham-sized hands he used on me whenever his fury got too big for him. I, on the other hand, was not only forbidden to express anger or unhappiness of any kind, I was forbidden to cry even after he had hit me. Boys don't cry, after all. He was a dangerous stranger everyone else seemed to love. That he has learned to cry (and that, in one way or another, it was I who taught him to) is part of his journey to me. It was my father, after all, who gave me permission to cry at Aunt Helene's funeral mass (after my mother had told me to stop). But as a child, my father was not there, even when he was there (and he made an effort, to be fair).

A friend of mine named Clark—now dead, of course, as virtually all my adult gay friends are—told me once of the shock he felt one day when he discovered men's shoes in his mother's bedroom closet: "Does Daddy *live* with us?" I could not have felt more estranged from my father than that, could not have felt his contempt more, could not have felt more that I was disappointing him because I didn't like sports and I didn't like building things and I was afraid of heights and cried on the submarine during a class trip to the Brooklyn Navy Yard (where I discovered claustrophobia) and I didn't like anything that Real Boys like as a matter of uncomplicated course.

Meanwhile, my mother would ask for my help not only in choosing her clothing and helping her accessorize for a night out but with dressing her as well. My father demanded labor as well as gratitude in exchange for room and board: mow the lawn, wash the car, clean the garage, and keep a civil tongue in your head. There was no end to the number of chores they could come up with to keep me from being myself. By the time I was in high school, I would invent things to do to please them. I would prepare dinner. I would paint the house. Anything to win the love they didn't have to give. That was my strategy to take the heat off being different: I would be perfect in all the other ways imaginable even though my parents made one inexcusable parental blunder after another.

Soon, of course, secrecy was part of my life. Cutout dolls were hidden under the eaves. My drawings of dresses and suits and swimwear—long into junior high school—were stashed under my bureau. My mother discovered them while "cleaning" my spotless room (just as she discovered my stash of marijuana some years later). She turned them over to my father, who tore them up and threw them away. I was forbidden ever to draw dresses again, and my hatred for my parents (and for myself) deepened.

It is a predicament to be an only child of such parents: Those one relies on for nurture are the agents of asphyxiation, of emasculation. To cut to the chase, so to speak, I felt castrated by my mother and ridiculed by a father who let her do it.

I would, of course, stay home from school whenever I could to avoid the daily humiliations of classmates, especially after my mother went back to work when I was thirteen. Once I wore her penny loafers to school, because I was not allowed to have any of my own (I was never allowed to buy my own clothes or choose what I wore to school). I was so thrilled to be wearing them, as they were the *de rigueur* rage of 1961. I was finally feeling at least marginally part of a group, but my foot had not come off the lowest school bus step and onto the concrete sidewalk before some budding femme fatale shrieked, "He's wearing girls' shoes!"

And I wore them all day, because there was no going home, and all day long, wherever I went, people pointed at me and screamed: "He's wearing girls' shoes." I didn't know there was a difference between boys' penny loafers, and girls' penny loafers, but there was—and everybody knew the difference and could recognize it, except me. What episode could be more quintessential?

Exactly why I was so attracted to women's clothing has more to do, I believe, with the pathological way in which I was enmeshed in my mother's emotional life (I can call it "incestuous" without a trace of hypocrisy or apology) than with wanting to be female—in the sense that I wanted male lovers or to bear children (all of which are part of me, of course), but attracted I was. Of course, given the difference between women's and men's clothing in the 1950s, what creative child would not prefer couture to haberdashery? Once when I was home alone, I dressed myself from head to toe in my mother's clothes. (On another such occasion, I had rifled the house for adoption papers; another time I poked holes in my father's condoms so I could have a brother). I was looking at my drag self in my parents' bathroom mirror, not so much in admiration as trying to make the silvered glass deliver up some answers. Certainly there was some sense of satisfaction. Then I heard the car pull up.

I tore to the TV room window. It was my father and his best friend Eddie. They were already at the kitchen door with the key in the lock as I dashed past it and up the stairs. I ripped off the clothes (underwear included, at least what underwear I understood), stashed them in the linen closet in my own bathroom, jumped into the shower and scoured off the makeup.

I sauntered back downstairs, trying to act as nonchalant as possible. But my father knew, and that night there was a confrontation. And a lame excuse: I wasn't dressing in my mother's clothes. I was playing store. Playing store, it turned out, was not a significantly more appropriate activity for a boy than transvestism. We all agreed to pretend we believed each other's stories, and nothing more was ever said. Although I certainly got the message that I would be severely dealt with if I ever did such a thing again.

At thirteen I knew my feelings for other boys had something to do with sex. I certainly knew my feelings for Georgie Bowen in gym class had something to do with his zero-fat body (which happened to be black) and his adult penis (its color being more of a surprise to me than its size). My own sex organs were immature (and lost in the folds of baby fat that would eventually become postbaby fat). I couldn't keep my eyes off him.

As luck would have it—or the typical endocrine systems of obese adolescents—puberty arrived in my body years after my classmates were practicing for procreation. Until I was a senior in high school I could sing the highest soprano part in Handel's *Messiah*—and I did, with gusto, despite the rude commentary. (One of my favorite defense mechanisms has been a kind of robust defiance that is equal parts bravado and anger.) Luck certainly did have it that I went to a public school in a town that prized intelligence and creativity above athletic prowess. I was a loner, of course, and an outcast generally speaking, eating lunch at the losers' table in the cafeteria. But I found a measure of acceptance in the school drama club, where various eccentricities were held as pennants of personality rather than perversions. I was deeply in love with a boy named Ray, who was our school's leading actor, but I was not averse to female companionship either. Even now a high school friend remembers that I was constantly slipping behind the staircase to make out with Linda Smith (a vivacious cheerleader who was, like Georgie Bowen, African-American—and whom I was forbidden to take to my senior prom because she was). If I was dating girls—or at least wanting to date girls—it was never consciously *only* for approval (although I knew it would certainly win me some). There was enormous *normality* in being able to say aloud that you were attracted to someone, a huge cathartic feeling of release and relief—and I could say those things about girls, not about boys (at least that's what I thought in those days, and why my writing is so explicit in its descriptions of attraction for various men). Back at Great Neck High School, I could publicly recite an unabashed love poem for a girl named Donna as part of an initiation ceremony, but I could never have declared such feelings of affection for Ray, although they were similar (but deeper). I did, in fact, tell Ray I thought I was gay when we were, what, sixteen or seventeen? He shrugged. I told another childhood friend a bit later. He seemed nonplussed. Either everyone already knew (which is what I suspect) or other people cared a lot less than either my parents or I did that I might be homosexual (which is also partly true).

The theater became my home for many years. I have acting talent, even I knew that despite my penchant for undervaluing my gifts. And could anything have been safer for a boy who hated himself than to lose himself in the identities of others? Unfortunately, what looks like a tranquil lagoon in a tropical paradise may in fact be a minefield of hull-splitting coral.

It is significant, deeply significant, I believe, that it never occurred to me that there was nothing wrong with me. Not once do I ever remember saying, "There's *nothing* wrong with me" in response to the often asked question. Rather, I spent decades wondering, "What *is* wrong with me?" And the truth of the matter is that when I survey my life at its hemicentennial, entirely informed as it is by the deep and abiding loneliness of ten years living alone in a plague-ravaged landscape, I still think, what is wrong with me that I am so universally rejected by my community of queers?

Ironically, it was my sexual relationship with a woman that prompted my coming out to my parents as homosexual.

I'd met Judy in college, where I'd had sex with both men and women (with Judy and a baritone named Jules on the same night—my twenty-first birthday). The summer of love was fast upon us, and

I was loving all year round—anyone, basically, who would take off their clothes in my vicinity, and such people were not difficult to find when I was young. I hated myself, but many others didn't seem to share the low opinion.

It was 1970. I was in graduate school, at Yale, studying set and costume design. (I had asked for a sewing machine the previous Christmas, so I could make my own clothes, and I can still hear my mother's voice saying, "Your father will never buy a son of his a sewing machine for Christmas." Thanks for the unselfish support, Mom!) Judy was staying in my room. My mother called up while I was out getting the Sunday paper. When I called her back, I was full of shame, just as I was when she finally figured out that I was the one stealing all the money constantly missing at home. But this time I was not *only* ashamed. I was also *angry* that I should be made to feel ashamed for having a sex life. I was furious with my mother that she was "disappointed" that her twenty-four-year-old son was sexually active. (My mother's refusal to allow me any other avenue of affection beyond herself extended even to dogs, which I was, of course, forbidden although I had begged for one all my life.)

I wrote a long angry letter to my parents that included the essential information: Yes, I was sleeping with Judy. Judy was not the only woman I had ever slept with. And, truth be told, I preferred having sex with men.

But did I? Did I actually prefer the sex act with men, or was I just so desperate for connection with another male that the sex act became a symbol for the closeness, the alliances I'd never had? I still think my own particular homosexuality is related to my deep-seated, lifelong desire for a brother. And I am still not sure if I prefer gay male sex to heterosexual sex if I'm judging strictly on sensual lines. But the senses are fed by the emotions, and there is no doubt that I am libidinously, emotionally, spiritually more attracted to men than to women. At least that was true in the days, now apparently over, when sex was still available.

The early 1970s were confusing times. After some friends and I started attending Gay Liberation Front meetings in New York City in the fall of 1969, we established a chapter in New Haven. At one point I was the male cochair. I was having an affair with the female cochair, a Vassar lesbian named Ellen who had both a husband and a female lover. I met her through a former (gay male) roommate of mine, who was having an affair with her former (bisexual? female) roommate. The roommate also wound up sleeping with another (gay male) roommate of mine. By the summer of 1970, we were all pretty much sleeping with each other in various pairs and other combinations that generously included other friends. I wasn't clear whether we were being very retrograde or quite avant-garde, but I am rarely sure of anything. Certainly confusion was a small inconvenience to put up with for the sense of being desired that I was feeling for the first time.

An active sex life did not actually clear things up for me. At the time of my freewheeling sexuality, at least, I think I might have been and might still well be—essentially—bisexual, which is what I believe normal human sexuality is. But in 1970 it was considered politically incorrect to be bisexual, a cowardly sitting on the fence. Whether by predilection or upbringing, I had become something of an either/or, black/white person, and it was just *easier* for me to declare myself gay (winning kudos from my fellow queers) than to live in a world of constantly shifting boundaries and very strict legal sanctions that were infrequently imposed but inequitably applied when they were.

It was in a graduate school seminar in Elizabethan and Jacobean tragedy that I had my first epiphany with respect to sexual identity in the context of my *haute* hypocritical society. In *'Tis Pity She's a Whore* by John Ford, a brother and sister named Giovanni and Annabella fall in love (romantic, sexual, passionate love). They clearly violate the incest taboo, but their love remains somehow pure. The world in which they live, however, condemns it utterly, and all are brought to hideous, bloody ruin. I have been clear about my own role as a "sexual outlaw" ever since: There is nothing "wrong" with being a member of a sexual minority, a natural state in humans and other life forms. On the other hand, repression of normal sexual expression *is* wrong. More than wrong, it is evil, and the individuals, and religious and political institutions that lobby against sexual expression are the root and soul of evil.

At the age of twenty-five, I took a look at my life. Frequently suicidal, often flatly stoned, aimless, frightened and lonely, I had had three long-term sexual relationships with women: Judy, Kay (whom I met in London, where we managed to deflower each other before returning to the United States), and my Vassar wolf girl. I had had sex of varying kinds with a far greater number of men, but had never formed a satisfactory emotional relationship with one (and may not have yet, despite two long-term lovers in my past).

Both the men I did eventually fall in love with were small and feminine (still my "type"), and both preferred the passive (receptive) role in sex. I prefer the active (inserter) "role." Traditionally, of course, passivity is seen as feminine, activity as masculine; in the gay world a "top" is often considered more "male" than a bottom. But it seems to me that these rigidities of butch and femme (as lesbians call the poles) deny full emotional expression as well as variety in physical expression. To be sure, there are gay men who are "versatile," who are passive and active in equal measure. I am not one of them. And I am not now certain whether this is because my sexuality is inherently male/masculine or whether the influences of my upbringing have limited corporal expression. I am sure that one's identity (in traditional bipolar male-female, masculine-feminine terms—or in more complex arrangements) need not be directly related to one's preferred sexual position.

I suspect that the truth, if it were knowable, is that sexuality is completely free-floating, absent social strictures. And that should be the aspiration of society: creating mechanisms that foster natural expression, not imposing artificial constructs on human behavior that have nothing whatever to do with human behavior.

These days, I am a gay man of little currency in the youth-obsessed world of millennial queerdom. The acceptable gay male norm these days is of an overpumped hairless creature that more resembles a retouched photo than a human being. And that image is relentlessly reinforced in our collective community consciousness by our own press and the mainstream advertisers who perpetuate heterosexual stereotypes about gay and lesbian people in the pages of our own magazines.

I suppose I could still be there at the gym pumping up like the rest of my surviving peers (some of us having bought the youth-is-all lie and walking around quite ludicrous in skintight workout attire more appropriate for boys a half or third our age). Happily, life offers some insights even though it doggedly resists imparting the real gift of wisdom. And I am just too tired to try to keep up with a community I no longer recognize and which I no longer respect.

"We're like cartons of milk," a contemporary remarked, "and we've reached our expiration date."

"Old-fat-and-ugly" is pronounced—and conceived of—as a single word in gayspeak, and I am it. Men my age are considered predators, and some of us probably are. I walk down the streets of Chelsea and I am still, or at least I am once again, the wrong thing to be. Gay boys who weren't born in 1969 think muscles define homosexuality and they have become exactly as oppressive to me in their attitudes as the straight men of my youth and childhood were. They are the Real Gay Boys, and the rest of us are disposable, *ersatz*. Whether they are tops or bottoms of versatility itself, they are using their bodies as an assault against the self-esteem of other kinds of gay men. It is the saddest of all possible things to me that male-gendered queers have not learned a single lesson from oppression or liberation, that we have denied rather than embraced feminist awarenesses about body consciousness, and that they—we, I suppose, I have to say—continue to perpetrate the supremacy of a limited kind of gay maleness that happens to be identical to the heterosexual male model of the 1950s. Apparently fashions in fascism recur as often as clothing styles. In the heyday of the post-Stonewall Era it was possible to be this kind of gay man or that. Sex was as much about love as about politics (and rarely about power). It should never be necessary to be one kind of man or one kind of gay man to be accepted, to be loved. But we haven't learned this yet as a tribe, and we continue to take our sense of value from a system by which others are artificially devalued. We are attempting to find happiness at the expense of others and creating great unhappiness as a result. To acquire happiness at the expense of others is just as low as life gets. That is predatory. And it's a shame to see in this enormous pool we call the gay communities.

Ah, well. Maybe reincarnation will turn out to be true, and things won't be so bleak next time around.

Fourteen

The Boy Who Grew Up to Be a Woman

Jody Norton

I lay claim to nothing but my own nature. . . . What
seems different in yourself: that's the one rare thing
you possess, the one thing which gives each of us his
worth; and that's just what we try to suppress.
—André Gide, The Immoralist

In "Femininity," Freud describes the limits of psychoanalytic knowledge of the female as follows: "psychoanalysis does not try to describe
what a woman is—that would be a task it could scarcely perform—
but sets about enquiring *how she comes into being.*" I was born "male"
(whatever the contingencies of that term may be), and I lived my
childhood largely (at least visibly) as a boy. But I grew up to be a
trans woman. In this reflection, I want to trace the scenes and images,
the emotions and identifications, the desires and the fears that together with my body have shaped the human being I am.

I can't remember why it was me against them. I remember only that,
inarticulate with rage and frustration, I stood on the back porch of our
brick duplex in State College, Pennsylvania, swinging our discarded
Christmas tree at a circle of taunting children, trying my best to smash
them with that wilted emblem of the birth of love. Each time I swung
my awkward club at the boldest grins, they surged back, surflike,
amidst great mirth, leaving me high, dry, and impotently alone on my
tiny isle of pique. How long this ritual of exclusion would have con-

tinued I have no idea, had not my mother at length forced me to abandon my posture of *resistance*.

My mother. . . . I could recite a litany of meanings my mother had for me. She and I read by the hour, often desperately sad stories in which anthropomorphized animals lured me, as a reader, into profound identification with them, only to meet some unutterably cruel fate. *Bob, Son of Battle, Bambi*, and the stories of Earnest Seton Thompson were some of the tales we cried over. The most excruciating structural element of each story was that the courageous, loving animal protagonist died, leaving another who loved them behind, helpless to help them, and helpless to help himself (I say "him," because in my memory and I suspect in fact as well, the abandoned children—sometimes animal children—were always male).

These stories told me the story of my mother's grief for a father who had died when she was relatively young, and whose life she felt she could have saved (though he died of a heart attack). They were stories of guilt, of the responsibility for the death of the being you love most in the world. More precisely, they were, like *Bambi*, stories of responsibility for *being unable* to prevent that death. I learned to feel, and to bear, my mother's guilt—learned that, like her, I was unable to prevent death (and more generally unable)—because the characters I came to love in the stories we read died while I watched from the edge of their world, utterly powerless to help them, and thus utterly culpable and absolutely to be condemned.

The process of identification is complex. While I "knew" myself to be a boy, I came to want/to be my mother, perhaps in order that I might be protected from failing her in the way that she and I had failed to help her father—a failure for which the animal stories served as a compulsively repeated metaphor. Yet now, many years later, I realize that on another level I was in competition with her, in that I wanted to be my father's child bride. I wanted him to sweep me up in his arms, to carry me away, leaving only a "spoor of sparks flying from Dad's cigar," as the narrator of Edmund White's *A Boy's Own Story* puts it in describing a similar fantasy—though in my Daddy's case it would have been the sparks of a campfire, as he carried me into his tent, to his sleeping bag, to do with me whatever men do with women that makes them women.

When I say that I am a woman (which I never say without qualification) I sometimes simply mean that my desire is the desire of the little girl to incorporate the phallus: to have that big, uncircumsized thing stuck in/on her, to feel its massiveness inside her, and to become its power. Where the boy, according to Lacan, finds ways to announce "I am that," the girl says, "I want that." I am the girl.

My early cross-dressing experiences were not about seeing myself as a woman, but about presenting myself as one—and a sexy one at that. That is, they were very much about being seen by others—about exhibitionism, if you will. My girl cousins and my sister dressed me up in women's clothes (was I seven? eight?) and made much of me. I was a spectacle, a proto-drag queen (though I have little interest now in drag as such), provoking riveted attention, laughter, admiration (even, perhaps, a tinge of jealousy at my translucent femininity, which the girls, caught up in the need to respond satisfactorily to the social gaze, may have wordlessly wondered whether they could match). I recall vaguely being paraded for the grown-ups, and realizing, quite without consciousness, that I represented not a character in a play but myself as theater: Jody-as-drama, Jody-as-entertainment, Jody-as-performance.

Later, when I was nine, I, my sister (two years younger), and the boy and girl from across the street invented a theater of gender-as-sexuality. I, as the oldest boy (and the subject of considerable sexual curiosity on the part of the two girls), was the star—or rather the starlet, since my performances consisted principally of a series of feminine costumes in which I would appear, withdrawing only to reappear in a more scanty, more revealing outfit. I never came out absolutely naked. My ultimate outfit was a single cloth strap looping over my shoulder, down my back, between my legs, over my erect penis, and back up to my shoulder. Since the strap was made of a firm material, my stiff penis held it away from my body, so that "everything" could be clearly seen by the spellbound audience, with the intensely magnified eroticism that the illusion of reserve unerringly provides. One cannot satisfactorily be a peeping tom unless one has to peep into a place that is "covered"—that is, symbolically designated as taboo. Scopophilia, indeed, is not simply the desire to see, but to see the object of a desire that is itself off limits, behind the veil, through the looking glass, and so on. My self-revelation became infinitely sexier, then, precisely because it took a feminine form of self-presentation: a striptease act through which I objectified myself as the "female" object of the gaze, preserving my chastity—a nod to the feminine demure—with the modest restraint of a thong.

When I was a boy, I rarely consciously felt like a girl. Yet my girlness was never far from the surface, and was sometimes more visible to others—instinctively—than to me. I'll never forget the time that a favorite fantasy boyfriend of mine, who played on the tennis team with me in ninth grade, wanted me to be a girl for him in the locker room. I was sitting on a bench changing my clothes when I heard a voice say "go ahead!" I turned around to find him standing behind me with his jockey shorts lowered to expose his rapidly lengthening penis. He knew I loved to watch him romp naked in the shower room, he knew that I adored his cock and, in his own moment of exhibitionistic pleasure, he was inviting me to enjoy him, to pleasure him, and to be his conquest. Unfortunately, others noticed, and shouts of "fairies" put an end to the scene. A minute or two later, though, in the noisy chaos of the locker room, I noticed Bobby, with his cock now fully erect and surging in his briefs, so that I could get a real eyeful of his plump brown balls, standing on a bench and calling for the others to throw me in the shower. I would have loved to be a girl for them all.

There was one boy on the tennis team who was a year or two older than me, whose girlfriend I especially wanted to be. Eddie was tall and supple, with slim, attractive legs and golden-blond hair. He was really a god-boy. I would have liked to put on a really nice dress and have had him take me to a dance or somewhere nice. This was somewhat unusual for me at the time (when I was thirteen or fourteen), since I was usually attracted to boys my age or younger.

The sexual moments that stick with me most from my adolescence tend to be ones in which another boy modeled femininity for me, and in doing so, made me want both him and the elusive, sexy female identity he freely and beautifully took on. I saw "he" become "she" in a crystalline moment, like the sun shining down through a split in the clouds. I remember Eddie (another Eddie), Raymond's little brother who, while Raymond and I sat on a sofa watching TV, came and lay face down on the carpet in front of us and surreptitiously worked his pajamas down until his beautiful little white bottom was fully presented to us. His brother would admonish him to pull them up, and he would do so, and leave the room, only to reappear a moment later and resume his strip show.

I remember Jeremy, before ninth-grade Latin class one day, reaching over out of the blue and gently stroking my kneecap, with a beautiful girlish smile and enough sexual energy to set the desk on fire. He wanted me to be the man. But while I was thoroughly turned on by his feminine sexiness, I wanted to be "her" too—we would be girls together, and maybe find some tough-but-sweet boys like Lenny to play with.

Later, after my family moved to Massachusetts (when I was fourteen), I remember working for a weekend as a busboy at the Amherst College Commencement. Sitting around with several others, a gorgeous young auburn-haired beauty suggested, "I could put on a grass skirt and be your whore." After a moment's reflection, he added, "Your hair's so long, you could be a whore too!"

In Pennsylvania, I had been very well socially integrated: generally accepted by the run-of-the-mill; having my secret little sexy friends I flirted with; and tolerated by the tough kids—even liked by some of them, though of course a crucial symbolic space had to be maintained between us at all times. In Massachusetts, I knew nobody, was perceived as an egghead and a flute-playing queer, and was generally fair game for anyone who needed to act out their masculine insecurities—including some of my teachers. I remember being asked by my tenth-grade English teacher to get up in front of the class and describe what I liked about my favorite rock 'n roll music. My answer—that what I liked most was the memories special songs held for me (certainly a very "feminine" kind of attachment)—was met with scorn and disbelief on my teacher's part, though one girl stood up for me, saying that she could understand what I meant.

I gave up the flute by the age of sixteen or so, the burden of shame attached to it too great for me to bear. I remember at District Orchestra (the only "male" first flute player), drifting over with the girls during a break to listen as some of the flashier boys played r & b and rock riffs on the piano. It was a revelatory moment: fifty girls and me watching breathlessly as boy after boy starred for us. Once, one looked across to me, where I hung back behind the other girls. His look was mildly puzzled, but not unkind.

It has taken me many years to resolve my feelings of depression and pain around flute playing and classical music in general. They have always reminded me that I am not fit. Recently, sitting at a conference banquet table near the stage that Minnie Bruce Pratt had requested be reserved for a transgender caucus, I listened as she spoke of her youth in the South, and of the struggles she and others endured over their unacceptable sexualities and genders. At one point, she spoke of "boys who played the flute in school bands," and I suddenly realized that to have been a boy who played the flute in school bands was a mark of distinction: that to have been that kind of boy included me in a very special and wonderful "sisterhood." I will never again give in to shame about being a flute-playing sissy. I'm proud of the sissy I was, and the trans woman that sissy became. (And I will try, as well, not to be ashamed of the adolescent with hir collar turned up trying so hard to be tough. S/he was struggling hard to survive, and s/he used whatever tools s/he could find.)

Other femme boys—other feminine ideals—whom I both wanted and wanted to be like, came into and out of my life. I remember when we first moved to Amherst, I used to play with my sister and two other girls and a boy named Jamey, who might have been twelve or thirteen (a year or two younger than I). Jamey was quiet and shy, with lovely liquid brown eyes and dark brown hair. He liked to play with us, and was always cheerful, but never said much. I remember some game in which we would all end up wrestling around on the grass. I was able to touch, caress, even squeeze Jamey's blue jean-clad bottom, under the guise of this "wrestling." He never objected in the least, and to this day I wonder if he knew what I was doing. If he did, he must have enjoyed it. I ran into him some years later, when he was perhaps seventeen or eighteen. He was writing poetry, as was I, and we walked along together for a while and talked about the kinds of poetry we liked. He was still shy, still attractive. I don't know why I didn't try to start some relationship with him then. I must simply have been too afraid of rejection.

I met another boy who told me he liked to dress up in girl clothes. I was about to suggest that he and I get together and do that, but then he said he had been really put off because someone he was dressing with had approached him sexually—had turned out to be a "queer." Once again, I backed off for fear of rejection.

The real icon of trans kids in Amherst was Channing, whose self-presentation was overtly feminine, and who once offered to be cheer-leader for the street-freak touch football games. I remember one Halloween (still clueless as to who I really was, or was becoming) I had somehow dressed myself in a woman's white fake fur, waist-length jacket and gold (spray-painted) boots. I had no consciousness of being cross-dressed, or of femininity. I must have been thinking in terms of being "far out." I saw Channing arrive at the party I was at and give me a long, curious once over. I was clearly, if unexpectedly, a sister.

Some time after that—perhaps the summer when I was between college and a miserably lonely year of graduate school at Yale—I was with friends in Springfield and for some reason took a series of passport photos of myself in one of those $1-for-three booths somewhere. I had on a lavender ruffled shirt, girl-length hair, and I remember consciously posing myself with a "feminine" smile. The pictures came out well for what they were: the feminine quality shows through. I still have them now, years later.

That was as far as I got in those days—those days in which I wanted to be beautiful, tried consciously to camouflage myself as masculine, avoided women who wanted sexual contact with me, and had absolutely no idea how to be me. After I left Yale, feeling isolated, depressed, and full of unacknowledged self-loathing, I diverted my search for self into a defensive involvement with compulsive drug and alcohol use. Alcohol and drugs worked to cover up my anxieties about my gender and sexuality (for years I periodically swore off homosexual masturbation, and destroyed my pictures of adolescent boys). They also provided me with an extreme—therefore cool-street identity as one who lived on the razor's edge, and deserved respect for "his" fearlessness in the face of death. Because I wasn't physically tough, I pushed my risk taking so as to appear masculine, courageous, unafraid to die. Underneath my ambiguously gendered facade (long, beautiful brunette hair; flowing, lacy shirts; tight pants) was a repressed woman hysterically trying to be a man. Conscious but evaded was my knowledge of my attraction to boys and men. Beneath this shameful and terrifying awareness—though I've always been secretly proud of my desire, and would never want it to be other than it is (the defiance of the condemned, of Genet)—and entirely unconscious, was the ironic burgeoning of my "heterosexual" womanhood.

I eventually became addicted to heroin—there are a surprising number of feminine boy junkies, amidst all the other kinds—which I loved because of the rush, because of the emotional stasis it produced, and because I could "lean and dream" long, phantasmagoric, anxiety-free dreams. Again, it gave me a niche, and a job—each day the need to hustle money, and then to cop, which might be easy, or might involve hours of waiting, the anxiety of dealing with strangers or unreliable acquaintances, three-hundred-mile round trips to New York (with a gun in the glove compartment), and so on.

With smack, I could be a coded heroine—beautiful, ethereal, doomed; an updated version of the fin-de-siècle femme fatale Martha Vicinus writes of, whose predestination, writ large on her frail charismatic body, and dramatized in her face and gestures, and in the romantic script of her camera-ready life, is always death. I had, then, my feminine being (constructed as passive, penetrated and penetrable, irrational, dependent/independent, dramatic, symptomatic, and unconscious), but in a nascent and decidedly dark form.

I was always drawn to what Leon Pettiway calls the "subcultural shadows" of the street. But the street style that I created for myself was really a misreading: "street" and "style" were honest convictions, rather than attractions, at the gut level. But I was doing the wrong gender. My need for suffering—even more, for punishment—revealed both a deep "feminine" masochism, and my shame at my female spirit. In *Honey, Honey, Miss Thang: Being Black, Gay, and on the Street*, Keisha reflects, "I say by me getting hooked on heroin, that stuffed a whole lot of emotions." Dope froze me. In retrospect, I think I had to work very hard to repress all the guilt I had for letting my parents down (and at the same time, a lot of anger over their passivity). I also had to adopt a "fuck you" attitude that is not at all what I'm about at deeper emotional levels, in order to justify treating everyone I came across as a mark, available for one or another kind of hustle.

I was living in Boston at one point, and had come out with friends to Amherst and spent the night at my parents' house. My friends came to pick me up the next morning. It was one of those perfect, crystal clear October days—bright blue sky, sunshine on orange and gold leaves. As I drove off with them from my parents' house, I had an anguished feeling of being barred by my own unworthiness from enjoying the beauty of the day: I couldn't have this, because it belonged to, and was intended for, good people. In twenty minutes or so, we were somewhere else in town, getting off.

One night when I was living in an upstairs hallway on Wedgeworth Street in Boston—in a house in which, if you wanted some works, you just reached into the drawer of the kitchen table and took your pick—I tried to kill myself. I remember going to a party in Cambridge with my best friend Ramon—we had a homosocial relationship that ultimately tailed off when he began to get girlfriends—and realizing after a while that he was having a good time without me. I was crushed. I was always supposed to be the one he was interested in, even though I wasn't physically attracted to him at all. I went back to Wedgeworth Street, and I don't remember if I got off again or what, but I went into the bathroom, found a razor blade, and did a thorough job on both my wrists. Then I went back down and sat at the kitchen table. Eventually somebody noticed I was bleeding all over the floor, and there was a whole big scene. I ran out of the house and up the street. Several people ran after me and caught me and brought me back. A bunch of them drove me down to Mass. General, where the ER doctors put upward of fifty stitches in me.

As severe as my self-mutilation was, I regarded it at the time as merely a suicide gesture. I think now that I was indeed trying to die. That event constituted a surfacing of the tip of an iceberg of death that manifested itself both before and after this incident in a number of more or less intentional drug overdoses. I think now, also, that I wanted very much to *kill* myself, both as a way of positioning myself as female, within a kind of ultimate passivity, and as a way of punishing myself for the impulse to be that most despicable of all social criminals, the she-male (paralleled only, perhaps, by the he-shes Leslie Feinberg describes in *Stone Butch Blues*).

Later, in Boston, I was a kind of femme for Charley, an ex-football player who was a middle-level weed dealer. He had a girlfriend, but I was a kind of birl friend—a shadow girl who did the girl things without explicit sexual involvement. Nancy, a model-thin blonde who always wore a full-length cape, and I would steal expensive liquor out of the package stores, or grab take-out food off restaurant counters and run, while the men got in the way of pursuing waiters; or be boosted up by Charley into parked ice cream trucks we could squeeze our skinny asses into to rob the merchandise for Charley to sell out of *his* truck. We women were the ones who were the most daring, the most defiant, the most risk taking—and the most suicidal.

> I lie beside my sisters in the darkness, who pass me in the street unac-
> knowledged and unadmitted.
>> —Audre Lorde, *Zami: A New Spelling of My Name*

"You're throwing it like a girl," my Dad said, demonstrating how I put my right foot forward, and threw from the elbow rather than the shoulder. I learned how to throw a baseball "like a boy," but I was never any good at the national pastime, and suffered agonies of em-barrassment during the four years of Little League I was made to endure. My teams were the Elks and the V.F.W. They were stocked with tough, or would-be tough, little boys who appeared to enjoy being aggressive, and didn't much care whether the object of their aggression was on their team or another. Mastery was the point. And scorn the lot of anyone who wasn't assertive, masterful, pugna-cious.

It seems a terrible shame to me that American society cuts so many boys off from being feminine, or bigendered, or polygendered, in such rigid, punitive ways. No one wants to be the object of contempt. And so much beauty is lost, or never materializes: look at the eyelashes on that fifteen-year-old over there. Imagine what (s)he'd look like in a dress. . . . Imagine what (s)he'd look like *out* of a dress. Men are hand-some, sexy, scary, strong. But boys—some boys—are beautiful, with sweet, smooth skin—like girls. They are never allowed this beauty. Instead, they have to be as tough as they can, as soon as they can. They have to disavow soft smiles, fey gestures, same-sex sexuality, an interest in cross-dressing. They have to play Little League, and learn to spit.

I wish there had been other ways for me when I was a boy. I would have liked a chance to choose female clothing, a female name, and to go through a public ceremony of initiation and approval, as does the *alyha* child in Walter Williams's *The Spirit and the Flesh: Sexual Diversity in American Indian Culture*. I would have liked to have chosen to be a girl, or perhaps a two-spirit person, as in Amerindian cultures. But I could never have done this unless my family and my society had given me the cultural option, and the vital approval. I was a good boy, and I could never have chosen to be a bad boy, or willingly to bring contempt on my head for being a sissy, a pervert, a queer. That is why I tried so hard, for so many years, to be straight and male.

He stretched himself. He rose. He stood upright in complete nakedness
. . . and while the trumpets pealed Truth! Truth! Truth! we have no
choice left but confess—he was a woman.

                         —Virginia Woolf, *Orlando*

I feel bad for the boy who became a woman—not at all because
s/he became a woman, which was exactly what s/he was meant to
become, but because I don't think s/he got enough chance to love
hirself—all of hirself—as s/he was. I am sorry that this boy's fledg-
ling female spirit couldn't be cherished, and instead had to be
scrunched into uniformities of various kinds. I regret the whole social
atmosphere of masculine terror that was introjected into him. The
need to be tough and aggressive, good at fighting, never afraid; the
need never to cry or feel "feminine" emotions: these requirements of
1950s American culture were terribly destructive and life-denying, for
me and for thousands of other boys like—and unlike—me.

I also feel a great loss at not having been able to recognize and to
have recognized and valued my same-sex desire. From the time I
began to masturbate at the age of twelve, I already somehow knew
that my intense sexual interest in the boy across the street (acted out
in elaborate fantasy scenarios) was very "wrong," and very gender
inappropriate. In another world, another society, I might have been
happily, and approvedly, sexually active with any number of my
boyfriends, to the joy and satisfaction of us all.

My narrative doesn't have an ending, because my gender journey
is not complete. I understand my life to this point (insofar as it has
had a living meaning, rather than a dying one) as having been a
struggle to allow myself to claim the right to love, the right to desire,
and the right to be. Living for me now is an ongoing series of
transformations—yet composed through greater patience, and adher-
ing with more continuity, than ever before. That paradox—that one
can stay, moving—stands for me as a metaphor for transgender. May
we all stay where we love to be, moving as much as we need to.

Fifteen

The Golden Book of the Civil War

Paul Russell

Since I used to play with dolls, and since, in American culture, there is no mark of a sissy more telling than a boy's propensity for such play, I must confess at the outset that I am not now, nor have ever been, a sissy.

But why begin with such a disclaimer, if not to suggest the extent of the conflict within me as a gay man—for if I succeed in not being a sissy, then at the same time I fail to be one. And by failing to be a sissy do I not in some way fail to be authentically homosexual? Do I not disqualify myself from a certain respectable martyrdom at the hands of the ever vigilant gender police; do I not, indeed, even place myself at their service?

By being who I am do I not, in a sense, betray myself?

Memphis, 1962. My first day of school. As a reward for my anticipated good behavior—"Big boys don't cry"—my father has given me *The Golden Book of the Civil War (Adapted for Young Readers),* a handsome gift, and even though I break my part of the contract almost immediately (wrenched from the security of home, thrown in with children I have never before laid eyes on, I cry all day long), nonetheless I am held spellbound by the elaborate, full-color illustrations of the various fields of battle. These are not just schematic maps indicating troop movements with markers and arrows but incredibly detailed water-colors, aerial views showing in Breughel like detail the trees and riv-ers, the neat houses and new-plowed fields, and amongst all those finely rendered features the men, individual soldiers in drab gray or a dark, gemlike blue, who are engaged in the serious business of fight-ing one another to the death.

Perhaps most enchanting to my young imagination is a two-page spread depicting the battle of Shiloh, fought a hundred years earlier and less than a hundred miles away. From the upper corner of the left-hand page, where a Confederate surprise attack has overrun the Union encampment at Shiloh Church, one follows the sweep of battle down past the furious assaults along the Sunken Road, the murderous fusilades of the Hornet's Nest and Bloody Pond, the Peach Orchard where many blue and gray lie dead beneath the pink blossoms of April, to finish, at the lower corner of the right-hand page, with Grant's stand at Pittsburgh Landing, his back to the Tennessee River, that unyielding line of Union blue stretched across the fields and repulsing, from behind a cloud of cannon and rifle fire, wave after wave of tiny gray figures bearing the stars and bars of the Confederate battle flag.

Afternoons after school, I peruse those pages with rapt care; then, as the warm September sun slants through the trees, I go into the backyard, climb onto my swingset, and pull myself higher and higher in that much loved, fiercely repetitive motion. Only much later, this would become the comforting habit of after-school masturbation, the pleasure already contained in that innocent thrust and glide, the wonder of nearly achieved but always failing flight. As I pull myself in ever wider arcs, I daydream my way back into the battle I have only a few minutes earlier been contemplating, hovering over the carnage with gentle, wide-eyed curiosity—but more than that, with longing, as if I might catch in all that fury amid a pastel landscape something of the fullness of life itself.

Not long after that I must have asked for, and been given, my first set of toy soldiers, little plastic men no more than six inches tall, cast in the grays and blues of the Civil War. There is nothing inherently pleasing in their crudely molded forms; those individual figures hold no power to move me. Rather, it is their deployment on the field of battle that so inflames my senses. On a large piece of cardboard I draw roads and rivers in colored chalk; along with the set of soldiers have come some green trees and an arched stone bridge, all of plastic; wooden building blocks supply what uneven terrain I need for Seminary Ridge or the Little Round Top. Using the illustrations in *The Golden Book of the Civil War* as guides, I meticulously reconstruct great and pitiless battles: Manassas, Antietam, Chickamauga, Spotsylvania.

As a southerner, I of course rally around my Confederate brethren.

The Lost Cause is in my blood, all that glorious futility, the stirring idea that the defeated might prove more noble in their defeat than the victors in their victory. But I do not stop there in my sympathies, for against the desperate honor of the South are set the ruthless virtues of the North. And not the least among those virtues is the simple, irrevocable fact that the North won the war, and despite the valiant genius of Stonewall Jackson and Robert E. Lee and Nathan Bedford Forrest, won it massively. I have always understood the allure of absolute power, the irresistible seduction of a juggernautlike Sherman's march to the sea. But my admiration for the North is not just an admiration of its victorious power. At age six and seven and eight I find myself drawn to the Union side precisely because it is the enemy, and in sympathizing with the Union I am betraying my own loyalties as a Southerner. I have always, in nearly every situation, secretly been a traitor. In part, what I love about the Union Army is that it beat us, humiliated us, brought us low and made us pay dearly—us, the hated and despised South of which I am inextricably a part.

Thus I engage both sides of my battlefield with equal identification, compassion, and suffering—different and conflicted halves of myself arguing back and forth in my own internal civil war. But a strange thing happens within that house divided against itself. In the process of staging my battles, I invariably sprout a bone-hard little erection, and with that arousal comes an acute but directionless desire that is both pleasurable and painful, a charged and heightened emptiness to which my Civil War battles return me again and again: the irreconcilable split within my psyche—stern vanquisher and rapturously vanquished—incarnated as erotic excitement.

Into that exciting split enters the simple exhilaration of power, the sudden wealth in all those miniature destinies I manipulate on the board. And yet I understand quite clearly that I have no power at all to exercise, that my battles are entirely scripted by history, the winners and losers foreordained by *The Golden Book of the Civil War*. For my brave Confederates the war is always already lost, and surveying the battlefield I am not so much playing God as sympathizing with a deity I imagine not as all-powerful but as all-suffering, a deity given to looking down with helpless longing on the very catastrophes He Himself has set in irreversible motion. On Sundays my mother brings me regularly to the local Southern Baptist church, whose Calvinist lessons pay off handsomely in moments such as this.

Eventually there comes an afternoon when my younger brother and I are in the midst of setting up a terrific Shenandoah Valley skirmish, and I ask him—I am perhaps eight or nine, he six or seven—whether, like me, he gets hard in his pants when he plays toy soldiers. He looks at me uncomprehendingly, and I, having offered something generous and benign, immediately withdraw my innocent question, retreating guiltily into my own excitement, continuing to get aching, wonderful erections that will last a whole afternoon. But I am acutely conscious then, for perhaps the first time in my life, that the world I inhabit, with its secret pangs and pleasures, is not necessarily the world of others, and that I must be extremely careful not to give any of that world inadvertently away.

Playing with toy soldiers, of course, does not make one a sissy. War redeems, and as a child I was obsessed with war, preoccupied with it in ways that seemed, in context, entirely healthy. My whole peaceable household was curiously infused with the imagery of violence. Perhaps this was merely typical of the late fifties and early sixties, when families gathered around the television in the evenings to watch *The Texas Rangers* or *The Rifleman* or *Combat!* orgies of mayhem neatly sanitized for family viewing. My father believed strongly in what he called "manliness," which for him consisted primarily of self-sufficiency, moral courage, inner as well as outer strength, and a certain pared down, austere approach to life. He was a mathematician, and in his spare time he liked to build things: model airplanes, furniture, a sailboat, an elaborate A-frame clubhouse for his three sons, of whom I was the oldest. He once explained to me that the difference between men and women was that women liked everything to be prettified, while men would be content to live in a rough cabin with tools hanging from the walls. What I remember so vividly about that comment is my own implied agreement, as if I did not have to speak in order to be understood, as a son, to assent. But I also remember my fear that the comment, clearly meant to be instructional, might also a gentle rebuke for my own lack of interest in my father's various projects—my failure, despite my respectable passion for war games, to otherwise participate as enthusiastically as I should in the ongoing project of manhood.

Both my father and mother were, in their way, fiercely sexist: that is to say, they both believed that men and women were fundamentally different, and that to each there belonged a distinctive, naturally ordained set of traits. In practice, however, this could work itself out in complicated ways. As with most successful marriages, my parents' was rooted in compromise. My father had abandoned a promising college career as a football quarterback at Ole Miss in order to concentrate on his studies, eventually becoming an academic—though he remained conscientiously scornful of his more effete colleagues. After a brief flirtation in his teens with the idea of becoming a Methodist minister, he had come to see all religion as a necessary crutch for the weak but an impediment to the strong. For his future wife, a devout Southern Baptist, these views were profoundly upsetting, and it was only by agreeing to keep his doubts to himself and to allow her to raise her children as Southern Baptist that he persuaded her to accept his proposal of marriage. Likewise, my mother had abandoned some of her own more feminine inclinations in order to share with my father the burden of raising three sons to be men. She avidly participated in our camping and hiking ventures, and like my father made a show of disparaging, for the sake of her sons' development, the so-called "mushy" stuff—love songs on the radio, television programs that trafficked in romance instead of the sterner themes. That boys were meant to be men when they grew up was always quite clear in our family, though at the same time subtly subverted by my parents' privileging of the academic life: I was never discouraged, for instance, from staying indoors after school to read or do my homework instead of playing outdoors with the other kids in the neighborhood. I was never encouraged to take up sports, or join the cub scouts—things my younger brothers, when their time came, voluntarily undertook with enthusiasm. But then their pleasures were always less inclined toward the solitary than mine.

Though my mother had initially wanted a little girl—I always knew, growing up, that my name would have been Andrea had I been that little girl—she claimed to have changed her mind, and would frequently say, "I'm so glad in this day and age that I'm not raising a daughter." Nevertheless, as if in answer to some subliminal suggestion, from time to time I would awake from a disturbing dream in which I wore an ill-fitting, awkward dress that made me look grotesquely like my mother, or at least the way she appeared in old photographs from her childhood, long before she had met my father. In the dream I knew that I was a disappointment to my mother—but whether it was because of who I was in the dream or in real life, in either case the daughter she had never had, I could not tell. Similarly, when I preferred to stay indoors and listen to music rather than help my father in one of his innumerable projects, I felt I was a disappointment to him as well—perhaps even more so than to my mother, since this particular disappointment needed no dream to trigger it.

It was with a great deal of relief, as I grew older, that I saw my younger brothers succeed with my father in ways I could not. Silently I thanked them. My greatest fear had always been that they would somehow turn out to be like me—whatever it meant to "be like me."

Christmas, 1966. By no stretch of the imagination was G. I. Joe, that new and exciting innovation by Mattel, a toy soldier. Whichever way you looked at it, he was a full-fledged doll. I was vaguely aware of a larger cultural debate surrounding G.I. Joe's appearance on the scene— was the manliness of American boys in any way threatened by this new toy, or did the G.I. in G.I. Joe happily prevent him from being a "real" doll? Despite that, I can't recall my parents having any adverse reaction to their sons' participation in the latest toy craze, and my grandmother, perhaps missing the granddaughters she never had, even went so far as to sew G.I. Joe some civilian clothes, though the loud flowered shirts and maroon shorts she produced would undoubtedly have raised some eyebrows among Joe's fellow recruits.

I remember, at first, not being sure what to *do* with him. Dressing him up in various uniforms had little appeal for me. Even after he had acquired some companions—the striking blond Wehrmacht Joe with his elegant forest green uniform, butch black boots, and potato masher hand grenade, Banzai Joe with his tightly wrapped leggings, French Resistance Joe with his black knit turtleneck and fetching beret—I continued to prefer battlescapes flooded with hundreds of miniature soldiers.

Then one afternoon the boy next door introduced into the mix dolls of an altogether different sort, slimmer and prettier than any G.I. Joe, even girlish in comparison. Where Trent got those refugees from Planet Barbie—handsome Ken, his friend Allen, and Andy, the cute adolescent cousin—I have no idea. Suddenly everything changed— the way, I suppose, in certain prisons, or at least in the fever-dreams of Jean Genet, the good-looking kid in for some minor bout of thievery is led by the guards down a corridor of hardened, hungering criminals. And at the hands of our war-toughened vets, especially with no

Barbies or other comfort women around, things likewise went pretty badly for Ken and Allen and especially for frail, pretty young Andy.

If we could not, in our ten-year-old minds, conceive of love, then we could at least conceive of the next best thing, which was torture. Trent and I would huddle in the secluded space between the A-frame clubhouse and the back fence and concoct desperate scenarios in which the dolls, especially Skipper, had reason to shed their clothes. Was I the instigator of such scenarios? Trent, I remember, always got nervous when this turn of events occurred in our play. "My mom and dad'll get really mad if they find out we took their clothes off," he'd warn. At the time it seemed to me a strange worry. They were just dolls, after all. But of course they were more than just dolls. If the toy soldiers on the battlefield were pawns in a grand design, helpless in the grip of their predestination, these male dolls, naked and in the dire straits of our devising, carried within them a whole freighted cargo of agency and desire. If, for the South, the war was always already lost, for Andy, always about to be tortured, brutalized, raped, the future was deliciously unclear. In the person of G.I. Joe I could either stop that course of events or further it. And as always, I found myself of two minds: would I elect, at the last minute, to save Andy, to lavish on him my sweet mercies, or would I sternly see through the equally sweet torments I had in mind, and which I would suffer, in his person, as thrillingly as, in the person of G.I. Joe, I inflicted them?

Yukio Mishima reports that his first orgasm occurred when he stood, as a boy of eleven or so, before a painting of Saint Sebastian pierced by arrows. That he was, in that transcendent moment, both vehement archer and willing martyr I have no doubt. As for myself, I was too young ever to come behind the clubhouse during our grubbily transcendent games. But the sight of Andy naked and tied to a post, beaten and dominated by G.I. Joe and his brutal cohorts, perhaps— who knows?—even castrated by those soldiers of miserable fortune who carried their own mysterious lack beneath those manly uniforms: all that violence and threat of violence made me very nearly delirious with something not unlike love.

Raleigh Egypt High School, Memphis, 1970. A newly arrived freshman, I am terrified of the Phys. Ed. requirement. This is not the recess on the playground I have been able to manage in junior high, but instead something serious involving uniforms and jock straps and showers in the gym, the latter a dangerous, heartstopping vista of flesh I know I will never survive. While the others, unabashed, slip out of their gym shorts and T-shirts and head for the shower, some even flaunting their proud, dreamy cocks around which a first flush of hair is beginning to appear, I wait till the room is empty, then hastily change into my regular clothes and pray for my erection to subside. The task is made more difficult by the lingering image of Jeff Fowler's perfect, Andy-like body, especially that bobbing vital sign Andy has been missing all these years, and which in Jeff's case is red and angry-looking, as if, after his shower, he has towelled it fiercely into obedience.

"I hate Phys. Ed.," one of my classmates confides to me later in the day, and I heartily agree. "Especially having to get undressed," I tell him. "Oh," he says, "that part doesn't bother me. It's the exercise I hate." Once again, I find myself in the position of quietly withdrawing a casually offered observation. It is clear that most boys do not get their erections the way I do.

Then, after only a week or so of torment, I discover to my great relief that Marching Band can substitute for Phys. Ed., and instantly become interested in playing the clarinet. My mother, in particular, is pleased: a music major in college, a clarinet player herself, she met my father when she was a band director in West Point, Mississippi. In retrospect I can see that the marching band was a haven for others in flight like myself, though at the time I was blind to that particular bit of demographics. And not everyone was in the marching band to avoid Phys. Ed. Gabriel Patmos, for instance, was an avid athlete who happened to play the trombone as well, and it was with Gabriel Patmos that I fell in love.

I hesitate to confess, lest it seem less shattering than in reality it was, that this love first came to me in a dream. At the time I hardly knew Gabriel. He was a year younger than I, still in junior high, but because he was a talented musician he came next door to play with the high school band. In my dream Gabriel was leaving, going away on some great journey, and I had the dream-impression that this was a cause of deep sadness, that Gabriel was throwing his life away. He would be a traveler, a wanderer, a vagabond. He would disappear. The prospect of his disappearance filled me with such emptiness, such longing: if I could not go with him, which I couldn't, then I wanted to bid him good-bye. I wanted to tell him that he had my friendship. But the dream wouldn't allow me to find him. I searched everywhere—in a restaurant high in a range of luminous mountains, in a line of school buses, in an empty parking lot, in a vast field—but did not find him, and I awoke the next morning with a sense of unbearable loss.

It was as if my whole life, in a single stroke, had been changed forever. In the clear light of that shocked morning one thing above all else seemed absolutely necessary—I had to become Gabriel's friend. But who exactly was this thoughtful, gracefully sculpted boy of the husky voice and fiercely winning smile who had only recently moved to Memphis from the North? I could hardly be said to know him at all. Yet it was as if he contained within himself a great secret—which seemed to me at the time nothing less than the secret of how to live. I would learn from him, I thought; he would be my muse.

The campaign I undertook to win his friendship was ruthless, my courtship cunning. Without a second thought I abandoned friends like Trent on the sudden suspicion that they might seem, well, too much like sissies. My friendship with Gabriel was to be unsullied by any hint of its true nature—which I was sure, if he even suspected, would mean the end. And yet, about that "true nature" I myself was deeply divided. Certainly I wanted nothing more than to make love to Gabriel, but I convinced myself that the love I wanted to make was spiritual rather than physical. To accompany him on his great journey, to throw my life away with his seemed the greatest good. In a fit of difficult renunciation I forbade myself to think of him whenever I masturbated, substituting instead from my generous mental repertoire of other boys—a prohibition that only heightened the profane excitement of my occasional lapses. On the few occasions, in the changing room, when I saw him strip to his underwear in order to don the red and black uniform of the marching band sent my spirit reeling with a desire that was entirely of the body. Though I highmindedly reassured myself that I did not in the least want to suck the lovely cock my eager gaze could discern nesting in his slightly soiled briefs, the rebel in me would have given anything to hold its holy weight in my blasphemous mouth. No doubt it is telling that, of all the boys at Raleigh Egypt High, the one I would not allow myself to imagine wanting was precisely the one who provoked in me such a searing and unquenchable thirst.

Under the benevolent tutelage of our band director, a self-effacing, rum-tippling black man who was a trombonist himself, I began to compose music for the Concert Band, soulful suites with titles like

"Winds of the October Earth" and "Elegy for a Young Lord," music made for Gabriel that Gabriel eventually would play. Seldom has the trombone been elevated to such a prominent role: my greatest joy lay in penning the notes he would blow into his instrument and shape into music. And no nights were more sublime than those Friday nights when the Marching Band loaded onto a school bus for the long ride to a football game at some rival school far out in the country, and Gabriel, my good friend Gabriel, eased into the seat next to me for the journey. In those moments I could convince myself that my patient campaign had succeeded, and that I was poised at last to conquer the bucolic Pennsylvania of this northern boy's trusting soul—that soul which had already effortlessly conquered me.

The possibility occurs to me that I might, in those heady days of Gabriel, actually have made certain conscious and enduring choices about my sexuality. Not in the sense of choosing to desire boys, for I had always and helplessly done that (at age four or five I watch, with a sweet flustered agony I have no idea what to do with, as the four-teen-year-old who has come to do chores around my grandmother's house in Okalona, Mississippi—and who has, in a fit of unrepayable kindness, fashioned a hat for me out of a brown paper bag—sweeps the front porch with a simple male grace that is unutterable). I am talking instead about the particular configurations I allowed my sexuality to assume, the mix of sexual object choice and gender roles and whatever sense of identity may be said to encompass both. I remember thinking, as I gradually came to consciousness of myself at the age of fourteen or fifteen, that it was incumbent on me to do two things in order to be true to myself: to renounce religion, and to live what I thought of as an exemplary life. Of what that exemplary life would consist I was remarkably clear: I would be homosexual without being a sissy. In the Southern Baptist South, where our accents retained the lilt of our ancestors and where in the mountains to the east could be heard the twang of Elizabethan fiddle, I think I connected atheism with homosexuality in a way the late sixteenth century might have understood: as the mutually reinforcing pillars of a certain progressive conception of self. Or perhaps atheism and homosexuality were simply parallel rebellions against the twin constraints of compulsory faith and compulsory heterosexuality. Against compulsory masculinity, however, I could not even imagine a rebellion.

Not that I was particularly "masculine" in my pursuits. I did not play sports. I did not even particularly like the marching part of Marching Band. I was utterly indifferent to camping and hiking and the other outdoor activities my family enjoyed so much, preferring to stay indoors and read books or listen to classical music, to sit motionless on the living room sofa and daydream of symphonies I would one day compose, novels I would write, boys who would one day love me back. Despite all that, and no doubt aided both by my appearance—tall, authoritative, manfully hirsute—and by my constant vigilance for any signs that might betray me, I managed my deception well. If I often found myself speaking to Gabriel in a voice not entirely my own, the success of that voice in winning his friendship was remarkably satisfying nonetheless.

On more than one occasion during those years my manner was described as "gentle but firm." In that phrasing there seems to have been a kind of code at work: if people suspected, at some level, that I was not like the other boys, at the same time, since I had done nothing to antagonize and much to ingratiate, they were reluctant to characterize me in ways that might be demeaning or insulting. If I was, indeed, at heart a sissy, I had nonetheless kept it to myself and not flung it in their faces. The reward for my delicate compromise was this: in exchange for sustaining the conventions I was allowed my secret psychic life, which included the not inconsiderable benefits of friendship with Gabriel Patmos or later, Luke Pynchon, the complex, dark-eyed, Connecticut-born captain of the track team who would honor me, on the eve of our graduation, by writing in my yearbook the astonishing, impossible-to-fathom words, "I offer you the love of a friend."

And of what did these two notable—if deceitful—friendships for the most part consist? Long soulful talks, usually about religion, since my atheism had become something of a scandal around my very religious high school. Both Gabriel and Luke attempted to coax me back into the fold with a tender concern that was, in its way, powerfully erotic. Having no intention of converting to a religion I had disdained even as a child, I was nevertheless open to any attention either of those handsome Christians might direct my way; our conversations were, after all, an ongoing attempt at seduction. And when Gabriel pulled me down onto his living room floor to pray with him on my knees for salvation, it was like nothing so much as the prelude to that long-awaited kiss that would never happen.

In the end I was neither seduced nor converted, and neither were they. That the self I created and sustained so successfully in order to win those boys' friendship was built on a subterfuge that effectively destroyed any possibility of my ever having a real friendship with them is of course a sad and all-too-familiar story for so many gay men.

Oberlin College, 1974. On an October night perhaps thirty people crowd into the lounge at German House for a dance sponsored by the Gay Union. I find myself gyrating next to a strapping, broad-shouldered upper-classman whose name and face I cannot today remember. Has he selected me, or have I selected him? I do not know. But it is the first time I have ever danced with a man, the first time I have ever been in the presence of other homosexuals. He keeps calling me Paul-Doll, a name which I find both exciting and repellent.

In the corner, two boys from nearby Wooster College are dancing together. One is undistinguished, a short-haired, bad-complexioned lad in glasses—but the other, a slight boy with longish blond hair, wearing a brightly flowered shirt, tight white jeans, and a rolled-up lavender handkerchief around his neck, is the most beautiful boy I have ever seen in my life about whom I can say to myself, definitively, "He is gay." And the reason I can say that is not so much his presence at this dance but his clear effeminacy, the reassuringly unambiguous mark of his homosexuality which he carries in the fluid way he moves, the musical lilt of his voice, a certain expression in the eyes.

"Paul-Doll," my dance partner says into my ear. With each repetition of my new name, as if it were a command to divulge my true self, I attempt to be gayer. But what does that mean? After years of secrecy, I have no idea how I am supposed to behave, who I am supposed to be. I try to make my normally disciplined body limber. I try to be swishy. I roll my eyes and let my hands flap on wrists grown suddenly limp. Into my voice I introduce the barest hint of music, even perhaps the shadow of a lisp.

No doubt I present a sad, alarming spectacle, but after years of expert camouflage I am trying desperately to find the signs that will convey my identity as a homosexual to the room at large, and especially to that boy in the corner, who only returns with a look of cool disdain the stare of the straight-acting boy from Tennessee desperately attempting, for an evening, to play the queer. For I am possessed by the sudden awful certainty that only by becoming, at least for the moment, the bona fide sissy I have willed myself not to be can I find entry into the mysterious world of homosexual love toward which, incognito, I have spent years journeying. But now that I have arrived my disguise, I discover, is not so easily shed. My disguise, in fact, has become exactly who I am.

Free to be a sissy among sissies, I cannot. And so I cannot respond to my dance partner's implied command: I cannot make myself gayer than I am, which means I am not for him, nor am I for the other masculine-appearing men in the room. I do not want them; more successful versions of myself, they only frighten and intimidate me. No, it is the beautiful sissy dancing in the corner I want, the boy I have tried so hard my whole life not to be.

Upstate New York, 1997. For many years now I have lived in exile among the Yankees, and though the North will never be entirely my home, nonetheless I like it here. When the college where I teach is not in session I live a quiet, almost reclusive life, writing at my desk in the morning, working in my flower garden in the afternoon, then reading or listening to music after dinner. I enjoy the physical labor of a garden, digging beds in the soft, sandy soil, pulling weeds, getting my hands dirty in a pile of rich compost. The exercise tires me in a pleasant way. And the earth is not reluctant. My garden blooms abundantly, and as I sit on a summer evening on the bluestone patio I have built with my own hands, two or three hummingbirds will dart amid a drift of scarlet bee balm and the heavy scent of the old Alba rose Madame Legras de Saint Germain which gives the very air a kind of weight.

A southerner at home in the North, a pacifist whose imagination is infused with violence, a Calvinist who no longer believes in God. The civil war does not go away: it is always in the heart. The young men to whom I find myself inexorably drawn are slightly effeminate boys, ephebes who carry within their masculinity a certain beautiful flaw, a delicate betrayal of their promise as men. I am not talking about boys who do drag: that is too willful a surrender. Rather, I am talking about boys who beautifully resist, whose varying degrees of resistance are integral to their beauty.

When I was fourteen I went with a friend, someone I later dropped for fear Gabriel Patmos might think him too much a sissy, to see

Luchino Visconti's film *Death in Venice*. I hardly ever went to the movies in those days, but having seen the ad in the newspaper—a silhouetted boy walking out into the ocean as if to disappear—I somehow knew this was something I must find my way to at all costs. And I was not disappointed. Painfully erect in my jeans, I breathlessly watched the scene in which, on a beach deserted save for a distinguished writer in a lounge chair, the darkly muscular Jaschieu wrestles and humiliates delicate, moody Tadzio (the distinguished writer rising at the sight of this one-sided struggle, as if carried by the oceanic tide of his longing, as if attempting flight—only to fall back stricken into his chair). I have always loved the dangers faced by the Tadzios and Andys of the world, their vulnerability, the common scorn directed their way, the secret breathless exhilaration they provoke in those few like Gustav von Aschenbach and myself. I love in them, in other words, precisely what I would despise in myself. And if I am to be honest: even the athletic beauty of Gabriel and Luke, for whom I so diligently unmade the sissy in me, in retrospect contains within it the barest whisper of a question mark. It was that question mark, even if wrongfully interpreted, that drew me to them.

In the mid-1980s, my great love would be a nineteen-year-old boy of much grace and charm, fine-featured and slim-hipped, of feathery voice and hysterical laugh, and sporting, at least for a few months, a tousle of bleached blond hair. Though he wasn't gay exactly, many assumed he was, and one of the reasons they assumed that (the fact that he had, on occasion, allowed men to sleep with him might have been another) was his tendency to sometimes linger a little too long at the well-guarded borders of his gender. At those moments he captured me completely: I remember seeing him once in a short knit skirt and a white turtleneck, with a heavy loop of faux pearls around his neck, and the effect was both ravishing and oddly distressing. And perhaps not unconnected with this: I remember a dream in which he and I were walking hand-in-hand through a desert canyon and he told me, simply and matter-of-factly, as if he were about to embark on a great and terrible journey, that he had AIDS. The dream-moment opened up a dizzying hollowness in my heart, a yearning not unlike that I had once felt as I hovered over my battlefields' carnage as a boy, or toyed with Andy's last-minute reprieve from torture, or dreamed of losing a Gabriel Patmos I did not yet even know, a terrible yearning more or less identical with that which fuels the desperate enactments of identification, suffering, and compassion that take place every morning at my desk in my study. For what else is the novel but another battlefield on which the old conflicts endlessly reassert themselves, the precarious union brought again and again to the very brink of dissolution only to be saved for further, as yet unimagined crises?

At forty, I sometimes find myself wishing that I had had the courage, as a boy, to have been more of a sissy, to have taken the brave rebellious chances, to have risked society's disapproval rather than ratifying its strict prohibitions. It is useless, of course, to wish the past away. I am who I am, though even today, on occasion, when I am with certain gay men, especially those I don't know well, and to whom I am trying to communicate general goodwill, I find myself making small adjustments, discreetly assuming a campy persona that is as little my own as was the manly earnestness with which I engaged Gabriel and Luke in high questions of God and the soul. I am well aware, in those moments, of wearing another mask, this time put on not for the purpose of deflecting suspicions that I might be a sissy, that I might be gay, but of confirming those very suspicions.

As to who I "really" am, I have no idea. I suspect that our roles create us, and that without the tyranny of complex and even self-contradictory scripts, however utopian the alternative might seem, we would be for all intents and purposes mute. Given what I was, and where and when I grew up, I chose my own particular script—that of the sissy who is not a sissy—as my only means of survival: a way of participating in the pleasures of the sissy without renouncing the privileges of masculinity. If the price has been a continual and painful betrayal of certain parts of myself, I have nonetheless, down through the years, found within my civil war an undeservedly rich hoard of pleasures.

Select Bibliography

Tomboys

Benjamin, Jessica. "Father and Daughter: Identification with Difference—A Contribution to Gender Heterodoxy." *Psychoanalytic Dialogues* 1, 3 (1991): 277–99.

———. "Reply to Schwartz." *Psychoanalytic Dialogues* 2, 3 (1992): 417–24.

Blum, Alan, and Van Pfetzing. "Assaults to the Self: The Trauma of Growing Up Gay." *Gender and Psychoanalysis* 2, 4 (October 1997): 427–42.

Case, Sue-Ellen. *Split Britches.* New York: Routledge, 1996.

Chernin, Kim. *My Life as a Boy.* Chapel Hill: Algonquin Press, 1997.

Elliott, Mary. "When Girls Will Be Boys: 'Bad' Endings and Subversive Middles in Nineteenth-Century Tomboy Narratives and Twentieth-Century Lesbian Pulp Novels." *Legacy* 15, 1 (spring 1998): 92–97.

Fast, Irene. "Commentary on Jessica Benjamin's 'Father and Daughter: Identification with Difference'." *Psychoanalytic Dialogues* 2, 3:301–4.

———. *Gender Identity: A Differentiation Model.* Hillsdale, N.J.: Atlantic Press, 1984.

Fletcher, Lynne Yamaguchi. *Tomboys!: Tales of Dyke Derring-Do.* Lynne Yamaguchi and Karen Barber, eds. Los Angeles: Alyson, 1995.

Harris, Adrienne. "Gender as Contradiction." *Psychoanalytic Dialogues* 1, 2 (1991): 197–224.

———. "The Tomboys' Stories." In *The Softly Assembled Self: Developmental Theory for Relational Psychoanalysis* (in preparation).

Hughes, Holly. *Clit Notes.* New York: Grove Press, 1996.

Kiersky, Sandra. "Exiled Desire: The Problem of Reality in Psychoanalysis and Lesbian Experience." *Psychoanalysis and Psychotherapy* 13, 2 (1996): 130–41.

Lish, Jennifer D., Heino F. Meyer-Bahlburg, Anke A. Ehrhardt, Bayla G. Travis, et al. "Prenatal Exposure to Diethylstilbestrol (DES): Childhood Play Behavior and Adult Gender-Role Behavior in Women." *Archives of Sexual Behavior* 21, 5 (October 1992): 423–41.

Magee, Maggie, and Diana C. Miller. "What Sex Is an Amaryllis? What Gender Is Lesbian? Looking for Something to Hold It All." *Gender and Psychoanalysis* 1, 2 (April 1996): 139–70.

Massey, Carla. "Body Smarts: An Adolescent Girl Thinking, Talking, and Mattering." *Gender and Psychoanalysis* 1, 1 (January 1996): 75–102.

McEwen, Christian. "Come Down, Tree Climber!" *American Voice* 41 (1996): 109–23.

———. ed. *Jo's Girls*. Boston: Beacon Press, 1997.

Penelope, Julia. *Call Me Lesbian: Lesbian Lives, Lesbian Theory*. Freedom, Calif.: Crossing Press, 1992.

Rubin, Gayle. "Thinking Sex: Notes for a Radical Theory of the Politics of Sexuality." In Carol Vance, ed. *Pleasure and Dangers: Exploring Female Sexuality*, 267–320. Boston: Routledge and Kegan Paul, 1984.

Schwartz, David. "Commentary on Jessica Benjamin's 'Father and Daughter: Identification with Difference'." *Psychoanalytic Dialogues* 2, 3: 411–16.

Zevy, Lee, and Sahli A. Cavallaro. "Invisibility, Fantasy, and Intimacy: Princess Charming Is Not a Prince . . ." *Lesbian Psychologies: Explorations and Challenges*. Urbana and Chicago, Ill.: University of Illinois Press, 1987.

Sissies

Als, Hilton. *The Women*. New York: Farrar Straus and Giroux, 1997.

Berger, Maurice, ed. *Constructing Masculinity*. New York: Routledge, 1995.

Bullough, Vern L., and Bonnie Bullough. *Cross-Dressing, Sex, and Gender*. Philadelphia: University of Pennsylvania Press, 1993.

Corbett, Ken. "The Mystery of Homosexuality." *Psychoanalytic Psychology* 10, 3 (1993): 345–57.

Doty, Mark. *Firebird*. New York: HarperCollins, in press.

Isay, Richard. Letter to the Editor in *News: Newspaper of the American Psychiatric Association*. XXXII, 22 (November 21, 1997).

Kleinberg, Seymour. "Where Have All the Sissies Gone?" In *Alienated Affections: Being Gay in America*. New York: St. Martin's Press, 1980.

Manrique, Jaime. *Latin Moon in Manhattan*. New York: St. Martin's Press, 1992.

Mass, Lawrence. "Insight into Gender and Roles: (Some) Boys Will Be Boys." *Advocate* 26 (May 1987): 55–56.

———. "Sissiness as Metaphor: A Conversation with Richard Green." *Dialogues of the Sexual Revolution*, vol. 1. Binghamton, N.Y.: Hayworth Press, 1990.

McCann, Richard. "My Mother's Clothes: The School of Beauty and Shame." In David Leavitt and Mark Mitchell, eds. *The Penguin Book of Gay Short Stories*. New York: Viking, 1994.

Norton, Jody. "Brian Says You're a Girl, but I Think You're a Sissy Boy: Cultural Origins of Transphobia." *Journal of Gay, Lesbian, and Bisexual Identity* 2 (1997): 139–64.

Rivers, Ian. "Mental health issues among young lesbians and gay men bullied in school." *Health and Social Care in the Community* 3, 6:380–88.

———. "Lesbian, Gay and Bisexual Development: Theory, Research, and Social Issues." *Journal of Community and Applied Social Psychology* 7 (1997): 329–43.

———. "Violence against Lesbian and Gay Youth and Its Impact." In Margaret S. Schneider, ed. *Pride and Prejudice: Working with lesbian, gay, and bisexual youth.* Toronto: Central Toronto Youth Services, 1997.Roberts, Richard. "School Abuse: An Autobiographical Cross-Generational Study of Three Australian Gay Men." Paper presented at the 17th Annual National Lesbian and Gay Health Conference and the 13th Annual AIDS/HIV Forum.

Rofes, Eric M. "Making Our Schools Safe for Sissies." In Gerald Unks, ed. *The Gay Teen.* New York: Routledge, 1995.

Selvadurai, Shyam. *Funny Boy.* New York: Harcourt Brace, 1994.

Gender Identity Disorder

Bradley, Susan J., and Kenneth J. Zucker. "Gender Identity Disorder: A Review of the Past Ten Years." *Journal of the American Academy of Child and Adolescent Psychiatry* 36, 7 (July 1997):872–80.

Bradley, Susan J. Ray Blanchard, Susan Coates, Richard Green, et al. "Interim Report of the DSM IV Subcommittee on Gender Identity Disorders," *Archives of Sexual Behavior* 20, 4 (August 1991):333–43.

Coates, Susan. "Ontogenesis of Boyhood Gender Identity Disorder." *Journal of the American Academy of Psychoanalysis* 18, 3 (fall 1990):414–38.

Coates, Susan, and Person, Ethel S. "Extreme Boyhood Femininity: Isolated Behavior or Pervasive Disorder?" *Annual Progress in Child Psychiatry and Child Development* 1986:197–213.

Coates, Susan W., and Sabrina M. Wolfe. "The Etiology of Boyhood Gender Identity Disorder: A Model for Integrating Temperament, Development, and Psychodynamics." *Psychoanalytic Dialogues* 1, 4 (1991):481–523.

———. "Gender Identity Disorder in Boys: The Interface of Constitution and Early Experience." *Psychoanalytic Inquiry* 15, 1 (January 1995):6–38.

Fridell, Sari R., Kenneth J. Zucker, Susan J. Bradley, and Dianne M. Maing. "Physical Attractiveness of Girls with Gender Identity Disorder." *Archives of Sexual Behavior* 25, 1 (February 1996):17–31.

Friedman, Richard C. *Male Homosexuality: A Contemporary Psychoanalytic Perspective.* New Haven: Yale University Press, 1988.

Friedman, Richard C., and Jennifer I. Downey. "Neurobiology and Sexual Orientation: Current Relationships." *Journal of Neuropsychiatry and Clinical Neurosciences* 5, 2 (spring 1993):131–53.

———. "Psychoanalysis, Psychobiology, and Homosexuality." *Journal of the American Psychoanalytic Association* 41, 4 (1993):1159–98.

———. "Biology and the Oedipus Complex." *Psychoanalytic Quarterly* 64, 2 (April 1995):234–64.

Green, Richard. "Gender Identity in Childhood and Later Sexual Orientation: Follow-Up of 78 Males." *Annual Progress in Child Psychiatry and Child Development* 1986:214–220.

———. *The "Sissy Boy Syndrome" and the Development of Homosexuality*. New Haven: Yale University Press, 1987.

Money, John. *Love and Lovesickness: The Science of Sex, Gender Difference and Pair-Bonding*. Baltimore: Johns Hopkins University Press, 1980.

Stoller, Robert. *Sex and Gender: On the Development of Masculinity and Femininity*. New York: Science House, 1968.

———. *Splitting: A Case of Female Masculinity*. New York: Quadrangle, 1973.

———. *Presentations of Gender*. New Haven: Yale University Press, 1985.

Zucker, Kenneth J. "Psychosocial and Erotic Development in Cross-Gender Identified Children." *Canadian Journal of Psychiatry* 35, 6 (August 1990):487–95.

Zucker, K. J., and S. J. Bradley. *Gender Identity Disorder and Psychosexual Problems in Children and Adolescents*. New York: Guilford Press, 1995.

Zucker, Kenneth J., and Richard Green. "Psychosexual Disorders in Children and Adolescents." *Journal of Child Psychol. Psychiat.* 33, 1 (January 1992): 107–51.

Zucker, Kenneth J., Susan J. Bradley, and Mohammad Sanikhani. "Sex Differences in Referral Rates of Children with Gender Identity Disorder: Some Hypotheses." *Journal of Abnormal Child Psychology* 25, 3 (June 1997): 217–27.

Zucker, Kenneth J., Susan J. Bradley, and Claire B. Sullivan Lowry. "Gender Identity Disorder in Children." *Annual Review of Sex Research* 3 (1992):73–120.

Zucker, Kenneth J., Jennifer Wild, Susan J. Bradley, and Claire B. Lowry. "Physical Attractiveness of Boys with Gender Identity Disorder." *Archives of Sexual Behavior* 22, 1 (February 1993):23–36.

Zucker, Kenneth J., Debra N. Wilson-Smith, Janice A. Kurita, and Anita Stern. "Children's Appraisals of Sex-Typed Behavior in Their Peers." *Sex Roles* 33, 11–12 (December 1995):703–25.

Zucker, Kenneth J., Richard Green, Christina Garofano, Susan J. Bradley, et al. "Prenatal Gender Preferences of Mothers of Feminine and Masculine Boys: Relation to Sibling Sex Composition and Birth Order." *Journal of Abnormal Child Psychology* 22, 1 (February 1994):1–13.

Zuger, Bernard. "Homosexuality in Families of Boys with Early Effeminate Behavior: An Epidemiological Study." *Archives of Sexual Behavior* 18, 2 (1989):155–65.

Gender and Transsexualism

Bolin, Anne. *In Search of Eve: Transsexual Rites of Passage.* South Hadley, Mass.: Bergin and Garvey, 1988.

Bornstein, Kate. *Gender Outlaw.* New York: Routledge, 1994.

Devor, Holly. *FTM: Female-to-Male Transsexuals in Society.* Bloomington, Ind.: Indiana University Press, 1997.

Feinberg, Leslie. *Transgender Warriors.* Boston: Beacon Press, 1996.

MacKenzie, Gordene Olga. *Transgender Nation.* Bowling Green, Ohio: Bowling Green State University Popular Press, 1994.

Prosser, Jay. *Second Skins: The Body Narratives of Transsexuality.* New York: Columbia University Press, 1998.

General

Bayer, R. *Homosexuality and American Psychiatry: The Politics of Diagnosis.* Princeton: Princeton University Press, 1987.

Bem, Sandra L. *The Lens of Gender: Transforming the Debate on Sexual Inequality.* New Haven: Yale University Press, 1993.

Benjamin, Jessica. *The Bonds of Love.* New York: Pantheon, 1988.

Burke, Phyllis. *Gender Shock: Exploding the Myths of Male and Female.* New York: Anchor Books, 1996.

Butler, Judith. *Gender Trouble: Feminism and the Subversion of Identity.* New York: Routledge, 1990.

———. *Bodies That Matter: On the Discursive Limits of "Sex."* New York: Routledge, 1993.

Coates, Susan W. "Is It Time to Jettison the Concept of Developmental Lines? Commentary on DeMarneff's Paper, 'Bodies and Words.' " *Gender and Psychoanalysis* 2, 1 (January 1997):35–53.

de Marneffe, Daphne. "Bodies and Words: A Study of Young Children's Genital and Gender Knowledge." *Gender and Psychoanalysis* 2, 1 (January 1997):3–34.

Devor, Holly. *Gender Blending: Confronting the Limits of Duality.* Bloomington, Ind.: Indiana University Press, 1989.

Dimen, Muriel. "Deconstructing Difference: Gender, Splitting, and Transitional Space." *Psychoanalytic Dialogues* 1, 3 (1991):335–52.

Domenici, Thomas. *Disorienting Sexualities: Psychoanalytic Reappraisals of Sexual Identities.* New York: Routledge, 1995.

Fausto-Sterling, Anne. *Myths of Gender.* New York: Basic Books, 1985.

Flax, Jane. "Taking Multiplicity Seriously: Some Consequences for Psychoanalytic Theorizing and Practice." *Contemporary Psychoanalysis* 32, 4 October 1996.

Fuss, Diana. *Inside/Out.* New York: Routledge, 1991.

———. *Identification Papers*. New York: Routledge, 1995.

Gerber, Marjorie. *Vested Interests: Cross-Dressing and Cultural Anxiety*. New York: Routledge, 1992.

Herdt, Gilbert, ed. *Third Sex, Third Gender: Beyond Sexual Dimorphism in Culture and History*. New York: Zone, 1994.

Irvine, Janice M. *Disorders of Desire*. Philadelphia: Temple University Press, 1990.

Jennings, Kevin. *Telling Tales Out of School*. Los Angeles: Alyson, 1998.

Kessler, Suzanne. *Gender: An Ethnomethodological Approach*. New York: Wiley-Interscience, 1978.

Leary, Kim. "Race in Psychoanalytic Space." *Gender and Psychoanalysis* 2, 2 (April 1997):157–72.

Meyer-Bahlburg, Heino F. L., David E. Sandberg, Curtis L. Dolezar, and Thomas J. Yager. "Gender-Related Assessment of Childhood Play." *Journal of Abnormal Child Psychology* 22, 6 (December 1994):643–60.

Ramet, Sabrina Petra, ed. *Gender Reversals and Gender Cultures: Anthropological and Historical Perspectives*. New York: Routledge, 1996.

Sandberg, David E., Anke A. Ehrhardt, Susan E. Ince, and Heino F. Meyer-Bahlburg. "Gender Differences in Children's and Adolescents' Career Aspirations: A Follow-Up Study." *Journal of Adolescent Research* 6, 3 (July 1991):371–86.

Sandberg, David E., Heino F. Meyer-Bahlburg, Anke A. Ehrhardt, and Thomas J. Yager. "The Prevalence of Gender-Atypical Behavior in Elementary School Children." *Journal of the American Academy of Child and Adolescent Psychiatry* 32, 2 (March 1993):306–14.

Sedgwick, Eve. "How to Bring Your Kids Up Gay." In Michael Warner, ed. *Fear of a Queer Planet*. Minneapolis: Minnesota University Press, 1993. Reprinted from *Social Text* 29 (1990).

Contributors

Kim Chernin has published thirteen books of fiction, nonfiction, memoir, and poetry. She lives in Berkeley, California, where she practices as a psychoanalytic consultant. Her most recent book is *The Woman Who Gave Birth to Her Mother*, Viking/Penguin, August 1998.

Ken Corbett is a Candidate at the New York University Postdoctoral Program in Psychoanalysis and maintains a private practice in New York City.

Sara Cytron has been a stand-up comic since 1987 and also works as a Human Resources Specialist in a hospital. She is also, in her mid-forties, a law student embarking on her next career.

Dianne Elise is a Member and Faculty at the Psychoanalytic Institute of Northern California and on the Adjunct Faculty of the California School for Professional Psychology. She maintains a private practice in Oakland, California and is author of a number of psychoanalytic publications on female development, gender, and sexuality.

Anne Fausto-Sterling is a Professor of Medical Science and Women's Studies in the Department of Molecular and Cell Biology and Biochemistry at Brown University. She is the author of *Myths of Gender: Biological Theories about Women and Men* (Basic, 2d ed., 1992). Her latest book project, tentatively entitled *Body Building: How Biologists Construct Sexuality*, has a projected publication date of summer 1999 (Basic, forthcoming).

Judith Halberstam is Associate Professor of Literature at UC San Diego. She is the author of *Female Masculinity* (Duke University Press, 1998) and writes a film column for *Girlfriends Magazine*.

Arnie Kantrowitz is a professor of English at the College of Staten Island, City University of New York. His essays, poems, stories, and reviews have appeared in the *New York Times*, the *Village Voice*, the *Harvard Gay and Lesbian Review, Lambda Book Report*, the *Advocate, Gay, Gaysweek, Outweek, QW*, and other publications. He lives in New York City with his lover, Lawrence Mass.

Lawrence M. La Fountain-Stokes is a writer and academic, born and raised in San Juan, Puerto Rico. He is currently Assistant Professor in the Department of Spanish and Portuguese at the Ohio State University (Columbus). Larry has published extensively in Claridad (Puerto Rico) and in other publications in Cuba and the United States. His first book of short stories is under consideration for publication in Mexico.

Michael Lassell is an award-winning writer. He is the author of *Poems for Lost and Un-lost Boys, Decade Dance*, and *The Hard Way*; editor of *The Name of Love, Eros in Boystown*, and, with Lawrence Schimel, of *Two Hearts Desire*. He is articles director for *Metropolitan Home* magazine and a former editor of the *Advocate, L. A. Weekly, L. A. Style*, and *Interview*. He holds degrees from Colgate University, California Institute of the Arts (where he served on the faculties of the School of Theater and the Division of Critical Studies), and the Yale School of Drama.

Harriet Malinowitz is Associate Professor of English and Director of Women's Studies at Long Island University, Brooklyn.

Shannon Minter is a staff attorney for the National Center for Lesbian Rights (NCLR) and Director of NCLR's Youth Project, which provides legal information and assistance to lesbian, gay, bisexual, transgendered, and transsexual youth who have been abused or discriminated against in the mental health system.

Jody Norton teaches in the Department of English Language and Literature and the Women's Studies Program at Eastern Michigan University. S/he is the author of *Narcissus Sous Rature: Mule Subjectivity in Contemporary American Poetry*, forthcoming from Bucknell University Press. S/he has written extensively on gender and transgender, and is currently at work on a book on the cultural origins of transphobia.

Richard R. Pleak is Assistant Professor of Psychiatry, Albert Einstein College of Medicine. At the Long Island Medical Center, he is Director of the Child and Adolescent Psychiatry Residency Program, the Sexual Identity Service (SIS) and the Long Island Lambda Clinic (LILAC) for Gay, Lesbian, Bisexual, and Transgendered Youth.

Paul Russell is the author of the novels *Sea of Tranquility*, *Boys of Life*, *The Salt Point*, and *The Pederast* (forthcoming), as well as a work of nonfiction, *The Gay 100: A Ranking of the Most Influential Gay Men and Lesbians, Past and Present*. He teaches at Vassar College.

Naomi Scheman is Professor of Philosophy and Women's Studies at the University of Minnesota. A collection of her papers in feminist epistemology, entitled *Engenderings: Constructions of Knowledge, Authority, and Privilege*, was published in 1993 by Routledge. Her subsequent work attempts to connect the reading of Wittgenstein with the theorizing of diversely transgressive forms of subjectivity.

Lee Zevy is the founder of the Lesbian Therapists Referral Network, and one of the founders of Identity House, a peer counseling center for gays, lesbians, and bisexual and transgendered clients, where she continues to be a staff therapist who trains, supervises, and teaches. She is past president of the New York City Coalition for Women's Mental Health. She is a contributing author to *Lesbian Psychologies* and continues to write and publish on lesbian developmental psychology. After completing her training with the New York Institute for Gestalt Therapy in the 1970s she began a private practice which she maintains today.

Index

Adaptation, as goal of GID therapy, 120

ADHD. *See* Attention deficit/hyperactivity disorder

Adolescence: female, crisis of, 156; gender dysphoria in, 46–47; heterosexuality in, pull toward, 150, 217–220; lesbian experience of, 191, 193; tomboy's transition into, 154–156, 215–216; transsexual, 266–267

Adornment: girlyboys and, 130–131, 256–257; tomboys and, 166

Aestheticism: of girlyboys, 130–131; of tomboys, 193

Aggression: girlyboys and, 122–125, 232, 233, 240–241; trans woman and, 272

AIDS, in lesbian identity, 86

Alienation, tomboy, 157–158

Ambiguity: advantages of, 84; versus androgyny, 175; identity, preference for, 86–87; personal emphasis on, 224; sexual, social response to, 183

American Academy of Pediatrics, policy statement on "Homosexuality and Adolescence," 28–29

American Indian culture, gender in, 272

Anderson, Dennis, 45

Androgyny: versus ambiguity, 175; childhood tomboyism and, 160–161; feminist dissatisfaction with, 163–164; homophobic effects of promoting, potential for, 164; ideological import of, 161; positive implications of, 160; versus tomboyism, 159

Annie Get Your Gun (musical), 149

Anomaly, versus pathology, 3

Anti-Semitism: and Jewish identity, 72; protection from, suspicious forms of, 66; racism and, 81

Anxiety: of girlyboys, 125, 258; and ho-

mosexual involvement, 21; of lesbian adolescent, 218–220; separation, gender dysphoria and, 46; of tomboys, 213; of transsexual, 269

Atheism, homosexuality and, 283, 284

Attention deficit/hyperactivity disorder (ADHD): as diagnostic alternative to GID, 37; gender dysphoria and, 46

Bailey, Michael, 167

Bathroom, as active gender zone, 174

Behavioral approach, to GID, 15–17, 39–40

Bell-Metereau, Rebecca, 171, 179 n19

Bem, Sandra L., 163–164, 178 n14

Benjamin, J., 145

Berenbaum, Sherry, 167

Bidwell, Robert, 28

Binary divisions, 53, 236

Binder, Jan, 96 n20

Biology, and cross-gender behavior in children, 24–25, 42

Birth: identity ascription at, 77–78, 79–80, 83; sex assignment at, 97 n26

Bisexual orientation, 260

Body: changing nature of, 55–56, 76; gay men's stereotypes about, 261–262; girlyboy's concern about, 121, 125–126; intersexed, surgical interventions upon, 178 n15; woman's, conceptualization of, 194 n20

Bornstein, Kate, 75, 77, 78

Boy(s): beauty of, 272; disidentifying with mother, 143–144; films portraying, 170, 171, 175; gender-dysphoric, adult outcomes of, 38–39; gender-dysphoric, special qualities of, 45; gender oppression of, 272–273; GID in, 10, 14–15, 35; homosexual. *See* Girlyboy(s);

Boy(s) *(Continued)*
  rebel icons of, 170; tomboy's envy of,
  213; with and without shirts, 237;
  woman's transformation into, 199–208
Boyarin, Daniel, 63, 82, 86, 89, 90, 91,
  100 n44
Boyarin, Jonathan, 82, 89, 90, 100 n47
Bradley, Susan, 13, 38, 118
Brain, lactation and changes in, 56
Butch, continuum of masculinity related
  to, 195 n28
Butler, Judith, 69

Call Me Lesbian (Penelope), 187, 191–192
Camp: girlyboy's experience at, 232–234,
  238; tomboy's experience at, 216–217
Canguilhem, Georges, 3
Categorical imperative, 64
Categorization: gender, youthful female
  masculinity and, 158; of GID, 116; ho-
  mosexuals' difficulty with, 112
Center, placement at: forces determining,
  68; queering of, strategies for, 90, 92;
  sensitivities regarding, 67. *See also*
  Privilege
Chasseguet-Smirgel, J., 144, 145, 146
Chodorow, N., 144
Choice: in homosexuality, stigmatization
  of, 62; of identity, 80–81; sexual, influ-
  ence of early behavior on, 187
Christianity: compared with heterosexuality, 63; identity, presumption of,
  93 n8; male-gender utopianism in, 63
Christianormativity, 62–63; and hetero-
  normativity, 63; identity requirements
  of, 79; queering of center of, 92
Clit Notes (Hughes), 133
Clitoris, normal size of, parameters for,
  178 n13
Clothing: girlyboys and, 130–131, 256–
  257; tomboys and, 166
Club, gender as, 173
Coates, Susan, 14, 45–46, 118–120; perspective on GID, 1
Conformity: in American culture, 252;
  and health, conflation of, 116; and
  transgression, in girlyboys, 133. *See
  also* Nonconformity
Convention, versus stability, 113
Cooking, girlyboys and, 128, 243–244

Corderi, Victoria, 167
Cortisone therapy, for prenatally androgenized girls, 165, 178 n14
Cowgirl, 149–150, 215
Creativity, of girlyboys, 131–133, 249, 255–
  256
Cross-dressing experience, early, 256–
  257, 265
Cross-gender behavior: biology and, 24–
  25, 42; clinically significant, 37–38; and
  predisposition to homosexuality, 38–39;
  redirection of, 119–120; *See also* Gender
  Identity Disorder
Cross-gendered identification: versus
  gender mixing, 170; and homosexuality, 111–112
Culture: and gender, 55, 68; and gender
  oppression, 272–273; as rationale for
  GID treatment, 17, 27, 41; and tomboy
  phenomenon, 142

Dance: gay men and, 285; girlyboys and,
  243, 251
Davenport, Charles, 38, 43
Death, trans woman's attitude toward,
  264, 271
Deisher, Robert, 28
Democratizing privilege, 65
Descartes, René, 64, 65
Desire: language and, 158; lesbian, 205;
  in lesbian childhood, 182; lesbian de-
  nial of, 184–185; maternal erotic, 181,
  182; mirrored by parents, 183; trans-
  formed into identification, 173
Developmental paradigms, gay perspec-
  tive on, 112–113
Diagnostic and Statistical Manual (DSM),
  35; treatment of homosexuality in, 1,
  12
Diasporic identity, 86, 90, 238
Discrimination, diagnosis of GID and, 37
Dissociation, 221
Distress, as rationale for GID treatment,
  17–18
Dolls, boys playing with, 248, 274, 279–
  280
Domesticity, girlyboys and, 128, 131–132,
  243–244
Drug abuse, gender nonconformity and,
  270

DSM. *See* Diagnostic and Statistical Manual
Duty, versus inclination, 64

Effeminacy: problem of, 114–121; social construction of, 119, 120
Ego-integration, 136 n1; continuum of male femininity and, 114–115; early levels of, 134; and health, 136 n1; parent-child identifications and, 129
Ehrhardt, Anke, 34
Envy: in girlyboys, 126–127; in tomboys, 213
Ethical issues, in diagnosing and treating gender dysphoria, 43–44, 47–48
Even Cowgirls Get the Blues (film), 149–150
Expert essentialism, 74–75

Family: girlyboy in, 245–246, 249; Jewish, growing up as lesbian in, 210–220; lesbian in, 220–221; resemblance, and identity ascription, 87. *See also* Parent(s)
Family Research Council, 13
Fantasies, 135
Father(s): of gay son, 226–227, 254–257, 259, 277; identification with, preoedipal girl and, 145; of lesbian daughter, 209, 211–212; as love object, and girl's masculine identification, 141; of transsexual, 264, 272
Fausto-Sterling, Ann, 166, 178 n15
Feinberg, Leslie, 70, 96 n19, 187, 190, 271
Female andrenogenital syndrome, 165
Female-to-male transsexuals, 96 n23–97 n23; feminist suspicion of, 70
Femininity: Freud on, 263; male, as continuum, 114–115, 120–121; versus pain, in girlyboys, 115–116; and subjectivity, synthesizing, 148; as symptom, 117
Feminism: and homophobia, 164; and lesbianism, conflict between, 178 n11; punk rock culture and, 153–154; and reinvention of gender, 53; suspicion of transsexuals, 70; on tomboys, 162–163, 168–169, 171; and transsexualism, 85; view of gender, 68–69
Femme, lesbian, 195 n28
Film(s): boy, 170, 171, 175; depiction of

girls in, 170, 175–176; girlyboy's escape into, 227–229; tomboy, 171–176
Flamboyance, of girlyboys, 131–133
Freud, Sigmund, 110, 148; on femininity, 263; theory of sexual development, 182–183; on tomboys, 141
Friedman, Richard C., 2–3
Frye, Marilyn, 60, 78, 98 n31

Gabriel, Davina Anne, 98 n31
Garber, Jenny, 155
Gay Liberation Front meetings, 259
Gay man/men: childhood experience of, 107–137, 226–234; conflict within, 274, 285–286; heterosexual stereotypes affecting, 261; middle-aged, 261–262; relation to gender roles, 234–235; sex life of, 259–261
Gender: in American Indian culture, 272; binary system of, challenges to, 53; clubby nature of, 173; development of, theories of, 118–119; dictionary definitions of, 52; dimorphic versus hybrid, 165; expert determination of, 75; feminist reinvention of, 53; feminist versus transsexual view of, 68–69; girlyboy's experience of, 109–110; health, 111–121; identity, expectations for stability in, 84; mixed, girlyboy's experience of, 121; mystery of, 135; oppression, 272–273; and pain, 118; and psychic structure, blurring of, 110; rigidity of, arguments against, 90–91; sexological reinvention of, 52–53; and sexuality, separation of, 1; social construction of, 119; in Western society, 68
Gender-as-sexuality, theater of, 265
Gender dysphoria: in adolescence, 46–47; adult outcomes of, 38–39; in natural history of childhood, 38; psychopathology associated with, 45–46; treatment of, debate on, 39–40; treatment of, ethics of, 43–44, 47–48; use of term, 36. *See also* Gender Identity Disorder
Gender Identity Disorder (GID): in adolescents, 46–47; in adults, 11; and adult sexual orientation, 13–14, 42–43; as apotheosis of modernism, 116; behavioral approach to, 15–17, 39–40; in boys, 10, 14–15, 35; categorization of,

Gender Identity Disorder (GID) *(Cont.)*
116; in children, and adult sexual orientation, 19–21, 27, 38–39, 109; children referred for diagnosis and treatment of, 25–26; controversy surrounding treatment of, 13, 39–40; dangers of diagnosis, 189; debate on diagnosis, 35–37; diagnosis of, 9–11, 35–36; ethical issues in diagnosing and treating, 34–48; etiology of, theories about, 24–25; versus gender nonconformity, 114; in girls, 10–11, 35–36, 189; versus homosexual boyhood, 109; impact of treatment, 22–23; incidence of, 23; introduction of diagnosis, 12, 189; motivation of parents seeking treatment for, 21–22; parents' involvement in treatment of, 44–45; parents' motivation in treatment of, 21–22, 45; perspectives on, 1; phenomenology of, theories of, 118–119; as psychiatric diagnosis, 1–2, 35; psychoanalytic approach to, 14, 42; psychopathology with, 14–15; rationales for treatment, 17–19, 40–42, 44–46; research on, 14–15; short-term goals of treatment, 18; treatment of, 11, 13, 39–40, 47; treatment of, methods, 15–17, 39–40, 44–45, 119–120

Gender identity disorder of adolescence or adulthood (GIDAANT), 35

Gender identity disorder of childhood (GIDC), 35

Gender mixing, versus cross-gendered identification, 170

Gender roles: gay men's relation to, 234–235; in 1950s, 247–248

GID. *See* Gender Identity Disorder

GIDAANT. *See* Gender identity disorder of adolescence or adulthood

GIDC. *See* Gender identity disorder of childhood

G.I. Joe, 279–280

Girl(s): adolescent, crisis experienced by, 156; films portraying, 170, 175–176; GID in, 10–11, 35–36, 189; girlyboy's relations with, 241–242, 249, 250, 257–258; homosexual boy's desire to be, 254; latency period for, 149; masculine identification of, 141; masculinity of, 160; normalizing models of development, 169; prenatally androgenized,

164–165; rebel icons of, lack of, 170; rebellious, models of, 153–154; separation from mother, difficulty in, 144, 183; tomboy. *See* Tomboy(s)/tomboyism

Girlyboy(s), 108; aestheticism of, 130–131; and aggression, 122–125, 232, 233, 240–241; anxiety of, 125, 258; choice of term, 109; and cooking, 128, 243–244; creativity/flamboyance of, 131–133, 249, 255–256; and dancing, 243, 251; defined, 121; desire mixed with envy in, 126–127; and domesticity, 128, 131–132, 243–244; experience of gender, 109–110; femininity versus pain in, 115–116; first love of, 281–282; as label, 136 n2; maternal instinct of, 240–241, 248; and mothers, 127–130; Oedipal conflict in, 123; ostracism of, 254; and penis, 125–127; personal accounts of, 226–235, 236–244; play patterns of, 114–115, 130, 228–229, 237, 240, 275, 279–280; reclaiming of girl in, 133–135; relations with girls, 241–242, 249, 250, 257–258; sexuality of, 253–254, 257, 280, 281–282; and shame, 246–247, 248, 250–251, 259; and sports, 251, 252, 280–281

Gonsiorek, John, 28

Gopinath, Gayatri, 177 n

Green, Richard, 9, 13, 14, 38; longitudinal study of sissies, 108; on tomboyism, 177 n2

Greenson, R., 144

Growth, toward survival, in girlyboys, 133–134

Haber, Calvin, 42

Hagen, Marsha, 94 n14

Haldke, Lisa, 93 n9

Hale, Jacob, 87, 93 n8, 94 n15, 95 n19, 97 n25, 99 n39

Halperin, David, 61, 87, 94 n11

Hamer, Dean, 42

Harding, Sandra, 90

Harris, Julie, 172

Harry Benjamin International Gender Dysphoria Association (HBIGDA), 1997 Vancouver meeting of, 36–37

HBIGDA. *See* Harry Benjamin International Gender Dysphoria Association

Health: ego-integration and, 136 n1; gender, 111–121. *See also* Psychopathology

Heldke, Lisa, 97 n25, 100 n48

Hermaphrodism: challenge posed by, 178 n15; depiction in film, 174–175

Heteronormativity, 61–62; and Christianormativity, 63; experts policing, 76; homosexuality according to, 62; identity requirements of, 79; queering of center of, 92; resistance to, 87–88; and rigidity of gender, 90

Heterosexuality: adolescence and pull toward, 150, 217–220; compared with Christianity, 63; presumption of, 93 n8; privileged nature of, 61–62; social reinforcement for, 183–184

History, and identity, 80–81

Hoagland, Sarah, 78, 94 n12, 96 n20, 98 n31

Hollywood Androgyny (Bell-Metereau), 171, 179 n19

Homophobia: feminism and, 164; protection from, suspicious forms of, 66

Homosexual boyhood, versus GID, 109

Homosexuality: adult, GID in children and, 19–21, 27, 38; and atheism, 283, 284; choice in, stigmatization of, 62; cross-gendered identification and, 111–112; GID as reconceptualization of, 12; hate as defense against, 124–125; heteronormative representation of, 62; male, signifiers for, 109; male, trauma equation of, 117; mystery of, 110; need for, in definition of normality, 63; official depathologization of, 1, 12; as positive option, 40–41; predisposition to, childhood cross-gender behaviors and, 38–39; prevention of, effectiveness of, 22–23, 42–43; prevention of, as goal of treatment, 12–13, 18–19, 27, 40–42

Hormone therapy: girlyboys and, 232; for prenatally androgenized girls, 165, 178 n14

Horney, Karen, on masculinity complex, 142

Hughes, Holly, 133

Identification: feminine, 143, 144; versus identity, 134–135; of lesbians, 186–187; masculine, as attempt to win mother, 147–148; masculine, by disidentifying

with mother, 143–147; with mother, and ego development, 148; parent-child, and ego-integration, 129; parent-child, and homosexual development, 226–227; process of, 264; of tomboy, spectrum of, 187

Identity: ambiguity of, preference for, 86–87; ascription of, 77–78, 79–80, 83, 87; choice of, 80–81; Christian, presumption of, 93 n8; components of, 93 n9–94 n9; continuity of memory and, 59–60; cool-street, 269–270; diasporic, 86, 90, 238; expert essentialism and, 74–75; family resemblance and ascription of, 87; gay man's problems in establishing, 285–286, 288; gender, expectations for stability in, 84; girlyboy and repression of, 251; history and, 80–81; homosexual, development of, 21; versus identification, 134–135; Jewish, 91; opaque nature of, 71–72; religious versus natal ascription of, 79–80; separated from religion, 72–73; similarity with transsexual identity, 84; lesbian: AIDS in, 86; inhibition of, 190; Rich's conception of, 89; tomboy in, 193; memory of others and, 60, 75; name and, 157–158; natal ascription of, 77–78, 79–80, 83, 87; nationalist, diasporic identity as alternative to, 90; norms of, 58–59; policing of boundaries of, 88; as privileged access, 74; privileged access voluntarism and, 76–77; queer, 88–90; symbolic appropriation of, resistance to, 88–89; "traitorous," 90

Incest, as punishment of lesbian tomboy, 189

Inpatient therapy, for cross-gender behavior, 23

International Classification of Diseases, World Health Organization, 35

Isay, Richard, 36

James, William, 108

"Jew," 89

Jew(s): authentic, controversy over, 73; Christianormative representation of, 62–63; converts, intelligibility of, 72–73; identity, 91, 93 n9–94 n9; identity, opaque nature of, 71–72; identity, religious versus natal ascription of, 79–80;

Jew(s) *(Continued)*
   identity, separated from religion, 72–73;
   as test of social oppressiveness, 81;
   and transsexuals, commonality of, 67–
   68, 84
Jewish family, growing up as lesbian in,
   210–225
Johnson, Robin, 172
Judaism: conversion to, 81–82, 99 n38;
   distinguishing features of, from Christian perspective, 71–72
Juvenile unmasculinity, syndrome of, 117

Kampen, Natalie, 63, 97 n24
Kant, Immanuel, 64, 65
Kitchen, as girlyboy's domain, 128, 243–
   244
Klepfisz, Irena, 96 n22

Lactation, and brain changes in mother,
   56
Language, and desire, 158
Latency period: for girls, 149; for lesbians, 186; tomboys in, 147
Lebovitz, Phil, 38
Leighton, Anne, 78, 98 n31
Lenses of Gender, The (Bem), 163–164
Lesbian(s)/lesbianism: in adolescence,
   191, 193; AIDS in identity of, 86;
   butch, 195 n28; childhood experiences
   of, 180–181, 187–189, 209–225; definition of, 78; denial of desire by, 184–185;
   developmental continuum of sexuality
   of, 181–182; diagnosed as mentally ill,
   190; emblems, scripts, and symbols of,
   192; family relations of, 220–221; and
   feminism, conflict between, 178 n11;
   femme, 195 n28; first lover, 216–217;
   identity formation of, inhibition of, 190;
   identity, Rich's conception of, 89; internal psychosexual gendered representations of, 192; latency period for, 186;
   masculine identification of, 186–187;
   mental health problems of, 221–222;
   parental mirroring for, lack of, 183;
   parent characteristics of, 209, 211–212;
   prenatally androgenized girls and, 165–
   166; role models for, 191–192, 224; separatists, and transsexuals, 78, 83–84,
   98 n31; tomboyism and, 150, 164, 167–
   168, 186, 188; tomboy stage of devel-

opment, accomplishments during, 190–
   193; transformation into, 199–208; and
   transsexualism, 223–224
Lesbian Psychologies (Levy), 191
LeVay, Simon, 42
Levitt, Laura, 100 n47
Liberatory activism: criticism of strate-
   gies of, 66–67; twentieth-century, 58
Little Darlings (film), 173–174
"Looking Butch: A Rogue Guide to
   Butches on Film" (clip show), 177 n
Love: first, 216–217, 281–282; parent as
   object of, 141; and torture, 280
Lugones, María, 59, 87, 90, 92 n1,
   97 n24

McCullers, Carson, 156–158
"Macho boy syndrome," 167
MacKinnon, Catharine, 69
McNicholls, Kristy, 173
McRobbie, Angela, 155
Maladjustment, prevention of, as goal of
   GID treatment, 19
Male-gender utopianism, 63
Male-to-female (MTF) transsexuals: diffi-
   culties in understanding, 69–70; femi-
   nist suspicion of, 70; and lesbian sepa-
   ratists, 78, 83–84, 98 n31; as
   "naturalized" women, 82–83
Malinowitz, Harriet, 224 n–225 n
Man and Woman, Boy and Girl (Money),
   164–167
Man/men: burdens of, 202–203; homo-
   sexual. *See* Gay man/men; Girlyboy(s).
   See also Boy(s)
Marmor, Judd, 41
Masculinity: butch lesbian, 195 n28; fe-
   male, as assault on male privilege, 164;
   versus generalization of tomboyism,
   162–163; girl's aspiration after, 213–214;
   phallic narcissism as foundation of,
   123–124; youthful female, 160; and
   gender taxonomies, 158
Masculinity complex, 141–143
Mass, Larry, 235
Mass, Lawrence, 12
Maternal erotic desire, 181, 182
Maternal instinct, of girlyboys, 240–241,
   248
Meaning: as doing, 77; as privileged matter, contradiction in, 76–77

Member of the Wedding, The (film), 172–173
Member of the Wedding, The (McCullers), 156–158
Membership: by birth versus by choice, 82; gender as, 173
Memory: continuity of, and identity, 59–60; of others, and identity, 60, 75
Mental health problems. *See* Psychopathology
Meyer-Bahlburg, Heino, 12, 34
Meyers, Diana Tietjens, 94 n11, 97 n25, 99 n38, 100 n48
Michigan Women's Music Festival, 78, 98 n31
Mirroring, 183, 224
Mishima, Yukio, 280
Money, John, 38, 52; *Man and Woman, Boy and Girl*, 164–167
Monster, transsexual as, 76
Montaigne, Michel, 201–203
Morality, Kant's account of, 64
Mother(s): disidentification from, 143–147; of gay son, 226–227, 255–256, 259, 278–279; of girlyboy, 251; identification with, and ego development, 148; lactating, brain changes in, 56; of lesbian daughter, characteristics, 209, 212; as love object, and girl's masculine identification, 141; masculine identification as attempt to win, 147–148; omnipotence of, girl's escape from, 146; psychoanalytic view of, 129; separation from, girl's difficulty in, 144, 183
Mother-child relations: and GID, 1, 14; and girlyboys, 127–130, 227–231; and trans-woman, 264
Movies. *See* Film(s)
MTF transsexuals. *See* Male-to-female transsexuals
Mullins, Hillary, 182
Multiculturalism, 66–67
Multiple personality disorder, 60
Music, homosexual boys and, 267–268, 281–282
Mystery: gender, 135; of homosexuality, 110

Name(s), and identity, rigidity of, 157–158

Narcissism: in girlyboy's play, 114–115; phallic, as foundation of masculinity, 123–124
National Association for Research and Treatment of Homosexuality (NARTH), 36
Nationalist identity, diasporic identity as alternative to, 90
"Naturalized," term, 82; applied to MTF transsexuals, 82–83, 99 n35
New Woman's Conference, 98 n31
Nonconformity, gender, 3; versus GID, 114
Normal and the Pathological, The (Canguilhem), 3
Normality: conceptualization of, 2–3; definition of, need for homosexuality in, 63

Oedipal conflict: in girlyboys, 123; in tomboys, 142
Olson, Jenni, 177 n
Omnipotence, maternal, girl's escape from, 146
O'Neal, Tatum, 173
Oppositional defiant disorder, gender dysphoria and, 46
Ostracism: elimination of, as goal of GID treatment, 18, 19, 44; of girlyboy, 254; of transsexual, 263–264
Outsider: lesbian position of, learning to negotiate, 190–191; realization of status as, 260

Pain: versus femininity, in girlyboys, 115–116; gender and, 118
Parent(s): of girlyboy, 226–227, 251–252, 253, 254–257, 259, 277–279; involvement in treatment, 44–45; mirroring of desire by, 183; motivation in seeking treatment, 21–22, 45; response to child's sexual orientation, 43, 168; of tomboy, 209, 211–212, 214–215, 224; of transsexual, 264, 270, 272. *See also* Mother(s); Father(s)
Parent-child identifications: and ego-integration, 129; and homosexual development, 226–227
Passivity: in feminine development, 141; male homosexual, 137 n4, 261
Pathology. *See* Psychopathology

Peer rejection, elimination of, as rationale for treatment, 44
Penelope, Julia, 187, 190, 191–192
Penis: girlyboys and, 125–127; tomboys and, 144–145
Penis envy: disidentification from mother and, 144–145; in girlyboys, 126–127; social aspects of, 143
Perfection, standard of, 247
"Perinatally pinked," 79, 98 n30
Person, Ethel, 135
Pettiway, Leon, 270
Philosophy, privileged thinking in, 64–65
Piper, Adrian, 100 n45
Play: girlyboys and, 114–115, 130, 228–229, 237, 240, 248, 275, 279–280; tomboys and, 159–160, 166, 185–186, 214; transsexual and, 265–266
Potter, Nancy, 93 n6
Privilege, 60–61; democratizing, 65; disciplining apparatus of, resistance to, 61; gender classification and, 68; heterosexuality as, 61–62; male, female masculinity as assault on, 164; multiculturalist challenge to, 66–67; norms of, 58–59; and philosophical thought, 64–65; and subjectivity, danger of, 97 n25
Protection, suspicious forms of, 66
Psychic structure, 136 n1; gender and, blurring of, 110
Psychoanalytic approach: dogged features of, 129; to gender identity disorders, 14, 42
Psychopathology: versus anomaly, 3; conceptualization of, 2–3; degree of male femininity and, 114; in gender dysphoric children, 45–46; homosexuality-as-pathology, 1; lesbian denial of desire and, 185; lesbians and, 221–222; transsexuals and, 270–271
Puerto Rico, growing up in, 236–244
Punk rock culture: and feminism, 153–154; tomboyism and, 153–155, 159, 170–176, 176–177

"Queer," term, 87
Queer identity, 88–90

Race, mixed, compared with transsexualism, 95 n16
Racism: and anti-Semitism, 81; and gender oppression, 173; protection from, suspicious forms of, 66
Reagon, Bernice Johnson, 99 n31
Rekers, George, 13; perspective on GID, 1; religious bias of, 40–41; treatment methods of, 39–40
Religious converts: compared to transsexuals, 72–73, 75, 83; to Judaism, 81–82, 99 n38
Repression, GID therapy as, 120
Resistance, 85; to heteronormativity, 87–88; and solidarity, 86
Rich, Adrienne, 89
Robins, E., 39
Roiphe, Ann, 168–169
Role models, lesbian, 191–192, 224
Root, Michael, 97 n28, 99 n35, 100 n48
Rottnek, Matt, 96 n19
Russo, Anthony, 38

Saghir, M. T., 39
Schneider, Paul, 174
Scopophilia, 265
Sedgwick, Eve, 2, 12, 93 n7
Segall, Pamela, 172
Selfhood. *See* Identity
Separation anxiety, gender dysphoria and, 46
Sex: assignment at birth, 97 n26; binary system of, challenges to, 53; essential nature of, questioning of, 54–55; versus gender, 1, 52–53
Sexism, protection from, suspicious forms of, 66
Sex life, of gay man, 259–261
Sexuality: bisexual, 260; in boy's play, 276–277; choice of, influence of early behavior on, 187; continuum in development of, 181–182; developmental theories of, gay resistance to, 112; gay, development of, 253–254; genital, 182; girlyboy, 253–254, 257, 280, 281–282; pregenital, 181; tomboy, 180–195; of transsexual boy, 264–267, 268–269
Sexual orientation, adult: GID in children and, 19–21, 27, 38–39, 109; tomboyism and, 164; treatment for GID and, 13–14, 42–43
Shame, 133; girlyboy and, 246–247, 248, 250–251, 259
Silverman, Martin, 42

"Sissy": gay man's attitude toward, 274, 285–286, 288; implications of term, 109, 177 n2; threat of being called, 231
Sisterhood, of trans women, 268, 269, 272
Smith, Riawa, 98 n31, 99 n31
Socarides, Richard, 36
Social norms, shifting of, threat perceived in, 67
Solidarity, 92; resistance and, 86
Something Special (film), 174–175
Spelman, Elizabeth V., 94 n12
Spirit and the Flesh, The: Sexual Diversity in American Indian Culture (Williams), 272
Sports, girlyboys and, 251, 252, 280–281
Stability, versus convention, 113
Stoller, R., 144
Stone Butch Blues (Feinberg), 187, 271
Stryker, Susan, 68, 76, 77
Styrene, Poly, 153
Subjectivity: establishing, father identification and, 146; female lack of, 146–147, 148; and femininity, synthesizing, 148; privileged, danger of, 97 n25
"Sugar and Spice" (TV program), 167–169
Suicide attempts, gender nonconformity and, 271
Summer camp. *See* Camp
Support groups, 28
Surgical change, of transsexuals: illusion pursued by, 75–76; as social control, 178 n15

Television: girlyboy's experience with, 242–243; portrayal of tomboys on, 167–169
Temperament, as predisposing factor for GID, 24
Thompson, Clara, 142–143
Times Square (film), 172
Token reinforcement program, for GID treatment, 17
Tomboy(s)/tomboyism: adolescence and pull into heterosexuality, 150, 217–220; and adolescence, transition into, 154–156, 215–216; and adult lesbianism, 164, 167–168, 176, 186, 188; aestheticism of, 193; alienation of, 157–158; versus androgyny, 159; androgyny model of, 176; anxiety of, 213; definitions of, change in, 163; depathologizing of, 161–162; disidentification from mother and, 143–147; feminist position of, 162–163, 168–169, 171; fluid play space of, 185–186; Freud's explanation of, 141; good and bad models of, 162; identification of, spectrum of, 187; index of behavior, 166; as label, 148–149, 150, 186; learning process of, 185; in lesbian development, 190–193; as male impersonator, 179 n19; and maleness, aspiration after, 213–214; masculinity complex and, 141–143; as normative standard, damage done by, 160; Oedipal complex in development of, 142; origin of term, 193 n2; parents' response to, 214–215; personal account of, 210–215; pivotal day in life of, 180–181; play patterns of, 159–160, 166, 185–186, 214; prenatally androgenized girls and, 165–166; prevalence of, in latency period, 147; punishment for trespasses into "male territory," 188–189; punk (rogue), 153–155, 159, 170–176, 176–177; as rebellion against feminine role, 149; reduction of meaning of, 159–160, 170; role models for, 191–192; scientific observation of, dangers of, 167; sexuality of, 180–195; socially acceptable form of, 156; social tolerance for, 188; as stage in female development, 140; as strategy for separation from mother, 144; TV special on, 167–169; two models of, 154, 172; versus virilization, 166
Tordesillas line, 236
"Traitorous" identities, 90
Transgression, and conformity, in girlyboys, 133
Transsexualism/transsexuals: adult, GID in children and, 19–21, 38; defined as mental disorder, 11; female-to-male, 96 n23–97 n23; and feminism, 85; feminist suspicion of, 70; institutionalization of, 75; and Jews, commonality of, 67–68, 84; lesbians and, 223–224; and lesbian separatists, 78, 83–84, 98 n31; male-to-female, as "naturalized" women, 82–83; mixed race compared to, 95 n16; personal account of, 263–273; prevention of, as goal of GID

Transsexualism/transsexuals *(Cont.)*
    treatment, 18–19, 27; prevention of, effectiveness of, 22–23, 42–43; religious converts compared to, 72–73, 75, 83; surgical change, illusion pursued by, 75–76; tomboyism and, 164; understanding, difficulties in, 69–70; view of gender, 68–69
TransSisters (magazine), 98 n31
Turner, Victor, 87
TV program, on tomboys, 167–169

Vicinus, Martha, 270
Violence: in play, 280; protection from, suspicious forms of, 66. *See also* Aggression
Virilization, versus tomboyism, 166

Warner, Michael, 90
Williams, Walter, 272
Wittgenstein, Ludwig, 70, 71, 76, 84

Wittig, Monique, 95 n19
Woman/women: attachment of, 201; body, conceptualization of, 194 n20; homosexual. *See* Lesbian(s); Tomboy(s); "naturalized," 82–83; psychoanalytic view of, 129, 263; as scapegoats, in condemnation of odd men, 117; transformation into man, Montaigne's account of, 201–203; trans, personal account of, 263–273. *See also* Girl(s)
World Health Organization, *International Classification of Diseases*, 35
"World"-travel, 90
World War II: clinical interest in gender-atypical children after, 12; popularity of tomboy after, 171

Zinneman, Fred, 172
Zucker, Kenneth, 11, 13, 14–15, 38, 118; goals of treatment according to, 44
Zuger, Bernard, 38